Risking Difference

SUNY series in Psychoanalysis and Culture
Henry Sussman, editor

and

SUNY series in Feminist Criticism and Theory
Michelle A. Massé, editor

Risking Difference

*Identification, Race, and Community
in Contemporary Fiction and Feminism*

Jean Wyatt

State University of New York Press

Cover art: Paul Klee, *Two Heads*, 1932, 332 (A12), 81 x 85 cm, Öelfarbe und Bleistift auf Leinwand auf Keilrahmen, originale Rahmenleisten. Norton Simon Museum, the Blue Four Galka Sheyer Collection, 1953. © 2004 Artists Rights Society (ARS), New York / VG Bild-Kunst, Bonn.

Published by
State University of New York Press

© 2004 State University of New York Press

All rights reserved

Printed in the United States of America

No part of this book may be used or reproduced in any manner whatsoever without written permission. No part of this book may be stored in a retrieval system or transmitted in any form or by any means including electronic, electrostatic, magnetic tape, mechanical, photocopying, recording, or otherwise without the prior permission in writing of the publisher.

For information, address State University of New York Press,
90 State Street, Suite 700, Albany, NY 12207

Production by Judith Block
Marketing by Anne Valentine

Library of Congress Cataloging-in-Publication Data

Wyatt, Jean.
  Risking difference : identification, race, and community in contemporary fiction and feminism / Jean Wyatt.
    p. cm. — (SUNY series in psychoanalysis and culture) (SUNY series in feminist criticism and theory)
  Includes bibliographical references (p.   ) and index.
  ISBN 0-7914-6127-0 (acid-free paper) — ISBN 0-7914-6128-9 (pbk. : acid-free paper)
  1. American fiction—Women authors—History and criticism. 2. Feminism and literature—United States—History—20th century. 3. Women and literature—United States—History—20th century. 4. American fiction—African American authors—History and criticism. 5. Psychoanalysis and feminism—United States. 6. Psychoanalysis and culture—United States. 7. Identification (Psychology) in literature. 8. Multiculturalism in literature. 9. Group identity in literature. 10. Community in literature. 11. Race in literature. I. Title. II. Series. III. Series: SUNY series in feminist criticism and theory

PS374.F45W93 2004
813'.5099287—dc22   2003190066

*In the individual's mental life
someone else is invariably involved,
as a model, as an object, as a helper, as an opponent;
and so from the very first,
individual psychology, in this extended but
entirely justifiable sense of the words,
is at the same time social psychology.*

—Sigmund Freud
Group Psychology and the Analysis of the Ego

Contents

Acknowledgments ix

Introduction: I Want to Be You 1

Part I. Totalizing Identifications 19

1. The Politics of Envy in Academic Feminist Communities and in Margaret Atwood's *The Robber Bride* 20

2. I Want You To Be Me: Parent-Child Identification in D. H. Lawrence's *The Rainbow* and Carolyn Kay Steedman's *Landscape for a Good Woman* 42

3. Identification with the Trauma of Others: Slavery, Collective Trauma, and the Difficulties of Representation in Toni Morrison's *Beloved* 66

Part II. Structures of Identification in the Visual Field 85

4. Race and Idealization in Toni Morrison's *Tar Baby* and in White Feminist Cross-Race Fantasies 86

5. Luring the Gaze: Desire and Interpellation in Sandra Cisneros's "Woman Hollering Creek," Anne Tyler's *Saint Maybe*, Angela Carter's *The Magic Toyshop*, and Margaret Drabble's *Jerusalem the Golden* 119

6. Disidentification and Border Negotiations of Gender in Sandra Cisneros's *Woman Hollering Creek* 145

Part III. Heteropathic Identifications — 169

7. Toward Cross-Race Dialogue: Cherríe Moraga, Gloria Anzaldúa, and the Psychoanalytic Politics of Community — 170

Appendix: The Challenges of Infant Research and Neurobiology to Traditional Models of Primary Identification — 192

Notes — 209

Works Cited — 251

Index — 275

Acknowledgments

More than most books, *Risking Difference* is a product of collaborative thinking and discussion. Marshall Alcorn, Pam Bromberg, Lynne Layton, Todd McGowan, and Frances Restuccia read and reread the whole book at various stages; they contributed not only their time and infinite patience, but also new ideas that stimulated my thinking and enriched the argument. Adelaida Lopez, Roberta Rubenstein, and Ewa Ziarek gave me valuable suggestions for revising chapter 4. Sonnet Retman made many helpful suggestions for managing the tricky argument of that chapter. Jeff Berman, Joan Moschovakis, and Martha Ronk did sensitive, careful and precise readings of the Introduction. Raul Villa contributed a key idea to chapter 6; and Rita Cano Alcalá gave me new insights into Sandra Cisnero's work. Chapter 7 benefited from the readings of Elizabeth Abel, Wini Breines, Gabrielle Foreman, Jane Jaquette, Kalpana Seshadri-Crooks, and Victor Wolfenstein, who contributed shrewd and nuanced insights on the politics of race and identification; and Miranda Outman-Kramer's inspired restructuring suggestions helped me to reshape chapter 7. Hilary Neroni and Barbara Schapiro, readers for the press, read the manuscript with unusual care, tact, and insight. Judith Block, James Peltz, and Anne Valentine have been kind and encouraging editors. Because of the support of this vibrant intellectual community of readers, writing became less a lonely pursuit than a stimulating dialogue and exchange of ideas.

My student research assistant, Regina Clemente, was remarkable for her unfailing competence, hard work, and good cheer. I thank Cynthia Marugg for the painstaking and seemingly infinite copying.

Most of all, I wish to thank my husband Bob Braden, who nurtured my writing both literally, as cook, and inspirationally, as writing coach, for his unflagging support and love.

Parts of chapter 1 appeared in *Tulsa Studies in Women's Literature* 17.1 (Spring, 1998). A small portion of chapter 3 was published in *PMLA* 108.3 (May 1993); a small portion of chapter 4 appeared in *Journal for the Psychoanalysis of Culture and Society* 1.2, 1996; and a small portion of chapter 5 appeared in *Women's Studies* 25.6 (1996). A version of chapter 6, slightly altered, appeared in *Tulsa Studies in Women's Literature* 14.2 (Fall 1995). Parts of chapters 4 and 7 appeared in "Toward Cross-Race Dialogue" (*Signs* 29.3, Spring 2004).

Introduction

I Want to Be You

"Don't you mean, 'I Want to Be *Like* You?'" a rational friend asked when she read the title of this introduction. No: identification as I use the term in these pages is less deliberate, less conscious, less discriminating than the selective imitation of the other implied by the modest phrasing of "I want to be like you." "I want to be you," in its grammatical and logical impossibility, captures the global nature of the desire to become the other, to replace the other—a desire that, I will argue, undergirds everyday structures of feeling like envy and idealization. By identification I mean a confusion of self and other, impelled by the (usually) unconscious desire to be the other. For example, a spectator who watches an iceskater or a basketball player tenses his or her muscles in sympathy with the athlete's moves, losing for a moment the distinction between his or her own body and that of the other (Sandler 25).[1] A woman who looks at a catalog and sees a beautiful dress clothing a perfect body experiences a momentary confusion of her own image with that of the model—and, of course, buys the dress in an effort to make that momentary specular confusion a reality. In this book I analyze common interpersonal emotional dynamics that I claim are founded on such identifications. The quality of the totalizing identifications in part I is suggested by the spectator's holistic identification with the athlete's body in the example cited above; in part I's three chapters on envy and primary identification, the subject takes in the other as a whole, according to the wish to be her: no fine distinctions, no halfway measures, no selective discriminations here. Part II involves identifications based on a visual negotiation suggested by the second example above, in which the catalog shopper confuses her own self-representation with that of the model. Idealization and interpellation involve a visual appropriation of the other's image, as in Lacan's model of imaginary identification. The identifications in parts I and II cause trouble, both psychic and social, immobilizing desire and/or preventing the recognition of the other as subject. Part III focuses on the ways that the same problematic dynamics operate unacknowledged in multiethnic communities. Picking up the analysis of how power and identification work in community from earlier chapters, I argue in part III that a psychoanalytic understanding of such processes can not only uncover some of the sources of these unexamined tensions, but also suggest political correctives to them.

I would not wish to remain long with the impression produced by my introductory examples that identification is always temporary, fleeting. Rather, adults easily fall into such global identifications with the other because of a long habit of identification. Identifications with others prove both deep and lasting, causing changes in one's behavior, motivations, and self-representation as one molds oneself to resemble the admired model. Summing up the current psychoanalytic consensus, Laplanche and Pontalis state without qualification that "it is by means of a series of identifications that the personality is constituted and specified" (205). If identification is thus constitutive, and if earlier wishes and modes of thinking persist in the unconscious, as psychoanalysis tells us they do, then, I argue, the desire to be the other remains a motivating force in human relations throughout life.

It is of course Freud who gave us our basic understanding of identification as the primary relation to the other. In *Group Psychology and the Analysis of the Ego* he claims that identification is the first emotional tie: a baby wants to "be" the parent initially; only later does she or he develop the desire to "have" the parent as a love object (105). And, operating on the basis of an oral logic, the infant imagines becoming the parent by devouring him or her. To deal with adult versions of primary identification I expand Freud's insights past the infantile model by consulting various Lacanian theories of identification. Because Lacan's thinking is marked, as Jacques Alain-Miller said of him in a recent talk, by the conviction that "the subjective link with the Other is originary... [that there is] an essential connectedness to the Other, a fundamental dependency on the Other" (ALL), Lacan seems to have worked and reworked the model of primary identification proposed by Freud.[2] In chapter 1 I adopt Lacan's model of envy as the desire to be an other who appears to possess a fullness of being and heightened vitality that the subject lacks. Two Lacanian paradigms of parent-child relations, the parental structure of demand and the hysterical structure of identification with the desire of the Other, enable me to explore the origins of damaging identifications in the family (chapters 2 and 3). I claim that these concepts represent Lacan's transformations of Freud's primary identification between family members into fully articulated psychic and intersubjective structures. It is my own private speculation that Lacan—like me, like all of us who try to theorize identification—was fascinated by the mystery of how the other can be internal to the self, by the puzzle that we appear to be free-standing, self-enclosed autonomous individuals, yet the other is always already imbricated in us.

It is Lacan's more widely recognized paradigm of imaginary identification that founds my theories of idealization and interpellation in part II. As a transaction in the visual field only, imaginary identification differs from the totalizing, prespecular merger of self and other in primary identification. Imaginary identification, Lacan says, is "the transformation that takes place in the subject when he assumes an image" (*Écrits* 2). The first identification takes place at the mirror: the child sees in the mirror image an ideal of bodily unity and assumes identity with it; and this process "will be the source of secondary identifications" (*Écrits* 2). Having seen "his form materialized, whole, [only in] a mirage of himself, outside himself" (S I 140), the subject will ever after seek an idealized image "outside himself," in the form of the other and strive to assimilate it to his own image. At first glance, this visual style of identification would seem to be less invasive, less a violation of the other's autonomy than the Freudian model of primary identification. But this form of identification blocks recognition of the other as a separate subject, too. In order to shore up the illusion of a coherent, unified identity, Lacan writes, the subject identifies with "the empty form of the other's body" (S I 170). To reduce the other to an empty form is to denude him or her of subjectivity.[3]

Part III examines the play of identification within multicultural feminist communities. I argue that the often unconscious desire to identify with, to *be*, the racialized other, produces a number of the misrecognitions that complicate race relations among feminists. Contemporary feminist theorists of identification like Diana Fuss and Doris Sommer, seizing on the seemingly inescapable conclusion to be drawn from both Freudian and Lacanian paradigms that identification involves an assimilation of the other to the self and thus a violation of the other's autonomous subjectivity, have warned against any attempt to use identification as a political tool for bridging race or class difference. Thus Fuss points out "the imperializing character of many cross-cultural identifications" and Sommer warns that "identification is a murderous trope that reduces two to one, ... the calamitous dismissal of politics by feeling" (Fuss 8; Sommer 22). Yet a psychoanalytic rethinking of feminist community such as I attempt in chapters 1, 4, and 7 has to start from a recognition that pointing out the dangers of identification may not be enough. Making identifications with admired others is an inevitable consequence of the discrepancy between the desire of the subject for fullness of being and the inevitable gaps and instabilities of identity that Lacan describes so well. "What we have then," as Jannis Stavrakakis elegantly puts it, 'is not identities but identifications, ... a play between identity and its failure, a deeply political play.... Instead of identity politics we should speak of identification politics" (29, 30).[4]

It is most often white feminists who voice admiring identifications with feminists of color: here identification carries with it the convenient, though unintentional, effect of erasing the power differential between whites and women of color. That can have real-world political consequences, as an example drawn from the classroom will illustrate. In her women's studies classes, Sonia Kruks writes, white students often identify so strongly with the experiences of women of color in the texts they read that they overlook their own structural implication in racist systems. "It is as if they were personally exonerated from white racism by virtue of the depth of their empathy" and the intensity of their outrage at racism. In this situation, "vicariously 'becoming' women of color" replaces the need to examine the realities of their own positions in a social structure organized by race privilege and oppression (158)—or to think of giving up the benefits they derive from that structure. I argue that in feminist communities cross-race identification can have similar political effects.

Then, too, as Iris Marion Young has argued, communities, like individuals, tend to strive toward unity and identification, toward a solidarity that eclipses difference. In part III I cross disciplinary boundaries to invoke the theories of standpoint epistemologists Sandra Harding and Paula Moya and feminist political theorists Seyla Benhabib and Iris Marion Young to help me explore two competing needs of a pluralistic community: on the one hand, hearing what the other says in her own terms requires temporarily adopting her perspective; on the other hand, hearing what the other says in her own terms requires some corrective to the imaginary tendency to draw the other into identification and so confuse her perspective (and interests) with one's own. Chapter 7 explores a range of identificatory modes in social groups in order to theorize policies and institutional structures that might correct for the tendency to reduce difference to the same, yet allow for a temporary and partial identification with the other's standpoint.

Identification and Culture: Gender, Race, and Interpellation in Contemporary Fiction

As a psychological process, identification functions as a conduit of values from culture to individual; as a conceptual tool, therefore, identification theory mediates between the fields of psychoanalysis and cultural studies. Identification processes may be largely unconscious, but that does not mean they are outside the reach of culture. One identifies with what one wants to be, and what one wants to be is inevitably influenced by cultural definitions of desirability. My chapter 5 is devoted to interpellation, to exploring answers to the question that feminists since Simone de Beauvoir have often asked: What makes a woman actively desire to embrace the culture's gender definition as her own? And the literary texts in each chapter dramatize the ways that race, class, and culture shape women's identifications, making a mockery of the supposed antinomy between psychoanalysis and cultural studies: For how can desire and identification be separated from power relations, or the individual psyche from cultural formations?

The figures one chooses for identification are "already framed and constituted in a broader sociality," as Sara Ahmed has said (31). So, for example, Jadine in Morrison's *Tar Baby,* an African–American woman trying to succeed in the world of fashion, identifies both with a white Western model of beauty and with a figure who embodies an African ideal of womanliness; that contradiction reflects her social position, torn between two cultures. And Denver in Morrison's *Beloved* not only identifies with her mother's traumatic past, but also identifies at the level of the body with the collective trauma of slavery. Her hysterical deaf-muteness would seem to enclose her within the confines of her own body and disconnect her from the social world, but I argue that her exile from language is a symptom of history, that it enacts the damage inflicted on her ancestors by the culture of slavery.

Identification in the fictions I study here often traps women in cultural stereotypes of femininity. In chapter 5 I theorize interpellation, "the process whereby a social representation is accepted and absorbed by an individual as her (or his) own representation," to borrow Teresa de Lauretis's definition (12). I extrapolate three forms of interpellation from Lacan's notions of the mirror, the screen, and the gaze. First, I analyze female viewers' mirror identifications with culturally endorsed figures of femininity on the cinematic screen (a form of interpellation that feminist film theorists of spectatorship have discussed extensively).[5] The screen comes into play in Angela Carter's *The Magic Toyshop* and Anne Tyler's *Saint Maybe:* the characters regard themselves and each other through a superimposed screen of cultural stereotypes. Last, through a reading of Margaret's Drabble's *Jerusalem the Golden* I trace the effects of desire for a gaze that is forever elusive—effects that include the reproduction of feminine glamour.

While these fictions portray identification as a tool of gender interpellation, identification can also provide inspiration for breaking free of conventional gender ideology. Given the logic of identification, it is not surprising that women would embrace identification as a way to shed the constraints of femininity. Gender identifications are always imbricated in power relations and, I want to argue, in the desire for power. Either a woman can believe a patriarchal culture's false promise that if she successfully parades her desirability she will attract a man and thus gain the only power that counts—power over the man who loves her—and therefore adopt the current version of attractive femininity as her own. Or, restive with the lack of power imposed on her by conventional definitions of femininity, she might identify in order to experience firsthand a stronger, more liberated identity. The desire to be Zenia, a figure who seemingly escapes social constraints altogether, drives the actions of the three protagonists in Atwood's *The Robber Bride*. On the one hand, identification with Zenia arrests all three in fantasies of absolute power and jouissance. On the other hand, dealing with the envy and aggressivity that their primitive identifications with Zenia arouse in them teaches all three to accept a range of feelings previously outlawed by their own "good girl" ideology. And confronting those unruly emotions leads them to question the costs to community of subscribing to the ideal of sisterhood and to formulate a broader ethic of care, one that makes room for envy and ambivalence between women.

Some of Sandra Cisneros's short stories offer an optimistic vision of identification as a means toward individual growth and change. For example, Cleófilas, a Mexican woman in "Woman Hollering Creek," identifies with Felice, a Chicana whose stance on the border between Mexican and American culture gives her the flexibility to play with and recombine various cultures' gender roles. Identification here provides a short-cut to difference, allowing Cleófilas to experience, if only for a moment, how it feels to be another kind of woman and so break the hold of (what Cisneros presents as) the Mexican cultural imperative to be one kind of woman only. Yet such is the slippery nature of identification that conscious, voluntaristic identifications with a subversive gender model can be undermined by unconscious identifications. In Cisneros's "Never Marry a Mexican" the protagonist Clemencia throws all her conscious energy into resisting the cultural pressures to be a mother, disidentifying with her cultural mothers, La Virgen de Guadalupe and La Malinche as well as disidentifying with her blood mother; she chooses to identify instead with an icon of aggressive masculinity. Yet she identifies unconsciously and involuntarily but decisively with, precisely, a mother—the wife of her lover Drew.

Race, Identification, and Community: Extending Lacan's Three Registers to the Political

Whether psychoanalysis is capable of expanding to deal with issues of race—and with social issues generally—has been the subject of recent debate. Because Lacanian psychoanalysis operates by means of universalizing structures, it has been accused, with some justice, of "imagin[ing] subjectivity hermetically sealed off from other informing discourses and practices" such as race (Spillers, "All the Things" 142). Since Lacanian "discourse collapses the social into a symbolic register that is always everywhere the same" (Abel, "Race" 185), it tends to exclude the influence of specific cultures and specific historical moments on subjects.[6] Yet I find Lacanian psychoanalysis to be most useful when it is joined to specific cultural discourses, such as discourses of race in the United States.

In parts II and III of this book, I adapt Lacan's three registers—the imaginary, the symbolic and the real—to social and political uses, including an analysis of race relations between feminists. Briefly stated, the imaginary is the realm of the visual and of dual relations. Imaginary experience is rooted in the subject's relation to images, in the first instance the image of his or her own body and the image of the other; imaginary relations with the other are governed by dual structures like identification, envy, and aggressivity, which rest on the assumption of a fundamental interchangeability of self and other. The symbolic is the dimension of language and social order; it is the categories and structures of the symbolic that organize our experience and our understanding of the world. The Lacanian real is not the material world, but rather that which is excluded from the symbolic order: it is there, in the external world, but it escapes symbolic categories and so cannot be explained, cannot be made to yield meaning. In human experience, real, symbolic, and imaginary processes are of course always intertwined; I separate them artificially for purposes of analysis.

Race is discursively produced, a function of socially determined categories that "shape human difference in certain seemingly predetermined ways," as Kalpana Seshadri-Crooks says (4). Race belongs, then, to the symbolic order of language and social structure. But the discourse of race imprints its meanings on bodies; racial hierarchies work themselves out in a field of corporeal visibility. As a regime of visual imaging, the system of racial difference depends for its effects on the imaginary.[7] In chapter 4, I explore the nature of imaginary identification across race lines.[8] The comments of some prominent white feminist critics—Elizabeth Abel, Jane Gallop, Tania Modleski, and Jane Stembridge—attribute to certain black women a liberated self-containment and authority that they seem to wish they possessed. Because of their emphasis on the visualized corporeal aspects of the other woman's presence, these admiring identifications seem to me to be founded on the imaginary processes that Lacan traces back to the mirror stage. The hallmark of imaginary identification is the perception of the other as a coherent whole, self-complete and self-possessed. As can be seen in the passages I cite from these white women's texts, the process of identifying with the seeming wholeness of the other woman reduces her to an illusory self-consistency, obscuring the actuality of her complex, multifaceted subjectivity. Black feminist theorists Ann duCille, Deborah McDowell, and Valerie Smith speak back from their own texts, thus refusing to be reified as icons of personal strength and self-possession and reestablishing their complexity as subjects. So there is the beginning of a dialogue—but less a dialogue than a sequence of "scripts of confession" on the part of the white women and "scripts of accusation" on the part of the black women.[9]

Chapter 7 extends the discussion of feminist politics begun in chapters 1 and 4 to explore how imaginary, symbolic and real modes of identification play out in feminist multicultural communities. How does the real function in community? How could community structures effectively mobilize symbolic processes? I approach the answers to these questions through readings of Cherríe Moraga's "From a Long Line of *Vendidas*" and Gloria Anzaldúa's *Borderlands*. I argue that a conscious acceptance of the real as it functions in a multicultural community to thwart identification, and the deliberate institution of procedures to encourage dialogues governed by the symbolic, could work against the imaginary tendency to see in the other a replica of oneself or to assign to her an idealized difference. It might then be possible to make a partial identification with the cultural other that would enable one to perceive things from her point of view while continuing to respect her differences.

What is at stake here is the hope for a functional multicultural community, a subject explored in chapter 7. For if one does not identify with the cultural other to some degree, how can one be in a position to hear her point of view, to perceive things from her perspective, to see how things look if one stands in her shoes? The trick is to modulate the totalizing tendency of identification, to put into practice the idea of identifying "to a degree." As Abdul JanMohamed articulates such a nuanced identification, "a greater awareness of *potential* identity" could produce an "openness to the Other" while preserving "a heightened sense of the concrete socio-politico-cultural differences between self and other" (93). In rethinking community, and in particular feminist multicultural community, the emphasis has to remain on the cautionary terms—on the "potential" for identification, on a "partial" identification with the other.

Contemporary Discussions of Identification

Since identification is central to human development, the literature on identification is enormous.[10] For purposes of locating the present text in the contemporary critical conversation, I will sort current theories of identification into two lines of descent from Freud's two major paradigms of identification: primary identification and identification as a melancholy compensation for object loss. Some of the confusion around identification—but perhaps also the fruitfulness of the concept—stems from Freud's own vacillation between these two models. In "Mourning and Melancholia" (1917) Freud defines identification as a process that preserves in the internal world a love object lost in external reality. In *Group Psychology and the Analysis of the Ego* (1921) however, Freud argues that identification is primary: the desire to be the parent precedes object love—and thus necessarily the loss of the object. In *The Ego and the Id* (1923) the reader can see Freud wobbling between the two paradigms. He begins chapter 3 with a definition of identification as the introjection into the ego of a lost object (28) and then, on pages 29 and 30, teeters back and forth several times between a definition of identification as the first emotional tie to an other and a definition of identification as a compensation for object loss—hence a sequel to object love rather than its predecessor. (See Mitchell *Relational* 48–51; also Borch-Jacobsen, *Freudian* 215–16.) Freud ends this vacillation with an endorsement of identification as primary: identification with the parent "is not the consequence or outcome of an object-cathexis; it is a direct and immediate identification and takes place earlier than any object-cathexis" (31).[11]

What Freud was trying to protect or preserve by worrying this problem, why it mattered to him which comes first—identification or desire—is not of concern here. What is relevant is that those contemporary theorists who take as their point of departure the idea of identification as a melancholic compensation for lost love arrive at a very different place from those who begin with the concept of identification as primary. Recently, feminist theorists and queer theorists—perhaps following the lead of French theorists Julia Kristeva and Nicholas Abraham and Maria Torok—have focused on the second Freudian explanation of identification as a process that preserves a loved and lost object by making it part of the ego. Julia Kristeva theorizes melancholy as the result of a subject's unwillingness to give up the originary relation with a parent who is still undifferentiated from the self—the maternal "Thing," in Kristeva's words, not yet distinct as "mother"; the melancholic inscribes that primary preobject within, focusing her or his hatred and love on it. Abraham and Torok distinguish between introjection, which acknowledges the object as lost and deals with the loss through a modified identification, and incorporation, in which the lost object is "encrypted" within, preserved within an (imagined) space set aside for it in the body.[12] In the texts of both Kristeva and Abraham and Torok, the refusal to acknowledge loss results in the failure to enter language fully—for words originate in the child's need to substitute a symbol for the maternal body, and in the case of encryptment the mother is not lost.

Judith Butler and Diana Fuss creatively use the notion of melancholic identification to undergird a series of psychological processes. In *The Psychic Life of Power* Butler theorizes "gender identification [as] a kind of melancholy" based on the ego's incorporation of the forbidden love object, the same-sex parent (132). Because of the cultural taboo on homosexuality, the prohibited love for the same-sex parent cannot be recognized and therefore cannot be properly mourned; rather, the same-sex object is incorporated. Identification then replaces object love, as in Freud's theory of melancholia; and normative gender identity is established on a melancholic base—a base fraught, then, with the pathologies described by Abraham and Torok and Kristeva. Butler also analyzes political identifications. She questions identity politics by urging us to examine what is excluded when an identification is formed: any gender identification or political identification is constituted and secured by excluding other identities that return to haunt it; every insistence on a disidentification—I am not that—may hide an identification that has already been made and so must be disavowed (*Bodies That Matter* 111–19). While Butler does not advocate the resurrection of all excluded identifications, the complexity and resulting instability of identifications that she emphasizes opens up the possibility of "innovative dissonances" within the subject that can contest the fixity of gender and political positions (*Gender Trouble* 67).

In *Identification Papers* Diana Fuss states categorically that "all identification begins in an experience of traumatic loss and in the subject's tentative attempts to manage this loss" (38). But the range of identificatory paradigms covered by her book belies that emphatic closure: successive chapters deal with hysterical identification, oral incorporation, and the political uses of identification as a colonizing tool. Throughout, Fuss critiques Freud's repeated insistence that desire and identification "are structurally independent of each other" as a defense against allowing homosexuality legitimacy. At every turn, she says, Freud twisted theory to guard against "the possibility for new forms of identification to generate ever proliferating and socially unmanageable forms of desire" (67, 72).[13]

In the 1990s spokespersons for various marginalized groups sought to redeem melancholia from the standard pathological model of a "desperate" alternative that prevents healing (Schafer, 154–55) and reclaim it as an effective political weapon. Philip Novak, for example, argues that the losses sustained by African-American culture warrant a grieving that never ends, a constant rememorialization of losses that keeps faith with the past. Writing on *Sula*, Novak says, "[Toni] Morrison's efforts to transform mourning into melancholia are paradoxically therapeutic" (191). Michael Moon recommends that gay men respond to the catastrophes of AIDS by preserving the dead and their erotic attachments to them. As José Muñoz sums it up, "For blacks and queers... melancholia [is] not a pathology or a self-absorbed mood that inhibits activism, but... a mechanism that helps us (re)construct identity and take our dead to the various battles we must wage in their names" (355–56). In an even-handed assessment of such adaptations of melancholia to political ends, Greg Forter comments: "These authors help remind us that to establish a universal pattern of mourning and enjoin all victims of loss to follow it is to erase the particularities of lived experience, and often to delegitimate continued attachment to what a dominant culture deems unimportant or pernicious." On the other hand, Forter points out that melancholia is by definition an unconscious process that actually blocks the conscious memory of the lost person, not least "because it confuses self and other and so makes it hard for the other to become an object of memory or consciousness"; it is mourning rather than melancholy identification that would allow a full articulation of "what racism or homophobia or sexism has destroyed [so] that we can build a collective memory of it and seek to do battle in its name" (138–39).

Anne Cheng's innovative *Melancholy of Race* plots the intersections of race and several models of identification. The race melancholia that gives the book its title originates in the contradictory mandate of assimilation. Racialized subjects are enjoined to assimilate to "Americanness," but since after all "Americanness" means whiteness, bodies marked Asian are denied assimilation. "Because of the built-in impediment of racial difference, the prospect of assimilation for the 'Asian' is fraught with potential failure, shame, and humiliation, not to mention the threatening indictments of self-denial and self-beratement" (69). Those subjected to the pathogenic doctrine of assimilation encrypt not a lost beloved, as in the Freudian model, but "an impossible ideal" together with "a denigrated self" (72).[14]

Those critics who make their point of departure primary identification tend to emphasize, as I do, identification as an end in itself and the desire to identify as an ongoing motive force.[15] Mikkel Borch-Jacobsen argues that identification is the subject's primary desire. Elaborating Freud's argument in *Group Psychology* that identification is the first emotional tie to the other, Borch-Jacobsen contends that "the ego ... is born" through mimesis—a formation of the self as a copy of the other, as an incarnation of the other. And "the 'other' whose identity is incorporated ... sinks into an oblivion that precedes memory and representation, ... and it is 'myself'" (*Emotional Tie* 60). Borch-Jacobsen thus answers in the most radical way the enigma that I posed earlier: How is it that the other is always already imbricated in, internal to, the self? According to him, the self is from the beginning radically other to itself. If the other is the foundation of the self, human beings can no longer be thought to be coherent and self-identical.[16]

Most useful to my study of adult identifications is Borch-Jacobsen's point that this primal fantasy—I am the other—leaves a legacy of desire for identification. "Desire ... does not aim essentially at acquiring, possessing, or enjoying an object; it aims ... at a subjective identity. Its basic verb is 'to be,' not 'to have'" (*Freudian* 28). While Borch-Jacobsen's view of desire may be incomplete (for surely the desire "to have" also generates fantasies? Otherwise how would the business of marrying and having children get on? to say nothing of consumer capitalism) his emphasis on the desire for identification explains the basis of many adult fantasies. As I will argue, envy, idealization, and interpellation are based on the desire to be the one "whom one wishes to equal, to replace, to be" (*Freudian* 28).[17]

Theorists who consider identification to be motivated by a primary desire to be the other rather than by loss tend to see identification as part of ongoing relationships within the family. Thus Roy Schafer understands identifications with parental figures as both an essential element of a child's development and a means of enriching parent-child love relationships.[18] Jessica Benjamin continues this tradition of understanding identification as a relational process linked to other relational processes: "Identification is not merely an internal process, it is also a kind of relationship"; "to 'be' something, to act it in one's own body, is ... a crucial mechanism of maintaining closeness" (*Like Subjects* 124, 65). Defying Freud's vigilant separation of identification and object love,

Benjamin posits the existence of identificatory love: for the son, identification with the father is a means not just of securing recognition and gender identity; it is also "a special erotic relationship," a love relationship with his ideal (*Like Subjects* 124). And daughters yearn to have their identificatory love for the father affirmed and encouraged. In *Like Subjects, Love Objects* Benjamin addresses some of the same questions of identification and difference as the present work, albeit from an object relations rather than a Lacanian perspective.[19]

While the theorists surveyed above focus primarily on Freudian models of identification, my analytic framework is Lacanian. Kaja Silverman also theorizes from a Lacanian perspective and her work, like mine, focuses on the social implications of identificatory processes. Silverman's development of "heteropathic identification" in *Threshold of the Visible World* is a welcome reminder that identification can have positive effects. Following Max Scheler, Silverman labels heteropathic an identification through which one goes over to the other's position rather than assimilating the other to the self. My theory of partial identification has affinities with that model. Yet when Silverman suggests that idealization can provide the vehicle for such a heteropathic identification, I disagree. Starting from the same Lacanian assumption that I do in chapter 4—that idealization is a process conditioned by the original idealization and appropriation of the mirror image—Silverman arrives at a conclusion diametrically opposed to mine. While Silverman wants to encourage the idealization of African-American bodies in order to reverse their abjection in contemporary culture, I try to demonstrate through example how white idealizations of black women unintentionally erase them as subjects, arousing interracial resentment and misunderstanding.

Like Benjamin and Schafer, I take as my point of departure the notion that identification occurs with someone who is there and loved rather than with someone who is loved and lost; and with Borch-Jacobsen, I assert that identification is desired as an end in itself rather than as a compensation for loss. But while these three theorists' concern with disputing, developing, or revising Freud's theories leads them to focus on infancy and early childhood, I am more interested in following the workings of identification in adult relationships. I argue that if identification is the primary means by which the ego is constituted, then identification likely continues as the unconscious ground of many adult dynamics, such as those involved in envy and idealization. Because all of us live in communities—and increasingly in multicultural communities—it is important to recognize how identification figures in interpersonal processes where it has not been recognized, in particular how it distorts cross-race communications and how it plays out in the complex interactions between women in multicultural feminist communities.

THE SEQUENCE OF CHAPTERS

The three chapters of part I explore some of the complex ways that identification tangles with, enhances, blocks or reroutes desire. Chapter 1 discusses the dynamics of envy in feminist community, drawing on studies of contemporary academic feminists and the portrayal of a female support group in Margaret Atwood's *The Robber Bride*. Lacan's model of envy as an identification with a figure who appears to be complete, to preserve the object a intact, enables me to analyze both academic feminists' (muffled) envy of female superstars who appear to possess fame and the three protagonists' envy of Zenia in *The Robber Bride*. The novel dramatizes the force of envy: Tony's, Charis's, and Roz's desire to be Zenia is more powerful even than sexual desire, romantic love, and self-preservation. I argue that the feminist ethic of mutual support would serve women better, more realistically, if it were expanded to acknowledge feelings of envy and ambivalence between women.

Chapter 2 formulates a Lacanian structure for understanding how parental demand perpetuates primary identification between parent and child. In Seminar X Lacan describes the "structure of demand" that creates a neurotic subject: the parent takes the child as his or her object a, as an extension of self that will complete him or her. D. H. Lawrence's classic *The Rainbow* illustrates the Lacanian paradigm of demand, showing how the parental need for identification immobilizes a child's desire at the point of the parent's desire. In Carolyn Kay Steedman's *Landscape for a Good Woman* class loyalty cements a daughter's primary identification with her mother. And the text itself vividly dramatizes the effects of excessive parent-child identification on the grown-up child's consciousness: this is Carolyn Steedman's autobiography, but it foregrounds her mother's desires and needs, to the exclusion of the autobiographer's own.

Race complicates a similar structure of primary identification in Toni Morrison's *Beloved*, discussed in chapter 3: Sethe's maternal bond with her one surviving daughter Denver is "too thick" largely as the result of a perverse social system, slavery. Denver's hysterical symptom, deaf-muteness, literalizes and reifies Lacan's notion that "man's desire is the desire of the Other": the paralysis of mouth and ear express not Denver's own desire (which is for language), but her mother's desire that the family story of suffering and murder not be told, not be heard. Denver's hysteria "transforms the body into a textual utterance" (Fuss 116), as does any hysterical symptom: the symptom tells a story that is barred from language. But Denver's body, in thus confusing the linguistic and the corporeal, also tells a larger story: the unarticulated—and unarticulatable—history of slavery. Like Denver, the narrative itself exhibits some of the symptoms of trauma survivors: gaps in chronology, failed metaphors and silences testify to Morrison's own identification with the collective trauma of her slave ancestors.

The models of idealization and interpellation I construct in part II are derived from Lacan's notion of identification as an appropriation of the other's visual form. Idealization, I propose in chapter 4, functions largely through the ideal ego; formed through the assimilation of an idealized image of coherence external to the subject, the ideal ego continues to function throughout adult life as it did during the mirror stage, idealizing a human form external to itself and "assuming [that] image" as a part of itself (*Écrits* 2). The African-American woman Jadine in Toni Morrison's *Tar Baby* is fixated on the ideal ego and is prone to identifications with idealized figures, including an African woman who appears to Jadine to be a model of self-completion and racial authenticity. I juxtapose her idealization of a black woman with several white feminists' idealizations of black women, arguing that race makes a difference in idealization: white women can idealize black women with impunity, ignoring the material conditions that attach to being black in the United States and so feeling no pressure to change the way they themselves live. Jadine's idealizing identification with a black woman, on the other hand, threatens the material and psychic benefits she receives from her successful assimilation to whiteness. The white feminists whose comments I cite appear to be idealizing in Lacanian fashion, seeing in the other an idealized fullness of being that they lack. The misrecognitions and misunderstandings that result demonstrate the dangers to feminist community posed by the impulse to perceive the other in terms of one's own need for an ideal self-possession.

Chapter 5, on interpellation, focuses on the various ways that identifications in the visual field lure women into embracing femininity. The chapter theorizes three kinds of interpellation which persuade a woman to assume the cultural representation of woman as her own self-representation. First, the imaginary: the construction of the ego in the mirror stage, through a process of identifying with an externalized corporal image, makes the subject susceptible to mirroring identifications with the idealized figures of masculinity and femininity on the screens of television and cinema. A second model, which foregrounds symbolic identifications in the visual field, builds on Kaja Silverman's premise (in *Male Subjectivity at the Margins*) that the screen Lacan introduces in Seminar XI, the screen through which others gaze at the subject, is a cultural screen. The third and largest section of chapter 5 considers the paradoxical effects of the subject's desire for the real in the form of the gaze. The desire to captivate a forever elusive gaze inspires various poses that, inevitably, mimic the version of glamour that has cultural currency. My analysis of fictions by Sandra Cisneros, Anne Tyler, Angela Carter, and Margaret Drabble ties the identificatory processes associated with mirror, screen and gaze to the specific gender discourses of Britain, Mexico, and the United States.

Chapter 6 deals with three short stories by Sandra Cisneros which try out three different strategies for disemboweling deeply embedded gender identifications. In "Never Marry a Mexican" Clemencia tries to free herself from limiting identifications with both her mother and her cultural mothers, La Malinche and La Virgen de Guadalupe, through disidentification—and that strategy does not work. A better liberatory method, according to Cisneros's "Little Miracles, Kept Promises," is to reconstruct gender icons so you can live with them: Rosario uses the flexibility of a border perspective to understand La Virgen de Guadalupe as herself multiple and contradictory; and that allows her to identify with a redefined Guadalupe, a model of various disparate womanly strengths. In "Woman Hollering Creek," identification itself provides escape from gender constraints.

Chapter 7 picks up the discussion of feminist politics begun in chapters 1 and 4 to speculate on how dialogues across race lines might become more fruitful. My readerly "dialogues" with texts by Cherríe Moraga and Gloria Anzaldúa are meant to suggest how the real and the symbolic might function in the more embodied conversations of a multicultural feminist community. Through my own (Anglo) reading of Cherríe Moraga's autobiographical text, "From a Long Line of *Vendidas*," I model a cross-cultural conversation where the symbolic dominates, foregrounding difference. While imaginary identification depends on a visual perception of the other as a perfect whole that one appropriates in order to be whole oneself, it is more difficult to see the other as a unified entity when two persons speak—or, as in the present case, when I register my responses to a self-revealing autobiographical text—because new and different aspects of the speaker are revealed over time. Extrapolating from individual exchange to community, I explore the question: Are there ways to institute formal procedures in a community that would enhance the symbolic dimension of communication and thus mitigate—if never completely control—the totalizing tendencies of imaginary identification?

And I argue that certain passages in Gloria Anzaldúa's *Borderlands*—those in dense and difficult Spanish—resist the non-Spanish-speaking reader's attempt to understand, making an implicit statement that there are limits to what Anzaldúa cares to reveal about her own culture. To the non–Spanish speaker these passages function as the real: they remain opaque to meaning; they resist absolutely integration into the monolingual reader's symbolic system. The "real," understood as a resistance like Anzaldúa's to being completely known, could function in community as a reminder that social differences cannot be completely understood, that difference must be acknowledged and respected (Sommer 4, 27). Were such protections against the takeover of identification to be instituted in cross-race alliances, perhaps identification could be modulated so that one could identify temporarily with the other's perspective without usurping or distorting it.

In an appendix, I shift perspective altogether to view identification from the vantage point of relational psychoanalysis and more particularly from the standpoint of infant research. Responding to the claim of infant researchers like Daniel Stern that primary identification between mother and baby does not exist and that internalization is irrelevant to psychic development, I map out how identification processes would function within the neurobiological framework of infant research analysis. Provisionally adopting the notion of neuronal networks as the basis of subject formation, I argue that identification remains a useful conceptual tool even within the infant research model of early development.

Part I

Totalizing Identifications

The identifications in part I are based on the totalizing confusion of self and other that Freud called primary identification; but each chapter extends Freud's model by incorporating Lacanian theories of the complex interconnections between desire and identification. Chapter 1 theorizes envy; comments by contemporary academic feminists, together with Margaret Atwood's *The Robber Bride*, enable me to focus especially on the problematics of envy in feminist communities. Chapters 2 and 3 analyze the origins of identification in the family; they follow the workings of primary identification in a family stressed by the inequities of class (Carolyn Kay Steedman's *Landscape for a Good Woman*) and in a family where the primary bond between mother and child is distorted by the pressures of racial oppression (Toni Morrison's *Beloved*).

Chapter 1

The Politics of Envy in Academic Feminist Communities and in Margaret Atwood's *The Robber Bride*

Opening this book with a study of envy enables me to focus on the primary intensity of the desire for identification and to show the often unacknowledged workings of that desire both in community dynamics and in the relations between individuals. As Lacan defines it, envy springs from the desire to be an other who is perceived as lacking nothing, as completed and fulfilled by the possession of the object a. This other appears to have a heightened vitality and self-possession forever denied the subject. While later chapters unfold the complications in relations between white feminists and feminists of color that derive from the will to identify with the other's supposed self-sufficiency and wholeness, here I deal with a different feminist problematic: the denial of envy, a primitive form of identification, in the name of an ethic of sisterly support. My examples combine reports from contemporary academic feminists with a fictional model of the threat that envy poses to feminist community: Margaret Atwood's *The Robber Bride*. I argue that denying the existence of envy between women in order to preserve feminist solidarity actually undermines solidarity and that envy, along with other hostile feelings generated by the uneven distribution of power between women, needs to be theorized and integrated into the feminist ethic of mutual support.

In Seminar VII, Lacan offers a distinction between envy and jealousy through an anecdote drawn from St. Augustine's *Confessions*. Augustine reports seeing a little boy bitterly eyeing his infant brother at the mother's breast. This is envy, Lacan says—not jealousy: "*invidia* [envy] must not be confused with jealousy" (S VII 116). It is not what the baby *has* that his older brother wants: he has no desire for breast milk. What he wants is to *be* the figure of completion he sees before him. I want to make the same distinction: envy focuses on being, not having; envy targets what the other is, not what the other has; it is a form of identification.[1] "True envy," says Lacan, is "the envy that makes the subject pale before the image of a completeness closed upon itself, before the idea that the *petit a*, the separated *a* from which he is hanging, may be for another the possession that gives satisfaction, *Befriedigung*" (S VII 116). In the small boy's vision the breast stands in for the object a, completing the baby and thus enabling it to experience a closed circuit of "jouissance"—a total instinctual satisfaction. For Lacan, then, envy is the desire to be the other insofar as the other is perceived as self-complete and in possession of an untrammeled jouissance.

Behind the Lacanian structure of envy lies the subject's relation to the object a. Subjectivity is founded on lack: entrance into the symbolic order of language and social law enables one to become a subject, but the price of entry is the sense of losing some part of an originary wholeness, some piece of instinctual satisfaction. That loss is figured as the loss of a part-object—of a part once integral to one's body. Lacan explains the function of the object a in a matheme that represents the fundamental fantasy, the unconscious basis of desire: S<>a. The barred S represents the subject who has been depleted, on entry into the symbolic, by the deletion of the "object a," that part of the self that gave him or her (the illusion of) completion. The subject remains in a relation of attraction/repulsion (<>) to the lost object a. The "a" is a paradoxical object, "both that which is lost... and the trace of this loss, that which remains as a left-over to remind the subject of the lost jouissance" (Evans, "Jouissance" 26). This structure founds the unconscious; and from the unconscious it generates desire—desire for the ever-unattainable lost object.

Because the fundamental fantasy, S<>a, is indeed fundamental to the unconscious of all subjects, everyone is susceptible to the suspicion that someone else is able to actualize the fantasy of jouissance, to enjoy possession of the object a. This suspicion takes the form of the belief that the other is able to enjoy a heightened state of vitality, fulfillment, and jouissance. Lacan says in Seminar VII that he is struck by some of his patients' convictions that "jouissance [is] that which is only accessible to the other." Only the Germans, he says, have a word for this passion of envy: *Lebensneid*. "*Lebensneid* is not an ordinary jealousy, it is the jealousy born in a subject in his relation to an other, insofar as this other is held to enjoy a certain form of jouissance or superabundant vitality." (The translation reads "jealousy", but the word *neid* means envy, and Lacan is explicitly defining envy here.) The envy is extreme—"to the point of hatred and the need to destroy"—yet its intensity is remarkable given that it targets something that the subject can neither perceive nor "apprehend in any way": the elusive, hidden object a that the other supposedly possesses (S VII 237).[2]

The other's possession of the object a is an illusion, Lacan says: "The reference the subject makes to some other seems quite absurd, when we see him continually refer to the other ... as if he were someone who ... is happier than the analysand.... We don't need to see this other come and lie down on our couch ... to know that this [is a] mirage" (S VII 237). In other words, the other is not this mythical being fulfilled by possession of the object a, but an ordinary subject plagued by insufficiency like everyone else.

In actuality, then, no subject can possess the object a. But there is always someone else who *appears* to have the object a—and that is the basis for Lacan's definition of envy. As subjects founded on lack, we are all in the position of Augustine's small boy. From a position of lack, it looks like the other enjoys the plenitude provided by the object a. In *The Robber Bride*, that other is Zenia, who appears to the three protagonists to be "a completeness closed in upon [her]self," a being complete with the object a whose drive energies are intact—for she exercises sexuality and aggressivity without stint, inhibition, or limit—and who possesses a heightened potency and vitality. Accordingly, each of the three protagonists envies Zenia; the wish to be Zenia is in fact so powerful that it trumps even self-preservation and the desire for romantic love. In academic institutions, I argue in the first part of this chapter, it is often the female possessor of fame who becomes the target of envy. For the contemporary feminist academics whose comments I quote, the incompatibility between feminist principles and academic structures generates both envy and the denial of envy. Both feminist communities—the fictional one in *The Robber Bride* and the actual one in contemporary U.S. academia—would benefit, I contend, from expanding feminist ethics to include an analysis of envy.

ENVY, THE FEMINIST ETHIC, AND ACADEMIC COMMUNITIES

The structural inequalities of the academic world breed envy. And in the culture of the academic world the elusive Thing, the prized object that the other enjoys but that remains forever beyond one's own reach, often takes the form of fame. Envy of the other's seeming possession of the object a is always painful, as Augustine's small boy attests. But for feminists in the academy, envy of the other woman's fame is doubly painful because it sets up an internal conflict with the ethic of sisterly solidarity.

A quick review of the evolution of feminist ethics in the 1970s will provide a historical context for the discomfort with envy voiced by contemporary feminist academics. In the early days of the women's movement, female solidarity was first of all a political imperative, a prerequisite for effectively combatting the oppressions of patriarchy. The insistence on sisterhood also derived some of its energy from the patriarchal construction of women as (only) rivals for the man. In reaction, feminist ethics seemed to require an absolute loyalty: there was no room for jealousy or envy of the other woman—remnants, both, of the patriarchal order. Instead, women were expected to feel empathy for each other. Consciousness-raising, the practice of 1970s feminism, both validated women as subjects through empathic listening and maintained that their personal stories made sense only as they were shared, only as they were understood as connected to each other in a communal text of gender oppression. Empathy—uncritical and compassionate listening—was necessary to foster trust and unguarded communication. A euphoric celebration of sisterhood as empathy resulted: "You and I are feeling the same feeling" (Benjamin, "Omnipotent" 144). The encouragement of empathy between women received a boost from feminist psychoanalysis: Nancy Chodorow's influential *The Reproduction of Mothering* (1978) centered on the proposition that the prolonged period of primary identification between mother and daughter generates a heightened capacity for empathy in women. In theory as in practice, then, empathy was privileged while its presumed enemy, envy of the other woman, was avoided and denied.

As feminism gradually became integrated into the university, the clash of values between feminist principles and the principles governing academic structures exacerbated feminist ambivalence about envy. In her comprehensive and fascinating history of the difficulties that arose when feminist activism moved into the university, *Disciplining Feminism*, Ellen Messer-Davidow summarizes this collision of cultures: "Ensconced in our [academic] institutions, we [feminists] demanded inclusivity from systems of selectivity, we sought equality from orders of ranking, and we fought for parity in economies of scarcity" (213). Equality between women grounded the women's movement: solidarity was based on the notion that all women are subjected to the same oppression and that working toward one's own liberation is inseparable from working toward the liberation of all women from that same oppression.³ But the academic principle of selectivity works by denying to some what it grants to others: only some get appointments, only some are awarded tenure, only some are promoted. Yet the feminist ethic enjoins, Don't compete for scarce resources: cooperate. Don't be individualistic: think collectively. It turns out, however, that it is easier to put the collectivity first when the group is excluded from participation—because then it is clear that one's self-interest coincides with, and depends on, the efforts of the group to change the status quo—than it is when the group is incorporated into a structure that rewards individual achievement. The scarcity of success builds hierarchy where there was once solidarity—and that structural inequality generates envy. Yet for feminists negative feelings like envy are banned in the name of sisterly solidarity. It seems clear, then, why the contradictions between feminist ethics and university hierarchies would produce in feminists both envy and the muting and repression of envy.

Even more than material differences in rank, salary, and tenure status, the unequal distribution of intangibles like fame and recognition generate envy in the academic world; that is because of the particular makeup of the professorate. The university operates on the basis of exclusivity—only those who have excelled academically get tenure track positions—so the men and women selected will likely have gone through years of training to "star": they are likely to have been high achievers throughout their school years and thus to have accepted that they would be measured and evaluated at every turn and to have learned to perform in return for abstract signs of recognition like grades and honors. Throughout the years of preparation for the Ph.D. the academic pay-off for accomplishment is recognition. And once inside the professorate, it is again recognition (it is certainly not money) that is the prize: for publications that get read and cited—how many times? for charisma in teaching—how laudatory are her evaluations? how large is her student following? To star is by definition to outshine others—to involve, then, dynamics of competition and envy.

Fame is notoriously something one can never get—or, more precisely, never get enough of; and—recalling the Lacanian structure of envy—fame is also what the successful academic star seems to possess and enjoy. In other words, in the academic world fame often functions as stand-in for the object a. To explore the subject's relation to fame as object a, I here anticipate my discussion of the gaze in chapter 5. I posit that the desire for fame is the desire for a universal gaze and that the disappointments of fame, the hollowness of fame, stem from a mistaken understanding of the nature of the gaze.

Lacan theorizes this mistake in Seminar XI: on the one hand, Lacan describes Merleau-Ponty's phenomenological model of the gaze; on the other hand he presents a psychoanalytic model of the gaze—the gaze as object a. It is the disjunction between these two "truths" about the human experience of the gaze that, I claim, explains both subjects' hunger for such universal abstractions as fame and recognition and the impossibility of "getting" enough fame and recognition to satisfy. In Seminar XI Lacan seems at first to adopt Merleau-Ponty's idea that "we are beings *who are looked at*, in the spectacle of the world" (S XI 75). The gaze is not on the side of the subject, but "on the side of things" (S XI 109), so that as a human being in the visual field one always feels "looked at." Then, however, Lacan makes a distinction between his own notion of the gaze and Merleau-Ponty's by saying that this "ultimate gaze . . . is an illusion" (S XI 77). The gaze is actually the point of invisibility in the visual field; it is missing; it does not exist as such, and so it can stand in for the object a, which is after all only the inscription of a lack. "The *objet a* in the field of the visible is the gaze" (S XI 105). The paradoxical situation of the subject in the visual field produces desire: one wants to be the object of the Other's desire, one wants to be desirable to this gaze that seems to regard us from all sides; but the desire is unappeasable, because the gaze is after all only a manifestation of the object a and as such has no existence in the external world. So, as Joan Copjec says, "if you are looking for confirmation of the truth of your being or the clarity of your vision, you are on your own; the gaze of the Other is not confirming; it will not validate you" (36).

I claim that the desire for fame is a desire to be the object of the universal gaze that appears to surround us. And the hollowness of fame is an effect of the disjunction between the seeming existence of the world's gaze and the fact that the gaze in actuality does not exist. For, as Lacan is careful to say in differentiating his work from Sartre's, the gaze never coincides with the look of a particular individual; nor for that matter would it coincide with the individual looks of thousands. What one wants is the world's gaze. No matter how many individual persons look with admiration on one's work or oneself, the number of particular admirers can never add up to the generalized gaze that one craves. That remains forever elusive: it is nonexistent, a manifestation of the object a and so "just an objectification of a void" (Žižek, *Sublime* 95). The desire for fame *is* the desire for the gaze—for the gaze that always eludes us. So one can never get enough.

No one possesses the object a. But there is always someone else who *appears* to have the object a. And that is the basis for envy. In the uneven distribution of status and fame in the academy, there is always a woman who appears to possess fame. As with Lacan's clinical cases, so with academics: one looks to the other who appears to have it all— who appears to enjoy the absolute fame that one covets, but can never get, for oneself. One envies her the seeming possession of the gaze, of the object a; one would like to be her. In a professorial population schooled in the idea that external recognition equals self-worth, of course the inequalities of fame give rise to envy. Yet the feminist ethic of sisterhood disallows envy between women: so the enviers cannot admit their unsettling feelings of competitiveness toward a female "star"— perhaps even to themselves.

The feminist scholars and students that Evelyn Fox Keller and Helene Moglen interviewed for their study, "Competition: A Problem for Academic Women," reported a high degree of anxiety about their own feelings of envy. On the one hand, respondents made such statements as "We compare ourselves with women, not men" and "The success of men doesn't threaten me, but the success of women does" (22–23); on the other hand, they expressed fear at such admissions: "Competition with women gets close to things that are really very scary" (23). The reluctance to acknowledge envy and competition, like other negative feelings toward women, stems from a faith in—or, perhaps more realistically, a nostalgia for—the idea "that basically all women are bonded together," as Jane Gallop says in a dialogue with Marianne Hirsch and Nancy Miller ("Criticizing" 361, 352). A woman does not want to articulate feelings of envy toward other women for fear of disrupting feminist solidarity.

Yet, as a case study presented by Keller and Moglen shows, envy unacknowledged and unarticulated in discourse makes its way into yet more hostile behaviors that are yet more disruptive of feminist solidarity than a straightforward expression of envy would be. Identified as one of three outstanding feminist scholars in her discipline, the woman Keller and Moglen call "Greta" is consequently watched closely by her female colleagues for signs of "unsisterly" behavior, for lack of support for junior women—which they are not slow to find. They accuse her of a lack of generosity and she in turn "feels betrayed by a begrudging sisterhood" (32). Unable to confront and bring into discourse their own feelings of envy, the junior colleagues (I would say) displace their own guilt for "unfeminist" sentiments onto the superstar, who then becomes the depository of blame for "unfeminist" behavior.

Keller and Moglen conclude, "Envy (and their intense discomfort with it) seems to be the emotion talked about with the most urgency by the women with whom we have spoken. It is this, primarily, that makes competition with women so much more acute and painful... than competition with men" (32). Such an urgency and ambivalence—an envy denied as soon as expressed—calls for inclusion in feminist analysis.

Undergirding feminist guilt about envy is the assumption that envy and competitiveness among women are products of patriarchal thinking, to be extirpated along with other internalized patriarchal structures (Michie 6–7). But the distinction between jealousy and envy becomes important here. Certainly, a phallocentric system that values man as subject and positions woman as less-than-subject puts pressure on a woman to "get" a man to complete her and validate her existence, making the man the scarce resource for which women compete. The result is jealousy: the desire to have what the other has. Either the woman has a man, and I want him, or I have a man and I fear she will take him away. That fear structures her as "the other woman," not a subject interesting in her own right, not a potential friend, but a threat to my well-being, a potential enemy. While feminist analysis has thus provided a framework for understanding jealousy as the product of a value system that privileges the male, envy remains to be analyzed.

Jane Gallop relates a graduate student fantasy that opens up an alternative theoretical approach. "There is a graduate student fantasy that if you stand up after a lecture and ask a devastating question you will get to take the place of the lecturer. They will lose everything they have and you will get it" ("Criticizing" 364). Gallop repeats the idea on the next page, this time making explicit the generational gap between established academic women and aspiring junior women: "The daughter trying to gain a voice for herself must kill the mother" (366). The fantasy throws into sharp relief the difference between the principles of the women's movement and those of the academy: in a world of scarce resources, it's you *or* me—instead of *we*, fighting together and winning through together. And one's own shock at hearing a fantasy about "killing the mother" drives home the point that envy is incommensurate with the ethic of sisterhood.

I would say the underlying structure of this fantasy is quite primitive. Its calculus goes: there is only one position, and there are two of us: therefore you must go so I can be in your place. And here the structural difference between jealousy and envy comes into play: jealousy is a three-person structure, with two rivals vying for the possession of a third; envy rests on a two-person structure, in which the one wants to be the other. Jealousy may well be the product of a male-dominant culture; envy, I would argue, has a different origin. Lacan notes the aggressivity attached to identification, saying it stems from "a rivalry over which is the self and which the other, which the ego and which the replica" (Gallop, *Reading* 62); but in my opinion his account does not explain the origin and logic of this aggressivity as well as does Freud's model of primary identification. In *Group Psychology and the Analysis of the Ego*, Freud asserts that identification constitutes the baby's first relationship with the other: "Identification is the original form of emotional tie with an object"; "[the other] is what one would like to *be*" (107, 106). This first other is necessarily a parental figure. In infancy, Freud says, we process relations in an oral mode; so the wish to be the beloved parent takes the form, "'I should like to eat this'" ("Negation" 237). The first identification thus entails the destruction of the other: "the object that we long for and prize is assimilated by eating and is in that way annihilated as such" (*Group* 105).

Melanie Klein draws her definition of envy from this original relationship to a parental figure, but she moves away from the Freudian base when she goes on to posit a "primary envy"—an impulse to "spoil and destroy" the omnipotent other, based on the perception that the breast "possesses everything that [the infant] desires" but keeps "its unlimited flow of milk and love...for its own gratification" (213). Thus, according to Klein, in adult life "envy is the angry feeling that another person possesses and enjoys something desirable—the envious impulse being to take it away or to spoil it" (212).[4] To my mind, the primacy that both Freud and Lacan accord to the desire to be the other is sufficient to explain envy—both its originary moment and its adult form—without resorting to Klein's hypothesis of a primary envy.

Countering Klein, I would argue that the venom of envy, the bitter desire to denigrate the other, is a secondary effect of the subject's frustration that he or she cannot *be* the other. In order to mitigate the pain of being oneself and not the other, one strives to "alleviate the sense of our disparity by lessening [the] other," as Samuel Johnson said (197).

Gallop, Hirsch, and Miller discuss a phenomenon that I claim constitutes an enactment of this spoiler impulse—the "trashing" of feminist pioneers' work ("Criticizing" 364-66). "A certain generation of feminist theorists . . . have really gotten it from all sides: Elaine Showalter, Nancy Chodorow, Sandra Gilbert and Susan Gubar, Carol Gilligan" ("Criticizing" 364). I would say that the scholars named here, who wrote the seminal texts of second-wave feminism, are in the enviable position of superior prestige, influence, and fame; so other women "trash" their scholarship. The dynamic of envy described by Samuel Johnson is surely at work here: If I cannot be her and have her fame, then I will denigrate her work till she no longer seems enviable, till she no longer stirs these painful feelings of longing to be what she is—and I will take a lot of satisfaction in thus restoring the balance between us![5]

Yet the aspiration to be the other, even if one takes into account the accompanying urge to disparage her success, does not fully account for the spite attributed to envy by previous moralists[6]—nor for the vehemence of the contemporary feminist "trashing" of feminist mothers and the graduate student fantasy of matricide. Freud's theory, however, provides a rationale for the aggressive underside of envy which is consistent with the primitive intensity, violence, and resistance to the reality principle of these fantasies. If it is true, as psychoanalysis tells us, that earlier wishes and modes remain in the unconscious, envy may well draw its ambivalence from the early mode of identification Freud ascribes to infancy: I love the other and therefore want to be her; I want her destroyed so I can take her place.

If envy, the desire to be the other, along with its component of aggressivity, is as basic to human relations as Freud and Lacan assert, and if envy is continually stimulated by the culture of academic institutions, then the feminist imperative to be kind to your sisters—"the omnipresent injunction to play nice and don't be trashy" (Zwinger 190)—won't work; it is fruitless to expect, as Keller and Moglen say that women in academic communities often do, "that competition, conflict and envy can be avoided if only we are good enough" (33). As the examples cited above show, and as Keller and Moglen argue about competitive feelings generally, denial of envy doesn't prevent the feared disruption of feminist bonds. "Competition [and envy] denied in principle, but unavoidable in practice, surfaces in forms that may be far more wounding, and perhaps even fiercer and more destructive, than competition that is ideologically sanctioned" (Keller and Moglen 34). The feminist insistence on solidarity here works against solidarity: what the ban on envy and other competitive feelings between women prevents is not envy, but creative solutions to the problematics of envy.[7]

What is called for, what is indeed overdue, is an analysis of the power relations between women and within feminism.[8] As part of that analysis, feminists could begin to theorize envy as an inevitable product of the power disparities between women. In the context of the academy, that would entail a recognition of the structural inequalities that engender envy and a more complex and detached approach to collegiality; to enter envy and its attendant hostilities into the discourse of feminist solidarity might allow us to imagine relations of support flexible enough to accommodate ambivalence, competition, and envy.

COMMUNITY AND FEMINIST ETHICS IN *THE ROBBER BRIDE*

The Robber Bride reflects the ethic of loyalty that governed the second-wave feminist movement of the 1970s and 1980s—and hence affected Atwood's middle-aged protagonists. The small community of Tony, Charis, and Roz is implicitly governed by the feminist ethic of unqualified support for one's "sisters." A fourth character, Zenia, poses a challenge to this ethic: uninhibited by any principle of care or consideration for others, Zenia indulges every impulse of aggressivity, sexuality, and greed: in particular, she steals away the beloved partner of each of the three protagonists in turn. Zenia's actions challenge the feminist ethic of solidarity; and the emotions that she both expresses and arouses in other women—envy, rage, hostility—point to what that ethic leaves out. The resolution of the novel supports my argument that feminist ethics needs to become more inclusive, to incorporate an analysis of envy, ambivalence, and hostility between women into the reigning ethic of emphatic support.

Through the three protagonists' treatment of Zenia, *The Robber Bride* implies that while feminism has liberated some of women's capacities from the stranglehold of gender training, it has not been bold enough. In the Victorian version of womanhood that feminism has effectively deconstructed, woman is a self-sacrificing, self-effacing angel who ministers to husband and children, directly intuiting and satisfying their needs and desires while having no needs or desires of her own. The purity of her love for children and husband is angelic as well. *The Robber Bride* suggests that feminism preserves the "angel" stereotype in at least one dimension of female experience: women are still expected to be pure in their feelings toward other women, to care for them without ambivalence.

The name, Zenia, is a transliteration (with a change of the initial letter) of *Xenia*, the guest-host relationship sacred to the ancient Greeks. It was the duty of the Greek citizen to include the stranger in his household, to give the stranger a substitute home, to make of the stranger (*xenos*) a friend (*philos*). Similarly, each of the three protagonists protects, shelters, and nurtures Zenia, extending familial care to "the other woman" (*xeina* or *xene* is the feminine form of the word for stranger/guest).[9] Each woman, going over her memories, pinpoints the moment that Zenia came over the threshold, welcomed into the home: "[Tony] opened the door wide and in came Zenia, like a long-lost friend, like a sister, like a wind, and Tony welcomed her" (128); "mutely Charis holds out her arms, and Zenia stumbles over the threshold and collapses into them" (250); "Roz opens her heart, and spreads her wings, her cardboard angel's wings, her invisible dove's wings, her warm sheltering wings, and takes her in" (412). The Greek obligation to offer the stranger shelter has become the sacred duty of "taking in" and taking care of the other woman (and to the detriment of caring for the self: Zenia's sexual appetite for men destroys the domestic happiness of each woman in turn). Atwood thus implicitly links the Greek duty to care for the stranger to the feminist directive that all women should care for and nurture each other. By insisting on universal and unfailing support for other women, Atwood implies, the feminist ethic fails to account for negative feelings between women—especially envy.

The women's responses to Zenia's depredations illustrate the potency of envy. The three protagonists, I claim, see Zenia as a figure of jouissance who defies the law of the symbolic order that every subject shall be constituted by lack. In terms of Lacan's paradigm for envy, they look at Zenia as the small boy looks at his blissful brother at the breast: they assume that she is in secure possession of the object a. Accordingly, they want to be Zenia: and that desire for identification with a figure who seems to possess untrammeled potency, freedom, and vitality is stronger than self-preservation, sexual desire, and romantic love. For each of the three protagonists in turn, despite ample evidence that Zenia is a robber of husbands (hence the title), insists on keeping Zenia near and so exposes, and predictably loses, her beloved mate to Zenia's seductions.

What makes Zenia such a compelling target for identification? I argue that *The Robber Bride* constructs Zenia as the impossible figure who is *in actuality* complete with the object a. No subject can possess the object a; but Lacan names two mythic figures who do—the *père-jouissant* and ~~The~~ Woman. As I understand Lacan, these mythic figures play out the subject's impossible dream of attaining the object a and thus experiencing a jouissance without inhibition or limit. Through an analysis of Lacan's essay on *Hamlet*, I will argue that Zenia, like Claudius in *Hamlet*, is positioned as such a figure. In *The Robber Bride*, then, envy is the desire to be an other who does not just appear to, but actually *does*, possess the object a and so experiences unmitigated jouissance. Like Claudius (in Lacan's reading) Zenia functions as a double for the protagonists—not in the usual sense of the subject's mirror image, but in Lacan's more specific sense of the uncanny double who incarnates the fundamental fantasy, the fantasy of the subject completed by the object a.[10]

Identification and Desire: The Lacanian Double

Lacan's essay, "Desire and the Interpretation of Desire in *Hamlet*," provides a way into understanding the central puzzle of *The Robber Bride*: Why does each protagonist, even when forewarned, put her own happiness at risk by exposing the man she loves to Zenia's obvious seductiveness and known rapacity for men?

Lacan's analysis begins with the fundamental fantasy discussed earlier—$\mathcal{S}<>a$—and develops the implications of this structure for the workings of desire. The price of entering the symbolic order and so becoming a subject is the sacrifice of unified being, figured as the loss of an integral part, the object a. The formula for fantasy, $\mathcal{S}<>a$, represents the subject in a relation of attraction to the lost object a. This structure founds the unconscious; and from the unconscious it generates desire: "Desire ... finds in the fantasy its reference, its substratum, its precise tuning in the imaginary register ... in an economy of the unconscious" ("Desire" 14). "How does [the subject] respond then to the necessity of mourning [for the lost thing, for the object a]?" With "the composition of his imaginary register," says Lacan ("Desire" 48): that is, as I interpret it, the subject searches for the semblance of the object a, the lost part of the self, in some object in the external world. "Something becomes an object in desire when it takes the place of . . . that self-sacrifice, that pound of flesh which is mortgaged in his relationship to the signifier" ("Desire" 28). In normative desire, the subject finds a substitute in the outside world for the lost object a: the object of conscious love fantasy "takes the place of what the subject is symbolically deprived of," so that "the imaginary object is in a position to condense in itself the virtues or the dimension of being and to become that veritable delusion of being (*leurre de l'être*)" ("Desire" 15).

It is a delusion that the loved object is worthy of love, since it is lit up by virtue of its position in the subject's structure of desire, not by virtue of its own merit. But that delusion is normative: "In the fantasy [i.e., the relation of the subject to the substitute object] an essential relationship of the subject to his being is localized and fixed" (16). That is, desire is anchored to some object in the subject's local reality; this anchoring has the advantage of orienting the subject away from the self and toward the external world.[11]

Hamlet's desire was once on track, directed at Ophelia. But now he reviles her: once loved, once adequate as substitute for the lost object, she is no longer: Why? Because Hamlet is fascinated by Claudius, who presents a much more compelling object than an attractive woman—the image of the self completed by the object a. Claudius embodies jouissance: he acts as if the sacrifice that Lacan stipulates as the price of entry into the symbolic order never took place—as if he never had to sacrifice "that pound of flesh." His drive energies are intact: he acts out uninhibited aggressivity (he kills his brother the king) and uninhibited sexuality (he takes his brother's wife into his bed). In other words, he operates on the level of jouissance, indulging every impulse, immune or oblivious to the Law of the Father that sets limits on action.[12] As Lacan points out, the death of a king—in the myth of the primal horde or in *Oedipus Rex*—is usually followed by the translation of the actual father into the Law of the Father. In *Hamlet* the king is killed, but what succeeds him is not the Law of the Father; rather, the *père-jouissant* remains on scene—not a father abstracted into social law, but a father who acts out all his impulses, sexual and aggressive.[13]

Hamlet knows what he wants: he wants to kill Claudius. But he cannot act because of an overlap and confusion of two dimensions. Normally, the structure $S<>a$ inhabits the unconscious, whence it generates desire for substitute objects. When Hamlet confronts Claudius, he sees the central fantasy structure of his own unconscious—that is, the fantasy of possessing the lost wholeness, of integrating the object a: he cannot strike down an existence that inhabits his own unconscious (50). Hence, Lacan says, Hamlet can kill Claudius only when he has received his own mortal wound and knows it, when he has severed "all narcissistic investments" (51), including investment in the impossible dream of regaining intact being and jouissance.

Freud defined the uncanny as the appearance in the outside world of something familiar, yet strange—something once known, then repressed; and he listed the double as one of the manifestations of the uncanny ("The Uncanny"). Lacan refines that notion, so that the uncanny comes from an encounter with an other subject who embodies not just any signifier repressed from consciousness, but the original object, the object of primal repression that created the unconscious—the object a. "*Das Unheimliche*, the uncanny, ... is linked not, as some believed, to all sorts of irruptions from the unconscious, but rather to an imbalance that arises when [the unconscious fantasy structure, $\$<>a$] decomposes, crossing the limits originally assigned to it, and rejoins the image of the other subject" ("Desire" 22). The object a materializes in the body of "the other subject," and that is the moment of the uncanny. Although he does not use the term here, I claim that this is Lacan's version of the double: not a figure of the imaginary, not the mirror image of the subject—for the mirror image lacks the unspecularizable object a; not a figure in the symbolic, not the image of the barred subject, constituted by lack; but a figure of the real, a reflection of the self at the level of the unconscious fantasy that the subject can be completed by possession of the object a.[14]

Lacan's definition of the uncanny explains Zenia's hold on Tony, Charis, and Roz: they see in her the integration of the object a, the completion of the self impossible in the symbolic order to which they belong. And, as Mladen Dolar says of Hoffman's doubles, "because the inclusion of the object entails the emergence of the lost part of jouissance, [the double] is somebody who enjoys, ... who commits acts that one wouldn't dare to commit [and] indulges in one's repressed desire" ("I Shall Be" 13–14). Zenia is likewise a figure of unrestricted jouissance, indulging every sexual and aggressive impulse without limit. Jouissance is impossible within the symbolic order and exists only in the real. That is, the full and unlimited expression of aggression and sexuality is impossible to the symbolically castrated speaking subject. "The real is what must be excluded in order for the subject as a speaking being to constitute itself" (Dean 15). Zenia, like the Claudius of Lacan's interpretation, is a figure of the real—a figure who evades the ineluctable law of symbolic castration.[15] Zenia's power, vitality, and impulsiveness are intact because she has not made "that self-sacrifice," forfeited "that pound of flesh" necessary to entry into the symbolic (Lacan, "Desire" 28).

How then can Zenia be a subject? My answer would be, she is not a subject. First, textually speaking Zenia is not a subject because she never gets to be the subject of narration, so her thoughts and feelings are never recorded; no subjectivity, no inner world, confronts the reader directly. More pertinent to a Lacanian analysis, she exists outside all structures fundamental to the symbolic order. The Name-of-the-Father orders the network of intersecting signifiers that gives each subject a position in relation to other subjects. Zenia's birth is nowhere recorded (two archivists, Harriet the detective and Tony the historian, agree that "according to the records . . . she was never born" (518; see also 420); and Zenia has no surname, carries no name-of-the-father ("Zenia didn't seem to need a name" [141]). So she has no stable place in the kinship structure governed by the Name-of-the-Father, but fabricates a different origin and family history for each listener. Likewise, she refuses the symbolic fate of the dead—to be replaced by a signifier, by the name recorded on the gravestone. She returns after her supposed death, after her funeral, "more alive than life itself"—because, as Slavoj Žižek says, the living dead exist outside the symbolic and so have "access to the life-substance prior to its symbolic mortification" ("Grimaces" 47).

But, it will be objected, the symbolic order also designates the order of language, and Zenia certainly speaks. Yes, but because she does not acknowledge herself as a named object in a system of named objects, positioned by a signifier, she is capable of traveling up and down the signifying chain, capable of unlimited substitutions. That is, she lies. So signifiers appear to be subject to her rather than she to them.

The symbolic is also a social order. The "I" is a signifier that places me in relation to other signifiers within a system; and that position is necessarily limited by the structured relation to other positions; as subject, I recognize not just the other subject, but the relational system that governs us all. One accedes to one's subject position by accepting that it is limited—that *is*, by renouncing jouissance. Zenia, like Claudius in *Hamlet*, does not acknowledge her position as a signifier in relation to other signifiers, nor the necessity of abandoning jouissance as a prerequisite for joining such a system. "Raging unchecked" (152), she exercises sexuality as if there were no Law regulating desire, taking any man she likes, regardless of whom he "belongs" to in the civic order of marriage; likewise, she recognizes no limit to aggressivity, leaving only "scorched earth" (35) when she finishes with each protagonist in turn.

The three protagonists are unable to act effectively in Zenia's presence because, like Claudius in *Hamlet*, she is out of place in the symbolic order they inhabit. She is the real, that which exceeds the symbolic order, that which no signifier can represent, that which those within the symbolic order are at a loss to account for: "She's a given. She's just there, like the weather" (498). Atwood is careful to show that each protagonist has lost, or repressed, something specific that Zenia embodies; but more broadly, each protagonist of *The Robber Bride* encounters in Zenia Lacan's "uncanny," the piece of the real, the object a, that she has had to renounce as part of the symbolic compact; and she is fascinated by the image of an uncastrated self capable of unfettered and unlimited self-expression.

Now I can hazard an answer to the riddle of desire in *The Robber Bride*. Each protagonist's desire is for her man—clearly, unequivocally; yet each, ignoring clear warnings of Zenia's "robber bride" propensities, is intent on keeping Zenia near and thus placing the man she loves in harm's way: Why doesn't each woman move in the direction of her desire? Desire is motivated by the absence of the object a. For desire to operate—for the subject to seek a substitute object in the world—the original object, the piece of the real called the object a, has to be missing. If it is present, there is no lack and so no desire. Or (another way of saying the same thing), the subject's fantasy ($<>a) channels desire not outward, toward the external substitute for the object, but back upon the self, in a compulsion to regain the impossible unity barred by the symbolic. Each protagonist would like to be Zenia—and the desire to *be* the one with access to the jouissance afforded by the object a is much stronger than the desire to *have* the man, the (substitute) object of desire. Desire loses its way, ensnarled in identification. As Hamlet knows what he wants—he wants to kill Claudius, and says so repeatedly—so Tony knows what she wants: she wants West; he is her happiness. Yet when Zenia returns and takes him away, Tony is paralyzed, like Hamlet, by a narcissistic attachment: "part of what Tony feels is admiration. Despite her disapproval, her dismay, all her past anguish, there's a part of her that has wanted to cheer Zenia on, even to encourage her.... To participate in her daring, her contempt, her rapacity and lawlessness" (184). Zenia incarnates Tony's jouissance, untrammeled by Law.

ENVY AND THE ETHIC OF CARE IN *THE ROBBER BRIDE*

While *The Robber Bride*, rich in psychological complexity, is larger than allegory, on one level it functions as a parable of a feminist community's integration of envy into an ethic of mutual nurturing. At first, the three protagonists of *The Robber Bride* follow a code that requires that they care for each other in a purely supportive way that excludes all negative feelings—including envy. Thus Roz, feeling lonely, "thinks wistfully of the dinnertime tableau at Tony's house [Tony and West at the dinner table], then decides that she is not exactly envious.... Instead she's glad that Tony has a man, because Tony is her friend and you want your friends to be happy" (441). The upsurge of envy, the desire to be Tony in the moment of the conjugal meal, is followed by denial. Feminist orthodoxy replaces spontaneous emotion, as Roz dutifully recites the rule that one must empathize with one's friend, be happy in her happiness.

Yet envy is the feeling that Zenia arouses in each of the protagonists: each wants to be in Zenia's place, to take over her attributes, her power—to replace her and to be her. I will give an account here of the sources of Roz's envy only, since for my purposes Roz represents an exemplary feminist subject.[16] She is the character most influenced by feminism: she has participated in consciousness-raising sessions and produced a feminist magazine. She envies Zenia because Zenia embodies what she has been denied, first by the social code of gender and now, in relation to other women, by feminist principles. The experience of feminist consciousness-raising has opened Roz's eyes to some of the limitations of gender, but it has only reinforced her obligatory goodness to other women. She lives by what Carol Gilligan has identified as a specifically female "ethic of care": a view of the world as "a network of connection," a web of interconnected subjects so constituted that if someone in need pulls on the thread that connects her to an other, that other is expected to respond. Roz recalls Zenia exclaiming, "'Fuck the Third World! I'm tired of it!' ... It was a selfish, careless remark, a daring remark, a liberated remark—to hell with guilt! It was like speeding in a convertible, tailgating, weaving in and out without signaling, stereo on full blast and screw the neighbours, throwing your leftovers out the window" (109). Zenia's "Fuck the Third World!" defies an ethic that insists on the "response" in responsibility. Roz, tired of always "try[ing] so hard to be kind and nurturing" (332), envies Zenia the vitality that comes from putting the self first, heedless of consequences to others. Against Roz's vision of her own timid moral self "tiptoeing through the scruples" (442), hobbled by consideration for others, she imagines Zenia speeding, tailgating, throwing her garbage out the window. "Roz—although shocked... had felt an answering beat, in herself. A sort of echo, an urge to go that fast, be that loose, that greedy, herself, too" (109). What wears Roz down is the eternal sameness of giving to others, all her other potencies damped down, "muffled," by "her Lady Bountiful cloak" (442). Weighted down by her own "goodness," she longs for excess—longs to enact "some great whopping thoroughly despicable sin.... she would like to be someone else. But not just anyone... she would like to be Zenia" (442–43).[17]

To give her obsession with Zenia a name, Roz reviews the "Seven Deadly Sins" and realizes that her sin is "Envy, the worst, her old familiar, in the shape of Zenia herself, smiling and triumphant... *Let's face it, Roz, you're envious of Zenia. Envious as Hell*" (118). Roz pictures Zenia as a figure in the style of medieval allegory—an embodiment of the envy she both enacts and arouses in other women.[18]

The envy foreclosed from the feminist ethic that governs the small community of Roz, Charis, and Tony materializes in Zenia—and her presence makes that ethic founder. Or so I read the present-day sequence that opens the novel. Long after Zenia has stolen away their men, long after they have attended her funeral and seen her ashes scattered (they think), the three protagonists are having a companionable meal at the Toxique Cafe when Zenia comes in the door, seemingly risen from the dead—and her intrusion immediately destroys their solidarity. Their friendship has been based exclusively on caring for each other after each of Zenia's man-stealing depredations. After Zenia stole each woman's man, the other two moved in to comfort and soothe. Roz "rocked Tony back and forth, back and forth, the most mother that Tony ever had" to comfort her for the loss of West (210); "Tony makes Charis a cup of tea [and]... wraps Charis in a blanket" after Zenia runs off with Billy (317); and Tony and Charis mother Roz with warm baths, massages, and tuna casseroles after Zenia robs her of Mitch. The images of devoted maternal nurturing suggest that the feminist ethic has carried forward one aspect of the Victorian "angel of the house" stereotype, transformed into a sororal imperative: a woman must now extend the care once accorded to family members to other women. I would not say that Atwood is advocating that women abandon an ethic of mutual care: after all, the three women gain both from giving and from receiving care, enabling each other to revive from loss and to regain a measure of self-esteem. But the text does show that the ethic of care, like any ideology, lives by the exclusion of some important realities.

After having attended Zenia's "funeral," and in the absence of a crisis that would call on their nurturing skills, the three women have continued to see each other, but their relations lack intensity. Although the focus of their reunions is Zenia—metaphorically, "she's here at the table . . . we can't let her go" (32)—"they don't talk about Zenia" (31). They do not reveal aspects of themselves that are not part of the ethic of care—do not reveal, for instance, their envy of and rage against Zenia. Their friendship has grown correspondingly pale and one-dimensional: they meet mainly to commemorate, Tony thinks, "like war widows or aging vets, or the wives of those missing in action" (31). Zenia embodies what is left out of the feminist ethic of mutual support: usurping the place of the woman in each of the three heterosexual couples in turn, she enacts envy in its most primitive form: get out of the way, I want to be in your place. And her actions can be interpreted at best as a reckless fulfillment of her own impulses, regardless of the consequences to others, at worst as a no-holds-barred aggressivity toward other women.

When Zenia makes her reappearance at the door of the Toxique Cafe where the three women are lunching, she both represents and evokes in the others the envy and aggressivity they have been repressing. Because they have barred these elements from their friendship, the bond of mutual aid immediately disintegrates at their resurgence: each woman thinks privately that the others will be of no "help in the coming struggle" against Zenia (39). Roz, imagining how she will take a knife to Zenia's jugular, "knows" that the other, peaceable, women will be of no help: she does not need "Tony's analysis of knives through the ages or Charis's desire not to discuss sharp items of cutlery because they are so negative" (116). Tony "hasn't shared her plans with Roz or Charis. Each of them is a decent person; neither would condone violence. Tony knows that she herself is not a decent person" (455). Just at the moment that the reappearance of Zenia calls for devising a common strategy for confronting her, sisterhood, powerless to deal with the anger and ambivalence between women that it has excluded, disintegrates. The three women, stumbling out of the Toxique, melt away from each other in silence.[19]

The concluding dinner of the three women at the Toxique is structurally parallel to this first meal, but it represents a more substantial communion. Their conversation, which takes up the 70 pages of the novel's penultimate section ("The Toxique"), is thus extended because it frames the narrative of each woman's final encounter with Zenia. Each has gone alone, that day, to Zenia's hotel room, and each has "killed" Zenia. That is, Tony went to Zenia armed with a weapon and a plan for murder, Charis enacted a murder on the spot (or thinks she did), and Roz played out multiple scenarios of killing Zenia. In the event, Zenia indeed died that day, as the three women find out after dinner. (The text mystifies the cause of her death, so that the reader cannot tell whether one, or, more probably, none of the three killed her.) While on the plane of psychological realism each of the three has ample motive for revenge—Zenia has "robbed" each of her beloved partner—the coincidence of three separate "murders" and the victim's actual death on a single day defies the reality principle and begs to be read outside the conventions of literary realism.

What the three women are acting out is the Freudian logic of envy, based on primary identification. Each of the three has envied Zenia, wanted to "be" her. Roz remains aware that her desire to be Zenia is a fantasy. But for Charis and Tony, the boundary between self and other sometimes blurs completely: Charis, especially, incorporates her ("[Charis] thinks about being Zenia"; "Charis has part of Zenia inside herself" [300, 302].) The three "murders" enact the primitive complement to envy. Like the graduate student fantasy recounted by Jane Gallop, the plot turn here recapitulates the strategy that Freud attributes to the infant: the other side of wanting to be the parental figure is the wish that he or she would disappear. Where the one wants to be the other, aggression results: the other must be removed so the one can take her place.

Feminist psychoanalysis has reinforced the feminist ethic of empathy—most obviously through Nancy Chodorow's emphasis in *The Reproduction of Mothering* on the extended mother-daughter identification that gives women permeable ego boundaries and enables them to experience what the other is feeling. The ambivalence central to Freud's model of the first identification challenges Chodorow's version of a pacific female-female relationship by emphasizing that a love that identifies with the first other and an envy that wishes her out of the way coexist. Both envy, the desire to be the other, and empathy, the capacity to imagine what the other feels, are reminders that human relations begin in identification and that human beings as a result are not the self-enclosed, solitary individuals that they appear to be, but are instead open and permeable to each other's experience and emotions.

The surreal events of the last day can be read as Atwood's attempt to bring envy, with its attendant ambivalence and violence, into the text of female friendship. It is important to *The Robber Bride*, and to the nuances of its critique of feminism, that the protagonists kill Zenia only in fantasy. " 'I must have been a little crazy,' [Tony] says, 'to think I could actually kill her.' 'Not so crazy,' says Roz. " 'To *want* to kill her, anyway' " (468). The crucial act here is a speech act: as each woman tells the story of her attempted murder, she brings her destructive feelings toward a woman into the female community's discourse, where they can be accepted as part of a complex and contradictory mix of feelings toward women. So long as the feminist ethic of sisterhood insists on empathy and denies envy and ambivalence between women, it leaves individuals to go off by themselves, like Charis, Roz, and Tony after the initial luncheon, to confront alone their guilt over hostile feelings toward women or to spin out the monstrous plots of private revenge fantasy. When the three characters bring their envy and rage into the conversation, these feelings can be contextualized, seen to coexist with positive feelings toward women. Charis, Tony, and Roz continue to care for each other, but their mutual support is more meaningful now that it is based on a fuller understanding of *all* that they share. I would suggest that feminist community can provide support to women on a realistic basis only when it acknowledges feelings of envy and ambivalence between women and learns to integrate them into an ethic of mutual support.

Chapter 2

I Want You To Be Me

Parent-Child Identification in D. H. Lawrence's *The Rainbow* and Carolyn Kay Steedman's *Landscape for a Good Woman*

What are the family dynamics that prolong totalizing identifications between parent and child? In the texts under study in this chapter and the next—*The Rainbow*, *Landscape for a Good Woman*, and *Beloved*—it is the parent who requires that the child function as an extension of him- or herself, or, in Lacanian terms, as the object a that will complete the parent. The misdirection of parental desire and its devolution into demand maintains a primary identification between parent and child and prevents the child from establishing him- or herself as a separate subject of desire and language.

In Lacan's model, maternal desire is the crucial factor that forces a child to separate from its identification with the mother. Lacan's emphasis differs from the Freudian account, where the baby experiences a primary identification with the mother—"either at one with her or striving to be at one with her" (Greenberg and Mitchell 161)—until the father intervenes; by laying claim to the mother, the father in Freud's theory refutes the infant's immediate and total possession of her and thus forces the child to enter into new relations of desire and identification. In Lacan's model the father functions more as a reference point for the mother's desire, while the key factor is that "maternal desire goes *elsewhere*," forcing the child to confront "the traumatic 'fact' that it is not her immediate and sole object" (Shepherdson, *Vital* 126). In pointing elsewhere, maternal desire opens up the field of the

Other beyond the infant and thus the possibility of other objects—for the child as well as the mother. The realization that maternal desire targets something beyond itself inaugurates desire in the child (a process I will shortly describe in more detail).

The same realization propels the child into language. The fort-da parable, dear to Lacan, can serve as an example. When the mother goes away, the baby is compelled to create signifiers to fill the void of her absence—and little Ernst does, vocalizing for the first time the syllables "da" [here] and "fort" [away]. In other words, when the mother's desire propels her away from the infant, he has to develop a substitute for her, a signifier that can serve in her absence. The fort-da illustrates the reduced role Lacan gives to the father, who is "present" in this anecdote only as the presumed destination of the mother's desire. Lacan everywhere depreciates the role of the actual father and reduces him to "paternal metaphor"—the representative of language, of "the symbolic operation, the primordial metaphoric substitution, by which the symbolic order of difference and mediation is established" (Shepherdson, *Vital* 135). What serves as a wedge between mother and child is no longer the castrating father, but language—signifiers that mediate between persons, signifiers that establish difference and distance.

The key term is then the desire of the mother. And when something goes wrong with maternal desire—when for some reason the mother's desire no longer points the child toward the field of the Other—there will be effects not only on the desire of the child, but also on his or her language function. In *The Rainbow, Landscape for a Good Woman,* and *Beloved,* parental desire does not function properly as desire, but devolves into demand. (In *The Rainbow,* it is paternal desire that goes astray, but the father's taking the place of the mother figure makes no material difference in the structure of parent-child relations that Lacan calls demand. For Lacan, the term "mother," like the term "father," designates a position in a structure—"a place and a function" (Rose, "Introduction" 39)—which does not necessarily coincide with a specific gender.)[1] Whereas desire is indeterminate and always moving on—"in its essence, a constant search for something else" (Fink, *Lacanian* 90)—demand is unchanging. Parental desire in each of these texts becomes a demand for primary identification, for the conflation of self and other. And that substitution of demand for maternal desire affects each child's capacity for desire and language. In *The Rainbow,* Ursula's development of desire is blocked as a result of meeting her parent's demand to reflect and contain *his* desires and feelings. In *Landscape* the daughter/narrator seems incapable of articulating any desires of her own, and her language, instead of streaming ever forward, becomes snagged on the key signifier of maternal desire. And in *Beloved*, primary identification with the mother effects an arrest in both desire and language: Denver's hysterical deaf-muteness signifies not her own, but her mother's desires; and her speech and hearing are literally paralyzed.

A child can escape imprisonment in primary identification through a process that Lacan calls "separation" (S XI 213–15)—a specialized use of the term that addresses specifically the separation of one's own desire from one's parent's. "Separation" requires both the recognition of lack in the parent and the capacity to substitute signifiers for the parent's desire. When the parent, however, stubbornly hangs onto the child, allowing no distance between them, there is no lack to set the process of signifying substitutions going, and the child cannot get his or her desire into motion. In *Écrits* and Seminar XI, and more fully in the unpublished Seminar X ("Anxiety"), Lacan describes the neurotic structure of desire ($\$<>D$) that results from the parent's taking the child as his or her object a—as the missing part that completes the self. D. H. Lawrence's *The Rainbow* fleshes out this formula by describing, with a meticulous attention to psychological detail, a series of interactions that weld the desire of the child to the demand of the father. The parent-child dynamic theorized by Lacan and dramatized by Lawrence can serve as explanatory paradigm for the primary identifications in *Landscape for a Good Woman* and *Beloved*, and more specifically for the laming of the child's desire in both texts.

"He Took Ursula for His Own": The Child as Object A in D. H. Lawrence's *The Rainbow*

In Seminar X, Lacan describes the structure of demand, a parental structure that produces the child as a neurotic subject—defined by Lacan as someone whose fundamental fantasy structure is $\$<>D$ instead of $\$<>a$. As explained in chapter 1, the fundamental fantasy structure of the normative subject is $\$<>a$, where $\$$ represents the subject divided by the symbolic order, $<>$ signifies "bound to" or "in a relation of attraction to," and the object a denotes the lost primal object the subject unconsciously believes is necessary to his or her being. The object a is the object-cause of desire, engendering the subject's movement from one object to the next in search of the always-already-lost, never-to-be-found object that would fill the gap in the subject.

The crucial step in the formation of a subject of desire ($\$<>a$) is the child's recognition of the mother's lack, a process described as "separation" in Seminar XI (213–15). At first, Lacan says, the child tries to be the object that will satisfy the mother's desire. It is only when the child realizes that the mother's desire is always on the move, searching for something, never satisfied with what she finds, that the child gives up the quest to be the sole object of maternal desire and recognizes that the mother's lack is fundamental, irremediable. The child then realizes that she, too, is lacking, presumably because "man's desire is the desire of the Other"—meaning, in this context, that the child identifies with the mother's form of desiring. As Bruce Fink says, "Man learns to desire *as an other*, as if he were some other person" (*Lacanian* 54). (While "the desire of the Other" generates multiple meanings in the Lacanian text, one sense of the Other is the mother as the first representative of the big Other or symbolic order—"the Mother *qua* primordial figure of the Other," as Žižek says (["Body" 69]).[2] Through identification with the mother's lack, the child discovers its own fundamental lack, the object a—or, as Lacan puts it, "One lack is superimposed upon the other" (S XI 215).[3] Rather than remaining fixated on the question of what the parent wants, his or her own desire gets going. Or, to return to the terms of Lacan's formula, the process of separation results in the child's establishing its own fundamental fantasy, in imitation of the mother's: $\$<>a$.

In the parental structure of demand that Lacan refers to in Seminar XI and describes more fully in Seminar X, both parent and child exhibit a faulty structure of desire. For the parent, the fundamental fantasy could be represented (although Lacan himself does not so represent it) by $\$<>$ the child; in the parent's perception, the child completes him or her, so that the lack that propels desire disappears. As for the child, Lacan says that the child "transports the function of the a into the other" (S X, 5 December, 1962), meaning that he or she visits the problem of the object a, or lack, only within the fantasy structure of the mother; and there she solves it by becoming the object a that fills the gap in the mother; the child need not, then, deal with lack (the object a) as a property either of her mother or of her own subjectivity. As Lacan expresses it, the child puts the parent's demand (for love, for completion) there, where the object a should be, so that the formula for neurotic structure is $ \diamond D$. In the place of the object a, forever lacking, is the demand (D) of the parent, always there: "the demand comes here improperly at the place of what is elided, the object a" (S X, 12 December, 1962). The mother's demand fills out the child's being. Not being able to establish him- or herself as subject on the basis of lack, the child cannot become the subject of her own desire (always synonymous with lack in Lacan's thinking), but instead remains attached to the mother's demand.[4]

D. H. Lawrence's classic description of the relation between an overbearing parent and an accommodating daughter in *The Rainbow* will serve not only to give the texture of lived experience to Lacan's formula of demand, but also to provide a paradigm for the contemporary narratives of overidentified parent-child relations in Steedman's *Landscape for a Good Woman* and Morrison's *Beloved*. *The Rainbow* shows, with an attention to emotional and psychological detail unmatched in literature, both the parent's—in this case, the father's—need for a totalizing identification and the child's responses to that need.

Lawrence makes it abundantly clear, from Will's relation with his wife Anna before Ursula is born, that he feels incomplete and wants someone (originally his wife) to make him whole through a primary identification, a complete and lasting fusion with him. When Will "t[akes] Ursula for his own" while she is still a tiny baby (254), he is trying to make up for an acute sense of insufficient being by annexing another to the self. Placing the child in the position of the object a, the part that will complete the self, annihilates the recognition of the child as a separate subject and assimilates her to the self. When the fantasy of a primary identification lives on, unmodified, in a parent, it becomes a danger to the child.

The expressions that convey Will's feelings for Ursula appear at first to be harmless clichés of parental love: "So Ursula became the child of her father's heart" (255); "he had set his heart on her" (254). But the literal sense of the heart as an internal organ underlies the conventional phrases, so there is a latent sense of Will placing the infant within the confines of his body.

Heart images also convey the effects of the father's assimilation on the baby: "Her sleep-living heart was beaten into wakefulness by the striving of his bigger heart, by his clasping her to his body for love and fulfillment" (263). Will's heart "beats" Ursula's heart into a rhythm akin to his own, though it is only an infant heart, with its own internal rhythm. The verb "beat" retains all its meanings here, as a heartbeat and as a term of physical abuse: to "beat" the infant's heart into an adult tempo that matches Will's own is a kind of physical violence that stands for the emotional violence of forcing a baby's feelings into alignment with adult feelings.

As Ursula grows, her heart remains in thrall to Will's heart: "Her heart followed him as if he had some tie with her" (263). For example, when she is four and Will is angry and irritable, "It was then that his child Ursula strove to be with him. She was with him, even as a baby of four, when he was irritable and shouted and made the household unhappy.... When he was disagreeable, the child echoed to the crying of some need in him, and she responded blindly. Her heart followed him" (262–63). Although "she suffered from his shouting" (263), her primary response is not her own fear—the fear a small child might well feel at a parent's rages—but a mimesis of her father's feelings. She "echoes" in her own internal world "the crying of some need in him" and responds "blindly" to it—"blindly" because the crying need is invisible, belonging not to the external display of anger but to Will's underworld of emotion, where Ursula is "with him," "within his darkness" (259).

A refrain of excess—"too soon," "too near"—indirectly comments on the incommensurability between the adult demand and the child's capacity for response:

> Her father came too near to her. The clasp of his hands and the power of his breast woke her up almost in pain from the transient unconsciousness of childhood. Wide-eyed, unseeing, she was awake before she knew how to see. She was wakened too soon. Too soon the call had come to her, when she was a small baby, and her father held her close to his breast, ... clasping her to his body for love and for fulfillment. (263)

Despite the overtones of incest, Will demands a union that is identificatory, not sexual. The violation is psychic. Ursula is forced to see—and bestow recognition—"before she knew how to see"; the call for empathy is age-inappropriate, beyond her capacity, and so gives her "pain." The chorus of "too soon," "too near" forms a lament for the child's forced maturation.[5]

The demand is presented through the "too near" relation of bodies, as Will "clasps her to his body for love and for fulfillment" (263). Lacan deploys a similar image of bodies clamped together to convey the overclose relation of the parent "who allows absolutely no space between [him]self and the child" (S X, 12 December, 1962): the "mother on his back." "This relation of lack on which [the child] establishes himself, which makes him desire, is... disturbed when there is no possibility of lack, when the mother is always on his back" (S X, 12 December, 1962).[6] A child cannot establish itself as a subject of desire when there is a lack of lack, when "the mother is always on his back" so that there is no absence to set both desire and the signifying function in motion. By a happy coincidence, *The Rainbow* figures the overidentified relation between parent and child as a similar burdensome joining, the one glued to the other's back (although the positions are reversed.) When Ursula is five years old, Will demands that she dive with him from a high canal bridge, repeatedly risking both their lives; the child "hold[s] herself fixed to [his back]" (267) as they dive naked into the canal. Lawrence thus pictures Ursula's body as an extension of the father's body, as the object a that completes him. That overclose identification "fixes" her in a single position, immobilized at the point of his demand.

Both Lacan and Lawrence focus on the loss of childhood mobility as a symptom of a pathological attachment to the parent. Lawrence depicts normal childhood consciousness as a free movement among the flowers, insects, and playthings that offer themselves to the child's attention (261, 263). In contrast to the images of nature through which Lawrence describes the fluidity of attention proper to early childhood, a mechanical image depicts the unchanging nature of the demand. Will asks Ursula "for love and for fulfillment, asking as a magnet must always ask" (263). And Ursula orients herself, ceaselessly, to the lodestone of her father's emotional being: "still she set towards him like a quivering needle" (263). The destructive quality of the father's unending demand—feel my feelings, want what I want, be me—is conveyed by the replacement of the human by the mechanical: Ursula is fixed, permanently stationed at the point of her father's demand. Rather than discovering the parent's lack and thence, through identification, recognizing her own lack and thus becoming a subject of desire in motion—$\$<>a$—Ursula is arrested at the D, at the point where she completes the parent ($\$<>D$). "In the neurotic's fantasy ($\$<>D$) instead of ($\$<>a$), the subject adopts... the Other's demand—that is, something that is static, unchanging" (Fink, *Lacanian* 186–87, n. 2). Mobility gives way to stasis.

Consequently, Ursula's desire is lamed. As an adult she suffers from a lack of erotic mobility. For example, she always returns to Anton Skrebensky rather than seeking another object—though she always finds him unsatisfactory. And rather than try out a variety of erotic experiences with him, she adopts a single posture in relation to him: when they dance, when he kisses her, when they make love on the dunes, she mentally "kills" him, "destroying him in the kiss" (368). The demand of her father was that she give herself up to him entirely. Now Ursula can conceive of heterosexual relations only as a power struggle: either she submits to the other and he takes her over, or she obliterates him and survives intact. What she has lost is the play of desire—the fluidity of movement as one seeks first one substitute, then another, for the missing and motivating object a. She remains fixed in a single position of defensive autonomy that she figures to herself as an identification with the moon: "she was cold and hard and compact of brilliance like the moon itself" (366). As the moon, she is whole, sufficient unto herself, lacking nothing: "she was hard and bright as ever, intact" (366). But that refusal to acknowledge lack and desire ends in making her like the moon indeed: when Skrebensky turns back to look at her lying in the sand, after their final sexual encounter on the dunes, he sees "the unaltering, rigid face like metal in the moonlight, the fixed, unseeing eyes, ... the motionless, eternal face" (532–33).

To be fully human, according to Lacan, is to be in motion, roving down "the rails—eternally stretching forth towards *the desire for something else*—of metonymy" ("Insistence" 167). It is in seeking (and never finding) the lost object that the subject is propelled into motion, and that motion is life: "all that exists lives only in the lack of being" (S VII 294). Ursula's fixation in a posture of self-sufficiency that rules out lack and desire is inhuman by Lawrence's standards, too: in the passage above her living face is finally reduced to an immobility characterized as inanimate—"unaltering, rigid, ... like metal, ... fixed, ... motionless."[7]

LANDSCAPE FOR A GOOD WOMAN AND THE SIGNIFIER OF MATERNAL DESIRE

Landscape for a Good Woman dramatizes a similar arrest in desire, and it enacts the linguistic analogue of that arrest. Both the structure and the narrative discourse of *Landscape for a Good Woman* betray the narrator's ongoing identification with her mother, an identification that is "primary" in the standard psychoanalytic sense of the term: it rests on a conflation of self and other, on a fusion of the self-representation with the representation of the other. This is an autobiography, and the subtitle promises "A Story of Two Lives"—the author's own and her mother's. But although the narrator introduces her story by saying, "It has a childhood at its centre—my childhood, a personal past—and it is about the disruption of that fifties childhood by the one my mother had lived out before me" (5), it seems that the mother's life not only disrupts but displaces the life of the self, the *autobios*, that one would expect to find at the center of an autobiography. Rather than showing the processes of identification at work, as *The Rainbow* does, the text of *Landscape* itself dramatizes the structure of primary identification.

The task that Steedman sets herself is to articulate "the politics of envy"—the desire to have what one cannot get—that ruled her mother's life, to enter that envy into a political analysis, as the subjective side of class inequity, and to validate it, as an envy "proper" to those who live in a state of dispossession (123). Well and good. But what is lacking is the narrator's own economy of desire. What does she, the narrator, want? And how does she feel about not getting it? It is the mother's desires alone that fill the autobiography; so the text performs a variation—indeed, several variations—on Lacan's dictum that "man's desire is always the desire of the Other" (S XI 58). I will argue that the mother's desire presents itself in such a way that the child Kay cannot easily become a subject of desire in her own right. On the one hand, the mother's desire devolves into demand—the same demand for a definitive, ongoing primary identification that Will makes on Ursula in *The Rainbow*: be a repository for my desires and feelings. On the other hand, the mother replaces desire with need: in the gap where maternal desire might be, indeterminate and indeterminable, the mother always names a specific material object and implies that it will satisfy her need. So the child cannot discover the unnamable desire, the crucial lack that would enable the process of "separation" that Lacan describes. Consequently, the adult narrator, like her childhood self, remains overly attached to what the mother wants and needs, and her own desire stalls.

That hitch in desire is reproduced at the level of the text. First, the New Look dress—object of the mother's desire—becomes the obsessive focus of the narrator's text, as it apparently was of her mother's life. Second, the narrator's discourse adheres loyally to the stubbornly materialist discourse of the mother. Over its length, *Landscape for a Good*

Woman compiles a virtual inventory of the material objects denied the mother by an unjust class system. It is true that thus entering maternal need into a signifying system enables the author, finally, to begin moving away from her discursive identification with the mother: she evolves a language of her own (composed of fairy-tale signifiers); and from the vantage point of that separate personal discourse she sees her mother anew. But something escapes this symbolic resolution: the primary identification, the impossible conflation of "her" and "me" persists in a blurring of the boundary between self and other even in the final pages of the narrative.

Steedman's text is in many ways innovative: as Victoria Rosner has written, it critiques the stories that Western culture tells itself about childhood—including autobiography, history, and psychoanalytic case study (9). Perhaps Steedman's most original contribution is the insertion of class into the developmental stories of psychoanalysis. Her memoir thus answers the call of such psychoanalytic critics as Elizabeth Abel and Hortense Spillers to expand psychoanalysis "to incorporate issues of social difference" and so make it "useful . . . for theorizing [the social] order's intervention in the production of diversely gendered subjects" (Abel, "Race" 185). In Steedman's revisions of psychoanalysis both the preoedipal bond and the oedipal problematic are formed not through family dynamics alone, but in the intersection between the parental figures and "the social world outside the front door" (Steedman 72). As Abel has pointed out, it is a representative of class hierarchy who figures as the third term in Steedman's oedipal crisis, when a forest keeper shouts at her father for picking bluebells and wrests the flowers from his hand: the white roots of the bluebells lie exposed, limp, withering on the bank, in a fairly explicit metaphor of her father's social castration. He could not embody the Law for the child because his "position in [the] household was not supported by recognition of social status and power outside it" (Steedman 72).

Primary identification also originates in a moment of class contempt. Shortly after the birth of Steedman's sister, a visiting social worker insulted her mother: "This house isn't fit for a baby!" The position of primal importance that Steedman gives this scene implies that Steedman's primary identification with her mother is based on class loyalty, cemented by sharing her mother's hurt pride. She speaks as if it were she who had suffered the insult, as if her mother's determination to protect herself henceforth from the injuries of class were her own: "I will do everything and anything until the end of my days to stop anyone ever talking to me like that woman talked to my mother" (2). Primary identification becomes a form of class solidarity.[8]

Similarly, Steedman reformulates the traditional definition of primary identification, transforming it into an economic structure. She claims that in nineteenth-century accounts of working-class girlhood, "the primary identification with a mother figure that modern psychological accounts have presented, was elaborated . . . by recognition of an economic duality. In becoming a worker like her mother, and in her precise understanding of the terms on which she was sent out to work, in her detailed knowledge of how money was got and laid out, the little girl showed an economic identification with her mother that was not shown by little boys" (89–90). Since Steedman refers elsewhere in the text to Nancy Chodorow (86–87), it seems safe to assume that Chodorow is included among the "modern psychological accounts" of primary identification; Chodorow's theory is that the fluid ego boundaries between mothers and daughters—their prolonged primary identification—originates in the mother's unconscious definition of the daughter as an extension of herself. It would seem that Steedman is self-consciously replacing Chodorow's psychoanalytic theory with an economic explanation: the daughter identifies her labor with her mother's. Later in the text Steedman introduces Henry Mayhew's interview with the "little watercress girl" as an example of this maternal identification through the medium of work: the little watercress seller understands who she is through an exact understanding of her function as a worker, and her mother validates that identity through an appreciation of her work and of the money her work brings in. The little watercress seller is Steedman's "mirror image," she says (141), substituting the recognition of an economic counterpart for Lacan's specular identification with visual form. Steedman finds comfort in identifying with the watercress seller, in "find[ing her]self . . . in the little watercress girl, the good and helpful child, who eased her mother's life" (141). As Victoria Rosner has said, this desire "to turn the child into herself, and herself into the child" is a kind of wish-fulfillment, "a desire to endow another with a better version of one's own childhood" (Rosner 20, 18). The emphasis on labor as the basis of an identificatory bond—both between Steedman as reader and the watercress seller and between the watercress seller and her mother—reinforces Steedman's contention that primary identification, her own primary identification with her mother included, is class-based, an effect of economic conditions.[9]

While this account of a primary identification that is class-specific and based on material conditions supplies a necessary corrective to the universalizations of psychoanalytic theory, it performs its own exclusions. Namely, it excludes the emotional and psychological details of the mother-daughter dynamic that might explain Steedman's ongoing identification with her mother. Notations of that primary identification surface every now and again: "whilst hating her, I was her"; "she, myself, walks my dreams"; "knowing that I was her" (55, 61, 19). These references are presented as bare statements of fact, without explanation or elaboration. Given that the narrative is meant to be the story of Steedman's childhood, descriptions of interactions between mother and child are oddly rare. Only at the end of the text does Steedman articulate the structure of demand: "She made me believe that . . . I was her. . . . If you expect children to be self-sacrificing and to identify with the needs of others, then they often do so" (141).

In place of a psychoanalytic model, Steedman sets out to explain her mother within an exclusively socioeconomic theoretical framework: coming out of a working-class childhood of economic privation, "she wanted: a New Look skirt, a timbered country cottage, to marry a prince" (9). Yet in the midst of this stringently materialist explanation for maternal desire, one passage gives a glimpse of the mother's demand for a primary identification and Steedman's attitude toward it: "In a social world, it is the social that people want—fine clothes, a house, to marry a king; and if these desires are projected on to a child, and if she comes close to the feeling that they are her own desires as well as her mother's, then that social world itself may provide her with some measure of their quality and validity and help her to stand to one side, momentarily detached from her mother's longing" (106–07). The narrator's situation is cloaked in the generalized abstractions of "the social," "the child" and "the mother" that Steedman habitually uses when she gets close to a description of her own relation to her mother, but both the problem—the demand for primary identification—and a possible solution are articulated here. The mother, regarding the child as a receptacle for her own feelings, has projected her desires into the child; consequently, the child grows up assuming "that they are her own desires as well as her mother's" (107). Lacan's notion that "man's desire is always the desire of the Other" finds its extreme and pathological form here. And Steedman maps out a possible escape route: if she can place her mother's desires in a social context, that will allow her to see them more objectively—to "stand to one side, momentarily detached from her mother's longing" (106–07). Steedman understands class analysis ("the social") to be the means of gaining this measure of detachment.

A subtext of personal motivation emerges here for a moment, complicating the stated purpose that Steedman reiterates as "a central theme of this book" (12): to represent the consciousness of the working-class mother and thus supply the gap in Marxist theory as well as male working-class autobiography; both, Steedman claims, have denied working-class women "a complicated psychology" either by leaving them out altogether or reducing them to a stereotype (12, 92). Hence her explanation of her mother's feelings within the strictly economic terms of class analysis. Steedman does give dignity to her mother's desire for material things by articulating them in a political language and tying them to a collective history of class. But the above passage (106–107) supplies a second, understated purpose for the composition of the present work: to distance herself from her mother's desires, to extricate herself from her assigned function as receptacle of her mother's feelings by locating those feelings in an external matrix of socioeconomic factors. Thus, it is not only a theoretical commitment to class analysis, but a personal desire to escape primary identification with her mother that motivates Steedman's presentation of her mother's thinking as an effect of social conditions alone.

The autobiographical part of *Landscape for a Good Woman* begins with a dream—a dream that Steedman intends to represent the longings of the dispossessed, of working-class women, but which, from my viewpoint, encapsulates the structure of primary identification:

> When I was three, ... I had a dream ... a woman hurried along ... she wore the New Look, a coat of beige gabardine which fell in two swaying, graceful pleats from her waist at the back.... She hurried, something jerky about her movements, a nervous, agitated walk, glancing round at me as she moved across the foreground. Several times she turned and came some way back towards me, admonishing, shaking her finger.... she entered a revolving door of dark, polished wood, mahogany and glass, and started to go round and round, looking out at me as she turned. (28)

Two pages later comes the waking analogue: the narrator remembers her mother "looking across the street at a woman wearing a full-skirted dress, and then down at the forties straight-skirted navy blue suit she was still wearing, and longing, irritatedly, for the New Look."[10]

The narrator assigns central interpretive value to the dream as the key to the text and, indeed, to her life (28).[11] The dream represents the centrality of the "politics of envy" to her mother and thereby to her own childhood. The New Look coat would require an extravagance of cloth—twenty yards—inaccessible to a working-class woman who is also a mother. The New Look is the signifier of her mother's desire for "fine clothes, glamour, money; to be what she wasn't" (6); and Steedman intends the dream to represent the impact of that wanting on her mother's life, on her own life, and on the everyday consciousness of working-class women in general. The subjective aspect of class inequality, overlooked by Marxist analysis, is this "subterranean culture of longing for that which one can never have"(8).

But this is Kay's dream, not her mother's. Dreams express wishes, Freud says. Yet it is not Kay who wants a New Look coat, but her mother. From what place does the dreamer desire? From the place of the mother. The dream mimics the structure of desire that the child Kay observed in waking life—the mother's look of longing at the other woman's New Look dress: the dreamer incorporates the scopic structure of the mother's desirousness, so that now it is she who stands gazing at the object of desire, the New Look. At the age of three, Kay is locked into a primary identification so complete that her mother's desires take the place of her own.[12]

The text of *Landscape for a Good Woman* is structured like the dream: that is, the narrator's own desires are nowhere in the text, while what her mother wants is central, ever-repeated. I hazard the explanation that the mother's desire, though so oft-repeated, is not desire in the Lacanian sense, but deviates into need, on the one hand, and into demand, on the other. Kay's mother presents herself as a subject of need. Lacan makes a distinction between need, demand, and desire in the following way: need is related to biological need, an organic thrust toward a concrete object that will satisfy. Human needs must be channeled through signifiers, and signifiers can express only a portion of what the subject wants. What can be expressed emerges in a series of demands; what cannot be articulated is repressed, becomes unconscious, and is then subject to the laws of displacement and condensation: that residue is desire. And desire, because it escapes the conscious logic of the symbolic and is subject to unconscious processes, emerges in "the paradoxical, deviant, erratic, excentric, and even scandalous character by which desire is distinguished from need" (Lacan, "Meaning" 80; see also Muller and Richardson 335).

The quest of the child, Lacan says, is to discover the desire of the Other—and here the Other refers to the first other, "the Mother *qua* primordial figure of the Other" (Žižek, "How to" 69). Because desire cannot be captured in language, the child cannot locate the desire of the mother in what she says. So the child is always probing beyond the parent's words, probing for what remains unspoken, asking: "*He is saying this to me, but what does he want?* . . . and all the child's whys reveal . . . a *Why are you telling me this*? ever-resuscitated from its base, which is the enigma of the adult's desire" (S XI 214). But at the age of three, Kay already knows what her mother wants—the New Look; here is no enigma. That is because, I argue, the mother always names exactly what she wants—over and over, it would seem from Steedman's representation of her—and what she wants is always a specific material object. There is nothing ambiguous, nothing for a child to search for in the interstices of speech, no undercurrents rippling away from the names of concrete objects. Desire cannot be satisfied: it is insatiable, always in pursuit of the next object; Kay's mother always implies that the material thing she names will fill her need. "What she actually wanted were real things, real entities, things she materially lacked, things that a culture and a social system withheld from her" (7). And *Landscape* itself mimes the maternal need by presenting, throughout, statements of objects the mother wanted (9, 22, 24, 30, 31, 38, 43, 46, 47, 59, 70, 88, 113, 118, 121, 123, etc.)—always, with the exception of the wish to marry a prince, concrete things. Although I am bending Lacan's definition of need a bit here—for Lacan, need is primarily biological and it cannot be rendered fully in language—I argue that the mother presents herself as a subject of need because her articulation fastens unswervingly on the concrete material objects that will satisfy her and because there are no shadows around her words where desire would seem to escape on all sides, nothing like "what we call desire, [which] crawls, slips, escapes" from the blanks in the mother's discourse, eluding a child (Lacan, S XI 214).

Kay cannot, then, establish herself as a subject of desire. For in order to establish herself as subject of desire, a child must perceive the mother's desire as desire—that is, as a lack in constant search of fulfillment. "Desire has no content as such. Desire functions much as the zero unit in the numerical chain—its place is both constitutive and empty" (Rose, "Introduction" 32)—"empty" because it is the blank space where words fail. If the child sees that her mother's desire is always in movement, never satisfied, then her lack becomes apparent:

there is a desire that cannot be filled. Then identification serves not as the glue that holds mother and child together, but as the lever that springs them apart. Perceiving the lack in the other, the subject can (still through identification) recognize her own lack in response: neither you nor I has the missing piece, we are both empty, both forever seeking what we do not have. I must seek fulfillment elsewhere—following the lure of the ever-receding object a. Only thus, by establishing "the central lack in which the subject experiences [it]self as desire" (Lacan, S XI 265), can the child become a desiring subject.

It does not seem, then, that the child Kay, or at least the discursive child-self created by the text, ever became a subject of desire. Her desires are nowhere in the text. She does follow the Lacanian program in one respect, though: Lacan's statement that "man's desire is always the desire of the Other" signifies that the child adopts the structure of the parent's desiring, "learns to desire as an other, as if he were some other person," and therefore "desires in the same way as the Other" (Fink, *Lacanian* 54). For there are moments when Steedman the narrator expresses desire as if it were need.

> State intervention in children's lives was . . . experienced, by me at least, as entirely beneficent. . . . I think I would be a very different person now if orange juice and milk and dinners at school hadn't told me, in a covert way, that I had a right to exist, was worth something. My inheritance from those years is the belief (maintained with some difficulty) that I do have a right to the earth, . . . the sense that a benevolent state bestowed on me, that of my own existence and the worth of that existence—attenuated, but still there. (122–23)

Desire reduces to need, to biological need: the state supplies what the organism requires for physical survival. Steedman's determinedly materialist assessment of what she needs imitates her mother's exclusive focus on material things.

Yet although need seems to supplant desire here, desire can be deduced from what is said—and not said. (Steedman's discourse places the reader in the position of Lacan's child trying to fathom the parent's unspoken desire—on the watch for tips, tokens, hints and clues to what remains hidden behind the words: the narrator's desire.) Overtly adhering to a discourse of material consumption, the narrator's gratitude to the state contains a covert reference to a scarcity that goes beyond a shortage of milk and orange juice. If she were not in want of the basics of maternal nurturance, she would not find them in the milk and orange juice supplied by the state. Nor, if there were an adequate supply of maternal love, would she need the assurance of the state that she has the right to exist and that her existence has value.

In the fashion of desire, the longing for a maternal nurturing that is not there can also be inferred from between the lines in the passage that contains the waking memory of the mother's desire for the New Look, which I quote here in full: "[she was] looking across the street at a woman wearing a full-skirted dress, and then down at the forties straight-skirted navy blue suit she was still wearing, and longing, irritatedly, for the New Look; and then back at us, the two living barriers to twenty yards of cloth" (30). The New Look coat is central to Kay's fantasy because its position as the mother's object of desire means that *she* is not the object of her mother's desire. "I was born in the year of the New Look, and understood by 1951 . . . that dresses needing twenty yards for a skirt were items as expensive as children" (29). Either/or: Either Kay or the New Look. Born in the same year, they are interchangeable—but also mutually exclusive. The child Kay (and the adult narrator, too, it seems) continues to define herself in a rigid binary with the New Look as the opposite term: She is not it. It is only by negation that the originary meaning of the phrase, "Man's desire is always the desire of the Other," comes into view—the child's wish to be what the first Other desires: "If the desire of the mother is the phallus, then the child wishes to be the phallus so as to satisfy this desire" (Lacan, "Meaning" 83). That originary desire—to be wanted—can be discerned here only in the negative: Kay is not what her mother wants. She is the negation, the thing of no value, the obstacle blocking attainment of the thing of value.

Seeing the world through her mother's eyes, Kay sees herself not as a subject but as a figure in her mother's drama—or, more precisely, as a figure on her mother's balance sheet. For example, Kay's mother gave birth to her as part of an exchange: her plan was to trade a baby for marriage to Kay's father. Since the exchange never took place—her father never married her mother—Kay's existence has not been paid for. Steedman the narrator, intent on her stated purpose of revealing the inner life of working-class mothers and children, claims that the economic terms of her origin illustrate normal working-class childhood: "Many [working-class children] had to learn that being alive ought simply to be enough, a gift that must ultimately be paid for. Under conditions of material poverty, the cost of most childhoods has been most precisely reckoned, and only life has been given freely" (109). Thus maternal ambivalence is attributed exclusively to class: as Elizabeth Abel says, "The narrator represents ambivalence as the psychic property of the working-class mother who loves her children but simultaneously resents the hardships they impose" ("Race" 194). But while it is true that children in an economy of scarcity are more aware of the costs of their maintenance than children in privileged situations, not all working-class mothers see their children solely as financial burdens. In remaining true to a class analysis, in generalizing from strictly economic determinants, Steedman inadvertently narrows the working-class maternal subjectivity that she is trying to defend to a set of purely material desires and a purely instrumental relation to one's children. Nor do all working-class children define themselves exclusively in terms of what they cost their parents. The narrator, on the other hand, defines herself strictly by means of her mother's economic calculus, as the object of exchange in a deal that failed: since her father never paid up with marriage, Kay's existence is a debt outstanding. Permanently outstanding—for she acknowledges the impossibility of ever compensating her mother for her life: "There was nothing we [Kay's sister and herself] could do to pay back the debt of our existence" (17). So imbued is the narrator—still—with her mother's world-view that a child is "a difficult item of expenditure" (90) that precludes a better material life, that she thinks it would have been better never to have incurred the debt of her existence, better never to have been born: "it would have been better that it hadn't happened that way, hadn't happened at all" (104); "things might be better if one wasn't there at all" (96).[13]

This radical absence of self-worth, this lack of faith in the right to exist, can be traced to a second deviation of the mother's desire, into demand. At the same time that Kay's mother presents herself as a subject of need, she also structures her relations with her daughter in terms of demand—the demand that Lawrence's *Rainbow* illustrates so well: Feel what I feel, reflect my desires, reflect my frustrations, be part of me. In response, the daughter feels that she belongs not to herself, but to her mother: "Children are always episodes in someone else's narrative, not their own people, but rather brought into being for particular purposes"; "You come to know that you are not quite yourself, but someone else: someone else has paid the price for you, and you have to pay it back. You take on ... the capacity to know exactly how someone else is feeling" (122, 105). The language of exchange shows that the narrator is still thinking like her mother: she is the commodity in her mother's failed exchange; so she has to pay her back by supplying her with some commodity of value—specifically, the gift of "knowing exactly how someone else is feeling" and of feeling with her.

Unwilling, or unable, to put into words how she feels about this maternal dynamic, Steedman inserts a supplement into her narrative which articulates what she cannot: a passage from Alice Miller's *Prisoners of Childhood*, a work that enumerates the injuries to the child that result from a parental demand for primary identification. Miller articulates the demand in the language of Hans Kohut's self psychology rather than in the Lacanian discourse that I have been using; but if the explanatory model is different, the demand is the same. The parent requires that the child mirror her feelings and the child obliges by becoming exquisitely sensitive—permeable—to the parent's feelings.

The splice of the two texts occurs in the following passage:

And so, there come into existence children who are:

intelligent, alert, attentive, extremely sensitive and (because they are completely attuned to her well-being) entirely at the mother's disposal and ready for her use. Above all they are transparent, clear, reliable and easy to manipulate. (Miller 28)

They are, in fact, children who have been made good. (*Landscape* 105)

Steedman then describes herself as "good": "You grow small, and quiet, and take up very little room. You take on the burden of being good, the burden of the capacity to know exactly how someone else is feeling" (105). Of Miller's account of the mother's part, Steedman includes only the lines that excuse—but also put into words—the mother's lack of empathy: "Each mother can only react empathically to the extent she has become free of her own childhood" (105; qtd. from Miller 28). Miller goes on to say—but Steedman characteristically does not quote this part—that the mother who needs constant affirmation from her child is incapable of providing her child with empathy, with the mirroring that the child needs in order to experience her feelings as valid and claim them as her own. The child, then, loses track of her own feelings. Children in this situation "have all developed the art of not experiencing feelings, for a child can only experience his feelings when there is somebody there who accepts him fully, understands and supports him" (Miller 10). In the place of her own feelings, the child contains and reflects the feelings of the mother—as does the text of *Landscape for a Good Woman*: the mother's desires for material goods and the mother's rage at material deprivation are foregrounded and highly colored, while the narrator's rage at her own deprivations is missing.

The vocabulary of *Landscape* also reveals Steedman's ongoing primary identification with her mother. Her discourse is faithful to the mother's discourse of exchange, cost, and commodity. Only economic privation counts as privation: she never mentions (except by indirection, as in the example of the state's nurturing) the economy of scarce *emotional* resources that she was subject to (even when she cites her sister's "bitter resentment against our childhood.")[14] And she catalogs the material things that would have assuaged her mother's class envy. The paradigmatic example of these items is the New Look. Steedman marks the moment when she first put a name to her mother's desire: "It was with the image of a New Look coat that, in 1950, I made my first attempt to understand and symbolize the content of my mother's desire" (24). In the Lacanian interpretation, it is the intervention of symbolization (rather than the father per se) that frees the child from primary identification with the mother. Developing a point Lacan makes in Seminar XVII, Bruce Fink says: "It is through language that the child can attempt to mediate the Other's desire, keeping it at bay and symbolizing it ever more completely" (*Lacanian* 58). The child can escape fixation at the point of the parent's desire by entering that desire into a signifying system that requires substitutions and by using words as a wedge to open up a space between self and other. At the age of three, then, the child Kay pins her mother's desire to a signifier, the New Look, so she is well on her way to full participation in the symbolic order—or is she? As Lacan says, "to reduce the function of the subject to nomination, . . . to a label stuck on something . . . would be to miss the whole essence of language" (S XI 237). Naming the mother's desire is indeed the first step away from the mother and toward language, but finding that symbol is not enough: in order to enter the mother's desire fully into a signifying system, the first signifier has to be placed in relation to other signifiers that modify it ($S1$—$S2$). The New Look is central not only to the three-year-old's dream, but also to the adult narrator's text: it crops up again and again (9, 24, 28, 30, 31, 40, 47, 121, 142). The lack of modification, the looping back again and again to the New Look—a static image that always means the same thing—shows that the mother's desire is not fully entered into the endless series of substitutions that characterizes the signifying system. The New Look seems to have some of the weight of a unary signifier—a signifier that has dropped out of the continual slippage of the signifying chain and assumed a petrified meaning. And I would argue that the New Look functions as a unary signifier not only because it is the sign of a primary attachment to the mother's desire but also because the daughter/narrator's own viability is at stake. The New Look coat was the object that she saw her mother explicitly prefer to the two potential objects of maternal love, herself and her sister. The master signifier (S1) is often construed as the subject's point of entry into the signifying chain (S2); thus, for example, as Charles Shepherdson illustrates this relationship, a man's professional role, "rural family doctor," stands as the S1 in relation to the set of S2s that constitute "the body of medical knowledge" ("Epoch" 190). In Kay's mother's brutal system of material exchange, the New Look is the signifier of what would be there if the child Kay were not there. It would seem, then, that Steedman's point of entry into the symbolic field is not the signifier that designates *her* in relation to the signifying chain, but the signifier that stands for *what she is not*. And the dominance of that signifier of her negative worth is consonant with the self-erasure that rules the memoir, with the absence of the *auto* from the autobiography. Or, to return to Lacan's notion that it is the intervention of the signifying function that can free the child from primary identification and state the problem in a more positive way: the New Look continues to function as a traumatic signifier, arresting the flow of words and dooming the narrator/daughter to repetition because Steedman has not yet narrativized the effect *on herself* of her mother's obsession with worldly goods.

In the last few pages she does just that: she puts into words how it feels to be effaced as a human being, treated as a thing of no worth. And she shifts from the relentlessly materialist discourse that marks her continuing identification with her mother's worldview to a discourse of fairy tales that gives her metaphors for her own feelings of anger, deprivation, and desire. Does putting her mother's desires into words throughout the text of *Landscape for a Good Woman* then work a Lacanian resolution to the problem of a fixation at the level of primary identification? It would seem so, yet the ending does not present a textbook-perfect cure.

All along, images from fairy tales, unintegrated into the mainstream narrative, have been suggesting a different story from the carefully objective description of the socioeconomic circumstances of the mother's material desires. As Elizabeth Abel has shown, "the disavowed story of daughterly ambivalence returns through the middle-class discourse of fairy tales, ingeniously manipulated to encode a subversive psychoanalytic subtext to the daughter's faithful narrative of class" ("Race" 195). Steedman's borrowings from "The Snow Queen" and "The Little Mermaid" focus on the figures of the Snow Queen and the witch, "call[ing] into question," as Abel says, "the narrator's legitimization of working-class mothering" ("Race" 195). Throughout the text, references to witches bob up like images of a repressed anger against the mother.

In her last interview with her mother—after a hiatus of nine years, an unexplained chronological gap that corresponds to the narrative gap where her resentment of her mother might be articulated[15]—Steedman makes the link between the witch and her mother explicit: "When she opened the door, she looked like a witch" (140). I see this as the beginning of a new discourse which expresses Steedman's feelings about her mother directly. She goes on using fairy-tale images to describe the mother-child dynamic: "We were truly illegitimate, outside any law of recognition: the mirror broken, a lump of ice for a heart" (142). The broken mirror and the heart of ice derive from "The Snow Queen," where under the snow queen's influence a shard from the devil's mirror enters the eyes of the child Kay and turns his heart to ice. In the present text heart of ice and broken mirror represent, apparently, the mother's coldness and her failure to mirror the daughter. The indictment of faulty mothering is put into words. Does the emergence of signifiers for Steedman's own feelings about her mother indicate that putting the mother's wants into words through the length of the narrative has effected a cure, that the writer is freed from subjection to the mother's needs, freed to feel her own frustrated desires and put those feelings into words? Yet the grammatical structure is ambiguous; "the mirror broken, a lump of ice for a heart" are sentence fragments: to whom do they refer? The mother, refusing all along to do the empathic work of mothering, has always been a broken mirror for the daughter. But it is the adult narrator who, in this last meeting, refuses for once to mirror the mother, so the broken mirror could represent the daughter. Likewise, it would seem that Kay hardens her heart against her mother in this scene, refusing pity—so the heart of ice may belong to Kay (and she has throughout identified with the boy Kay and wondered if her heart, too, were frozen [46]). On the other hand, it was the mother who originally withheld love, so it may be the mother as Snow Queen who is represented by the "lump of ice for a heart." Or the frozen heart could be a property of both, the mother's coldness resulting in the deadening of the child's emotions. The refusal of grammatical attribution to one subject or the other maintains the ambiguity of primary identification, traits mirrored back and forth between the two in an infinite rebound.

Yet I would argue that the introduction of fairy-tale signifiers does indeed signal a new freedom from primary identification. The fairy-tale images can be called "a discourse of her own" because reading fairy tales had been an emotional resource in her childhood, Steedman recalls. They gave her "a means of analysis, . . . a way of seeing what is happening" (106)—an analytic device with which to interpret her mother's behavior. I assume that she found in reading fairy tales a world apart from her mother's need, a world where she could wander free of her mother's emotional control and find analogues to her own experience. The substitution of signifiers from fairy tales for the rhetoric of economic motivation and material goods signals her return to a discursive space wrested from her mother's influence. For in the passage that introduces the fairy-tale imagery, quoted here in full, she puts into direct discourse, for the first time, the structure of demand—the pressure on her to identify with her mother: "She made me believe that I understood everything about her, she made me believe that I was her: her tiredness, the pain of having me, the bleeding, the terrible headaches. . . . If you expect children to be self-sacrificing and to identify with the needs of others, then they often do so" (141). And she describes, also for the first time, what it feels like to be forced to "identify with the needs" of the other: "I was really a ghost who came to call. That feeling, the sense of being absent in my mother's presence, . . . was what it had always been like. We were . . . outside any law of recognition: the mirror broken, a lump of ice for a heart" (142). Whereas Steedman has heretofore described herself from the mother's point of view, as an object of exchange or as the obstacle to the New Look, she now puts into words what it feels like to be reduced to the container for the mother's feelings, what it feels like to be effaced as subject: she is an "absence" in the presence of the mother, "a ghost," a cipher whose subjectivity is on permanent loan to the other.

At the end, then, the narrator states directly how she feels about the maternal dynamic and describes the mother from a new standpoint and in a new language—her own. Indeed, to argue as I have been doing that the daughter is enslaved to the materialist discourse of the mother throughout because she keeps to the mother's language of economic deprivation and material goods is to underestimate the personal motive that Steedman mentions, in passing, for framing her mother's behavior within an exclusively socioeconomic analysis: placing a mother's desires within the context of the social world might help a daughter "to stand to one side, momentarily detached from her mother's longing" (107). It would seem, from the new distance the narrator has achieved at the end, that she has succeeded. Or, in Lacanian terms, Steedman has managed a separation from the mother by turning the mother's desires into signifiers ("she wanted X, . . . she wanted Y. . ." [9, 22, 24, 30, 31, 38, 43, 46, 47, 59, 70, 88, 113, 118, 121, 123, etc.]); and she has connected the mother's feelings to an entire signifying context by tying the mother's complaints about wanting and not having to a rhetorical tradition of social protest descended from the Chartists to people in her mother's hometown (112–21) and by linking the mother's stories to stories of other working-class women—her mother's mother and grandmother, the little watercress seller, and so on. From a Lacanian perspective, Steedman has been practicing the saving art of substitution, entering maternal desire into a chain of symbolic substitutions and so freeing herself from attachment to the one signifier, the New Look—master signifier both of her mother's desire and of her own negative worth—that has dominated both her mother's text and her own.

Yet an ambiguity lingers; primary identification is tenacious. Despite the linguistic resolution, despite the transformation of dream into the written word—for the structure of the autobiography repeats the structure of the New Look dream, foregrounding the objects of the mother's longing while eclipsing the desires of the narrator—it would seem that the "writing cure" is only partially successful. For the confusion of desire with the desire of the Other, the conflation of self and other, persists—and still at the level of the unconscious: "She, myself, walks my dreams" (61).

Chapter 3

Identification with the Trauma of Others

Slavery, Collective Trauma, and the Difficulties of Representation in Toni Morrison's *Beloved*

If *Beloved* is a novel about the "crisis of subjectivity" suffered by slaves (Morgenstern 114), it is also about the crisis of subjectivity transmitted to the descendants of slaves. What are the identification processes that account for the intergenerational transmission of trauma? What is the psychic mechanism of transmission, especially in cases where the traumatic event remains unspoken, untold? What are the effects on the second-generation trauma survivor's capacities for desire and language? And what is the identification mechanism that enables someone to suffer the symptoms of collective trauma, of a traumatic past experienced by a whole group of people but not by the sufferer herself? In *Beloved*, I will argue, both a character and the narrative voice play out the effects of identification with a traumatic past not their own.

Denver, the daughter of the ex-slave Sethe, did not herself experience slavery; but the deaf-mutism that immobilizes her for two years is a sign of her identification first with the specific trauma suffered by her slave mother and second with the dehumanizing trauma inflicted by slavery on all her slave ancestors. As in Freud's classic cases of hysteria, Denver's deaf-mutism is a symptom of past trauma: the body expresses what the voice cannot say. It is, however, not Denver's own traumatic experience that her deaf-muteness expresses, but the experience of her mother. The story of Sethe's infanticide has not been told, cannot be told: it is "unspeakable," and Sethe wants it to remain that way (58).

Denver lives out what Lacan calls the "desire of the Other" at the level of the body, enacting her mother's pathological desire that the story of her child-murder not be told, not be heard.

Like the symptoms of the trauma survivors Freud treated, Denver's deafness and mutism are hysterical: that is, they are without physiological cause. Identification is the mark of the hysteric, Freud says in the *Interpretation of Dreams:*

> Identification is a highly important factor in the mechanism of hysterical symptoms. It enables patients to express in their symptoms not only their own experiences but those of a large number of other people. It enables them, as it were, to suffer on behalf of a whole crowd of people" (149).

That insight opens the door, as Elin Diamond says, "to understanding identification as a social as well as a psychical relation" ("Rethinking" 89). Denver's substitution of the body for language expresses an identification with the trauma of her enslaved ancestors, who were likewise denied access to language and reduced to bodies.[1]

I will argue, finally, that the narrative discourse of *Beloved* sometimes mimics the concretisms of second-generation children of trauma victims. Ilse Grubrich-Simitis, describing patients who are children of Holocaust survivors, observes that second-generation subjects of a collective trauma often exhibit a concrete way of thinking and speaking, including an inability to understand or to use metaphor. Although Grubrich-Simitis does not say so, her patients' "concretism" can be read as a form of identification with the literal quality of their parents' traumatic reminiscences. As is well known, traumatic events do not become part of narrative memory but come back in concrete forms, as flashback or recurrent nightmare: "It is as if the thing itself returns, as opposed to its representation" (Morgenstern 103). The narrative voice of *Beloved* falls into similar "concretisms" when it approaches an idea connected with slavery, such as the body or the past. The narrative voice stutters, so to speak; it aims for the substitutions of metaphor but falls back into the literal. Like the language of a second-generation trauma survivor, the novel's language bears the mark of inherited trauma: it dramatizes Morrison's identification and solidarity with her slave ancestors.

At the heart of the narrative is a conflict between the therapeutic necessity to translate the untold story of slavery into language—a need to tell that propels the narrative—and a textual resistance to that therapeutic imperative, a resistance carried out by the text's refusal of some of the constitutive substitutions of language. Ultimately, *Beloved* "is the story of its own impossibility," as Naomi Morgenstern has said (116). It strives to put the traumatic past of slavery into language, and it both succeeds and fails; the failure is itself eloquent, showing the inadequacy of the representational capacities of language to encompass the collective trauma of slavery.

Hysterical Identification and the Desire of the Mother

Denver's enactment of her mother's desire is a symptom of her overclose connection with her mother—of a primary identification whose first cause, as in the texts of Lawrence and Steedman, is the parent's lack of boundaries. Here again, it is the parent's need that produces the daughter's extended identification with her mother.

Sethe defines herself as a maternal body whose connection to its offspring remains unbroken, and that self-definition includes Denver within the compass of the maternal body. The contours of Sethe's self-image as maternal body appear during the narrative of her escape from slavery and journey toward freedom in Ohio. On the one hand, that journey is presented as an epic of maternal heroism, as Sethe both gives birth against seemingly insuperable odds—alone in the wilderness, wounded and exhausted—and gets her mother's milk to the nursing baby she has sent ahead to Ohio. While celebrating the courage and determination that she draws from her attachment to her children, the narrative of her flight to freedom also dramatizes the problematics of her maternal self-image. During the journey, Sethe experienced her own existence only in relation to her children's survival, "concerned" not for her self, but "for the life of her children's mother." She thought, "I believe this baby's ma'am is gonna die" and pictured herself as "a crawling graveyard for a six-month baby's last hours" (30, 31, 34). Sethe continues this roundabout self-definition through the many images of nursing that picture her as the sustaining ground of her children's existence; even after they are weaned, her bond with them remains so strong that she continues to picture it as a nursing connection (100, 162, 200, 216). And her maternal identification is so complete that it allows Sethe to take the life of her baby because she believes that child to be "part of her" still. Thus, when the slave catchers come to recapture Sethe and her children and return them to slavery in the South,

Sethe "collected every bit of life she had made, all the *parts of her* that were precious and fine" and attempted to kill them all; she succeeded in killing one—the nursing baby who returns in the body of Beloved (163 [emphasis mine]).[2]

Sethe's self-definition maintains her in a primary identification with her children: so long as she continues to define herself as the gestating enclosure of their being or as the life-sustaining provider of their milk, she thinks of herself as fused with them. While Sethe and the revenant Beloved are in a classic primary identification, I focus on the less obvious case of Denver, for many other critics (myself included) have written on the primary dyad of Sethe and Beloved.[3] Suffice it to say here that Sethe perceives no boundary between herself and her baby, returned in the body of the nineteen-year-old Beloved, and that Beloved, thinking always as a one-year-old, "experiences herself either at one with [her mother], or striving to be at one with her" (Greenberg and Mitchell 161). The relation between Sethe and Denver is not such an obvious case of primary identification. But Sethe's references to Denver sometimes fail to be age-appropriate. When Sethe introduces "my Denver" to Paul D, the ex-slave she has not seen for 18 years, Paul D says to Denver, "Last time I saw your mama, you were pushing out the front of her dress" and Sethe responds, "Still is, provided she can get in it" (11). Does Sethe then think of Denver still as the baby she carried in her womb? When Paul D informs Sethe, "[Denver]'s grown," Sethe replies, "'Grown don't mean nothing to a mother. . . . In my heart it don't mean a thing" (45). In relation to her children, Sethe seems to be arrested in time, to live still in the moment she was carrying and nursing them.

The arrest of the child's development in the mother's imaginary is reflected in Denver's failure to move forward developmentally—in particular, to enter fully into language. After a year of learning to read at the home of Lady Jones, Denver became deaf and dumb for two years, "her hearing cut off by an answer she could not bear to hear" (103): that answer would have informed her that her mother killed her baby sister. Denver's loss of hearing, prolonged from age seven to nine, is a hysterical symptom: that is, a symptom with no physiological basis. It reproduces the desire of the mother—that the story of the baby's murder remain unspoken, the act unnamed, the memory repressed.

Denver's hysterical deafness performs a kind of literalization of Lacan's dictum that "man's desire is the desire of the Other." Under better circumstances, what the child takes over when its desire becomes the desire of the Other, as chapter 2 explains, is the *structure* of the Other's desiring. The child identifies with the lack in the parent and, superimposing its own lack on the parent's lack, recognizes and assumes possession of its own lack and thus its own desire (always, in Lacan, synonymous with lack). The child becomes, like the parent, a subject of desire in eternal quest of the eternally elusive object a. In this best case scenario, then, identification with the other's desire as a lack that cannot be filled gets the subject going, as she follows the metonymy of desire from one (unfulfilling) object to the next.

But in the case of hysteria, as Lacan explains it, the child's desire remains in a mimesis of the parent's desire, pegged to the parent's original object and dependent on the support of the parent's desire for its existence. In Seminar XI, Lacan gives an example taken from Freud to explain the dynamic—the case history of Dora. Dora complained to Freud that her father, who was having an affair with Frau K, had made a bargain with Herr K—my daughter for your wife—and that consequently Herr K kept pressing seduction on her ("Fragment"). While Freud insists that Dora is in love with Herr K and that her love rests on the unconscious basis of her (oedipal) love for her father, it becomes plain from what Dora herself says that Frau K figures as her object of desire. What interests Lacan in this narrative is that Dora is identified with her father and later with Herr K ("Intervention" 97, 99)—identified, in both cases, with the male desirer of Frau K. That identification, Lacan says in Seminar XI, provided what was "necessary to her"—"the link ... with that third element that enabled her to see the desire" (S XI 38). That is, Dora could only know her own desire for Frau K ("see her desire") by ascertaining the desire of the father (or of his stand-in, Herr K) and putting herself in his position. Lacan emphasizes the purely identificatory uses of Herr K to Dora when, both in "Intervention in the Transference" and in Seminar XI, he points out that Dora dismissed Herr K when he made the statement, "I am not interested in my wife," or, as Lacan translates it in "Intervention," "My wife is nothing to me" (S I 38, "Intervention" 101). "The reward was instantaneous: a hard slap" which put an end to their relationship. Lacan imagines Dora's logic thus: "If she is nothing to you, then what are you to me?" ("Intervention" 101). If Herr K is indifferent to his wife, then he can no longer serve Dora as the identificatory support for her desire, and he is of no further use.[4] To come into existence, the hysteric's desire needs to be relayed through the intermediary position of a desiring subject.[5] Desire depends upon identification. Lacan rereads Freud, then, to show that the desire of the hysteric mimes, in a concrete and absolute way, the desire of the other.[6]

The hysterical case dramatizes, at its pathological extreme, the tendency of every child to take in and identify with the desire of the parent: as Lacan says, one's "desire is *always* the desire of the Other." The dynamic here may be exaggerated, but they cause us to question how far the sense of owning one's own desire is an illusion: to what extent is the desire that propels action "a desire of one's own" and to what extent is it a mimesis, absorbed unawares, of the first Other's desire?

As in Freud's model of hysterical conversion, Denver's hysterical symptom enacts the content of a repressed desire. But it is not Denver's own desire that her deafness expresses. Denver's primal desire, what Morrison calls Denver's "original hunger," is not for silence but for language—for the "sentences [which] rolled out like pie dough," for the "page[s] and rule[s]" that Denver "ate up" with gusto (118, 121, 247). Denver remembers the year of learning language skills at Lady Jones's "school" as a kind of lost oral jouissance—delight in "the capital *w*, the little *i*, the beauty of the letters in her name, the deeply mournful sentences from the Bible Lady Jones used as textbook" (102). So it is not her own desire that her body expresses, but "the desire of the Other," as in Lacan. Sethe will not, cannot tell the story of the infanticide. Denver's empty ear and empty mouth reproduce in a corporeal language the empty place at the center of the text where her mother's story of the infanticide should be. Her deafness and muteness enact "the unspeakable" (58, 199), as if to keep her mother's silence intact by locking it up in her body.

The Time of Trauma

Denver's identification with her mother extends to an enclosure in her mother's time. For Sethe, the past has not passed: rather than being placed in a temporal continuum, the past occupies space in the present—notably in the house haunted by concrete materializations of the past. Denver is enveloped in her mother's time-space continuum: for her, too, the past is always there, waiting to happen again. Contemporary theorists of posttraumatic stress disorder have extended Freud's notion of traumatic repetition to describe the anomalies of traumatic memory. Since a traumatic event, because of its unexpectedness or horror, exceeds the cognitive structures available to process it, it is not experienced like other life events: it resists comprehension as it is happening and it eludes processing by narrative memory. "Not having been fully integrated as it occurred, the event cannot become . . . a 'narrative memory' that is integrated into a complete story of the past" (Caruth 153). Rather, trauma victims experience the past as involuntary flashbacks that have a concrete character: the traumatic event comes back as if it were happening again—without the usual blurring, transforming, generalizing effects of memory.[7]

The past comes back to Sethe in vivid pictures over which she has no control: "and suddenly there was Sweet Home rolling, rolling, rolling out before her eyes . . . it rolled itself out before her in shameless beauty" (6). Not "she remembered," but "there it was." (See Morgenstern 111). Sethe's house is crammed full of the past: "When she woke the house crowded in on her: there was the door where the soda crackers were lined up in a row . . . the exact place on the stove where Denver burned her fingers . . . There was no room for any other thing or body" (39). Time is spatialized: each act sticks to the place where it occurred, usurping the space where something new might happen. Sethe has suffered the trauma of the infanticide and before that the assorted traumas of slavery, so it is not surprising that her recollections bear the hallmarks of traumatic memory.

What is surprising is that her daughter Denver, who has not lived through slavery and was a newborn at the time of the infanticide, deals with the past in a similar way. She does not suffer from flashbacks per se, since she has not experienced the traumatic events that would flash back; but she waits, constantly vigilant, for the past to recur. Thus she cannot leave her mother's house and yard because she is always expecting the appearance of the slave catchers who once came into the yard and triggered the infanticide: "the thing that happened . . . could happen again. Whatever it is, it comes from outside the house, outside the yard, and it can come right on in the yard if it wants to. So I never leave this house and I watch over the yard, so it can't happen again" (205).

We can perhaps see a mechanism for the intergenerational transmission of trauma in the explanation of time Sethe gives Denver:

> Some things go. Pass on. Some things just stay. I used to think it was my rememory. You know. Some things you forget. Other things you never do. But it's not. Places, places are still there. If a house burns down, it's gone,

> but the place—the picture of it—stays, and not just in my rememory, but out there, in the world.... Someday you be walking down the road and you hear something or see something going on. So clear. And you think it's you thinking it up. A thought picture. But no. It's when you bump into a rememory that belongs to somebody else. (36)

What Sethe passes on to Denver here is a traumatic model of time. She teaches the distinction between ordinary memory—some things you forget, some things you remember—and the memory of trauma, wherein the traumatic past reappears as a concrete presence: you bump into it. It is a thing, not a "thought-picture." And it reimposes itself: it is involuntary—again, not "she remembered," but "there it is."

Consequently, Denver understands the past only as reenactment. When her mother nearly dies of starvation, after devoting herself to Beloved and sustaining her with her own substance—a nursing fantasy writ large—Denver realizes she will have to leave her mother's house to get food or they will die. Yet she finds herself unable to move, imprisoned within her mother's time—a time that, clinging to places, is always happening again: "Out there ... were places in which things so bad had happened that when you went near them it would happen again.... Denver stood on the porch ... and couldn't leave it" (243). Ashraf Rushdy asserts that Denver shares her mother's refusal to confront the past; I would say, rather, that she has absorbed her mother's concretistic understanding of the past. To her, too, things that happened in the past are not translated into mental concepts but manifest as concrete things you can bump into.

She crosses the threshold into social discourse only when the voice of the dead Baby Suggs, her grandmother, speaks out: "You mean I never told you ... nothing about how come I walk the way I do and about your mother's feet, not to speak of her back? I never told you all that? Is that why you can't walk down the steps? ... Know it, and go on out the yard" (243–44). And Denver does. Why is that speech enabling? To a child afraid to step out into the world, the particulars of how that world damaged her grandmother and mother are hardly reassuring. It is the speech act itself, the voice of the grandmother putting the past where it belongs, into oral history, that frees Denver to enter the present.[8]

So Denver finally moves—out of the stasis of primary identification with her mother which, in *Beloved*, entails a paralysis both of desire and of time itself. However belatedly (she is by now 18) Denver takes the crucial step from the imaginary of mother-daughter fusions to the symbolic order of language and society. She goes straight to the place of verbal nurturance, the house of Lady Jones, the woman who had taught her to read some 10 years earlier. She begins to pursue a desire of her own—"the original hunger" for words (118, 121)—by learning to read and write. And to speak: although the effort of describing her family's situation "seemed big to Denver," "nobody was going to help her unless she told (253)"; so Denver must begin to tell the story of her family's suffering, begin to enter a traumatic past into narrative.

What Baby Suggs does for Denver is take a traumatic family history—"a history that literally has no place, neither in the past, in which it was not fully experienced, nor in the present, in which its precise images and enactments are not fully understood" (Caruth, 153)—and place the dislocated events in a temporal sequence. Paraphrasing Julia Kristeva, Claire Kahane writes: "The enunciation of noun plus verb places the subject in linear time" (15); even more does an entire narrative align us with "a linear ... unfolding" (Kristeva 192). The temporal continuum of beginning, middle, and end appears to be the antidote to the dislocated, disjunctive moments of trauma.

Slavery, the Discourse of Bodies, and Freud's "Talking Cure"

It would seem, from Denver's saving move from hysterical symptom and temporal stasis into the order of language, that the text endorses narrative as the cure for trauma. Denver is arrested in the traumatic time of her mother in part because Sethe has never told her the story of the infanticide. So Denver cannot process the event through narrative comprehension and memory, but instead processes it through the body. She does not know the past, yet her body and her unconscious know; they continue to process the information, but they cannot offer resolution—only the repetition of corporeal symptom and recurring nightmare. The arrest of Denver's development shows how urgent is the need for a story that will make sense of the baby's death, mark the baby's disappearance, and lay her and the past she represents to rest. Baby Suggs's integration of the disjunctive moments of trauma into the coherent timeline of narrative liberates Denver from the temporal paralysis she shares with her mother. So the novel appears to drive toward the resolution of trauma through a version of Freud's "talking cure." Freud understood a hysterical symptom to be telling a story that could not be put into words. "Since hysteria was a malady of representation, the cure was worked through representation. If the hysteric converted verbal symbol into corporeal symptom, the talking cure would return her to the spoken word" (Kahane 15).[9] In *Beloved*, there is a similar drive to put the traumatic past into narrative and so "cure" all the characters who suffer from the legacy of slavery. But there are narrative forces that resist that resolution. *Beloved* remains true to the traumatic past of its characters by reproducing, in a variety of ways, the resistance to language characteristic of trauma.

First, the stubbornness of the body, its refusal to give way to the word, is a reminder of the traumatic nature of the slaves' sufferings: most of the characters, in one way or another, put the body in place of the word. In so doing, they are not only testifying to the "unspeakable" nature of trauma itself, but they are also reproducing a specific trauma, the subjection of slaves to an order that defined them as bodies and denied them the position of speaking subjects.[10] Slaves were barred by law from learning to read and write. Thus deprived of the distinguishing mark of human being—language—they were treated like bodies intended only for production and reproduction.[11]

Various forms of torture—whippings, mutilations, rape, the bit, the irons—continuously informed the slaves that they were in fact just bodies. And they got the message: as Richard Brodhead reports, slave narratives "foreground the embodiedness of whipping, the bodily enacted and bodily received nature of its disciplinary transaction" (141–42). To torture the body is to "unmake language," as Kristin Boudreau asserts: "the experience of vivid pain dismantles language itself, so that pain results in the impossibility of any intelligible utterance" (456, 455).[12] These punishments had a pedagogical purpose—not only to teach slaves their powerlessness in relation to the absolute authority of the white masters, but also to reduce them to bodies. As Elaine Scarry writes of contemporary uses of torture:

> What the process of torture does is to split the human being into two, to make emphatic the... latent distinction between a self and a body, between a "me" and "my body." The "self" or "me," which is experienced on the one hand as more private, more essentially at the center, and on the other hand as participating across the bridge of the body in the world, is 'embodied' in the voice, in language. The goal of the torturer is to make the one, the body, emphatically and crushingly *present* by destroying it, and to make the other, the voice, *absent* by destroying it. (48–49)

The physical violence that seems arbitrary in slave narratives is in fact part of a systematic attempt to reduce slaves to bodies deprived of language.[13] We can see the efficacy of such treatment in Juan Francisco Manzano's *Autobiography of a Slave*. When Manzano begins to describe his torture at the hands of his owners, he says: "I draw the veil" and stops; he cannot say it. Not just in the moment of torture is he deprived of voice; he continues bereft of language, unable even now to put the experience of torture in his own words or give it his own meaning. He cannot become the speaking subject of his own experience.

In *Beloved* the crisis of subjectivity that is the legacy of such practices is expressed through the substitution of body for language. Thus, for example, the story of Sethe's whipping is carved on her back in a clump of scars; despite Paul D's continued prodding, Sethe does not relate the story of her beating, so it remains in a "hieroglyphics of the flesh" inscribing the slave owners' code; and Sethe herself remains "a body whose flesh . . . bears the marks of a cultural text" that labels her a slave (Spillers, "Mama's Baby" 67). Baby Suggs reckons up the damages of slavery through an inventory of body parts: "slave life had busted her legs, back, head, eyes, hands, kidneys, womb and tongue" (87). Once freed, she comes to the idea of self-possession through connecting with her hands—no longer the possession of the slaveholders, but her own: "These hands belong to me. These *my* hands" (141).

When Baby Suggs finds her vocation as preacher to the ex-slaves in Ohio, her sermons address the bodies of the worshippers:

"Here in this here place, we flesh . . . Love it. Love it hard. Yonder they do not love your flesh. They despise it. They don't love your eyes; they'd just as soon pick em out. No more do they love the skin on your back. Yonder they flay it. And O my people they do not love your hands. Those they only use, tie, bind, chop off and leave empty. Love your hands! Love them. Raise them up and kiss them. Touch others with them, pat them together, stroke them on your face 'cause they don't love that either. *You* got to love it, *you*! And no, they ain't in love with your mouth. Yonder, out there, they will see it broken and break it again. . . . No, they don't love your mouth. You got to love it. This is flesh I'm talking about here. Flesh that needs to be loved. . . . And O my people, out yonder, hear me, they do not love your neck unnoosed and straight. So love your neck; put a hand on it, grace it, stroke it and hold it up. And all your inside parts that they'd just as soon slop for hogs, you got to love them. The dark, dark liver—love it, love it, and the beat and beating heart, love that too." (88)

Baby Suggs is not preaching spiritual salvation or moral elevation. Still less is she recommending a talking cure. Addressing the specific gougings, whippings, and mutilations the ex-slaves have suffered, Baby Suggs tries to heal at the level of the body, where the damage to subjectivity has occurred. Love is the antidote, but not love of God nor even self-love: loving each body part, the ex-slaves need to reclaim their bodies before they can find a voice and a self.

Denver's deaf-muteness memorializes the abuses of slavery. In addition to signifying the "unspeakableness" of the infanticide, the final trauma slavery inflicted on her mother, the bodily symptom enables her "to suffer on behalf of a whole crowd of people," as Freud describes the plasticity of hysterical identification (*Interpretation* 149). Foregoing language and putting her body there, where the speaking subject should be, reenacts the communal trauma of slavery—the violent stripping of voice and will from the captive body. "Taking the place of a discourse that cannot be uttered" (David-Ménard 3), Denver's body remains loyal to the essentially traumatic nature of her ancestors' suffering: the body speaks what the tongue cannot.

Storytelling versus Unspeakability

Like its characters, the narrative discourse of *Beloved* both embraces and resists the "talking cure." On the one hand, the narrative momentum of *Beloved* derives from the drive to translate the traumatic past into narrative and thus lay it to rest. The text gestures to the "underrepresented" history of slavery, to "history's absences" (Anderson 137), to the fact that "the victim's own chronicles of [slavery] were systematically submerged, ignored, mistrusted, or superseded by 'historians' of the era" (Holloway 516); and it tries to fill that gap through the imaginative recreation of slaves' personal experiences.[14] On the other hand, narrative discourse balks at some linguistic practices, as if to show the incommensurability of the slaves' sufferings with the expressive resources of language. The narrative exists only through the medium of words, so it cannot adopt Denver's show of loyalty with the trauma of her ancestors by physically putting a body there, where language should be. But it can resist the substitutions of language for trauma in other ways—namely, in a series of "concretisms" commonly associated with trauma. Naomi Morgenstern summarizes the tension at the heart of the novel's narration: "*Beloved* is both the text that has been excluded from the canon—the story that now demands its place, a place for the stories of slaves ... and the story of its own impossibility: how can there be a story of trauma?" (116).[15]

On the positive side, *Beloved* continually expresses the value of storytelling. Beloved embodies the accumulated sufferings of slavery, and it is through her that the past demands containment in narrative. In her one monologue, she speaks in the voice of a child on the Middle Passage, a child torn away from her mother through the originating trauma of slavery, the capture and transport of Africans to slavery in North America. She speaks in a series of disconnected images and sentence fragments divided by large spaces, where the lack of punctuation avoids even the minimal closure of sentences. This fragmented syntax approximates the unintelligibility of trauma, which comes back in invasive images that have no connective logic. As Morgenstern says, "someone who suffers from recurring nightmares or invasive and oppressive hallucinations is suffering from senselessness or meaninglessness" (103). Readers are forced to share at least partially in the dislocated time of trauma, since the text gives them no clue about how Beloved—a grandchild of the generation that came over on the slave ships—comes to inhabit the space and time of the Middle Passage. This is the time of trauma—impossible to anchor in a chronological sequence; as Beloved says, "All of it is now it is always now" (210).[16] Materializing in hallucinatory forms in the present, never fully experienced in the past, trauma lies "outside the boundaries of any single place or time" (Caruth 8).

The jumbled incoherence of Beloved's language both insists on the trauma that the captive Africans suffered and asks to be made sense of, as the temporal disorientation she voices both insists on the impossibility of laying to rest a past of suffering that haunts the present and begs for containment within the linear time of history. I say "begs for containment" because Beloved herself does just that. Beloved is not only the baby that Sethe killed, but—as the generic name Beloved suggests—the embodiment of all the loved ones lost through slavery, beginning with the Africans who died on the slave ships.[17] As the embodiment of the traumatic past, Beloved continually demands that her mother and sister put that past into stories; and she is pacified, momentarily given rest, by their telling. "Denver noticed how greedy she was to hear Sethe talk"; storytelling "became a way to feed her," to gratify her (63, 58).

This storytelling is beneficent for Sethe as well: Sethe had long ago decided that everything in her past life was "unspeakable," yet when Beloved asks, Sethe is able, finally to put at least part of the past into words. In response to Beloved's prompting, she tells the story of losing her mother—a traumatic loss that she is able only now to narrate and so begin to process consciously.[18] Enregistering the losses of the past then triggers a crucial retrieval.

> [Sethe] was remembering something she had forgotten she knew. Something privately shameful that had seeped into a slit in her mind... the woman called Nan who... was around all day, who nursed babies, cooked... and who used different words. Words Sethe understood then but could neither recall nor repeat now.... But the message... she was picking meaning out of a code she no longer understood.... Nan [saying] "Telling you. I am telling you, small girl Sethe."... She told Sethe that her mother and Nan were together from the sea. Both were taken up many times by the crew. "She threw them all away but you. The one from the crew she threw away... the others from more whites she also threw away.... You she gave the name of the black man. She put her arms around him. The others she did not put her arms around. Never. Never. Telling you. I am telling you, small girl Sethe." (61–62)

When Sethe pushes the past out of her mind, because "every mention of her past life hurt" (58), it comes back involuntarily, in the unwanted hallucinatory images described earlier. When Beloved demands stories about slavery, Sethe is able to organize the past in narrative form and thus become the speaking subject of her own experience. So far, the text endorses Freud's talking cure. But storytelling does more.

Storytelling in *Beloved* is healing because it enables the characters to connect with the oral tradition of their ancestors and thus enact their continuity with them. When Sethe tells the story of her mother, she reconnects not only with her mother and with her surrogate mother Nan, but also through Nan with the lost language of her mothers and with the African ancestors who spoke it. Storytelling thus begins to heal not only Sethe's breach with her mothers but also that larger breach, that "monumental collective psychic rupture" with the homeland, Africa, represented by the Middle Passage (Christian 364).[19]

But there are limits to the power of "telling." When Sethe tries to explain to Paul D her attempt to kill herself and her children to prevent their reenslavement, she finds speech blocked: "Sethe knew that the circle she was making around... the subject would remain one. That she could never close in, pin it down for anybody who had to ask" (163). Sethe is never able to articulate the central trauma of her life, her murder of her baby girl.[20] A gap remains at the heart of Sethe's story— and at the heart of the novel. That gap is filled by the presence of the dead baby: her death not having been sublated onto the abstract level of signifiers, the ghost baby is there, embodied, a concrete presence.

Textual practice seconds and supports Sethe's resistance to telling. Despite the novel's affirmation of the value of storytelling, despite the narrative drive to move the past into the containment of verbal history, the narrative discourse resists symbolic processes in a series of "concretisms," or literalizations. Ilse Grubrich-Simitis, describing patients who are the children of Holocaust survivors, claims that second-generation subjects of a collective trauma think and talk in what she calls "concretisms." "[Concretism] is a characteristic specific to some of those patients whose parents, having survived extermination camps, had to deny their traumatic experiences. These patients frequently regard what they have to say as thinglike. They appear not to regard it as something imagined or remembered, as something having sign character. The open-ended quality of fantasy life is missing. Instead the expressions have a peculiarly fixed and unalterable quality" (302). To identify with a traumatized parent is apparently to be, like the parent, "haunted by the literality of events" (Morgenstern, 103) in a way that permeates all aspects of one's thinking and speaking. These second-generation subjects are, for example, incapable of using metaphor (Grubrich-Simitis 304–07).[21]

I want to argue that at certain points the text of *Beloved* reads as if it were itself a second-generation trauma survivor, fixated at the concrete level of language. Toni Morrison says that she wants her work to "bear witness" to the past ("Memory" 389). Bearing witness to slavery must, to be sure, involve putting the slave subjects' experiences into words. But "bearing witness" to the *traumatic nature* of slaves' sufferings implies a loyalty to the inexpressibility of trauma, to its incommensurability with the representational capacities of language. Sometimes the narrative discourse of *Beloved* does indeed balk at metaphor and exhibit the literalism typical of second-generation trauma survivors, seeming to mime the resistance of trauma to narrativization.[22] When the text touches on a legacy of slavery—the past, for instance, or the slave's body—the narrative discourse often turns literal, as if it suddenly loses access to the figurative dimension of language.

For example, the family's house is haunted—haunted by the past, by the traumas suffered under slavery. Language reinforces this materialization of the past by refusing spatial metaphors. When Paul D finds Sethe again after an absence of 18 years, he feels out his chances for establishing a relationship with her by asking if "there was some space" for him, and then again if she "could make space for him" (45). The phrase "making space" is clearly a metaphor for "accepting a relationship." But the text refuses the metaphor. That is, Paul D has to make a space for himself quite literally. When the house begins shaking violently to scare him out, he fights back: "Holding the table by two legs, he bashed it about, wrecking everything, screaming back at the screaming house" (18). He has to "make a space" for himself in Sethe's life more literally than any suitor in literature before him. The narrator later comments that the house is so crammed with materializations of the past that "there was no room for any other thing or body until Paul D . . . broke up the place, making room, . . . then standing in the place he had made" (39). And now readers can see that the novel's opening sentence, "124 was spiteful. Full of a baby's venom" (3), is to be taken quite literally: the "full" in "spiteful" is no figure of speech. The house is so full of the "spite" born of slavery that "there was no room for any other thing or body." Thus the language mimics the haunting by getting literal, sticking to the concrete level of things, coming as close as words can come to the materialization of things in space.[23]

Or take the passages that describe an ex-slave's body. Paul D stands behind Sethe, cupping her breasts from behind in a display of tenderness. Sethe thinks to herself, "What she knew was that the responsibility for her breasts, at last, was in somebody else's hands" (18). The phrase "in somebody else's hands" usually functions as a metaphor meaning that it is someone else's "responsibility"; in this passage the hands are literally there. A similar slippage occurs in the next sentence, where Sethe describes being "relieved of the weight of her breasts" (18). Because the term "weight" appears within the usually figurative phrase "relieved of the weight of," readers assume that it is a metaphor for responsibility—that is, "relieved of the responsibility, the mental burden." But the modifying phrase "of her breasts" gives weight back its literal meaning. Like Denver's clinging to a corporeal reenactment of collective trauma, the text's refusal of verbal substitutions for the body expresses solidarity with the slaves who were subjugated by a discourse of bodies. The fall from metaphor, the failure to enter fully into the play of substitutions that governs language, constitutes a resistance to translating trauma into the abstract register of language.

Contemporary trauma theory carries on Freud's faith in the talking cure: to move trauma from the body into verbalized expression is to cure the patient. But *Beloved* throws into doubt the possibility of a narrative cure for the trauma that was slavery. Throughout the narrative, concrete bits of the past resist transformation into the figurative level of language, just as bits of the traumatic past claim concrete being in the haunted house. That resistance to the endless variety of metaphor that could give new meaning to experience, that clinging to the fixity of a single concrete level of brute fact, is, I think, a way of remaining loyal to the trauma at the heart of the ancestors' experience. Morrison's refusal to enter the sufferings under slavery fully into the substitutions of language is a sign of respect for the essential incomprehensibility of trauma, its "affront to understanding" (Caruth 154). Morrison's concretisms constitute a kind of second-generation signature, a declaration of identification and solidarity with the trauma suffered by her slave ancestors.

The Traumatic Real and the Impossibility of Narrative Closure

Morrison's text is, finally, closer to Lacan's skepticism about the power of the symbolic to heal all than it is to Freud's faith in the talking cure. After the story of Sethe and Paul D reaches its heterosexual closure, with Paul D persuading Sethe to accept the subject position in language ("Me? Me?") and to accept the separation between parent and child necessary to entry into the symbolic order (271–73), two additional pages depict a left-over, something that couldn't be encompassed within the narrative resolution: Beloved herself and the past she embodies—slavery.

In Lacan's view, too, the symbolic is not all-encompassing: there is something left over, left out of the symbolic, something which cannot be captured within the symbolic's logic of limit and differentiation: namely, the real. The real always exceeds the symbolic, with its definitions and categories, and so remains indeterminate: it is "this something faced with which all words cease and all categories fail, the object of anxiety *par excellence*" (S II 164). It can erupt into the symbolic at any moment and disrupt our understanding of reality, which is organized by the logic of the symbolic. The last two pages put the exiled Beloved in the space of the real—promising perhaps a future disruption of our common-sense reality.

This afterword, formally distinct from the main text, focuses precisely on the gap in the symbolic order: it first describes the deficiencies of language and then evokes what escapes language, what exists in the gap—the indeterminate. Beloved will not be remembered, the text says, because "nobody anywhere knew her name"; she is "disremembered and unaccounted for" because "they could not remember or repeat a single thing she said, and began to believe that... she hadn't said anything at all. So, in the end, they forgot her too" (274). Beloved doesn't have "a name," so she has no position in the kinship network organized by the Name-of-the-Father; she could not make her way into the symbolic order through speech (they cannot remember her saying anything); so she is "disremembered," excluded from historical memory.[24] The various organizations of the symbolic—language, history, narrative, kinship—cannot encompass Beloved. Morrison's oft-repeated line, "This is not a story to pass on," acknowledges the failure of her own narrative to capture the tragedy of Beloved and the larger tragedy of slavery that she represents.[25] Beloved is the real, in Lacan's terms—"that which resists symbolization absolutely" (S I 66). At the same time Morrison insists on the continuing existence of that which escapes symbolization. She evokes something just beyond the grasp of conscious knowledge— "the rustle of a skirt" half-heard in sleep that "hushes when they wake," the photograph of a close friend or relative that suddenly "shifts," so that "something more familiar than the dear face itself moves there," footprints by the river that "disappear, as though nobody ever walked there" (275). All these half-glimpses of the lost Beloved convey the idea of something intermittent, fragmentary, ephemeral, something that eludes the categories of symbolic knowledge but is nonetheless there.

This epilogue is symmetrical with the epigraph: Beloved wandering lost occupies a space parallel to the "Sixty million and more" of the epigraph—a space *hors-texte*, outside the narrative frame. The "Sixty million and more" are the lost of the Middle Passage: having perished in the slave ships midway between a place in African history and a place in the history of North American slavery, these lost souls never made it into any text. Lost still, they remain stranded in the epigraph, their human features erased beneath a number. The phrase "and more" indicates the residue excluded even from the body count of the epigraph, unaccounted for by any text—like Beloved at the end. In the historical dimension that always doubles the personal in *Beloved*, the ghost represents all the loved ones lost to slavery.

Beloved is the traumatic real, the empty center around which the signifiers march—attempting to capture, but never managing to capture, the real at the gaping heart of the signifying chain. What the infanticide is for Sethe—the traumatic real that cannot be put into words; what the infanticide is for the novel—the empty place at the center of the text where Sethe's narrative of the baby's death should be: that is what slavery is for the sociosymbolic order that we in the United States inhabit—the trauma at the core of our national history and identity.

The story of Beloved finally cannot be told: "it was not a story to be passed on." But it also "is not a story to pass on": it cannot "pass on," or die (275, 35). Wandering lost in the epilogue, beyond narrative closure, Beloved and the "unspeakable" tragedies of slavery that she embodies continue to haunt the borders of a symbolic order that excludes them.[26]

Part II

Structures of Identification in the Visual Field

Lacan's model of imaginary identification is based on the baby's original appropriation of the mirror image as the core of the ego and so rests on a transaction in the visual field: the subject appropriates the other's visual form in order to incorporate it into the ideal ego. In the next two chapters I extrapolate from Lacan's statements a process of idealization and a process of interpellation built on the misrecognitions of the imaginary. Idealization, I posit in chapter 4, is set into motion by the discrepancy between the ideal ego, formed on the basis of the mirror image's consistency and cohesion, and the subject's actual incoherence and incompletion: that discrepancy makes the subject hungry to take in again, as at the mirror, an external bodily form that promises wholeness and mastery. The consequent reduction of the other to the "empty form of the body" (S I 170) results in a misrecognition of the other—and I explore the resentments and misunderstandings that such idealizations produce in feminist community by citing some specific white feminist idealizations of black feminists, together with the black feminists' responses. Chapter 5 theorizes three forms of gender interpellation based on negotiations in the visual field. While the first process closely follows the mirror-stage experience—the subject takes in the bodily outline of the figures glamorized on the cinema screen—the other two processes are based on the subject's response first to the screen and second to the gaze, features which complicate the visual field in Lacan's later work. The salience of photographs in all the novels explored here points to the stasis characteristic of imaginary identification: whether she is clinging to the ideal ego which closes off growth and change like Jadine in Morrison's *Tar Baby* (chapter 4) or posing for an ever-elusive gaze like Carter's and Drabble's protagonists (chapter 5) the subject is arrested, frozen in the moment of imaginary identification.

Chapter 4

Race and Idealization in Toni Morrison's *Tar Baby* and in White Feminist Cross-Race Fantasies

> The real woman, the pure being-in-itself, is always the other woman.
> —Jane Gallop

In this chapter I explore some of the political consequences of idealization, first in a (fictional) African-American woman's experience and second in the relations between contemporary white feminists and African-American feminists. In Toni Morrison's *Tar Baby* idealization is complicated by the stresses of race. The African-American protagonist Jadine idealizes two contradictory and mutually exclusive models of beauty, reflecting the conflict of her allegiances to white and black cultures. She models many of the processes generated by the ideal ego, including idealization. Although Jadine's attachment to the ideal ego may be extreme, exaggerated as it is by the complicated pressures of race, her orientation toward self and other reflects the dynamics of the ideal ego as it operates more generally in imaginary identifications.

In the second section, some prominent white feminists' idealizing comments on black feminists enable me to explore white fantasies of black women's power and authority. I claim that an attention to cross-race idealizing fantasies can uncover some of the impediments to communication between different racial constituencies within feminism, some of the sources of mistrust that have plagued organizers of feminist communities—whether these are academic women's studies departments or activist groups. A full understanding of the misperceptions between white women and African-American women would have to be grounded in a historical study of raced relations in the United States—such as Hazel Carby's account of the painful history of African-American slaves' relation to their white mistresses or Wini Breines's illuminating study of the divergences between white and black feminists' perceptions and memories of the civil rights and early women's movements.[1] Indeed, I do touch briefly on the historical determinants of gender envy across race, on what I like to think of as an emerging comparative genealogy of white and black women's gender roles. The differences in social pressures on gender formation in white and black families go some way toward explaining the origins of white women's idealizations of black women. But more generally, I argue that it is not only the historical context of power relations in which contemporary race relations are inevitably embedded, nor the racially skewed economic and social structures in which we live, that impede communication between white and black women: processes of idealization and identification also generate misunderstanding and mistrust. Idealizing identifications tend to obstruct a perception of the other as the center of her own complex reality—as, in a word, a subject. And, as black feminists' commentaries on white women's idealizing fantasies of them make clear, they do nothing to change actual power relations or to bring about economic and social justice. Indeed, white feminists' focus on the individual power of a black woman obscures and distorts the power differential between white and black, inadvertently communicates the message that a "strong black woman" does not need any help from white women—in combating racism, for example—and so perpetuates the actual imbalance of power between white and black women.

In the final section of this chapter I explore the impact that raced power relations and the material conditions attached to them have on imaginary processes of identification; that is, I contrast the social and economic consequences for Jadine of idealizing a black woman with the consequences for white feminists of idealizing a black woman.

Lacan describes imaginary identification as "the transformation that takes place in the subject when he assumes an image" (*Écrits* 2). The first identification occurs in the "mirror stage": the young child sees in his or her mirror-image an ideal of bodily unity and assumes identity with it; that image becomes the core of the ego. And this process "will be the source of secondary identifications" (*Écrits* 2): having seen "his form materialized, whole, in a mirage of himself, outside himself" (S I 140), the subject will ever after seek an idealized image in the human form—that is, in the form of the other's body; and the impulse will be, as at the mirror, to take in the perfected form of the other and assimilate it to the subject's own self-image.

What enchants the baby at the mirror is that the image of its bodily form appears to have what it lacks: the human gestalt seems to promise unified being. The subject's first identification is itself, then, an idealization (Lacan suggests as much when he calls the mirrored image "[the baby's] ideal form" [S I 176]). That is, the bodily image in the mirror presents a unified ideal in contrast to the baby's felt experience of the body, which at this stage before the development of motor control is a jumble of sensations and impulses. The process that I am calling idealization follows the same lines. Because the adult subject continues to experience herself as fragmentary and inconsistent, she hungers for that originary illusion of wholeness and finds it projected, again, onto a human form in the external world: "It is in the other that he will always rediscover his ideal ego" (S I 282). And, as before the mirror, he or she will identify with that idealized visual form. "The ideal ego always accompanies the ego . . . [and] continues to play a role as the source of secondary identifications" (Dylan Evans, *Dictionary* 52). As Jannis Stavrakakis puts it, the ego is forever dependent on the other "due to the need to identify with something external, other, different, in order to acquire the basis of a self-unified identity" (18). The tell-tale mark of idealization—and of the imaginary identification that necessarily accompanies it—is the perception of the other as a seamless whole, self-complete and self-possessed.[2]

What psychoanalysis is arguably best equipped to contribute to the study of race is an analysis of "the fantasies organizing the meaning of racial and ethnic identities," in Chris Lane's words (1). Race is to be sure a symbolic discourse, "a certain structure of signification . . . that has its own logic or law that invests us as subjects with a semblance of coherence," as Kalpana Seshadri-Crooks says (24–25).[3] But fantasies of race play out in the visual field and so bear the mark of the imaginary. In the examples that follow, the various fantasies of authenticity, power, and wholeness projected onto the racialized body of the other dramatize the imaginary dimension of race thinking.

Fortifying and Defending the Ideal Ego: Jadine in *Tar Baby*

While much has been written about the role of the ego ideal, a position in the symbolic with which the subject identifies and that supplies him or her with "an internalised plan of the Law," a guide to his or her place in the symbolic order (Dylan Evans, *Dictionary* 52), less attention has been given to the ideal ego and its imaginary functions. Since the ideal ego generates many of the intrapsychic and interpersonal operations that take place in the visual field, including identification and idealization, it seems important to gather Lacan's scattered references to it into a coherent explanatory model. The ideal ego is the self-image appropriated from the mirror reflection and internalized as the nucleus of the ego. The ideal ego functions throughout life as the source of secondary identifications (Lacan, *Écrits* 2). Because there is a gap between the unified ideal ego and the fluctuating and fragmented actuality of the subject, the subject hungers for identifications with others' bodily forms through which the subject can replenish the ideal ego. That desire for imaginary identification results in the reduction of the other to "the empty form of the body"—the form that makes mirror-style assimilation possible (S I 170). The consequent erasure of the other's complex subjectivity is problematic, as the examples of white feminist idealizations of black women in the next section of this chapter will show.

On the other hand, the ideal ego creates a problematic relation to the self: it is this internal conflict that I explore in this first section, through the text of Toni Morrison's *Tar Baby*. The ideal ego is structured by the visual form of the body, so it leaves out the body as process—leaves out its perpetually shifting energies, for example, and the changes that aging produces. It is the seeming permanence and stability of the object in the mirror that, over against the baby's chaotic inner world, makes the bodily image a target for idealization in the first place: Lacan refers to the mirror image as a "statue" and emphasizes the stasis it imposes by referring to the baby's fascination as "spatial captation" and "formal fixation" (*Écrits* 2, 4, 19; see Ziarek, "Toward a Radical" 62, Borch-Jacobsen, *Lacan* 52). That initial arrest is reinforced by the need to defend the idealized bodily image against the baby's "organic disturbance and discord" (Lacan, "Reflections" 15). Thus some of Lacan's figures of speech imply not only stasis but defense, as in his description of the baby's assimilation of the mirror image as an "assumption of the armour of an alienating identity, which will mark with its rigid structure the subject's entire mental development" (*Écrits* 4). What the baby internalizes as the ideal ego is a static picture of the self, a "rigid structure" which, as the metaphor of armor suggests, has to be defended "throughout the subject's entire mental development" against continuing signals of the body's fragmented and shifting actuality. In Lacan's schema, then, the subject is the site of a warfare between a fixed self-image—the ideal ego—and the temporality of the body, whose physical processes, shifting impulses, and changes through time are always putting pressure on a rigid self-representation that excludes them.[4]

In humans generally, according to Lacan, the idealized picture of the self founded on the mirror image forms an obstacle to growth and change—or, to use Lacan's figure of speech, it becomes a bottleneck:

> the initial outburst of appetite and desire comes about in the human subject via the mediation of a form which he at first sees projected external to himself, at first in his own reflection. . . . This image is the ring, the bottle-neck, through which the confused bundle of desires and needs must pass in order to be him, that is to say, in order to accede to his imaginary structure." (S I 176)

The impulses arising from the lived experience of the body have to pass through the bottleneck of the ideal ego in order to enter the subject's self-construct. When they do not match the self-image, they cannot get through: and that defense keeps out potentially revitalizing energies. In *Tar Baby*, the protagonist Jadine's stubborn attachment to the ideal ego forecloses possibilities for growth and change offered by both the body and the African-American culture she denies. In an interview, Morrison says of Jadine's encounter with the woman in yellow in Paris: "Someone assaulted her self-image" (Ruas 106). In fact, *Tar Baby* could be described as a book-long assault on Jadine's self-image from the corporeal and cultural energies that she has thrived by excluding; and it ends with Jadine repulsing all these assaults to reaffirm the narrow bounds of the ideal ego and the exclusions that support it.

Jadine introduces herself to the character Son (and to readers) in a scene that shows her attachment to the ideal ego and her corresponding rejection of the corporeal processes that would threaten that idealized image. Having triumphed over the automatic exclusion of African-American women from the Western beauty ideal to become a successful model (and triumphed over the exclusion of African Americans from higher education to get an advanced degree in art history), Jadine has "made it" in the white world. At the beginning of the novel, she has left Paris, the site of her career success, to return to the African-American aunt and uncle who raised her—servants now on the Caribbean estate of the white American Valerian. Confronting Son, the underclass black man who has insinuated himself into the Caribbean mansion, she introduces herself by handing him a fashion magazine "with her face on the cover" (116). That phrase reproduces the misrecognition of the mirror stage: it is not actually her face on the cover, but the image of her face. By identifying with the specular image of herself, Jadine subjects herself to a self-alienation like that of the mirror stage, but with a cultural dimension: she would not have made it onto the cover of a Parisian fashion magazine if she had not tailored her face and body to the aesthetic of white Western beauty.[5] (This is not to suggest that Jadine is passing for white; billed as "the copper Venus," she has evidently preserved a degree of racialized difference—just enough to please a white fashion world that welcomes a touch of the exotic.)

Over against this mirrored image of herself, the scene introduces the corporeal processes that threaten its disintegration. When Jadine says that Son smells like an animal (he has not bathed for the week that he has been hiding out in Valerian's mansion), Son says, "'I smell you too'" (122). Afterward, Jadine cannot stop extrapolating from Son's remark: "she felt... shame.... He had jangled something in her that was so repulsive, so awful... she was the one he wanted to smell"; and that means "that there was something in [her] to smell and that [he] smelled it... And no sealskin coat or million-dollar earrings can disguise it" (123, 125). Jadine's success as a beautiful image on the page and her concomitant repulsion toward smell seem to validate Freud's intuition that because the leading indicator of the civilizing process is the repression of smell, together with an abhorrence of the bodily odors that remind man of "his earlier animal existence" (*Civilization* 46, n. 1), the attraction of sexual odors will be increasingly replaced by visual erotic stimuli—replaced, in Muriel Dimen's words, by "the smooth, deodorized, but nevertheless (or therefore) very sexy body, posing on the page" (16). But while Jadine can achieve the glamour of the distanced, visualized body by parading the "sealskin coat and million-dollar earrings" of the photo spread, she cannot control the internal flows of the body that produce odors. In Lacan's terms, the smell participates in the real of the organism, in the physical processes excluded by the idealized visual image of the self. Jadine's body creates a smell, and no lavish adornment of the visualized body can disguise or stop it.

Jadine's shame at being perceived as a body with natural odors triggers an immediate displacement: she projects her own body, with its problematic physical flows, onto a female dog in heat recalled from childhood. "One dog sniffing at the hindquarters of another, and the female... letting herself be sniffed... [the male dog] had just come out of nowhere, smelled her ass and stuck his penis in, humping and jerking and grinding away while she stood there bearing . . . his whole weight . . . and other dogs too, waiting, circling . . . to mount her also" (124). Jadine had felt sorry for the dog, especially after a man cracked her over the head with a mop handle to chase her away—"she who had done nothing but be 'in heat' which she couldn't help but which was her fault just the same so it was she who was beaten" (124). What bothers Jadine is not so much the dog's pain as her lack of agency: the dog herself "had done nothing" while the body alone, taking its own course, made her the victim of dogs and men: "the dog was 'in heat,' which she couldn't help." The memory is triggered by Son smelling something analogous in Jadine: "He had managed to make her feel that the thing that repelled her was not in him, but in her . . . she was the one he wanted to smell. Like an animal. Treating her like another animal and both of them must have looked just like it in that room. One dog sniffing at the hindquarters of another" (123). So there is some animal energy, or heat, in Jadine that she cannot control, any more than the female dog can control being in heat, and Son has discovered and exposed it.[6]

I argue that it is not sexuality that Jadine fears—for she goes on to experience a joyously uninhibited sexual relationship with Son—but rather a sexuality that leads to maternity. She projects the real of her body onto a female dog whose body is possessed by the processes of fertility. It is an uncontrollable sexuality that Jadine fears—the fertile body taking over for its own reproductive aims.

The urgency of her displacement reveals one reason why Jadine clings to the specular image of herself. The ideal ego—represented here by the idealized form on the magazine cover—is based on a mirror image that was attractive in the first place because it promised mastery over the body: "the sight alone of the whole form of the human body gives the subject an imaginary mastery over his body, one which is premature in relation to a real mastery" (Lacan, S I 79). In making the mirror image the nucleus of the ego, the baby assumes mastery over a unified body; but that mastery is "premature"—in other words, illusory—for the baby's reality is one of uncoordinated limbs and chaotic impulses. Built on an illusion of mastery, the ego continues in the false perception of itself as autonomous, self-defined master of a well-regulated body. Jadine's allegiance is to the visualized self-image that appears, as in the mirror stage, to guarantee control over the body; but that apparent mastery is always at risk, threatened by the bodily processes outside the compass of the specular image. Her disparagement of the natural body as "animal" and her move to rid herself of it by projecting it onto the dog, demonstrate Jadine's horror of losing control of her own body through reproductive processes that would put others—the inseminating male and the developing embryo—in charge of her body and transform her, unawares, into a maternal woman.

Tar Baby deploys mythic figures to suggest the repudiated elements of Jadine's identity—both the processes of an alienated body about which she would prefer to know nothing and the elements of black culture from which she is estranged. Later in the novel, when Jadine has gone with Son to visit his black hometown, a whole troop of female figures—some from Jadine's past, some from the black community of Eloe, almost all mothers—invade Jadine's bedroom and flourish their naked breasts at her (258). One of them, the "woman in yellow," thrusts three eggs toward Jadine, completing the iconography of the maternal body with a representation of the female ova and confirming that it is the maternal breast, the maternal body, that is making demands on Jadine.

Jadine's own breasts are never described directly, but pictured in the fashion magazine as "six centimeters of cleavage supported (more or less) by silver lamé" (116). This description clarifies the reason why, when Jadine insists to the night women, "I have breasts too," they ignore her: "They didn't believe her" (258). Cleavage is the emptiness between the breasts, enhanced by artificial supports to appear seductive; the night women's breasts are flesh, substantial. Their breasts are made for giving milk; Jadine's breasts are meant for show. Jadine sees the women's breasts as "sagging," "soft, loose bags" (262, 261) because she fears what motherhood would do to her: take away the glamour of the high, pointed breasts intended to parade sexual attractiveness and thereby take away her individual success as a beauty, turning her into just somebody's mother.

Jadine's allegiance is to the visual image of the body rather than to the body's internal processes. Jadine reads the night women's pantomime to mean that they want her to "settle for fertility rather than originality, nurturing instead of building" (269). The women are presumably trying to reveal and encourage the maternal dimension of Jadine's own body. She perceives them as hostile and even life-threatening because they imperil a self-image based on entirely different uses for her body: they "were all out to get her, tie her, bind her. Grab the person she had worked hard to become and choke it off with their soft loose tits" (262). Jadine perceives the demand that she transform herself into a maternal body as a death threat.[7]

So far, I have been discussing the bodily energies that threaten Jadine's ideal ego as if they were separate from the pressures on Jadine from African-American culture. But the demand that Jadine become a traditional mother is embedded in black culture and history, as Morrison presents it. Jadine's experience of nearly losing her life in the "*Sein de Vieilles*," a swamp on the Caribbean island that, like a tar pit, sucks her down, illustrates how *Tar Baby* continually links issues of gender to race. The swamp is arguably associated with the history of slavery through the common factor of white colonization: once a river, it could no longer flow after the white colonizers despoiled the natural landscape of the island, and it "now sat in one place like a grandmother and became a swamp the Haitians called Sein de Vieilles" (10). Raped, violated, and rendered useless by the white colonizers who imposed their own ruinous designs on nature, the "old grandmother" *Sein de Vieilles* has a historical parallel in the African people devastated by enslavement.[8]

When Jadine inadvertently steps into the tar pit, the scene enacts her dread that an embrace of her black cultural heritage would reverse the course of her upward mobility, pulling her down and leaving her mired in an oppressed and backward-looking black community. But the tar-pit allegory includes a gender prescription that is part and parcel of Jadine's resistance to African-American culture. The mythic figures of the *vieilles* (the ancient ones) hanging in the trees above the tar pit sing their own praises while Jadine struggles in the tar below: they celebrate their "exceptional femaleness," which is characterized by the power to hold things together, and they assume that she will want to be just like them (183). In interview, Morrison endorses their values, lamenting the "tragedy" that Jadine "wasn't a Tar Baby. . . . she could not hold anything to herself" (Ruas 102).[9] Just as the breast, under cover of the French signifier *sein*, follows Jadine into the tar pit called *sein de Vieilles*, so the demand that she be a certain kind of woman always accompanies the demand that she submerge herself in black culture. To be worthy of the African-American tradition, this text says in many different ways, a woman needs to embrace the "ancient properties" of black women who, throughout a history beginning with the forced separations of slavery and continuing through the divisive pressures of a racist economic and social system, have been able to hold their families together. In *Tar Baby*, the imperative to maintain connection with African-American cultural traditions includes a directive to conform to a traditional definition of black motherhood.

Jadine's claim that "There are other ways to be a woman," as she says to Ondine, comes under siege both from within and from outside the text. Ondine replies to her, "There ain't but one kind of woman": a "real woman" takes care of family (282, 281). And Morrison in interview stands behind Ondine's opinion, criticizing Jadine for being "cut off [from] her ancient properties"—including "that quality of nurturing [which] is to me essential" (Ruas, 104).[10]

Both Jadine's experiences of suffocation—nearly swallowed up by the tar pit and nearly asphyxiated by the "loose soft tits" of the night women—enact the near-death not of the subject, I would argue, but of the ideal ego. In Lacan's schema, bodily energies are always threatening the limited imaginary ego with disintegration, and "the loss of an imaginary integrity implies a kind of death" (Boothby 350). Yet for Lacan this is a paradoxical death, for it also revitalizes the subject: the shattering of the ideal ego clears a path for the previously excluded vital forces of the organism to make themselves known (Boothby 349). Indeed, the places that Jadine associates with the suffocation of the "person she had worked hard to become" (262), the tar pit and the black community of Eloe, are potentially sources of cultural revitalization. Both are like the briar patch into which Br'er Rabbit is thrown at the end of the Tar Baby tale—comfortable and life-enhancing to those who are at home there (for Son, firmly rooted in black culture, perceives the tarpit as a safe haven and sees Eloe as a kind of Eden, a garden of origins), but suffocating to those whose self-definition is predicated on leaving blackness behind. And the breast-waving women represent something in Jadine—the life-giving properties of the female body. The two death traps, the tarpit and the bedroom at Eloe, offer the possibility of integrating the energies—cultural and physical—that Jadine's ideal ego, tailored to the requirements of white culture, has excluded.[11] But those incipient desires cannot make their way through the "bottleneck" of the ideal ego—for the effort to integrate them would spell the demise of the white-identified and slimmed-down model self-image.

The Ideal Ego and Idealization:
Jadine and the Woman in Yellow

So far, I have elaborated the problematic intrapsychic relations set up by adherence to the ideal ego—particularly the way that the ideal ego blocks bodily processes and impulses toward change from entering into and expanding the subject's self-image. Here I turn to the implications of the ideal ego in relation to others. Because the ideal ego, based on the vision of a unified self, is always at variance with the subject's shifting, inconsistent, fluid actuality, it requires repair: that is, it requires new identifications with a visual form that appears to have the characteristics of the mirror image—unity, coherence, mastery. The outline of the other's body seems to promise, as once before the mirror, a unity and coherence that the subject lacks. Thus the ideal ego is always on the lookout for a visual form that it can idealize and incorporate.

In a flashback to the scene of her success in Paris, Jadine remembers an encounter with a woman who seemingly incarnated the wished-for integrity of being:

> The vision materialized in a yellow dress. . . . The vision itself was a woman much too tall. Under her long canary yellow dress Jadine knew there was too much hip, too much bust. The agency would laugh her out of the lobby, so why was she and everybody else in the store transfixed? The height? The skin like tar against the canary yellow dress? . . . Two upside-down V's were scored into each of her cheeks, her hair was wrapped in a gelee as yellow as her dress. . . . She had no arm basket or cart. . . . just her many-colored sandals and her yellow robe. . . . The woman . . . opened a carton from which she selected three eggs. Then she put her right elbow into the palm of her left hand and held the eggs aloft between earlobe and shoulder. She looked up then and they saw something in her eyes so powerful it had burnt away the eyelashes. . . Left arm folded over her waist, right hand holding three chalk-white eggs in the air, and what will she do with her hands when she reaches the door? they wondered. . . Each one of the [shoppers in the aisles] begged in his heart that . . . she would float through the glass the way a vision should. She did of course . . . that woman approached [the door] with the confidence of transcendent beauty and it flew open in silent obedience. . . . Along with everybody else in the market, Jadine gasped." (45–46)

The woman in yellow reincarnates the gestalt unity perceived in the mirror. For Jadine's relation to the woman in yellow is purely visual (she sees her only for a moment and never speaks to her). And the black woman's self-assured presence seems to embody the illusion of complete and integrated being attached originally to the mirror image. She sweeps through the supermarket with absolute mastery, ignoring the conventions of shopping cart and egg carton, doing everything her own way, ruling her world, even making the door open "magically" to let her out (46). Seeing her self-possession awakens in Jadine a desire for her—to see her, to be her—which Morrison describes as a "hunger" that "never moves, never closes" (46). The "hunger" is the desire to incorporate—albeit through the eye, not the mouth—the perfected form of the other and add it to the ideal ego. The ideal ego is always "hungry," always in need of supplements to shore up its image of self-sufficiency and self-possession.

The legacy of the mirror stage is anything but simple, as Jadine's example shows. On the specular plane, on the plane of bodily forms where Jadine is at home, the woman seems to incarnate a wholeness and self-possession like that of the mirror image; those qualities compel identification. Yet the woman in yellow also embodies cultural values that conflict with the ideal ego that Jadine has lived (and succeeded) by. Her skin is "like tar against the canary yellow dress," her fingers "tar-black," her clothing African (45, 46). Jadine is not passing for white: her publicity rhetoric describes her as "the copper Venus," suggesting that her color makes her just exotic enough to appeal to the white fashion industry. For "copper" has a valence quite different from "tar," suggesting the glamour of tanned bodies (as in "Coppertone") and thereby the privilege—which belongs to white women only—of playing with skin color and transforming it. "Tar," by contrast, is unambiguously black. Further, the woman's "unphotographable beauty" suggests a world of uses for the body different from the reification of Jadine's body on the covers of glossy magazines: the full breasts and hips suggest the capacity to bear children and nurse children. Jadine's white-identified and maternity-denying persona has been founded on the exclusion of precisely what the tar-black skin and full-bodied presence of the woman in yellow represent.

Why then does Jadine idealize and identify with her? On the cultural plane, Jadine is divided: as a black subject who has assimilated to white culture, she feels a suppressed attachment to black culture—as her attraction to Son, with his "tar-black skin" and dreams of an all-black community marked by "the smell of tar and its shiny consistency," suggest (119–20).[12] Jadine has proved herself sensitive to a culture's ideals—for has she not perfectly adapted body and mind to the requirements of success in a white-dominated world?—so she can perfectly well read the values of black culture when they are represented visually, as they are in the woman in yellow. In the woman's body, the wholeness and self-sufficiency that awaken imaginary desires for incorporation are coupled with an ideal of maternal black womanhood that combines female fertility with loyalty to the race. Jadine identifies with the woman in yellow, as her subsequent actions show. Upon seeing the woman in yellow she immediately turns her back on Paris and career success to return to her African-American family, Sydney and Ondine.

At the risk of unduly complicating my argument—for my aim here is to describe as clearly and comprehensively as possible the operations of the ideal ego and the imaginary identifications it generates—I want to do justice to the complexity of visual relations in Morrison's text by pointing out how the spectacle of the woman in yellow dramatizes the interactions of ego ideal and ideal ego. After the woman in yellow has walked out of the market, Jadine catches one more glimpse of her through the plate-glass window—"and there, just there . . . the woman turned her head sharply around to the left and looked at Jadine. . . . and with a small parting of her lips, shot an arrow of saliva between her teeth down to the pavement" (46). Spitting is an expression of contempt for Jadine's assimilation, for her mimicry of a white-fashioned model of exoticized beauty. The humiliation latent in the visual field comes from the fact, as Sartre observed, that it is not only I who look at someone: someone is also looking at me. The woman in yellow looks at Jadine from the position of "ego ideal." In Seminar XI, Lacan modifies his original description of the mirror experience by including the figure of the mother who holds the baby up to the mirror. It is her admiring gaze that allows the baby to admire itself; and Lacan names the place of that validating gaze the ego ideal. Prior to identifying with its image, the baby has to identify with the position of the one who admires him, with the "ego ideal, in so far as from there he will feel himself both satisfactory and loved" (S XI 257). Žižek sorts out this double identification. "Imaginary identification is identification with the image in which we appear likable to ourselves, with the image representing 'what we would like to be'"—that is, identification with the ideal ego. "Symbolic identification [is] identification with the very place *from where* we are being observed, *from where* we look at ourselves so that we appear to ourselves likable, worthy of love" (*Sublime* 105). The place "from where we are observed" is a position in the symbolic—hence the term, "symbolic identification." The mother in Lacan's parable inhabits the symbolic order and necessarily mediates its values. The woman in yellow looks at Jadine from a position securely within the African-American symbolic—or, more accurately, the Afrocentric symbolic—and mediates its cultural values. She occupies the place of ego ideal whose gaze establishes the matrix within which the self-image appears lovable—or, as in this case, unlovable, despicable. The look from the position of the ego ideal conveys massive disapprobation here—and, according to the Seminar XI paradigm, that matrix of contempt would prevent the subject from admiring her own self-image.[13]

A reader of *Tar Baby* may well wonder, If career success is what is gratifying to Jadine, and if she rejects everything about black culture, then why isn't she in Paris, following up on her success as a model, rather than spending her time with her black servant aunt and uncle and, even more questionably, with homeboy Son in his all-black hometown in Florida? Jadine herself is mystified. Looking back on the incident with the woman in yellow, she reviews the events of that day: she had heard that she passed her exams for an M.A. in art history and that she would appear on the fashion magazine cover, and, exultant, she was preparing to celebrate her dual success with a lavish dinner-party—so "why leave the show? cable to old relatives? . . . and split to Dominique . . . when everything on her shopping list was right there in Paris? . . . She couldn't figure out why the woman's insulting gesture had derailed her—shaken her out of proportion to incident" (47)—why it had radically changed her course. Jadine recognizes the magnitude, if not the meaning, of the life-changing impression she received from the woman in yellow. According to my interpretation, the "vision" of the woman in yellow changes Jadine's course because the power of the imaginary lure to identification is enhanced by the symbolic authority of the ego ideal: on the one hand, the woman's full-bodied presence and seeming integrity of being compel Jadine, always under the sway of the ideal ego, to make an imaginary identification; on the other hand, the woman's look invalidates the model self-image that has long served as Jadine's ideal ego. For someone attuned to the visual, and to the cultural values subsumed in the visual, the combination is irresistible. Jadine swallows the ideal whole—Afrocentric values along with the imaginary wholeness—as can be seen from her return to her black family. That revisiting of her "roots" is an unconscious attempt, apparently, to approach the blackness and femaleness of the woman in yellow, whom she idealizes as the embodiment of Authentic Womanhood: "that woman's woman—that mother/sister/she" (46).

Jadine vacillates between identifying with the photographic image of herself and identifying with the form of the woman in yellow—two icons endorsed by the two cultures to which she belongs. For idealization does not take place in some isolated psychic space: rather, the objects chosen for idealization are "already framed and constituted in a broader sociality," as Sara Ahmed says of identifications generally (31). The features of the woman in yellow have an immediate appeal for Jadine because at some level she knows that African-American cultural tradition endows with central importance the black motherhood and racial solidarity embodied in the woman in yellow. Jadine's own figure in the fashion magazine is likewise not a random target of idealization: as an image manufactured by the fashion industry and designed for circulation in a marketplace dominated by white values, it is a culturally standardized and endorsed product. And Jadine, who is caught psychically in the imaginary relation and culturally in the polarization between black and white, can only oscillate between idealizing identifications with the two cultures' ideal figures.

The concrete realities of living out an African-American identity turn out to be more difficult than the imaginary act of putting on the other woman's seeming integrity of being. (The third part of this chapter broadens the context of imaginary identification to explain the economic and social factors that make it harder for a black woman than for white women to sustain an imaginary identification with a black woman.) While tar and breasts, signifiers of black culture and the maternal body, continue to haunt, taunt, and harass Jadine throughout the novel, ultimately the defense of the original ideal ego holds. In the end Jadine is on an airplane flying back to Paris and (presumably) career success in the fashion world. Disconnected from everyone and every place, she feels triumphantly autonomous: "Now *she* felt lean and male" (275). Although the male self-image seems at first quite different from that of alluring female model, it only represents a further narrowing of the imaginary ego to embody a more complete self-sufficiency. For autonomy in white Western culture is associated with the male: as Jessica Benjamin says, "A touchstone of adult masculinity [is] the devaluation of the need for the other" (*Bonds* 171). And just as masculinist autonomy rests on a denial of the subject's actual dependency on others, so Jadine's insistence that she will do just fine by herself begins to sound hollow by dint of repetition: "So what if she was alone"; "Aloneness tasted good"; "no more dreams of safety... she was the safety she longed for" (275, 290). Jadine's affirmation of a lean and male autonomy equips her for the ethic of white individualism, summed up in the American dream that the individual can, entirely alone, achieve any ambition by dint of hard work and education; but it divorces her from the African-American ethic of interdependence that her aunt Ondine and her lover Son have been preaching throughout the novel. So Jadine's revised self-image is culturally alienated, cut off from the African-American tradition of the tar woman who holds people together. It is psychologically alienated as well, representing as it does a new version of the absolute self-sufficiency and self-possession of the ideal ego.[14]

To claim a corporeal self-image that is "lean and male" is also, of course, to reject "breasts." Adopting the structuring imago of the male body effectively negates the image of the fertile female body that has been haunting her. Jadine is all the more distanced from the materiality of her body, all the more encased in the abstraction of the ideal ego. As Lacan says, the ego, "if too developed, ... stops all development" (S I 74). While allowing in impulses to bear and nurture other lives, like the acceptance of her cultural heritage, might have revitalized and broadened Jadine's consciousness, her self-image becomes ever more narrow, ever more hardened against the reproductive potentials of the female body.[15]

Cross-Race Idealization and Misrecognition in Feminist Community

Jadine idealizes a black woman at the level of the specularized body. The writings of some white academic feminists betray a similar tendency to idealize black women: that is, prominent feminist critics Elizabeth Abel, Tania Modleski, and Jane Gallop seem both to idealize a black woman and to ground that idealization on the visualized form of the body. African-American feminist scholars Ann duCille, Deborah McDowell, and Valerie Smith have responded by pointing out what these idealizations elide, such as the historical context and material conditions in which African Americans become women. The sequence of white idealizing statements and black feminist critiques give the impression of a dialogue—but a failed dialogue. Cross-race misrecognitions based on idealization, I would argue, contribute to the misunderstandings between white feminists and African-American feminists, impairing our ability to work together toward common goals.

My analysis of the idealizing comments of Elizabeth Abel, Tania Modleski, and Jane Gallop only pushes forward the exploration they themselves have initiated. Gallop, for example, self-consciously exposes her own fantasies about black feminist critics because she thinks they are "not just idiosyncratic" (*Conflicts* 364), but typical of the tendency among white female academics to exoticize black women. I see the analysis of cross-racial idealization in the pages that follow as my contribution to this common project of uncovering the racial thinking that divides white from black within the feminist community. As Jean Walton describes it, "the project now is to investigate, in specific and detailed ways, local constructions of racialized identification and desire, especially in those areas where the discourses of psychoanalysis and feminism intersect and enrich each other" (40).[16]

I argue that idealizations of the racialized other are rooted in the same process I have described in relation to Jadine—the original idealization of the bodily form in the mirror. And just as Jadine targets for idealization a woman who seems to embody what she lacks—black cultural authority and full-bodied fertility—so, I argue, the idealizations of the white feminists discussed below are motivated by the idealizers' felt lacks. The child at the mirror tries to make up for lack, for its actual *manque-à-être*, its incomplete being and incoherence, by identifying with the seeming fullness of its reflected image. This process does not end with childhood. Because of the incommensurability between the static picture of the ideal ego and the chaotic discontinuities of subjective life, the ideal ego requires supplements—new idealizations, new incorporations of a seemingly complete human form. What is striking in the examples of idealization that follow is that the body often figures as the site of the ideal; even when it is the black woman's mental qualities or cultural authority that the white feminist in question admires, she tends to perceive those qualities in terms of the racialized body.[17]

Elizabeth Abel's article, "Black Writing, White Reading," a survey of various white feminist critics' readings of African-American women writers' texts, constitutes a compendium of the fantasies of difference that white academic women project onto black women.[18] In the spirit of including herself in her scrutiny of race-inflected readings, Abel begins by presenting her own reading of Toni Morrison's short story, "Recitatif." As Morrison herself says, "'Recitatif' was an experiment in the removal of all racial codes from a narrative about two characters of different races" (*Playing*, xi). Because the story gives confusing and contradictory clues to the racial identities of Twyla (the narrator) and Roberta, its ambiguity brings to light "the unarticulated racial codes that operate at the boundaries of consciousness" (Abel, "Black Writing" 472). Abel read Roberta as black, she says, because Roberta seems to be more "in the know" about the social scene—political and cultural—

than Twyla and because Roberta seems to inhabit a more imposing body. As a girl Roberta is apparently better mothered and better fed than Twyla; as an adult, Roberta, like her mother, is large in stature ("Black Writing" 473). These details are in the text. But why should Abel therefore read Roberta as African American? The woman who hungers for what the other has—Twyla "perceives Roberta as possessing something she lacks and craves" ("Black Writing" 473)—is read as white; Roberta, the one who has what it takes, is read as African American. (That a different reading is equally plausible is demonstrated by the interpretation of Abel's African-American graduate student, Lula Fragd, who reversed the attribution of racial identities: Fragd, following cultural, economic, and historical cues, read Twyla as black and Roberta as white [471–75]). Abel characterizes her own reading as "pivoting not on skin color, but on size, sexuality, and the imagined capacity to nurture and be nurtured, on the construction of embodiedness itself as a symptom and source of cultural authority" ("Black Writing" 474). If Abel "reads envy into Twyla's narrative gaze" at Roberta, that is because the black woman appears to be the site of power. But since Abel perceives that power in terms of cultural and social authority, why the emphasis on the body?

Tania Modleski's account of her affection for the Whoopi Goldberg character in a series of Hollywood comedies suggests a cause for white women's location of potency in the African-American woman's body. After a sophisticated deconstruction of the Goldberg role as a product of dominant (racist) cinema that assigns masculine body language to Whoopi Goldberg in order to show that despite her best efforts at mimicry a black woman is "not quite/not white"—that is, not quite a woman—Modleski confesses to being drawn to Goldberg's character all the same. Although "it places me in an uncomfortable position" (that is, it makes her complicit with the racist strategies of dominant cinema), watching the Goldberg character is "empowering" because her body language "represent[s] a liberating departure from the stifling conventions of femininity" (133).

The last comment suggests what Abel's interpretation also hints at: idealizations that fix on the body have more to do with the ideologically constructed position of the white middle-class idealizer than they do with the idealized African-American subject. The body, as Susan Bordo, Pierre Bourdieu (*Outline*), and Peter Stallybrass and Allon White have argued, is an important site of social control. Through seemingly trivial routines, habits, and restrictions, bourgeois culture is "made body," in Bourdieu's phrase (94; qtd. in Bordo 13). Ruling conventions of gender and race as well as class are inscribed in the body. White middle-class femininity requires a general contraction of the body so that a woman may take up as little space as possible in a kind of permanent physical deference to the imposing size of men. Middle-class Anglo women tend to sit with knees and feet together, elbows at our sides, abandoning airplane armrests to men; and the nineteenth-century Anglo-American equation of a refined sensibility with physical delicacy has become the contemporary injunction, "Above all, be thin."[19] While a white middle-class woman might not be aware most of the time of a gender discipline that "goes by itself," she might well experience her dissatisfaction with her own cramped body in the form of envy of an African-American woman who seems more physically free and expressive, less inhibited about taking up space. Modleski says she finds the Whoopi Goldberg character empowering because her body language overturns the norms of femininity (read white femininity.) And Abel "reads envy into Twyla's narrative gaze" first at Roberta's mother, whose body is "bigger than any man's," then at Roberta herself, who as an adult has hair "so big and wild I could hardly see her face" and wears "earrings the size of bracelets" (Morrison, "Recitatif" 247, 249; qtd. in Abel "Black Writing," 473). Abel in fact identifies Twyla as white in part because her body seems "socially harnessed" in contrast to Roberta's larger and more self-expressive body ("Black Writing" 473).

Jane Stembridge, a white woman who was one of SNCC's early staff members, explicitly identifies the lack in herself that makes an African-American woman the target of envy. Observing Fanny Lou Hamer's public presence, Stembridge writes: "[Fanny Lou] Hamer... knows that she is good.... If she didn't know that,... she wouldn't stand there, with her head back and sing! She couldn't speak the *way* that she speaks and the way she speaks is this: she announces. I do not announce. I apologize" (Stembridge, qtd. in Giddings 301). It is the authority of Hamer's speaking voice that Stembridge admires, from a self-acknowledged sense of her own disabled function. As in body language, so in speech, Anglo middle-class women are socialized to be demure and unassuming, hedging their statements with self-disparaging qualifiers (Stembridge's "apologies") and advertising powerlessness through soft tones and hesitant inflections (see Henley 69). Stembridge concludes that Hamer has been trained differently from herself: she has not been "taught" to demean and diminish "herself, her body, her strong voice" (Stembridge, qtd. in Giddings 301).

It would seem, then, that middle-class white women tend to glorify the physical presence of the other woman because of specific gender- and class-based deficiencies that they see made whole in her. When I idealize you, I see in you the qualities that I lack, the qualities that I would like to have. For lurking within the white feminists' idealization of African-American women is the wish to be what the other is—to have her authority or her rhetorical mastery or the power of her physical presence, the qualities that, in the white observer's perception, make her effective in the world. And regardless of the exact qualities that they admire in the other woman, they locate this idealization at the site of the body—seeing, as Abel says, "embodiedness itself as a symptom and source of cultural authority" ("Black Writing" 474). The gestalt of the human form continues to serve as a primary symbol of unified being. We always desire a wholeness which we have not, and we always attempt to possess it through a repetition of the mirror-stage process of assimilating the seemingly coherent bodily image of the other.[20]

Ann duCille objects to a range of such white academic feminist idealizations; most relevant to the present discussion, she suggests that white feminists' obsession with the bodies of black women is a process of racial othering, claiming that for "white women ... black women are newly discovered foreign bodies, perpetually other" (105). In locating their idealizations at the level of the black woman's body, the white feminists in this study are indeed repeating the gesture of equating the black subject with the body which founds racial categories. As Frantz Fanon, for example, describes his encounters with the gaze of whiteness—"I am overdetermined from without. I am the slave ... of my own appearance" (116)—the black subject is reified as body, immediately categorized as other.[21]

The (failed) dialogue between Jane Gallop and Deborah McDowell (or rather between their two texts) illustrates one more psychic impediment posed by idealization to the perception of racial others as subjects. In a conversation with Marianne Hirsch and Nancy Miller recorded in *Conflicts in Feminism*, Gallop confesses that although she has seen Deborah McDowell only once and never spoken to her, she nonetheless feels a strong "wish for McDowell's approval. For McDowell, whom I do not know, read black feminist critic ... African-American women ... are the people I ... try to please in my writing. It strikes me that this is not just idiosyncratic" ("Criticizing" 363–64). She describes her relation to the (unknown) McDowell as a "transference" ("Criticizing" 363); and what transference means to her, she explains in her essay on Annie Leclerc, is "the subject presumed to know" ("Annie" 152). So Gallop projects onto Deborah McDowell "the subject presumed to know," an idealized figure of ultimate discursive authority who knows (and judges). She has gotten over her idealization of Lacan, she explains; and now "McDowell has come to occupy the place [that Lacan once occupied] in my psyche" ("Criticizing" 364). Whether that is the place of the ideal ego or the ego ideal, Gallop does not say; what is clear is that, as a "place" internal to Gallop's subjective world, it eclipses the place of Deborah McDowell as a separate subject in the external world. Gallop inadvertently lays bare the appropriative move that is part of idealizing identifications. If the ideal ego is not only at the start, but continuously, an idealized version of the self at variance with the subject's actual incoherence, it always requires supplements from further idealizations; the ideal ego needs to be repaired by taking in the idealized image of the other and adding it to the idealized self-image. Idealization, then, obscures the complex reality of the other subject not only by turning her into an undivided and perfect whole; idealization also obliterates the separate existence of the other through assimilation.

In *"The Changing Same,"* Deborah McDowell speaks back as subject and so demolishes her status as venerated fantasy object. McDowell aligns Gallop's use of her name with Harriet Beecher Stowe's use of Sojourner Truth's name. Stowe "assimilates Truth's complex life story" to her own rhetorical purposes, McDowell says, reducing the name Sojourner Truth to a "counter" in her own rhetorical game. In the same way, Jane Gallop reduces the name Deborah McDowell to a "counter" representing the category "black feminist critic," thus "reducing the humanity" of Deborah McDowell to serve the needs of Gallop's own rhetoric (174). A better alternative, the analogy with Stowe implies, would be to consider McDowell as a subject in the context of her own "complex life story"—or, more relevant here, to consider Deborah McDowell in the context of her own complex black feminist critical writings.[22]

Imaginary identifications such as these have the unintended effect of erasing the other woman as subject. Cross-race idealizations also erase the historical and political context in which she became a subject. For example, a white woman's wish to identify with a black leader like

Fanny Lou Hamer and so possess her rhetorical mastery or the power of her physical presence overlooks the situated nature of those qualities—ignores the possibility that black women leaders do not just "have" authority, but have developed ways of inhabiting and projecting body and voice as resistance, as a political strategy within a context of racial oppression. A more substantial recognition of a black woman's authority and presence than the wish to identify with her would involve a study of the raced history that has produced black female gender roles.

African-American feminists Sheila Radford-Hill and Joan Morgan provide a historical context for the strong black woman role which casts a different light on white idealizations of a black woman's personal power and presence. Morgan locates the origins of the stereotype in slavery. The idea that black female slaves were strong enough to endure any pain and keep on going justified slave-owners' abuses, including rape: "the black woman's mythic 'strength' became a convenient justification for every atrocity committed on her" (Morgan 98). In the liberation movements of the 1960s, Radford-Hill points out, the same stereotype came in handy to both black nationalists and white feminists: a strong black woman could be counted on to bear the blows of sexism and racism and "still render service" (Radford-Hill 1086). The mythic identity that emerges from history to inform contemporary black gender identities is, as Michele Wallace defines it, "a woman of inordinate strength, with an ability for tolerating an unusual amount of misery and heavy distasteful work. This woman does not have the same fears, weaknesses, and insecurities as other women but believes herself to be and is, in fact, stronger emotionally than most men" (107).[23]

Radford-Hill explains why, in spite of these historical abuses, contemporary African-American mothers often pass on to their daughters a version of the strong black woman gender role:

> As black mothers in the 1970s, we were keenly aware of what [degradation, discrimination, and disrespect] we had faced as young adults. Although we hoped that our daughters would be spared the effects of racism and sexism, we feared otherwise, so we raised our daughters with the capacity to build a self-concept that could withstand male rejection, economic deprivation, crushing family responsibilities, and countless forms of discrimination. In our view, the most effective antidote to having our daughters' lives destroyed by their experiences with racism and sexism was to build and maintain an intact self. To develop such a self-concept required us to pass along a variation of [the Strong Black Woman stereotype] (2002, 1086).[24]

To Radford-Hill, and presumably the maternal generation for whom she speaks, instilling the strong black woman identity is an adaptive response to the nexus of power relations in which black daughters are located—a form of maternal protection for daughters' self-esteem against the ravages of sexism and racism.

Young black women writers like Morgan, Lisa Jones, Veronica Chambers and Kimberly Springer—the "daughters" of the generation for whom Radford-Hill speaks—describe the psychic burdens of living up to the strong black woman role. Morgan writes that having "internalized the SBW credo—No matter how bad shit gets, handle it alone, quietly, and with dignity"—she "sank deeper and deeper into denial" (90). The emotional price of repressing her own needs in order to act always as "the dependable rock for every soul who needed me" was ultimately total breakdown.[25] As Kimberly Springer points out, Morgan's welding of the three words into the single unit "strongblackwoman" conveys the unrelenting pressure of having to be *always* in control and invulnerable: "there is the expectation in the Black community that Black women will be all three, *at all times*" (Springer 1070). As cure, Morgan claims for herself and her generation "our God/goddess-given right to imperfections and vulnerability" (Morgan 110). In her illuminating analysis of Morgan's, Chambers', and Jones's cultural/autobiographical works, Springer observes that for all three young black writers, the solution is redefinition—"opening up to the future as fallible human beings and not women of mythical proportions" (Springer 1069).

When white women idealize black women for embodying the strength that they themselves would like to have, then, they inadvertently champion and reinforce an oppressive, even damaging and dehumanizing gender identity. And, as Valerie Smith says, the "association of black women with reembodiment" is especially problematic, for it "resembles rather closely the association, in . . . nineteenth-century cultural constructions of womanhood, of women of color with the body and therefore with animal passions and slave labor" ("Black Feminist" 45). Smith refers here to the ideology of slavery, but her reference to "reembodiment" calls up a whole series of historical precedents for the displacement onto black bodies of the corporeal energies repressed by white middle-class socialization.[26]

Idealizing the racialized other has real-world political consequences. Abstracting a woman's personal strength from the social conditions that fostered her development of those strengths protects the white idealizer from having to confront the adverse material conditions that attach to being black in the United States and the daily insults and injuries of racism. This not-knowing bars the white idealizer from feeling any urgent need to change the racially skewed distribution of power and resources in the United States—or to give up the benefits that she derives from it.

The responses to white idealizations from the African-American feminists I have quoted here raise questions about Kaja Silverman's project to utilize idealization as a tool for changing racial stereotypes. In *Threshold of the Visible World* she argues that a cinematic practice that idealizes the racialized bodies that Euro-American culture currently stigmatizes—and her central example is the male black body—will make viewers identify with them in a positive way and so change the value attached to blackness. Silverman's aim is to enlarge the idealizing capacity of subjects beyond identification with "the self-same body" and to encourage, rather, idealizing identifications with "bodies which diverge as widely as possible both from ourselves and from the cultural norm" (37). But locating idealization at the level of the body is a tricky business: the objections of Valerie Smith and Ann duCille to the "othering" of black women's bodies remind us that idealizations of the black body are inevitably embedded in a history of reducing African-American subjects to their bodies and then using those objectified bodies to serve the self-elevating purposes of white ideology. Of course, it is these demeaning images that Silverman wants to counteract—but a focus on the visualized body maintains the binary of white skin/black skin and so supports, even if the valuation is inverted, the absolute difference of racial categories.

In the eight years since Silverman wrote *Threshold of the Visual World* (1996) there has indeed been a shift in the cultural valuation of black bodies: now cachet attaches to figures who depart from the white norm, figures whose racialized features, like Jadine's, are exoticized and glamorized. But that revised aesthetic has not resulted in meaningful changes in the race ideology that regulates everyday life, as Paul Gilroy says: "It is best to be absolutely clear that the ubiquity and prominence currently accorded to exceptionally beautiful and glamorous but nonetheless racialized bodies do nothing to change the everyday forms of racial hierarchy. The historic associations of blackness with infrahumanity, brutality, crime, idleness, excessive threatening fertility, . . . remain undisturbed" (22).

To move from the cultural to the psychoanalytic level of Silverman's argument: Silverman claims that one "can idealize, and so identify, at a distance from the self" (*Threshold* 74); she agrees with Lacan that identification always accompanies idealization, yet claims that one can make an idealizing identification with the other and still continue to see her as separate and autonomous, grounded in the particularities of her own subjective circumstances.[27] The cross-racial idealizations cited above reveal how problematic that assertion is. In most of these cases, idealization plucks the desirable subject out of her life context and transfers her into the idealizer's own frame of reference—or, in Gallop's heightened trope, into her own psychic structure. These examples throw doubt on Silverman's contention that one can maintain simultaneously "the ideality and the alterity of the other" (*Threshold* 105). To use the other to fill in one's own lacks is to perceive in the other only a figure derived from oneself, a figure who makes good one's own deficiencies; that projected ideal blocks the view of the other woman in herself, just as the idealizer's need to see the other as a perfect, undivided whole blocks the vision of her as a complex and contradictory subject. As Jessica Benjamin says, "To attribute difference to the other,... even to adore or idealize that difference, is not at all the same as to respect the other subject as an equal"— as "an equivalent center of being" (*Like* 8).

RACE AND IDEALIZATION: THE LIMITS ON IDENTIFICATION

The juxtaposition of Jadine's idealizations in *Tar Baby* with the white feminists' idealizations reminds us that although the imaginary relation with the other may be universal, as Lacan says, it is always inflected by the local and historically specific context of the viewer. There are limits to both Jadine's identification with the woman in yellow and the white feminists' identification with the black women that they idealize, but the limits are contoured differently by the relative power attached to white and black in the United States.

Jadine's idealization of the woman in yellow rehearses the specular processes of idealization and identification in a virtual imitation of the Lacanian text. The relation to the woman is purely visual: they do not speak; and the text repeatedly describes her appearance as a "vision" (45). The fullness of her bodily presence, together with the self-possession of her gestures, seems to incarnate the dream spawned by the original mirror-stage identification, "the dream of a complete presence-to-itself founded upon the wholeness of the perceptual gestalt" (Boothby 354). As Lacan says, when the subject perceives a bodily shape "which once again allows the subject to reproject, to recomplete, to *feed*..., the image of the *Idealich*," he retrieves "the jubilant assumption of the mirror image... along similar lines." The subject "literally loses himself" in the other's image and "identifies" with it in a repetition of "the fundamental mechanism around which everything relating to the *ego* turns" (S I 171). The impulse, as at the mirror, is to take on the perfected form of the other and make it into the image of oneself, to add it to the ideal ego. Because Jadine perceives the form only of the woman's body—not yet the meaning of its inner processes—that idealized bodily outline can "*feed*" (Lacan's emphasis) what Morrison describes as her "hunger" for the woman in yellow (46)—a hunger to be her, as we know from Jadine's subsequent choices: she immediately leaves Paris to return to her black family in an apparent attempt to take on and live out the racial authenticity figured by the idealized woman in yellow.

Jadine's vision of the woman in yellow appears, then, to have much in common with the white feminists' idealizations: like them, Jadine sees in the black woman a monumental authority of presence; and she perceives the woman's body and gestures, all of a piece, as evidence of her integrity of being and her mastery over the world around her. And like the white idealizers, Jadine sees her own lacks made good in the black body—but these are lacks specific to her own race and class position. Having abandoned the qualities emblematized by the woman's full body and tar-black skin in order to make herself into the model admired by the white world, Jadine lacks exactly what the woman in yellow embodies. The bodily form of the woman in yellow offers a supplement to the ideal ego—as in Lacan, a replenishing of its deficiencies. But whereas the white women can sustain the idealization of black women indefinitely because underneath they know that they cannot be black, Jadine, a black woman, could well move into the position of the woman in yellow, living out the solidarity with black culture and practice implied by the woman's tar-black skin and claiming for her own the fertility implied by the woman's ample hips and bosom. Consequently, her idealization of the woman in yellow is unstable and fraught with conflict; to sustain the idealizing identification, she would have to give up the material advantages gained by her long identification with the specularized model of herself as (white-defined) beauty.

The text freights Jadine's white-identified ideal ego with suggestions of artifice: existing only on the flimsy pages of a fashion magazine, her self-image is paper-thin, mere surface, a commodity packaged to sell in a white marketplace. By thus charging Jadine with artifice, the narrative implies that Jadine, in assimilating to white culture, is living a lie. As Valerie Smith says of African-American discourses of authenticity generally, that charge of artifice "assumes the existence of a particular type of black subject that is more authentic than any other" (*Not Just Race* 68).

In *Tar Baby*, the site of that black authenticity is the woman in yellow—a woman seen as complete and harmonious in herself. I would argue that the notion of an authentic racial identity bears some affinity with mirror-stage illusions about the wholeness and integrity of the ideal woman. Indeed, Toni Morrison herself seems both to idealize the woman in yellow and to connect her psychic wholeness with racial authenticity. In answer to interviewer Nellie McKay's inquiry about how the woman in yellow could have such an impact on events when she is glimpsed only for a moment, Morrison answers that "such people do. The genuine article only has to appear for a moment to become memorable" (McKay 148). It is the fleeting visual perception of the other woman that makes an impression, she goes on to say, because "she is a real, complete individual who owns herself.... There is always someone who has no peer, who does not have to become anybody. Someone who already 'is'" (McKay 147). Morrison does not treat the woman in yellow as a type of mythic figure here, but assumes that "such people" exist. To discover in the woman in yellow, and those like her, a person who does not "become" but "is" is to repeat the gesture of idealization which, following the mirror-stage model, attributes permanence, totality, and "being-in-itself" to the other woman. Morrison seems to be following the pattern of the white feminist idealizers and of Jadine in attributing wholeness and self-possession to the other woman—she is "real, complete ... owns herself." While in most of her writing Morrison complicates this kind of ontology, in this interview she appears to participate in the imaginary relation herself.

Morrison's remarks also link (what I would call) the mirror-stage illusion of the other's complete presence-to-herself to the notion of an unadulterated racial identity. Morrison explains that the woman in yellow constitutes a reproach to Jadine "because of her *blackness*! It is when she sees the woman in yellow that she begins to feel inauthentic"; the woman in yellow makes Jadine feel "inauthentic," she continues, by reminding her of her betrayed "authentic self" (McKay 147, 148). The notion of racial authenticity is dubious not only at the level of biology, where the history of genetic mixing makes such a thing impossible (as Jadine's light skin is always silently attesting), but on the cultural level as well. Since African-Americans in the United States must live within, negotiate with, and be influenced to some degree by the hegemony of white cultural values, there is arguably no such thing as an authentically black subject—one who has kept his or her commitment to African-American culture pure, uncontaminated by white cultural values—just as, on the psychic level of idealization, there is no such thing as a simple, noncontradictory subject, true to a single core self and completed, once and for all. Rather, it could be argued, as Valerie Smith does, that "all identities are inauthentic," since "all identities are discursively produced and under negotiation" (*Not Just Race* 67). An authentic racial identity is itself an imaginary identity, and in the same fashion that characterizes the imaginary identities attributed to "the other woman" in the idealizations that I have reviewed: it is pure, unadulterated, whole, and unitary.

By focusing on the artificiality of Jadine's identification with a white system of values, *Tar Baby* shifts blame from the system of racial inequality in which Jadine is trying to survive to the assimilated subject herself. But it is the existence of a racially divided structure of opportunity and reward that pushes Jadine toward assimilation. Jadine's fear of the limitations imposed on her as a black woman in the United States is dramatized in the scenes of the tar pit and the night women's visitation: she feels dragged down by the tar—symbol of her black cultural heritage, as I have tried to show—and suffocated by the breasts of the women who would impose the community's definition of black womanhood on her. She imagines immersion in black culture as a return to a communal ethos that would spell the death of the successful individual, of "the person she had worked hard to become" (262). While the life-and-death terms of these episodes are produced by Jadine's exaggerated fears of what an adherence to the legacy of black culture would do to her, an economic reality lies behind the melodrama of being stuck in the tar: to identify as black would indeed be a drag on her upward mobility. In the racially divided system in which she lives, a wide range of opportunity is reserved for whites; to be black is to live with limited economic opportunity. It is not Jadine's ambition that deserves criticism, but the racial inequality that makes her choose between a loyalty to family and race and the American dream—supposedly open to everyone—of success earned through hard work and education, unhampered by ethnic identity. While Ondine in the novel and Morrison in interview focus on Jadine's selfishness and materialism (markers of her identification with whiteness), her story of assimilation could be viewed, like the passing narratives of the 1920s, as a marker "of the space between white privilege and black disempowerment" (Smith, *Not Just Race* 60).

Thus, despite the narrative opprobrium cast on Jadine's identification with a white ideal, there are compelling reasons for her to stick with the original idealization, to continue to identify her ideal ego with the specularized image of herself as glamorous model which has brought her personal and financial success in a white-dominated world. To sustain the identification with the woman in yellow, to move into the racial loyalty that the woman in yellow embodies, she would have to give up too much.

By contrast, a white woman can maintain an idealizing identification with a black woman with impunity, because there is no possibility of actually being the black woman she admires. Indeed, because the white feminists in my study depend on the visual image to give them information about the other woman—they perceive her wholeness, her integrity of being, at the level of the specular body—they are, unawares, invoking a visual binary which assures them that they are white. Since whiteness, itself unspecified and unmarked, is defined by negation, as the absence of blackness (as whatever the African-American is not), the white American reminds herself of her own racial identity when she perceives the other woman as black. In the scopic negotiation of idealization, the underlying visual binary is always reassuring the idealizing white woman that she cannot be black. So she can entertain the fantasy of being the black woman indefinitely.[28]

Depending on the visual to give them information about the racialized body (she is black, she is powerful) also moves the white women in my study into a scopic relation to the other that has historically been the province of whiteness. "The white man has enjoyed for three thousand years the privilege of seeing without being seen. It was a seeing pure and uncomplicated; the light of his eyes drew all things from their primeval darkness" (Sartre 7–8; qtd. in Doane, *Femmes Fatales* 223). Looking confirms the invisibility of the white subject (and thus his or her normative position) and the hypervisibility of the black subject. The white women in my sample do not mention their own bodies. Rather, they occupy the position of disembodied eye: they see but are not themselves seen. So although looking engenders the idealization of the black woman, so that she appears to be the locus of power in contrast to the lack thereof in the paltry white observer, the structure of looking actually reverses those power relations. Power remains with the one who sees: she describes, defines, categorizes, "knows" the other. The other, the embodied, is seen, categorized, known.[29]

Is it then an "exercise of whiteness" to play with the identification and idealization of a black woman? When it is a white woman idealizing a black woman, there is a built-in limitation to identification. As Ann duCille says of white writers who appropriate the experience of blacks to understand their own lives, the writer "takes symbolic wealth from the ... romanticized black body but retains the luxury of ignoring its material poverty" (110).[30] The white women in my study can idealize and identify with the putative strength of a black woman while bracketing the other attributes of being black: they need not participate—even imaginatively—in the material conditions attached to being black in the United States. The specularization of difference is always reassuring them of their own unshakable privileged position within a racial binary. Jadine, a black woman, cannot so easily sustain the idealization of a black woman because she could actually shift into that identity position and so be forced to give up the dreams made possible by assimilation into white culture.

Finally, the tendency to idealize the woman of color is subtly racist in that the existence of distinct racial categories supports it. Idealization is paradoxical: at the same time that I identify with the other, taking in her image and making it part of myself, I also require her to be absolutely different so that she, unlike me, can be whole. Jane Gallop, in yet another example of confessional analysis, pushes to its extreme the tendency to emphasize the other woman's difference. She analyzes the source of her attraction to Marjorie Pryse's introduction to *Conjuring,* which characterizes the entire sequence of African-American women's writings as a single unified tradition originating in a "magic oral inheritance" from black foremothers who, barred from mainstream artistic expression, practiced alternative arts like conjuring, gardening and quilting. Gallop confesses: "I want the conjure woman. I want some special power that stands outside . . . white malestream institutions" (*Around* 175–76).[31] This desire to see black women writers as "outside" the academic institutions that constrain the writer echoes the primitivist longings of the white modernists who in the 1920s and 1930s found the black artists of the Harlem Renaissance to be a source of pure otherness, "outside" civilized white society. Indeed, as Rey Chow points out, this longing goes back at least to the eighteenth century: "Ever since Jean-Jacques Rousseau, the native has been imagined as a kind of total other—a utopian image" whose appeal comes from his "imaginary self-sufficiency" (49). To be within civilization, to participate in the symbolic order, is to forfeit wholeness, to be fragmented and incoherent, to live in disharmony with the ideal ego founded on the illusion of wholeness and self-sufficiency—and therefore to seek a support for that ideal ego in the "imaginary self-sufficiency" of someone who stands outside the civilized order that divides and oppresses oneself. Gallop goes on: "I want some ancient power that stands beyond the reaches of white male culture. I want black women as the idealized and exoticized alternative to European high culture. I want some pure outside" (*Around* 169). In order to imagine a whole, undivided subject, it is necessary to imagine him or her outside the mutilating repressions imposed by one's own social order. But then, one has an unconscious investment in the maintenance of racial categories that keep black women "outside" the mainstream: the more disenfranchised a black woman appears to be, the more she appears to be outside the sociosymbolic order and its constraints.

I have been arguing throughout this discussion that the seemingly innocent idealization of women of color has political effects: abstracting a woman's personal strength from the social conditions that fostered her development of those strengths protects the white idealizer from noticing the material conditions that attach to being black in the United States—and from feeling the need to do anything about them. As bell hooks says, white feminist activists' perception that black women are powerful has in the past convinced them that black women didn't need the feminist movement (*Feminist Theory* 45). (See also Michie 137). Idealization can engender political passivity, then: seeing an African-American woman as the locus of female power absolves me from acting on my own power to help her in her struggles—in the struggle to combat racism, for example.

Gallop suggests a corrective to "idealizing, exoticizing" longings to find a model who is purely other: "The pure is attractive... for white academics dreaming of an outside of Western culture. The pure is attractive, but we must try to affirm worldly impurity, inevitable mixity" (*Around* 171). The desire for a "pure" other with whom to identify returns us to the discourses of authenticity that posit a subject of racial purity uncontaminated by the dominant culture—to discourses that, I have suggested, form a subset of the desire to see the other as an embodiment of unified being. Her idea that we counter such desires by "trying to affirm wordly impurity, inevitable mixity" suggests, first, that we can "try"—that is, use our conscious will—to counter imaginary impulses which are unconscious; and, second, that we can turn current theoretical models of the subject to practical effect. We can, for example, counter the desire to attribute an indivisible pure autonomy and authenticity to the other woman by insisting on the multiple subjectivity of everyone—on the "mixity" of disparate and contradictory discourses that we all are.

The acceptance of the other as a complex, contradictory mix is a property of the symbolic, as is the process of viewing one's own imaginary longings from the detached perspective of a third term, a third position supplied by language, by analysis, by writing. In committing to print their vision of a black woman as a desired image of self-completion, the white feminists I have cited have inserted their fantasies into the symbolic order—and the symbolic is, for Lacan, the antidote to the distortions of the imaginary. Once the white women have published their idealizing fantasies, the black women who are their targets can respond as speaking subjects and so dispel their reification as fantasy objects. The act of moving idealizing fantasies of the other woman into the public space of the printed word enables the dynamic of dialogue to work on and throw into process the static objects of private fantasy. As Elizabeth Abel explains, the purpose of such an analysis is to "deepen our recognition of our racial selves and the 'others' we fantasmatically construct and thereby expand the possibilities of dialogue across as well as about racial boundaries" ("Black Writing" 498). Although it would be a stretch to call the exchanges recorded here a dialogue—they might better be described as a series of what Susan Stanford Friedman calls "scripts of confession" on the part of the white women and "scripts of accusation" on the part of the black women (Friedman, "Beyond"

8–11; *Mappings* 41–43)—the essential move into the symbolic realm of challenge and response has occurred, hopefully clearing the way for more fruitful cross-race dialogues.

The final chapter of this book (chapter 7) suggests several ways that feminists might consciously employ the resources of the symbolic to counter the political effects of imaginary identification across race and so work toward making such dialogues possible.

Chapter 5

Luring the Gaze

Desire and Interpellation in Sandra Cisneros's "Woman Hollering Creek," Anne Tyler's *Saint Maybe*, Angela Carter's *The Magic Toyshop*, and Margaret Drabble's *Jerusalem the Golden*

"In this matter of the visible, everything is a trap": so Lacan declares in Seminar XI (93). This chapter explores the ways that identification with visual images lures the subject into putting on the cultural representation of woman and making it her own. At the heart of my analysis is the relation between desire and interpellation. What motivates a woman to accept interpellation, what makes her want to embody society's definition of woman? This question is ruled out by Louis Althusser's theory of interpellation, but feminists have been asking it since Simone de Beauvoir first wondered why women embrace their own oppression.

Althusser's notion of interpellation preempts desire: the subject is constituted by interpellation, summoned to his or her appropriate subject position in the social structure. There is no choice; there can be no choice, since prior to interpellation there is no subject to choose, or to desire. The subject is "hailed" into his or her social position and compelled by that hailing to enact her given role. But, Judith Butler and Mladen Dolar object, why does the subject respond to that hailing? the turn toward the call presupposes a subject who actively chooses to obey.[1] In a similar vein, Anne Cheng asks, What pleasure inheres in the act of submitting to interpellation? (160 ff.)[2] My own approach to interpellation asks the old feminist question, most recently formulated by Teresa de Lauretis—What is "the process whereby a social representation is accepted and absorbed by an individual as her own representation"? (de Lauretis 12)—but tries to answer it in a new way by drawing on Lacan's models of interaction in the visual field. Lacan's notions of the mirror, the screen and the gaze suggest to me increasingly complex ways in which images in the visual field inspire the desire for identification and so "trap" the subject in gender roles; but this is not a passive, one-way process: the subject, too, is intent on trying to ensnare the gaze.

Lacan's "Mirror Stage" essay (1949) suggests a relatively simple process of interpellation based on the imaginary. The young child's identification with the image in the mirror, which provides the basis for the ego, institutes an aptitude for identification with visual images as well as a desire to be one with the whole and perfect image presented to him or her on a visual surface: hence the subject's susceptibility to the cultural ideals embodied in human figures on the movie or television screen. "Woman Hollering Creek" by Sandra Cisneros dramatizes the force of such identifications and also shows how imaginary identification blinds the subject to the symbolic coercion operating through the imaginary: Cleófilas and her girlfriends identify with the glamorous heroines of the *telenovelas* and thereby take in, unawares, the Mexican cultural representation of woman as she who suffers for love.

Whereas imaginary relations founded on the mirror stage are dual—the subject in quest of identification with his or her semblable—the visual field becomes more complicated with Lacan's introduction of the gaze in Seminar XI (1963–64). The second section of this chapter constructs a theory of symbolic identification mediated by the ego ideal—a look which reaches the subject from a site in the symbolic—and the "screen," whose operations Kaja Silverman describes in *Male Subjectivity at the Margins*. Silverman takes part of what Lacan says in Seminar XI—namely, that the gaze passes through a screen before it reaches the subject—and builds a theory of interpellation on it, interpreting the screen as a cultural screen and the gaze as a cultural gaze. While I disagree with Silverman's interpretation of the gaze, her interpretation of the screen is helpful in understanding symbolic identification. She attributes an "ideological status" to the screen: according to her, it is composed of the "culturally generated ... repertoire of images through which subjects are ... constituted"; and she concludes that "the subject can only be [seen] through the frame of culturally intelligible images" (*Male* 150). Since the gaze that Lacan diagrams in Seminar XI (diagram two) reaches the subject only by passing through this screen, it would align the subject with the cultural forms on the screen—and find that the subject either matches or (more likely) fails to measure up to the appropriate cultural image. I will use Silverman's adaptation of the Lacanian gaze as a model useful on its own merits for understanding symbolic identifications like those dramatized by Angela Carter in *The Magic Toyshop*. While Silverman's theory is indeed useful for thinking about one engine of interpellation—namely, the desire to fit the proper cultural shape—I maintain that Silverman stops short at the screen: that is, she focuses not on the gaze as such but on the cultural screen through which people look at each other.

My own interpretation of the gaze, which I develop in the third and longest section of this chapter, rests on the discrepancy between the two discrete models of the gaze that Lacan presents in Seminar XI. Lacan describes with approval Merleau-Ponty's notion of a gaze that appears to surround us on all sides: simply by virtue of being an embodied human being in the visual field, one has the continual sense of an imperceptible gaze "that circumscribes us ... makes us beings who are looked at" (S XI 75). Merleau-Ponty's decription is phenomenological and as such is an accurate description of how we experience the visible world. Yet in actuality, this universal gaze is only an illusion: according to Lacan, the gaze is actually the point of invisibility in the visual field (S XI 77). As the point of lack, the gaze can stand in for the object a, a purely structural function that designates what is absent: "The *objet a* in the field of the visible is the gaze" (S XI 105). The paradoxical situation of the subject in the visual field produces desire: "one's desire" is to be "the desire of the Other,"[3] to be desirable to the gaze that seems to regard us from all sides; but that desire can never be satisfied because the gaze, as a manifestation of the object a, does not exist. We are always in the position of K in *The Castle*, dependent on a generalized gaze to validate our being, yet incapable of securing, or indeed of making any contact with, such a validating gaze.

Clara, in Margaret Drabble's *Jerusalem the Golden*, dramatizes the dilemma of the subject in the field of the visible. Her object is to capture the admiration of a generalized gaze, so she throws her energy and intelligence into perfecting the visible surfaces that she hopes will seduce the gaze—style, manner, clothes, charm. She does indeed receive admiring looks from many persons. But, as Lacan is careful to stipulate by differentiating his own theory from Sartre's, the gaze is not the look; far from existing in an intersubjective dimension (S XI 100), it is an absence, "an unoccupiable point [which] indicates an impossible real" (Copjec 34–35). Clara, like all of us, can exist only in a relation of desire to the gaze, never in a relation of gratification. And how does that desire function as an interpellative force? It continually motivates the subject to put on a false, seemingly alluring simulacrum of the self, which inevitably mimics the contemporary version of the glamorous.

Moving from imaginary processes modeled on mirror stage transactions to symbolic identifications to the relation of desire between the subject and the Lacanian gaze, I argue that far from being mutually exclusive, the forms of desire generated by these three relations to the field of the visual work together to interpellate the subject.

Imaginary Identifications and Interpellation in Sandra Cisneros's "Woman Hollering Creek" and Anne Tyler's *Saint Maybe*

The imaginary, as a replay of mirror-stage processes, operates in a relatively straightforward way in Cisneros's "Woman Hollering Creek." In the opening scenes, which take place in Cleófilas's Mexican hometown, Cleófilas and her girlfriends watch *telenovelas* that repeat the same feminine qualities, embodied in variations of the same female figure. And that repetition produces a single-minded desire in the young spectators to imitate them. Lured by the stories' promise of a life rich in intense feelings and elegant clothes, the girls try to mirror the *telenovelas*' heroines, "copy[ing] the way the women comb their hair [and] wear their makeup" (45) and altering their dresses to capture the heroines' style. It is the body of the heroine that is clothed with glamour, and it is by way of their bodies that Cleófilas and her friends imitate and so try to appropriate that glamour. Located at the site of the body, this identification is wholesale—no fine discriminations or selective appropriation of traits here—suggesting its derivation from early processes such as those ascribed by Lacan to the mirror stage. The idealized figure is on a screen similar to the mirror, and like the mirror image she seems to embody wholeness, plenitude (i.e., the *telenovela* heroine has everything). As once before the mirror, so now before the television screen, the viewer is seduced by the idealized properties of the specular image into a misrecognition of the self in the external image. As once she put on alterity as the core of the ego, so now she puts on the culture's representation of woman, "accepting and absorbing [the social representation of woman] as her own representation" (de Lauretis, *Technologies* 12). In molding their bodies to the images of their heroines, Cleófilas and her friends think they are acquiring power—the power to command love and its apparent corollary, wealth. But it is of course the symbolic order operating through the processes of the imaginary; and what they are really absorbing is the cultural definition of woman as she who loves and suffers for love. Interpellation operates by repetition: even those who have it all suffer, as the title of one series indicates: "*The Rich Also Cry.*" The girls internalize the repeated message, telling each other: "To suffer for love is good. The pain all sweet, somehow" (44, 45). This training in the patient endurance of suffering in the cause of love (the "pain all sweet, somehow") prepares Cleófilas to accept her later role as battered wife.[4]

Identifications with figures produced by the media thus interpellate the subject along the lines of mirror-stage operations. Because one originally identified with the completed and seemingly perfect image in the mirror, one is primed to do the same with the idealized, seemingly perfect figure on the mirror of the television or cinema screen. And the fact that one identified on that first occasion with the gestalt of a body that is similar to one's own helps to explain gender interpellation: one is prepared to identify with the "self-same body"—with a body that looks like one's own. "The body provides the primary terrain across which the principle of self-sameness maps itself" (Silverman, *Threshold* 92). As feminist film critics like Mary Ann Doane ("Misrecognition") and Anne Friedberg have shown, mirror-stage identifications with the figures on the silver screen function as a powerful means of interpellation, no less powerful for following a simple psychological principle.

Anne Tyler's *Saint Maybe* makes the case that the television screen has the power to charm a whole family unit into an embrace of bourgeois ideology: the Bedloe family replicates the idealized family life of U.S. 1950s situation comedies. *Saint Maybe* makes Lacan's point, sketched in the diagram of seeing in Seminar XI, that looking at an object always means looking through an intervening screen; and it adds the concept that one looks not just at objects but at oneself, too, through a screen fabricated by the culture. The family sees itself in terms of the idealized family life portrayed in 1950s situation comedies. Usually, when one looks at oneself through the screen of cultural images, one sees that one doesn't match: there are excrescences and lacks which prevent a perfect fit. But it would seem that the middle-class family, at least in the United States, is trained to perceive that it does measure up, that it perfectly matches the image of the perfect family. Tyler describes a mechanism for adjusting one's vision to the requirements of the screen:

> When bad things happened—the usual accidents, illnesses, jogs in the established pattern—Bee [the mother] treated them with eye-rolling good humor, as if they were the stuff of situation comedy. They would form new chapters in the lighthearted ongoing saga she entertained the neighbors with: How Claudia Totaled the Car. How Ian Got Suspended from First Grade. (8)

Bee has the knack of transforming accidents, hardships, even failures, into gently amusing, heartwarming—and always quickly resolved—episodes of family life. Sometimes her 17-year-old son Ian wonders at the trick that enables his mother to edit life to the format of a half-hour slot; but obliged to live, as children must, within the closed reality of family mythology, he always ends up accepting her edited version of reality. "As for Ian, he believed it too but only after a kind of hitch. . . . For instance, from time to time he had the feeling that his father was something of a joke at Poe High—ineffectual at discipline, and muddled in his explanation of the more complicated algebraic functions. But Bee said he was the most popular teacher Poe had ever employed, and in fact that was true. Yes, certainly it was true. Ian knew she was right" (8). The ideal characters in the television family sagas are successful, happy, popular, and above all normal. If there is some doubt that a member of Bee's family is not successful, happy, popular, and normal she quickly readjusts the screen so that the family member can be seen only through the idealized image.

It is as if the Bedloes, and the middle-class white nuclear U.S. family they represent, had taken as prescriptive the opening words of Tolstoy's *Anna Karenina*: "All happy families resemble one another." The family has to "resemble" other families, match up to the norm; and they have to be happy. Self-congratulation is the most expedient means to assurance that they are indeed happy. "There was this about the Bedloes: They believed that every part of their lives was absolutely wonderful. . . . They really did believe it. Or at least Ian's mother did, and she was the one who set the tone. Her marriage was a great joy to her, her house made her happy every time she walked into it, and her children were attractive and kind and universally liked" (8).

Another form of self-congratulation (and self-reassurance) is the family photograph. Laura Wexler posits an integral connection between photography in its nineteenth-century beginnings and the bourgeois family that was in the process of establishing itself as the norm: "Middle-class people must have found in the very numbers of domestic photographs that filled their homes an assurance that real family life was coincident with the kind of families the photographs showed" (168). Indeed, the Bedloe living room is crammed with family photographs that reflect back to them an assurance that their family fits the middle-class norm (Tyler 10). Pierre Bourdieu and Marianne Hirsch have pointed out that family photographs tend to impose the conventions of the ideal family on the group, reducing individuals to the roles and relations dictated by family ideology. "When we are photographed in the context of the conventions of family-snapshot photography, ... we wear masks, fabricate ourselves according to certain expectations and are fabricated by them" (Hirsch, *Family Frames* 98).[5] And, I would add, when we look at the resulting photographs, mirror-stage processes collude with family ideology to do the work of interpellation. The Bedloes admire photographs of themselves that reflect back the conventional image of a family unified and happy, and thus they "know" who they are, sustained by the misrecognition of themselves in the idealized family image. The circularity of this photographic misrecognition is reflected in a holiday ritual: Mr. Bedloe takes Polaroid pictures of the family at Christmas, "each photo after the first one showing somebody holding a previous photo, admiring it" (23). The circularity of misrecognition is itself memorialized here: family members pose for the camera as the normative happy family and then admire, in the next photograph, the visible proof that they are indeed the happy family.

Visually interpellated by the family photograph as well as the television screen, the Bedloes put on the stiff poses and static smiles of the perfectly happy family even when there is no camera present: "Bee and Doug Bedloe sat side by side, smiling extra hard as if someone had just informed them that they were being photographed" (7). The image of the perfect family is essentially static.

This stasis makes the "happy family" brittle, vulnerable to the concrete material realities that family ideology excludes—like time and death. What defeats the Bedloe family mythology is the death of the eldest son, Danny, an apparent suicide. Bee, the family narrator, cannot encompass the tragedy within the cheery formulas of situation comedy. Faced with the death of a child, a tragedy whose long-term effects cannot be resolved within the temporal span of a sit-com episode, the family structure collapses. In Lacanian terms, the imaginary cannot survive the real.

Becoming a Picture: Symbolic Identification in Angela Carter's *The Magic Toyshop*

While Cisneros's Cleófilas enacts a straightforward, unmediated identification with the female figure on the television screen (and Tyler's bourgeois family mythology is apparently based on a similar one-to-one correlation between viewer and media image) the process of symbolic identification I will now describe incorporates two intervening terms, two terms that mediate between the subject and the images on offer in the culture: the ego ideal and the screen. In Seminars X and XI Lacan adds a representative of the symbolic register to the mirror stage, namely "that being that he first saw appearing in the form of the parent holding him up before the mirror," which Lacan calls "the ego ideal" (S XI 257); "in this so-called jubilatory moment when the infant assumes himself as a functioning totality... in his specular image, have I not always recalled the essential relationship to this moment, of this movement [when] the little child... turns back towards the one who is carrying him, who is supporting him, who sustains him, who is there behind him,... towards the adult, towards the one who here represents the big Other, as if to call... on his assent to what at this moment the child... seems to demand of him, to ratify the value of this image" (S X 28.11.52; see also S XI 257). In order to perceive the image in the mirror as lovable, the child has to identify first with the position of the mother who looks at him, with a position in the symbolic. Or, in terms of the interpellation of the individual into the symbolic position of woman that I am foregrounding here, one puts on an image not just because one perceives it as whole and perfect, but because it is first admired by someone who is a representative of the big Other, of the symbolic order. "Imaginary identification is always identification on behalf of a certain gaze in the Other" (Žižek, *Sublime* 106). This other who looks at me from a position in the symbolic order and approves my visual form enables me to find worth in the image and so assume it as my ideal ego. For example, when the woman in yellow looks at Jadine and spits in contempt of Jadine's self-presentation, she occupies the position of ego ideal in the symbolic register—or more specifically, in the local version of the symbolic that is the African-American cultural register. As the representative of that order her look has the power to invalidate the visual image Jadine presents to the world (as a woman assimilated to white beauty standards, adorning herself for a white lover, and so on). That lack of validation from the ego ideal shatters Jadine's faith in the image of herself as perfect model that has served her as ideal ego. This example is negative; in the positive case, it is a prior identification with the affirming look of an other who is positioned within the symbolic order, who represents the Other, that enables me to identify with an image and assimilate it as my ideal ego.

In order to fill out the process of symbolic identification and explore how it works in gender interpellation, I will combine Lacan's notion of the ego ideal with the "screen" which Lacan includes in his second diagram of the optical field in Seminar XI. His sketch diagrams a gaze ("point of light") which perceives the subject (labelled "the picture") through the intermediary of a "screen."[6] What is this screen? Lacan does not say. But Kaja Silverman identifies the screen as a cultural screen: "Although *Four Fundamental Concepts* does not do so, it seems to me crucial that we insist upon the ideological status of the screen by describing it as that culturally generated image or repertoire of images through which subjects are not only constituted, but differentiated in relation to class, race, sexuality, age, and nationality" (*Male* 150). Although I think that Silverman's explanation of the gaze as simply a cultural gaze misses the essential kernel of the Lacanian gaze as the real—and in the next section I present an analysis of the gaze *qua* real—I find her interpretation of the screen as a cultural screen useful because it adds a necessary term to the model of symbolic identification. Žižek has explained that the look of the ego ideal, because it is positioned in the symbolic, has the power to confirm (or discredit) my image. If, for purposes of understanding the function of this symbolic look in the process of interpellation, one puts the ego ideal—the point in the symbolic from which I am looked at—in the position of the gaze in diagram two, then the look of this other reaches me (the subject) only after passing through a cultural screen. It is, then, not only the other's position in the symbolic that gives him or her the authority to confirm (or withhold confirmation of) my visual form: it is the knowledge that the look of the other, this look from the symbolic, is measuring my form against some cultural norm, against a figure in the cultural screen.

For example, if I, a woman, walk past a group of men and one of them starts to observe me but quickly withdraws the look, implying that he does not see me at all, I know at some level that my image does not match the culturally preferred shape of woman in his imagination. Or—a better example, because Morrison's description of the language of eyes is so precise—when in *The Bluest Eye* the African-American child Pecola asks a shopkeeper to sell her some candy, he glances toward her, but "somewhere between retina and object, between vision and view, his eyes draw back, hesitate, and hover... he senses he need not waste the effort of a glance." This withdrawal of visual recognition, this "vacuum edged with distaste in white eyes," has the power to annihilate Pecola's self-worth—and it does, with lasting effects (*Bluest* 42)—because the look is authorized by the symbolic, or more specifically by the white-dominant racist symbolic order that governs the United States. Measured against the image of little girl on the cultural screen through which the shopkeeper looks at Pecola, she falls short: Pecola is not white. This symbolic look—unlike the "gaze as such," the real, which is invisible—*can* be located in the eye of a particular other. For purposes of understanding symbolic identification in the field of the visual, the "point of light" in diagram two, the point from which the subject is observed, can be aligned with the ego ideal; and the "screen" designates a screen of culturally endorsed forms through which this symbolic look must pass before it reaches the subject. Now, for the third term in the diagram: "the picture," which designates the place of the subject.

How exactly does the symbolic look, passing through a screen of culturally defined images, interpellate the subject? The screen is opaque, Lacan says (S XI 96). Since the social look can reach the subject only through the intermediary of an opaque screen, it can perceive the subject only as it matches her to an image on the screen. And what is the effect? Being mapped onto a field of preexisting images pressures the subject to adopt one of their forms. "To imitate is no doubt to reproduce an image. But at bottom, it is, for the subject, to be inserted in a function whose exercise grasps it" (S XI 100); that is, to be inserted in a picture superimposed by the screen's repertoire of cultural forms is to be "grasped" by the screen and made to conform to it. To take the particular case of gender interpellation: the social look lays the proper form of "woman" on the subject and then signals either approbation or disapprobation depending on how well the subject fits the image; either way, the social look pressures the subject to "become a picture," in Lacan's terminology (S XI 106)—to adopt the cultural representation of "woman" as her own self-representation. "If I am anything in the picture, it is always in the form of the screen," as Lacan says (S XI 97).

The opening scene of Angela Carter's *The Magic Toyshop* shows the process of gender interpellation operating through these three functions—ego ideal, screen, and picture—and the presence of all three is the more striking because there is no individual present to perform the function of ego ideal, or symbolic look.

> The summer she was fifteen, Melanie discovered she was made of flesh and blood. O, my America, my new found land. She embarked on a tranced voyage, exploring the whole of herself, clambering her own mountain ranges, penetrating the moist richness of her secret valleys, a physiological Cortez, da Gama, or Mungo Park. For hours she stared at herself... in the mirror... she posed in attitudes... Pre-Raphaelite, she combed out her long, black hair to stream straight down from a centre parting and thoughtfully regarded herself as she held a tiger-lily from the garden under her chin.... She was too thin for a Titian or a Renoir but she contrived a pale, smug Cranach Venus with a bit of net curtain wound round her head. (1–2).

As explorer of a New World, Melanie is presented as autonomous self-discoverer. But the trope of self-discovery and the idea of the body as uncharted territory are immediately mocked by the list of artists whose painted representations of woman direct Melanie's self-perception: Melanie's body is always already visually colonized. Lacan's first diagram of the optic field is operating here: in the first triangle, the subject sees an object only through an intervening membrane called "image."[7] Like the characters in *Saint Maybe*, who perceive themselves through a scrim of the idealized images of sit-com family members, Melanie can see herself only by way of the cultural images of Woman superimposed on her reflection.

It would seem at first that Lacan's second diagram does not apply: Melanie is alone in her room, so there is no eye present to act as the ego ideal. She seems to be engaged in imaginary negotiations only with her mirror and with the images of her culture. But, as Žižek points out, "imaginary identification is always identification *on behalf of a certain gaze in the Other*. So, apropos of every imitation of a model-image, apropos of every 'playing a role,' the question to ask is: *for whom* is the subject enacting this role? Which *gaze* is considered when the subject identifies himself with a certain image?" (*Sublime* 106). Indeed, Carter anticipates Žižek's question, "For whom?" "[Melanie] used the net curtain as raw material for a series of nightgowns... which she designed upon herself. She gift-wrapped herself for a phantom bridegroom" (2). Although Melanie has the illusion of "design[ing]...herself" by herself, for herself, in the privacy of her room, Carter's phrasing shows that she is designing an alluring self-image "for" a potential bridegroom, for the one who sees and approves from a position in the symbolic order.

Even in relation to the artists whose visions of femininity she imitates, it becomes evident that the symbolic look from the position of ego ideal is operating: "A la Toulouse Lautrec, she dragged her hair sluttishly across her face and sat down in a chair with her legs apart and a bowl of water and a towel at her feet. She always felt particularly wicked when she posed for Lautrec" (1). Melanie imagines Toulouse Lautrec looking at her, so to please the artist's gaze she "poses" for him in the guise of one of his painted forms. The artist's (imagined) look passes through the opaque cultural screen—here, the opaque canvas of his painting—alights on Melanie, and fits her to the figure on the screen/canvas. One is never in a dual relation with one's mirror, both Carter and Lacan show: the look of the other is there even if the other is not. Melanie thinks that the gaze is hers—that she is inventing herself in the visual field of the mirror. But between taking on the artist's image of woman and presenting that same image to his gaze, there is no room for an autonomous subject; such a closed circuit makes a mockery of self-invention. As Lacan's diagram insists, to believe oneself to be master of the gaze is to be deluded. One is, rather, in the position of the picture that the other's look, passing through the cultural screen, creates. Or, to appropriate Lacan's language, the look from the symbolic order—provisionally situated here in the eye of Toulouse-Lautrec—"inserts" Melanie into a cultural screen of images of Woman which "grasps" her and configures her to the screen's shapes, so that she "turns [her]self into a picture under the gaze." Melanie literalizes Lacan's notion that in the visual field the subject "becomes a picture" (S XI 106).

While Lacan's text is gender-neutral, in Carter's text it is of course a male look—from the bridegroom, from the Old Masters—that puts Melanie in her place, so that Melanie is doubly an object: not only the object of the symbolic look but also the feminine object required by systems of male desire and exchange. Melanie ends the scene by presenting herself as stereotype of femininity, veiled in a bridal costume, to the gaze of the world: "'Look at me!' she said to the apple tree . . . 'Look at me!' she cried . . . to the pumpkin moon" (16). Visually articulated into the cultural screen, Melanie leaves the prolonged cultural mirror stage of the novel's opening pages not as viewer but as spectacle, not as agent but as object: as "Woman" in a male-created imaginary.[8]

Margaret Drabble's *Jerusalem the Golden* and The Double Lure of the Gaze

The subject's relation to the gaze is one of desire, Lacan says: "At the scopic level, we are no longer at the level of demand, but of desire, of the desire of the Other" (S XI 104). And he repeats the phrase, "Man's desire is the desire of the Other" (S XI 115). If we understand the Other according to its usual Lacanian signification, as the sociosymbolic order, then the phrase yields two distinct interpretations, one relevant to the previous section's model of symbolic identification, one relevant to the present section and the real. In the first case, if "the desire of the Other" is taken to mean the desire of the sociosymbolic order and "man's desire"—or woman's—is to be what that Other desires, then the task is relatively straightforward: one can ascertain from scanning various cultural screens—fashion magazine photographs, television screens, the paintings of the masters, and so on—what characteristics are likely to please the social look, the look coming from the Other as social order; and one can try to imitate those characteristics as best one can. And if, as Silverman does and as I did in the previous section, one takes Lacan's second diagram of the optic field to be a sketch of symbolic identification, one can read it as a stark depiction of the motivating force behind conformity to what this social look seems to want. If I exist in the field of the visual *only* as "a picture" perceived by the social look, I must depend on that gaze for validation. I desire to "fit in," a figure of speech given literal force by Lacan's idea that I shape myself to fit the figures in the screen: "If I am anything in the picture, it is always in the form of the screen" (S XI 97). Interpellation is motivated, at this level, by a desire for the approbation of the social look. The reward is, as Judith Butler has explained the pay-off of interpellation more generally, the validation of one's social being (*Psychic* 130).

But "the desire of the Other" takes a more enigmatic turn if we think of "desire" as "lack." If "man's desire is the desire of the Other" and desire is synonymous with lack, as it is in all Lacan's writings, then what one wants is what is lacking in the Other. The Other, the sociosymbolic matrix that governs what we see of everyday reality, seems to be consistent and full—but it is lacking, Lacan says. "The Other, the symbolic order, is structured around some traumatic impossibility, around something which cannot be symbolized—i.e., the real of jouissance" (Žižek, *Sublime* 123). Just as the object a represents the lack in the subject, so Lacan uses the object a to represent the lack in the Other: the object a is the marker of the real that resists signication. Just as $S \lozenge a$, so also $\emptyset \lozenge a$.

And the stand-in for that lack in the visual field is the gaze. "The *objet a* in the field of the visible is the gaze" (S XI 105). The gaze is the point of failure in a visible world structured by the symbolic system in which we live. It is an "invisibility at the heart of the visible" (Shepherdson, "A Pound" 2). In short, the gaze as Lacan conceives it is absent. Now desiring to be the object of the gaze becomes a much more difficult proposition than in the case posited by Silverman, where the gaze is not distinct from the screen of cultural images through which it apprehends the subject. As the object a, the gaze is "just an objectification of a void" (Žižek, *Sublime* 95).[9] In order to be the desire of the Other in the visual field—to be what the Other lacks and wants—one would have to please a gaze that cannot be located, that cannot be read, that is missing. Where can one look for traces of a gaze that doesn't exist in order to attract it?

As the object a in the visual order, the gaze has no concrete presence, but it does have effects—and what I am interested in here are the effects on the subject. Because the gaze cannot ever be apprehended, because it is missing, it can stand in for the subject's fundamental lack, as one manifestation of the object a. Again, "*The* objet a *in the field of the visible is the gaze*," Lacan says, italicizing for emphasis (105). Contrary to his usual enigmatic and diffuse style, Lacan gives a painstakingly full definition of the object a here: "The *objet a* is something from which the subject, in order to constitute itself, has separated itself off as organ. This serves as a symbol of the lack, that is to say, of the phallus, not as such, but in so far as it is lacking" (103). The object a is an empty function that represents what is lacking. If the gaze is a stand-in for the object a, then human beings are in a relation of desire to the gaze, as Lacan explains: "In the scopic relation, the object on which depends the phantasy from which the subject is suspended in an essential vacillation is the gaze. Its privilege—and also that by which the subject for so long has been misunderstood as being in its dependence—derives from its structure" (S XI 83). The importance of the gaze derives from structure—from its structural position as a placeholder for the object a in the fundamental fantasy, the fundamental structure of unconscious desire, $ ◇ a$. In the field of the visual, the phantasy of the subject "from which he is suspended"—the founding structure of his participation in the visual field—is the usual phantasy $ ◇ a$, with the gaze in the position of object a.

The missing gaze then becomes the "object-cause of desire" in the field of the visible. As Joan Copjec explains, it is the combination of the subject's belief that there is something there to see, that, exactly at the point "where something appears to be invisible, this point at which something appears to be missing, . . . the point of the Lacanian gaze" (Copjec 34) the subject is impelled to launch an inquiry, to uncover what is hidden, what meaning is left unrevealed. The fact that the visible world seems to hide some ultimately meaningful gaze "is not treated by Lacan as a simple error": (35) rather, it is the discrepancy between the emptiness at the point of the gaze and the subject's belief that the gaze exists that generates the desire of the subject: "the subject [of desire] is the effect of the impossibility of seeing what is lacking . . . what the subject, therefore, wants to see" (Copjec 35).

While accepting Copjec's premise, I would like to push further the notion of a discrepancy between what the subject wants to see and what is in fact on offer, by analyzing the disparity between Merleau-Ponty's understanding of the gaze and Lacan's. Lacan devotes many pages of Seminar XI to a discussion of Merleau-Ponty's *The Visible and the Invisible,* and he seems to take Merleau-Ponty's ideas as guide to his own: "What we have to circumscribe, by means of the path he indicates for us, is the pre-existence of a gaze—I see only from one point, but in my existence I am looked at from all sides" (S XI 72); "I mean, and Maurice Merleau-Ponty points this out, that we are beings who are looked at, in the spectacle of the world" (S XI 75). The turns of phrase—"I mean, and Merleau-Ponty points this out," "what we have to circumscribe, by means of the path he indicates for us"—indicate acceptance. Lacan seems to embrace Merleau-Ponty's proposition that an inalienable dimension of being an embodied human being is the sense of being surrounded by a gaze, of being looked at from all sides: that is what circumscribes us as bodies in space. "That which makes us consciousness institutes us by the same token as *speculum mundi*.... that gaze that circumscribes us... makes us beings who are looked at" (S XI 75). Yet, Lacan says almost immediately, in actuality the gaze is always lacking in the world: it seems to belong to the order of things that look back at me, but it cannot be located. The gaze is the object a and so does not exist as such.

It becomes clear, then, why Lacan spends so much time describing Merleau-Ponty's theory, although his own ultimately diverges from it. Merleau-Ponty's theory is phenomenological, an explanation of how a subject experiences the world. As I read Seminar XI, Lacan agrees that experientially the subject, because he or she exists in space, in a visual field, has the perpetual sense of being "looked at from all sides." But that is an illusion: the "ultimate gaze... is illusory" (S XI 77). In actuality the gaze is a nothing, a purely structural function that stands for lack. In terms of the external world, it is the object a, the real that eludes the symbolic register of meanings that orders the world we see. In terms of the subject, it is the object a "which serves as a symbol of the lack" that founds subjectivity (S XI 103). The gaze lures us with the promise of a completing presence, but it is always missing. I would say that it is not only the lack of the gaze that powers desire, as Copjec asserts, but also the disparity between the dimension of experience described by Merleau-Ponty—"a dimension of experience in which the very fact of vision, the most 'natural' sensory experience, is haunted by a peculiar, invisible and tyrannical presence, a presence that cannot be seen, but that looks at us" (Shepherdson, "Pound" 7)—and the absence of the gaze in actuality.

The question then becomes, how exactly does the gaze as lack structure the subject's desire? And how does that desire operate as an interpellative force? Clara's pursuit of the gaze in Margaret Drabble's *Jerusalem the Golden* allows me to trace in more detail the concrete effects of a purely abstract gaze. Clara's desire is powered precisely by the gap between the phenomenological perception of a universal gaze and the actual nonexistence of that gaze.

Jerusalem the Golden shows how the idea of the gaze as object a complicates processes of identification. If one were to adopt the notion of the imaginary introduced in Lacan's mirror stage essay and Seminar I, one could make a perfectly coherent analysis of the protagonist Clara's identification with Clelia as a mirror stage identification with a more perfect and polished version of herself. For all intents and purposes, Clara becomes Clelia: she looks like, talks like, acts like Clelia. But behind her desire to be Clelia is the driving force of her desire to ensnare the gaze. What she recognizes when she sees Clelia is a person who has what it takes to lure the gaze, and she mimics her. Identification thus becomes an efficient way to acquire, in an integrated package, all the qualities that (supposedly) will please the gaze, fulfill the desire of the Other. But—the gaze does not exist, so Clara must always strive and never find; thinking the gaze will fill her, she must always go empty.

What does Clara want? The goal of her longing remains undefined. Drabble, like Lacan, aims at representing the unrepresentable—the indefinable allure of the gaze. While the novel contains an acute and concretely detailed observation of what Clara wants to escape—the unloving and unlovely world of her mother and the edge-of-the-lower-middle-class position and class credo that Drabble presents as the root cause of the mother's hostility to all beauty, grace, and feeling—what she desires is left vague. Foremost among Clara's motivations is the desire to say "all the right phrases" (14), to "like things . . . for the right reason" (11), to have the "right" dress and the "right" manner—but who is looking, who is judging? For whom does Clara put on the right opinions, the right clothes? For "people," evidently: the first three pages introduce her by way of her evaluation of other people's assessment of her. Her name, which had seemed for so long a liability, is now "an asset," for "people" declared when they heard it, "How delightful, how charming, how fortunate!" (5). Likewise, "time had converted liabilities other than her name into assets" (6)—her intelligence, for instance. Her intelligence, her beauty, are not meaningful to Clara for themselves—"she never learned to take simple pleasure in her abilities; they remained for her a means, and not an end" (7)—but count only as "assets" or "liabilities" in the central business of impressing "people." Because Clara does not tie this desire to please to any named individuals, the term "people" seems to indicate a generalized gaze that would acknowledge her worth.

How do you please a gaze that is "unapprehensible" (S XI 83), impossible to gauge? You remain alert to the qualities in other persons that seem to gain the approbation of "people," or a generalized gaze, and you imitate them. Clara, musing on her selection of friends in her three years of college, recognizes that "she had been attracted by surfaces, by clothes and manners and voices and trivial strange graces, and she had imitated what she had seen of these things in others" (107). Because she is intent on attracting the notice of the gaze, Clara is interested only in visible surfaces—clothes, manners, graces. Lacan says, suggestively, "if beyond appearance there is nothing in itself, there is the gaze" (S XI 103). Clara would agree with Lacan. Beyond appearance there is, for her, only the gaze. There is nothing *beneath* the appearance: Clara has no use for any inner world, in herself or in others, that might lie beneath the surface. Hence, she is alert only to the visible surface of others: for example, at the poetry reading where we first see her, it is the woman reader, Margaret, who elicits Clara's admiration because of her clothes, her manner, her dramatic style; Clara has no interest in her poetry (10–11).

So single-minded is Clara, from girlhood, in the quest of "the right thing" to appeal to the gaze, that she knows it when she sees it, embodied, in Clelia.

> She began to realize that she was in the presence of the kind of thing for which she had been searching for years, some nameless class or quality, some element... A kind of excitement filled her, not unlike the excitement more frequently experienced, of love.... she had wanted such people to exist, so dressed, so independent, so involved... here was a woman who was the thing that she had presupposed. (22)

Clara recognizes in Clelia a woman who has "it"—and in refusing to define "it" beyond "some nameless class or quality," Drabble approaches the difficult task of representing glamour—some *je ne sais quoi* which makes Clelia, in Clara's eyes, a likely object of the Other's desire. The degree of excitement that the meeting with Clelia generates, the sense of drama, of "a conjunction so fateful and fruitful" (8), begins to suggest what it is that Clara wants: not money, not power (unlike other ambitious working-class literary heroes), not—explicitly stated here—love, but rather a model that Clara can imitate in order to become the desired object of the gaze. A totalizing identification with one woman seems to offer a more quick and efficient mode of becoming the object of the gaze than the piecemeal imitation of her classmates' graces that Clara has practiced up till now.

While Clara tries to identify with Clelia wholesale—and Drabble uses metaphors of oral incorporation harking back to Freud's primary identification to emphasize the primitive nature of her efforts (129,

130)—it is primarily Clelia's style that Clara succeeds in capturing: the surface effects of manner, dress, and look that, I argue, are aimed at captivating the gaze. For how does one set out to be "the object of desire of the Other," the object of an unknowable gaze? As I read Lacan, one imputes a desire to the gaze and then tries to fulfill that hypothesized desire: "I would say that it is a question of a sort of desire *on the part of* the Other, at the end of which is the *showing* (*le donner-à-voir*)" (S XI 115). Lacan underlines "on the part of" the Other to emphasize that the desire one is trying to meet seems to originate in the gaze itself; the desire of the Other seems to come first, and the "showing" on the part of the subject is a response to that (supposed) preexistent desire. One decks oneself out in a particular guise, one appears to be one thing rather than another, because one imagines that one is responding to what the Other wants. One concentrates on the "showing," or, in the more literal French, on the "donner-à-voir"—on the given-to-be-seen. Clara acquires and displays the visual surface of Clelia, so that Gabriel, Clelia's brother, is amazed at the resemblance:

"Clara, you remind me of Clelia, at times you even look like Clelia, tell me, why do you look like her, now, at this instant?"

"I look like her... because I try to look like her, that's all. I bought this nightdress because it looks like hers, if you want to know. And I went into a shop to have my hair cut like hers." (207–208)

Lacan describes the relation to the gaze as a double lure. "Generally speaking, the relation between the gaze and what one wishes to see involves a lure. The subject is presented as other than he is, and what one shows him is not what he wishes to see" (S XI 107). Catering to the imagined tastes of an imagined gaze, one sends out a simulacrum of oneself designed to entrance the gaze. Thus, Clara, imagining Clelia to be the cynosure of all eyes, "shows herself" as Clelia. Lacan elaborates the notion of "showing" through the example of animals. "In the case of display, usually on the part of the male animal... the being gives of himself... something that is like a mask, a double, an envelope, a thrown-off skin.... It is through this separated form of himself that the being comes into play in his effects of life and death" (S XI 107). A human being does the same—why? What is the relation between mimicry and the gaze? "It is in this domain that the dimension by which the subject is to be inserted into the picture is presented.

Mimicry reveals something in so far as it is distinct from what might be called an *itself* that is behind. The effect of mimicry is camouflage" (S XI 99). To understand the implications of being "inserted into the picture," it is necessary to refer back to Lacan's second diagram of the gaze (note 6). I will consider what I regard as Lacan's primary sense of the gaze here, rather than bowing to Silverman's interpretation a cultural gaze. The gaze (or "point of light") is at the apex of the triangle, and through the mediation of the screen it targets the subject, which is labeled "picture." "To be inserted into the picture" thus means to be the object of the gaze: or, as Lacan puts it, I "turn myself into a picture under the gaze" (S XI 106). Mimicry is the mechanism for this insertion into the picture. I mimic what I think the gaze desires and so turn myself into the picture (supposedly) demanded by the gaze. And that display is the whole game. "Mimicry reveals something in so far as it is distinct from what might be called an *itself* that is behind" (S XI 99). The semblance that one displays to the gaze has no relation to some "authentic" being behind the show. It is oriented toward the gaze "in front," not to the expression of the being "behind." This is a different kind of alienation from the mirror stage alienation, wherein one defines an external image as oneself and takes it in to form the ideal ego. The alienation produced by the desire for the gaze produces a movement in the opposite direction: one sends out "a separated form of oneself" to create an effect. "The being breaks up, in an extraordinary way, between its being and its semblance, between itself and that paper tiger it shows to the other" (S XI 107). In an effort to seduce the gaze, Clara "shows"—or, in the more precise French, *"donne à voir"* (gives, in order to be seen)—a simulacrum of Clelia. Since Clara is engaged in a relation of desire for the gaze, it is useless to reproach her with a lack of authenticity. What counts is "the mask, the double, the envelope, the thrown-off skin" that she presents to the gaze (S XI 107).

Clara falls in love on the same principle by which she chooses a friend—by reference to some index of glamour, some infallible intuitive measure of what will appeal to the gaze. When she meets Gabriel, Clelia's brother, it is, she says, love at first sight; but more important, as the reader is immediately aware, it is recognition at first sight—the recognition of some quality that makes Gabriel a star. "She thought she had never seen anyone so sexy off the cinema screen in her life, ... and she was amazed that he should be allowed to wander loose around the world; she had ... always assumed that there was some system ... which selected such people and removed them.... She had thought that they would live, these heroes and heroines, in some bright celluloid paradise" (140). Others second Clelia's opinion that Gabriel is destined for the screen: his sister Annunciata says, "'You must let the world see you ... Nobody could ever get tired of staring at you.... One would as soon get tired of staring at Marlon Brando.... People would stare at you forever'" (146–47). Gabriel is "almost" a movie star, and movie stars come as close as humanly possible to being the object of the gaze as Merleau-Ponty would define it—a gaze that surrounds, that comes from all sides, a universal gaze. Association with Gabriel, like identification with Clelia, can provide Clara with a vehicle for becoming an object of the gaze herself, as the subtle instrumental counterpoint to her description of "falling in love" with Gabriel suggests: "Gabriel stood there in front of her, ... as mortal as she was mortal, or acknowledging her too as divine" (141); "some bright celluloid paradise ... from which Gabriel had perhaps fallen, for she might surely never ascend?" (140). The lingering question contains hope and ambition: attached to Gabriel, she too might "ascend," she too might be counted among the "divine."

It is this hope and ambition that Clara thinks she has realized at the end of the novel, when she commits herself to "a tender blurred world where Clelia and Gabriel and she herself in shifting and ideal conjunctions met and drifted and met once more like the constellations in the heavens: a bright and peopled world, thick with starry inhabitants" (252). The metaphor of "heaven" collects (at least) two meanings from the text: it is "Jerusalem the golden," the celestial city imagined in the hymn that attracted Clara in girlhood, not through any promise of spiritual revelation but through its evocation of the "radiancy of glory," the golden sheen of glamour haloing the city's inhabitants (37); and it is the celluloid heaven of the cinema screen inhabited by the images—only—of the beautiful people. Clara commits herself to a life of image in choosing to be with Clelia and Gabriel. For Clelia, Gabriel, and their siblings spend their adult lives poring over their pictures in family albums and "displaying" each other for admiring guests. "They displayed each other, they encouraged each other, they laughed, in the same key, at each other's jokes" (143). Because they look alike—"the same face stared out of all their photographs"—to display the other is to display the self, and to admire the other is to admire the self. Simultaneously spectacle and spectator, they provide a domesticated version of the gaze for themselves, a closed circle of "mutual admiration" (131,

143). Because Clara, having made herself over in the image of Clelia, now looks like them, too, she is qualified to move into the circle of adoring self-reflection.

Clara's concluding move into the Denham world involves a final renunciation of depth in favor of the Denhams' shining insubstantialities. Shortly before the ending, Clara is summoned back to Northam by the terminal illness of her mother and spends a few days uncovering her mother's past through reading her mother's journals, poems, and pictures. The encounter with her mother's youthful hope and desire brings Clara a moment of "shocked relief" at the recognition of their kinship: "she was glad to have found her place of birth, she was glad that she had however miserably pre-existed, she felt, for the first time, the satisfaction of her true descent" (241). The language of authenticity here ("her true descent") suggests that were she to pursue the encounter with her mother as subject, she would discover the "truth" of her origins and come to a better understanding of who she herself is. But Clara has no interest in such depth psychology. Abandoning her dying mother to drive off with Gabriel to join "the bright and peopled world" of the Denhams, she chooses seeming over being. For example, her mother's house represents to Clara a deeply embedded threatening all-encompassing identification with her mother.[10] She acknowledges to Gabriel that her mother's house is "part of me forever," but she denies him the sight of it: "I don't feel free of it . . . I can't be free, but there's no reason why I shouldn't be thought to be free, is there?" (251). What counts is what she is "thought to be," not what she is—appearance, not substance.

A fable read in childhood, "The Two Weeds," becomes a defining narrative for Clara's life course and throws an ambiguous light on her final destination. In the fable, two weeds grow on a riverbank: the first "conserved its energy," putting out only low brown shoots; the second "put forth all its strength into growing tall and into colouring itself a beautiful green" (39). The two weeds quarrel all summer long, the lowly weed calling its brother "grandiose" and the tall weed calling the other "mean and miserly." A beautiful girl picks the tall weed to decorate her dress, where "it blushed a glorious red and died content; the weed on the bank . . . laughed, and reflected that it would live till the next year. And it did" (40).

The tall weed chooses "showing," in Lacanian parlance. It throws its energy into the extravagant gesture, into a show of color and beauty—for whom? for the gaze. "How could this *showing* satisfy something,"

Lacan asks, "if there is not some appetite of the eye on the part of the person looking?" (S XI 115). Clara, like the weed, throws herself into a show of "beauty and extravagance" (Drabble 40) rather than clinging to the dull brown of lower-middle-class respectability like her mother. She chooses to put all her energy into color, into glory, into the extravagant gesture that will attract the gaze. As Lacan says, the gesture is not meant to lead to action, but to produce an effect on the gaze. Captivated by the *fascinum* of the gaze, one is frozen in a gesture (S XI 116–17). The weed blushes and then dies. And Clara deliberately chooses the frozen poses of the Denham "stars" in a heaven where there will be "no ending, no parting"—no action, then, but only "an eternal vast incessant rearrangement" of static gestures.

But using the fable as an interpretive tool does not provide a clear moral judgment on the novel's ending. The reader can align her or himself with the perspective of the dull brown weed and view Clara as the plant that has foolishly cut itself off from its root (as Clara has cut herself off from the maternal ground of her being) and cannot survive; or the reader can affirm Clara's extravagant gesture as a parallel to the weed that throws itself into useless beauty and dies—but dies content.

However, one's final assessment of Clara's chances for happiness in the self-reflecting circle of the Denhams is inevitably colored by the earlier scene, in Paris, of Clara's disappointment with the gaze. Although she has been told that she looks just like Clelia and although she feels "a whole new self... unfurling broadly and confidently within her" (215)—the self, presumably, that she has acquired through imitating Clelia—"she was not yet satisfied, she had not had enough, she had not had what she wanted, whatever it might be that she wanted" (221). Clara herself is baffled: she has Gabriel, she has the admiring looks of the various male admirers she has collected in Paris; yet satisfaction eludes her. That dissatisfaction is connected to the double deception that Lacan describes in relation to the lure of the gaze. "The relation between the gaze and what one wishes to see involves a lure. The subject is presented as other than he is, and what one shows him is not what he wishes to see" (S XI 107). Clara is "presenting" a new façade, in imitation of Clelia. And what she wishes to receive as reward for her performance is the approbation of the gaze—but "what one shows [her] is not what [s]he wishes to see" (S XI 107).

Clara begins to sense this disparity when she parades through the streets of Paris on the arm of Gabriel: "She was proud of being with

Gabriel, and the passing inquisitive glances of other women did not satisfy her craving for confirmation.... She wished to see in the eyes of others the dim, narrowing, receding vistas, the arches and long corridors through which she had traveled. She wished to set, through him, a value on herself" (206–07). Here Clara gets the social look I elaborated in section two of this chapter: the passers-by show through their glances that she and Gabriel do measure up to some cultural register of what is to be valued in masculine and feminine style—but that is not enough. I think we can read Clara's disappointment as an indication of the discrepancy between the belief in a gaze that looks at us from all sides (Merleau-Ponty) and the actuality of a gaze that is missing (Lacan). Clara wants to be the object of a universal gaze that surrounds her, remarking everything she does—all the "ways she has traveled," everything she has done and accomplished in order to achieve this moment of glory with Gabriel—a gaze that will validate her whole existence. It had originally seemed to her (as indicated by the half-phrases of ambitious hope that occur during their first meeting) that by attaching herself to Gabriel's movie-star persona, she could participate in the seemingly universal gaze that surrounds movie stars. But there is no such gaze. There is no witness. No one is looking. Or rather, persons are looking (the passing women, the admiring men) but the looks of particular individuals, no matter how many, can never add up to the gaze. The gaze is an empty function—it has effects, but no concrete existence; so it can never deliver the desired approval. "So, if you are looking for confirmation of the truth of your being or the clarity of your vision, you are on your own; the gaze of the Other is not confirming; it will not validate you" (Copjec 36). Sometimes this withholding of visual recognition is represented by Lacanians as the blind eye—"the gaze which sees nothing, but which stares out at us through the gaping holes of an eyeless face," as in the figure of the blinded farmer in *The Birds*) (Samuels, *Hitchcock's* 131). The blind eye looks but does not see you. But whether the gaze is blind or is nonexistent, the effect on the subject is the same: you cannot be the desire of the Other, you cannot win the approbation of the gaze, if the gaze cannot see you—whether that not-seeing is figured as a blind eye or as the blind spot, the gaping empty hole, in the symbolic. One fears, then, that the Denham domestication of the gaze will not, in the long run, serve: the admiration of particular individuals—even "golden" individuals like Gabriel and Clelia—will never be enough to satisfy.

THE GAZE AND INTERPELLATION

Fame is a similarly elusive property: as chapter 1 explains, I read the desire for fame as a desire for the gaze—for a gaze that appears to surround us yet is only an absence in the visual field. Alongside Clara's story runs a subplot concerning the hollowness of fame. Candida Denham, the mother of Clelia and Gabriel, is famous, by any objective measurement: she has written best-selling novels, her pen name, Candida Gray, is familiar to everyone, and, as the large collection of photograph albums in her living room attests, her picture has appeared in innumerable glossy magazines. Yet, as her daughter Clara remarks, Mrs. Denham "is always letting herself be interviewed, . . . she likes people coming to ask her questions about herself and how she makes coffee and . . . what kind of paper she writes on, she says it makes her feel as though she really has got somewhere in her life. It consoles her, without it she says she feels she hasn't moved" (104). Candida has all the evidence of fame that one could imagine. Yet without the reassurance of the interview—token of the world's immediate interest—she feels that "she hasn't moved" (104). It is not one more interview or one more photo spread that will make her believe "she really has got somewhere in her life," or even a hundred interviews and publicity photographs. Since the gaze never coincides with the look of particular individuals, no number of particular interviewers will suffice. The desire for fame is the desire for the gaze—for the gaze that always eludes us; one can never get enough fame to satisfy.

It is a tribute to the power of the gaze to enforce gender roles that Candida Denham puts on the role of supermother, that she feels that five novels are not enough—she must have five children too. And the act of having five children is not enough; she must display them, over and over, to the gaze. Publicity photos crowd the family photograph albums and the family living room. "There was one photograph in particular, that caught the whole family, in sudden clarity . . . Candida, . . . with a pile of her own books on a small table by her side, a baby on her knee, and four children ranged neatly around her." The picture is "cut out of a glossy magazine" and displays to the world the magnitude of Candida's productivity. She produces magically, excessively, in all fields at once. She is a worldly success, yet puts motherhood first. To seduce the gaze, Candida becomes a superwoman—a role that appears to have the cachet to attract the admiration of a generalized gaze.

Since the gaze has no objective existence, one can only imagine what it desires. And one's imagination is constrained by the evidence of one's social world. One looks around to see what subjects seem to have what it takes to win the approval of the world's gaze. And one imitates them. Thus Clara looks for an identificatory model who has "glamour," that indefinable something that appears to be alluring to the indefinable gaze. But glamour is tied into the style of the moment: the manner or the look or the aura that appears to have the power to seduce and captivate the gaze is inevitably a version of glamour that has cultural currency.[11] Thus Clara chooses Clelia as a model. Clelia's style manages to integrate the impossible contradictions of contemporary femininity. She combines independence—her manner is somewhat acerbic, proclaiming her freedom from the need to please—with a traditional desire to nurture: she takes care of others, taking into her home her boss's baby, for example, when its mother abandons it. In trying to be Clelia, Clara is identifying with a fashionable version of femininity—cool and autonomous, yet warm and nurturing.

Since on the one hand one can never, in the scopic relation, escape the desire for the gaze, and on the other hand one can never "get" the gaze, dependency on the gaze ensures its continuing power to enforce the current version of gender roles. Never succeeding, one keeps trying to put on the version of female glamour that will entrance the gaze. When Lacan added the notion of the gaze as object a to his original description of a visual experience governed by the imaginary, he increased our understanding of the desires that motivate visual identifications and so facilitate interpellation: not just the mirror-stage desire to identify with an idealized body, not just the response to the pressure of the social look to conform to the proper shape, but also the desire to be that which the invisible gaze finds desirable.

Chapter 6

Disidentification and Border Negotiations of Gender in Sandra Cisneros's *Woman Hollering Creek*

How can a woman struggle out of a limiting gender identification, how undo the work of interpellation? The protagonists of three stories in Sandra Cisneros's *Woman Hollering Creek* try out quite different strategies for breaking out of their assigned gender roles. Clemencia in "Never Marry a Mexican" tries disidentification: she disidentifies with her mother; she disidentifies with her cultural mothers, La Malinche and La Virgen de Guadalupe, by trying to live as their opposite; and along with these icons she repudiates the gender mandate of Mexican culture that women must be wives and mothers.[1] Going to the opposite pole of Mexican gender ideology, she identifies with the position of extreme masculinity represented by "El Chingón." But what is disavowed returns to haunt her; as Judith Butler argues, any gender identity is defined by its exclusions, and those excluded identities come back "to disrupt its claim to coherence" ("Imitation" 302). Rosario in "Little Miracles, Kept Promises" begins, somewhat like Clemencia, in all-out rebellion against the gender prescriptions embodied in La Virgen de Guadalupe. But rather than remaining stuck in repudiation, she engages in a dialectical process of imagining La Virgen from the standpoint of the various civilizations that have worshiped her—Nahuatl, Spanish, Mexican, Chicano, U.S.—and so expands the gender icon itself. Unlike Clemencia, who remains a prisoner of her culture's gender binary even as she struggles to escape it, Rosario is able to use a border perspective to recreate La Virgen as many-sided, capable of validating multiple ways of being a woman. The title story, "Woman Hollering Creek," endorses identification itself as a means for escape from a narrow and debilitating gender identity modeled on a third icon of Mexican femininity, La Llorona. "Woman Hollering Creek" offers an optimistic vision of identification as a bridge to difference and a means to change.

Disidentification in "Never Marry a Mexican"

More than in most cultures, in Mexican culture gender indoctrination and gender identity are bound up with mythic figures who crystallize the desirable and the undesirable traits of femininity: "We're raised with a Mexican culture that has two role models: La Malinche y la Virgen de Guadalupe.... there's no in-betweens," says Cisneros in interview (Aranda 65). She goes on to say that it's the internalization of those models that makes deviating from them so hard: "I found it very hard to deal with redefining myself or controlling my own destiny or my own sexuality. I still wrestle with that theme, ... writing about being good or bad" (67). Her character Clemencia "wrestles" with both figures, I will argue: that is, she enacts a ruthless aggressive sexuality as a repudiation of the gender traits attributed to La Malinche; and she repudiates the conventional maternal qualities embodied by La Virgen.

In exploring the influence of La Malinche on a contemporary Chicana's sexual identity, Cisneros joins forces with Chicana theorists like Norma Alarcón and Cherríe Moraga, who claim that the myth of La Malinche haunts the sexuality of virtually all contemporary Chicanas and Mexican women: "There is hardly a Chicana growing up today who does not suffer under [La Malinche's] name," says Cherríe Moraga (175). And Norma Alarcón, writing about the same legendary figure, says, "The pervasiveness of the myth is unfathomable, often permeating and suffusing our very being without conscious awareness" ("Chicana" 184).[2]

An Aztec princess sold into slavery, Malintzín, or Malinche, eventually became Cortez's translator; she was also his lover and the mother of their son, Don Martín, the first *mestizo*, of mixed Indian and Spanish parentage. Malinche also advised Cortez, giving away religious secrets of the Aztecs that allowed him to impose his authority on them. While the dignity and competence of the historical Malintzín, or Malinche, were apparently respected by both Indians and Spanish (Soto 15; Todorov 101), after independence Mexican storytellers pinned the blame for the Conquest on her complicity with Cortez, and more specifically on her sexual complicity. "Malintzín, also called Malinche, fucked the white man who conquered the Indian peoples of Mexico and destroyed their culture. Ever since, brown men have been accusing her of betraying her race, and over the centuries continue to blame her entire sex for this 'transgression.'" She is "slandered as La Chingada, meaning the 'fucked one,' or La Vendida, a sell-out to the white race" (Moraga "From a Long" 175, 174). While it would seem that mastering several languages, giving successful strategic advice, negotiating between Indians and Spaniards, and enabling the Conquest imply an active competence, Malinche is characterized not as doing but as done to: "in the very act of intercourse with Cortez, Malinche is seen as having been violated. She is not, however, an innocent victim, but the guilty party—ultimately responsible for her own sexual victimization" (Moraga "From a Long" 185). Lack of agency together with guilt: according to Chicana feminists, contemporary Chicanas and Mexican women have to bear the full weight of this paradox. Norma Alarcón comments, "The myth contains the following sexual possibilities: woman is sexually passive, and hence at all times open to potential use by men whether it be seduction or rape.... nothing she does is perceived as a choice. Because Malintzín aided Cortés in the Conquest of the New World, she is seen as concretizing woman's sexual weakness,... always open to sexual exploitation" (184). By virtue of having female genitalia, then, woman is sexually guilty—guilty of being open to the world.[3]

Clemencia in "Never Marry a Mexican" rebels against this passive sexual identity by imagining herself in the role of violator. Describing sex with Drew, the white lover with whom she had an affair sixteen years before, she says, "I leapt inside you and split you open like an apple. Opened for the other to look and not give back" (78). Clemencia not only takes the man's part—"I leapt inside you"—but she performs the violent actions attached to the verb *chingar*. Octavio Paz elaborates all the meanings of *chingar* in an effort to understand "the strange permanence of Cortés and La Malinche in the Mexican's imagination."[4] He concludes, "The ultimate meaning always contains the idea of aggression.... The verb denotes violence, an emergence from oneself to penetrate another by force" (76). When *chingar* is used in the narrowly sexual sense, "the *chingón* is the *macho*, the male. He rips open the *chingada*, the female, who is pure passivity, defenseless against the exterior world. The relationship between them is violent, and it is determined by the cynical power of the first and the impotence of the second" (77). To Clemencia, apparently, one is either the *chingada* or the *chingón*—and she chooses to be the *chingón*. "I split you like an apple" appropriates "the idea of breaking, of ripping open" attached to the usually masculine *chingar* (Paz 77). She imagines that this take-over puts Drew in her power: "You were ashamed to be so naked.... But I saw you for what you are, when you opened yourself for me" (78). Following the logic of the violator, who pries open what is closed to take possession of what is inside, Clemencia seeks to possess what is now revealed—Drew's private inner self. Her look appropriates the power to control and possess usually attributed to the male gaze ("to look and not give back").

Clemencia extends her sexual ravages to women's bodies, if only in fantasy. In the years since Drew left her, Clemencia has slept with other married men—often while their wives were giving birth. "It's always given me a bit of crazy joy to be able to kill those women like that... to know I've had their husbands when they were anchored in blue hospital rooms, their guts yanked inside out" (77). Now it is a woman's body which is violated, the insides "yanked" out, while Clemencia, the *gran chingón*, pursues a bitter, vindictive sexual satisfaction (Paz 77)—a kind of rape at one remove.

While Clemencia thus evades the stereotype of sexual victim, *la Chingada*, it is only by projecting it onto the other—the lover or the other woman—while leaving the gender binary in place. The pathology of Clemencia's gender identity inheres not so much in her choice of masculinity as in her acceptance of "the cultural rule that gender is a binary system" (Goldner 258). And that binary thinking imprisons her in a rigid sex role as surely as if the reversal had not taken place. Since masculinity and femininity are set up as polar opposites, allegiance to one of them forecloses all traits and desires associated with the other. To admit so-called feminine traits, according to this logic, would be to slide immediately to the opposite pole of femininity. Having identified with the hard, ruthless, closed pole of the gender binary—"I'm vindictive and cruel and I'm capable of anything" (68)—Clemencia cannot admit desires to nurture and protect, which would align her with the pole of open, vulnerable mother. To keep the renounced femininity at bay, Clemencia has to perform psychic acrobatics like those that feminist relational psychoanalytic theorists ascribe to the maintenance of a "normal" gender identity: "Consolidating a stable gender identity is a developmental accomplishment that requires the activation of pathological processes, insofar as any gender-incongruent thought, act, impulse, mood, or trait would have to be disowned, displaced, (mis)placed (as in projective identification), [or] split off" (Goldner 258). Clemencia follows these practices, her efforts redoubled in intensity by the need to resist, rather than accede to, the norm: she disowns, she projects, and she displaces desires for maternal intimacy.

The excluded identity of mother comes back to haunt Clemencia in the form of a defining, if unacknowledged, identification with, precisely, a mother—Megan, the wife of her former lover, Drew. Drew was Clemencia's lover 18 years ago, and she is now having an affair with Drew's and Megan's son—ostensibly to wreak revenge on Megan. True to her *chingón* discourse, Clemencia acknowledges only desires to give Megan pain; on the surface, she and Megan are in a structure of jealousy, rivals for the love of Drew. But her actions testify to a more fundamental structure of envy—to a desire to be Megan, actively mothering. (See chapter 1 for the distinction between envy and jealousy.)

On the night Megan gave birth to Drew's son, for instance, Clemencia positioned herself parallel to the birth process: "While his mother lay on her back laboring his birth, I lay in his mother's bed making love to [Drew]" (75). She has reenacted this imitation of birth many times, with other men:

> It's not the last time I've slept with a man the night his wife is birthing a baby. Why do I do that, I wonder? Sleep with a man when his wife is giving life, being suckled by a thing with its eyes still shut. Why do I do that? It's always given me a bit of crazy joy to kill those women like that.... To know I've had their husbands when they were anchored in blue hospital rooms, their guts yanked inside out, the baby sucking their breasts while their husband sucked mine. (76–77)

Clemencia expresses only contempt for the new mothers; but the mirror scenario—the husband sucking her breast while the baby sucks the mother's breast—betrays an unacknowledged identification with the act of mothering.

Addressing Drew's son mentally, Clemencia probes further into the workings of the maternal body:

> Pretty boy. Little clone. Little cells split into you and you and you. Tell me, baby, which part of you is your mother. I try to imagine... her long long legs that wrapped themselves around this father who took me to his bed. (77)

Here Clemencia follows gestation backward through the division of cells—"little cells split"—to the moment of conception and merges her own body with the mother's body: "her long long legs" refer to Megan's legs, but in the same phrase it is Clemencia whom "this father took to his bed." By conflating her body with Megan's, she imagines herself into the very act of conception. The various images of maternity suggest that Clemencia does not so much want to *have* Drew as to *be* Megan. Hence the claim that she, not Megan, produced the son—from an abstract site of power divorced from the body: "Your son. Does he know how much I had to do with his birth? I was the one who convinced you [Drew] to let him be born.... I'm the one who gave him permission and made it happen, see" (74–75).

In a flashback, Clemencia remembers her last evening with Drew. While Drew is cooking dinner, Clemencia plants gummy bears in Megan's private places—in her make-up jar, in her nail polish bottle, in her lipstick, in her diaphragm. On the one hand, this is a desire to wreak vengeance on "the other woman," in a language of signs comprehensible to women on both sides of the race barrier: "I was here." And to penetrate into a woman's most personal spaces is to enact the *chingón*. Yet the act of placing representatives of herself in Megan's lipsticks, nail polishes, and diaphragm also suggests a yearning to participate in those sites of femininity. The female underside of her *chingón* aggressivity is most obvious when Clemencia dismantles Megan's Russian babushka doll until she penetrates to "the very center, the tiniest baby inside all the others ... this [she] replaced with a gummy bear" (81). Clemencia substitutes her own signifier for the "baby" in the doll-within-a-doll's innermost compartment, symbolically interrupting the clones of generational succession, each a replication of the same, with her own "difference." Then, borrowing motherhood, Clemencia puts the purloined "baby" in her pocket, where "all through dinner I kept ... touch[ing] it, it made me feel good" (82). But on the way home she throws the "baby" into a stagnant creek "where winos piss and rats swim. The Barbie doll's toy stewing there in that muck. It gave me a feeling like nothing before and since" (82).

The episode expresses the full range of Clemencia's ambivalence, an ambivalence shot through with feelings of racial exclusion: as Megan's baby in Clemencia's pocket, the doll evokes Clemencia's "borrowing" of motherhood; as the toy of the "Barbie doll" (Clemencia's derisive label for Megan), the doll becomes metonymically identified with a Barbie doll, icon of white woman as idealized sex object. Clemencia's rage is directed not just against the woman who occupies the position she wants as Drew's lover and mother of his son, but also against the principle that race determines desirability.

Now, some eighteen years later, Clemencia is still simultaneously avenging herself on Megan and miming Megan's maternity by having an affair with Megan's son, to whom she plays mother: "You could be my son" (76).

While Clemencia's obsession with the motherhood that she consciously abjures is evident to the reader, it is not to Clemencia: images of maternity interrupt, like slips of the tongue, a monologue which is consistently power-oriented. For example, she paints and repaints Drew on canvas, boasting: "You're nothing without me. I created you from spit and red dust. And I can snuff you between my finger and thumb if I want to.... You're just a smudge of paint I chose to birth on canvas.... And if that's not power, what is?" (75). Clemencia is thinking power, but the word "birth" slides in, uninvited. Likewise, Clemencia boasts of the power she has over Drew and Megan's son:

> I sleep with this boy, their son. To make the boy love me the way I love his father. To make him want me, hunger... Come here, *mi cariñito*, Come to *mamita*. Here's a bit of toast. I can tell from the way he looks at me, I have him in my power.... Come to *mamita*.... I let him nibble.... Before I snap my teeth. (82)

Again, Clemencia's ostensible motive is power—sexual power over the son, which gives her indirect power over his parents. But the rhetoric of nurturing and maternal endearment that blends into the discourse of mastery suggests that the imitation of mothering continues, unawares.

Judith Butler argues that any coherent gender position—counterhegemonic positions like gay and lesbian identities as well as heterosexual identity positions—rests on the expulsion of other potential identities and other identity traits, which inevitably return to haunt the subject. And the more emphatically the subject insists on *not* being the rejected identity, the more likely it is that she is repudiating an identification that has already been made: "a radical refusal to identify with a given position suggests that on some level an identification has already taken place, an identification that is made and disavowed" (*Bodies* 113). Clemencia reiterates her stand outside conventional marriage and family—"'I've never married and I never will'" (69)—and continually announces her contempt for conventional wives and mothers. But her actions are at odds with her words. Contradicting the boasts that are meant to consolidate the counterhegemonic identity of masculine aggressor ("I'm vindictive and cruel, and I'm capable of anything" [68]) she acts out a mimesis of motherhood through all its stages—conception, gestation, birth, nursing, and nurturing.

Disidentification does not work, because the identification that is most emphatically refused, most insistently, repeatedly, refused, is likely to be one that is constitutive of the subject. Hence, it always returns to threaten the coherence of the gender position founded on its exclusion. At the story's conclusion, a gush of maternal desire not only disrupts, but (because it is the last line of the story) displaces the insistently macho narrative voice:

> Sometimes all humanity strikes me as lovely. I just want to reach out and stroke someone, and say There, there, it's all right, honey. There, there, there. (83)

This expression of a desire to soothe and console—in a word, to mother ("There, there, there" expresses a specifically maternal tenderness in two other stories in the collection, "Eyes of Zapata" [86] and "*Bien* Pretty" [154])—represents a return of the repressed that contradicts the ruthless tone of the whole preceding narrative. Here Clemencia expresses urges which belong properly to la Virgen de Guadalupe who, as Paz says, "consoles, quiets, dries the tears" of the Mexican people, her children (85). It would seem that Clemencia is acting out against an underlying identification with la Virgen as icon of maternal tenderness, as well as against the exploited female sexuality embodied by La Malinche.

Not surprisingly, given her emphatic rejection of woman's place, Clemencia also disidentifies with her mother, and in the same absolutist manner: "it was like if I never had a mother ... Like I never even had one" (73). But just as the wish to mother survives her disidentification with two of the "three Our Mothers"—"*Guadalupe, ... la Chingada (Malinche), ...* and *la Llorona*"—that Gloria Anzaldúa claims for all Chicanas, so Clemencia's identification with her biological mother's fundamental attitudes toward life survives disidentification (*Borderlands* 31, 30.) "Never Marry a Mexican" implies that it is impossible to deal effectively with the gender identifications mandated by the culture if one does not first deal with early identifications within the family.

Clemencia explains that she has not been able to mourn her mother's death because her mother, whom Clemencia disowned for marrying a white man, ceased to be her mother long before her death; but the metaphor that she uses to describe the absence of mourning explains more of Clemencia's relation to her mother than she is aware. Her mother, she says, was to her what its crippled leg was to a little finch she used to have: the leg got twisted in a bar of the cage, then "dried up and fell off. My bird lived a long time without it, just a little red stump of a leg." Like the injured leg, her mother was already dead for her before she died—so that her death was "like if something already dead dried up and fell off, and I stopped missing where she used to be" (73). "Where she used to be" was already an empty place. How can she mourn the absence of an absence?

But if one follows the metaphor to completion—past what Clemencia intends—it seems that repudiating the mother is not enough. Repudiating the mother—"like my ma didn't exist" (73)—leaves her still attached, as the analogy with the bird's dead but still connected limb suggests. The mother continues as a denied but still present appendage to Clemencia's living being. Just as the tactic of repudiation does not work for the cultural mothers, so it does not work for the biological mother: the traces of identification remain. For it was her mother who said "Never marry a Mexican." The mother's negative spirit, encapsulated in that command, remains to frame the negative space where Clemencia lives, as it frames the text. For while Clemencia sees her refusal to marry as a proudly independent stance, the insistent negatives of the opening pages, "I'll *never* marry. Not any man.... No. I've never married and never will" (68–69) are extensions of her mother's injunction. Or, in the language of Clemencia's analogy, the dead stump of the mother's negativity spreads its deadness across Clemencia's living potentials.

For example, take Clemencia's opinion of potential suitors:

> Mexican men, forget it. For a long time the men clearing off the tables or chopping meat behind the butcher counter or driving the bus I rode to school every day, those weren't men. Not men I considered as potential lovers. Mexican, Puerto Rican, Cuban, Chilean, Colombian, Panamanian, Salvadoran, Bolivian, Honduran, Argentine, Dominican, Venezuelan, Guatemalan, Ecuadorian, Nicaraguan, Peruvian, Costa Rican, Paraguayan, Uruguayan, I don't care. I never saw them. My mother did this to me. (69)

Clemencia's mother negated all Mexicans because her husband displeased her; Clemencia expands her mother's practice of racist splitting to negate all Latinos ("I never saw them"). She goes her mother one better by borrowing the Anglo habit of lumping all Latinos into a single monolithic identity—"Mexican"—a label that erases individual differences and distinct cultures to consign all brown-skinned persons to a single category. As in (racist) Anglo discourse, Clemencia's word choice blurs the distinction between race and class: "Mexican" here means busboys, butchers' assistants, bus drivers—working-class men lumped together under an ethnic label that in actuality designates a class, a class of brown-skinned servers. The negation in the mother's injunction, "Never marry a Mexican," multiplies across the pages of Clemencia's monologue until it negates marriage, motherhood, and, finally, Mexicans—all potentially fruitful features of Clemencia's identity position.

Butler contends that the more insistent the subject's disavowal of an identification, the more likely the identification is to be constitutive. Clemencia says: "It was like my ma didn't exist, . . . Like if I never had a mother. . . . Like I never even had one" (73). The disavowal of connection with the mother has to be repeated again and again because the effort to decouple does not work. "What cannot be avowed as a constitutive identification of any given subject-position runs the risk of becoming not only externalized in a degraded form, but repeatedly repudiated and subjected to a policy of disavowal. To a certain extent constitutive identifications are precisely those which are always disavowed" (*Bodies* 113).[5] Although Butler states the premise that compulsive repetition of disavowal is the mark of a constitutive identification, she does not explore the underlying process.

To understand the internal dynamics of disidentification, I return to the model of primary identification and trace its effects through Ralph Greenson's analysis of disidentification, "The Struggle against Identification." The subjects of Greenson's case histories—two male, two female—all rejected the same-sex parent and disavowed their identification with him or her. Indeed, "their entire way of life was predominantly an attempt to contradict" the evidence of identification. "They tried to deny any resemblance to the hated external object by adopting characteristics, actions and behavior which were in direct opposition to those qualities in the hated parent" (162). In moments of impulsivity, however, the subjects acted out behaviors identical to those of the repudiated parent: the women from time to time acted out their mothers' sexual promiscuity, alcoholism, or aggressivity; "the men did not just get angry, but became their angry fathers" (163, 164, 169). In all Greenson's examples, the subjects were terrified of being their parents and did everything they could to fend off the dreaded identification. In Greenson's view, this dread points to the primitive nature of the identifications: they derived from a very early period when there was no boundary between self and other, so that a renewal of the identification threatened a wholesale takeover by the hated parent. And this takeover was imagined in appropriately infantile terms, as a devouring (173–75). The underlying identifications were, in a word, primary identifications, governed by an oral fantasy "in which the object ... is assimilated by eating and is in that way annihilated as such" (Freud, *Group* 105; see Introduction and chapter 1).

Greenson's analysis makes it clear why it is "constitutive identifications" that, as Judith Butler says, are most vehemently and repeatedly disavowed. Repetition is a sign that the effort to construct a boundary between self and other fails. Such a boundary can be drawn between self and other in the external world—and indeed, the energy of repudiation often goes into denigrating the actual mother—but it is more difficult to construct a clear line of demarcation when the mother or father is part of the self. The repudiation is conscious, while the identification is unconscious, so the one cannot touch or modify the other. The unconscious preserves wishes and meanings from the earliest periods of life, as Freud explains, so it preserves an infantile identification with the mother where there was no distinction between self and other. Although one ordinarily differentiates from one's mother figure in many superficial ways, there must always linger an underlying identification with a parent who was in charge of one's body, who appeared for a time to be an extension of oneself: basic trust or mistrust of the world, anxieties about the body, attitudes toward food and sleep, are transmitted through that early confusion of self and other. Just so, Clemencia thinks like her mother—repudiating Mexican men *en bloc* and imitating her mother's habit of negation to negate the mother herself.

While repudiating the mother has become almost a norm among a particular generation of second-wave white middle-class feminists, where the dread of "becoming one's mother" is so widespread that it has been labeled as a specific phobia—"matrophobia"—it is more radical and unexpected in a Chicana daughter. Chicanas often write of their great love for and physical intimacy with their mothers and describe how they draw strength from their bonds with mother and grandmother (see, for example, Moraga, *Loving* 93–94; Chavez 251–69; Viramontes 117–24). Even when they are fighting to redefine themselves against traditional Mexican models of femininity, Chicana writers often find a new identity not through breaking with their mothers, but through revisioning their grandmothers' or mothers' identities and then identifying with that reconstructed maternal heritage. (For example, Esperanza in Cisneros's *House on Mango Street* remakes her great-grandmother, who was in actuality harnessed by patriarchy, into a wild horse of a woman; she then draws her own newly empowered identity from that reconstructed model.)

The magnitude of Clemencia's irreverence can be gauged from Cisneros's own response to the remark that, she said, inspired "Never Marry a Mexican." When her sister-in-law said, "I hate my mother," Cisneros told me, she was amazed and shocked. She explained that her sister-in-law was breaking a taboo in Chicano society, "where parents are saints, to be worshipped." Cisneros said that she immediately began to write "the story of hating one's mother," but all during the writing she felt like "bats and snakes were coming out of my mind—as in a Bosch painting—from the dark places," and she kept thinking, "I couldn't write *that*" (personal communication, Occidental College, Eagle Rock, California, March 21, 1995).

Although the Mexican cultural context makes Clemencia's repudiation of the connection with her mother more shocking than it would be in an Anglo daughter, the underlying psychological mechanism remains the same. The effort to eradicate a maternal identification that grounds Clemencia's way of looking at the world has to be repeated interminably, because it can never succeed. Likewise, Clemencia repeatedly, and histrionically, dramatizes a disidentification with gender, yet acts out a detailed, stage-by-stage imitation of the maternity she disavows. The plot emphasizes the futility of disavowing identification: despite her conscious repudiation of both her blood mother and her cultural mother Malinche, Clemencia remains caught in a repetition of their life stories. Although she detests her mother for marrying a white man, she herself undertakes a sexual liaison with a white man. And despite her determination to throw out the Mexican ideology that ties her sexuality to Malinche's, her life remains shackled to the Malinche story. For the conquering white hero Drew exploited Clemencia's talents and sexuality and then abandoned her, as Cortez abandoned Malinche after the Conquest. Clemencia's relation to her mother follows the Malinche script of betrayal and abandonment, too: La Malinche's mother sold her daughter into slavery in order to ensure that her husband's estate should go to her sons from a second marriage rather than to the rightful heir, Malinche; just so, Clemencia's mother disinherited Clemencia in order to pass Clemencia's father's house down to the sons of her second marriage ("My half brothers living in that house that should've been ours, me and [my sister's]" [73].)

"Never Marry a Mexican" can be read as a multi-dimensional demonstration of the principle that disidentification doesn't work: while the disidentifications and counteridentifications go on at a furious pace at the self-dramatizing surface of consciousness, all the underlying identifications remain in place—fixed, static.

Revisioning La Virgen de Guadalupe: Border Thinking in "Little Miracles, Kept Promises"

How then *does* one break out of a narrow and stultifying gender identity? Is one doomed to "be" one's mother and live out her story, as "Never Marry a Mexican" suggests? "Little Miracles, Kept Promises" presents a different, and more hopeful, way of negotiating with both gender and maternal identifications. Rosario thinks differently from Clemencia in a number of ways. First, rather than remaining in an imaginary rivalry with the mother, see-sawing between a primary identification and a disavowal which only testifies to the tenacity of the underlying identification, Rosario understands her own and her mother's position in symbolic terms: it is the ruling hegemony that imprisons both herself and her mother (and grandmother) in the role of passive, enduring, loving woman. Rather than blaming the mother as Clemencia does, she refers her mother's traits to a third term—the gender role of woman as represented by La Virgen de Guadalupe. Second, rather than accepting blindly the cultural binary of an integral masculinity and an integral femininity as Clemencia does, Rosario critically examines the rigidity of gender prescriptions, "refutes the logic of mutual exclusion" (Butler, *Bodies* 148), and works slowly toward a more flexible definition of gender. While Clemencia insists on a power-oriented masculine position that closes out all feminine traits, Rosario, far from insisting on a coherent gender identity, adopts a border perspective to recreate gender itself as multiple and contradictory. It is this border perspective that enables her in the end to reconstruct la Virgen de Guadalupe herself as a gender ideal that she can live with.

Rosario begins her letter to the Virgen with an outburst of anger. It appears that Rosario has been raging for years at La Virgen de

Guadalupe for "all that self-sacrifice, all that silent suffering"—for modeling the passive endurance of misery and oppression that she sees in her mother and grandmother (127): "I couldn't look at you without blaming you for all the pain my mother and her mother all our mothers' mothers have put up with... I wasn't going to be my mother or my grandma.... Hell no. Not here. Not me" (127). The build-up of negatives, the disidentification with the mother, the repudiation of a passive and abused femininity, all recall Clemencia's strategy of repudiation. But even at this stage, there is a difference:

> Virgencita de Guadalupe. For a long time I wouldn't let you in my house. I couldn't see you without seeing my ma each time my father came home drunk and yelling, blaming everything that ever went wrong in his life on her. I couldn't look at your folded hands without seeing my *abuela* mumbling, "My son, my son, my son"... Couldn't look at you without blaming you for all the pain my mother and her mother and all our mothers' mothers have put up with. (127)

Rosario notices how gender functions in her nearest relations to support gender hierarchy. The uncritical acceptance of Mary the Mild as ideal leads her mother and grandmother to "fold their hands" in response to male abuse; their patience and endurance support the abusive dominance of the male. Rosario has the ability to perceive and critique the social ideology that has formed her mother and her grandmother; rather than repudiating them, she routes her disidentification through the third term of la Virgen; because she disidentifies ("I wasn't going to be my mother or my grandma") by way of the symbolic representative of gender, she makes it clear that she is rejecting not a mother she hates, but a role she refuses.

Rosario's initial repudiation of the Virgen is based on the limited options the icon represents for Mexican women: she is—only—the tender mother who loves all her many children selflessly, patiently enduring their sins, always ready to comfort and console. But as Rosario's "dialogue" with the Virgen progresses, she reconsiders her from the perspective of a border subject. As Gloria Anzaldúa defines this position in *Borderlands/La Frontera,* the border subject, or *mestiza,* stands at the crossroads of three cultures—the Indian, the Spanish, and the Anglo; her soul is the battleground where the competing ideologies of these cultures collide, where "commonly held beliefs of the white culture attack commonly held beliefs of the Mexican culture, and both attack commonly held beliefs of the indigenous culture" (78). Because her survival depends on her flexibility, on her ability to move between different cultural perspectives, the *mestiza* cannot afford to invest in a single culture's version of reality. Further, she views each culture from the standpoint of the other: she "learns to be an Indian in Mexican culture, to be Mexican from an Anglo point of view" (79). She is positioned to look askance at the ideology of the one culture from the standpoint of the other.

Rosario moves away from an absolutist repudiation of the Virgen by taking advantage of her border position as a *mestiza*. She begins to consider the Virgen from the perspective of indigenous Indian culture. "I finally understood who you are. No longer Mary the mild, but our mother Tonantzin. Your church at Tepeyac built on the site of her temple. Sacred ground no matter whose goddess claims it" (128). The mythohistorical basis for the Virgen's identification with Tonantzin is that the Virgen de Guadalupe appeared to Juan Diego, a poor Indian, in 1531, at the site where Tonantzin's temple once stood on Tepeyac Hill. Speaking Nahuatl (the language of the Aztecs) she ordered him to persuade the Catholic Bishop to build a shrine to her on Tepeyac Hill (which he did). The Virgen de Guadalupe/Tonantzin thus combines in her person the diverse cultural streams of the Mexican people.[6] Rosario goes to the other side of the Indian/Mexican border to consider La Virgen as Aztec fertility goddess, fierce as well as loving. "That you could have the power to rally a people when a country was born, and again during civil war, and during a farmworkers' strike in California made me think maybe there is power in my mother's patience, strength in my grandmother's endurance. Because those who suffer have a special power, don't they? The power of understanding someone else's pain" (128). True to a border epistemology, Rosario does not settle on one side of the cultural border, not even on the side of power with Tonantzin the fierce, but returns to read Mary's (and her own mothers') capacity for endurance through the strengths of Tonantzin. Anzaldúa claims that seeing "through serpent and eagle eyes" (that is, through Mexican and U.S. eyes) enables the border subject "to shift out of habitual formations" (79); here, visiting the indigenous side of the border gives Rosario a new outlook on the feminine qualities her mother and grandmother embody, allowing her to define as power what she had previously perceived as weakness: her mothers' patience, endurance and empathy.

Then Rosario pushes multiplicity yet further: "When I learned your real name is Coatlaxopeuh, She Who Has Dominion over Serpents, when I . . . learned your names are Teteoinnan, Toci, Xochiquetzal, Tlazolteotl, Coatlicue, Chalchiuhtlicue, Coyolxauhqui, Huixtocihuatl, Chicomecoatl, Cihuacoatl, when I could see you as Nuestra Señora de la Soledad, Nuestra Señora de los Remedios, Nuestra Señora del Perpetuo Socorro, Nuestra Señora de San Juan de los Lagos, Our Lady of Lourdes, Our Lady of Mount Carmel, Our Lady of the Rosary, Our Lady of Sorrows" (128). Seeing her from the perspective of Spanish, Indian, and U.S. cultures, Rosario redefines the Virgen herself as a many-sided border subject. Moving back and forth across cultural borders, juxtaposing different cultures' sacred representations of woman, "break[s] down the unitary aspect of each new paradigm" (Anzaldúa, *Borderlands* 80), making imprisonment within any one culture's role prescriptions less likely.

One's strategy for breaking out of narrow gender identifications depends in large part on one's concept of gender. Clemencia tries to escape hegemonic gender constructions by attacking the external manifestations of gender. As if in a parodic (mis)understanding of Judith Butler's theory of gender as performance—constituted by the repetition of conventionally gendered behaviors and subject to subversion by parody, exaggeration, or counterhegemonic behaviors[7]—Clemencia seeks to rid herself of a culturally imposed gender definition through performance: all her gestures, her speech acts, and her mental acts too, dramatize a masculinized alternative to conventional femininity. She acts as if gender identity were only a mask to be put on and taken off at will, in no way linked to her own psychic history of identifications.[8] The upshot of not interrogating the history of her identifications with femininity, including the identification with her own mother, is that the dramatic performance of masculinity leaves the underlying femininity intact.[9] For what Clemencia actually does in the world, as opposed to what she performs in the confines of her own imaginary theater, is enact traditional "women's wiles": waiting ("I've been waiting patient as a spider all these years [for revenge on Drew's wife]," 75), jealous scheming against "the other woman," and manipulating men through giving and withholding sex. And the explosion of maternal desire that ends the story shows that it is only the external trappings of gender that have changed, not Clemencia's underlying identification with motherhood.

Rosario, by contrast, ends by saying, "When I could see you in all your facets, . . . I could love you, and, finally, learn to love me" (129).

If loving the Virgen is necessary to self-love, that is because the Virgen is "part of her," as Cisneros says of her own connection to the Virgen (Aranda 65). The assumption that Rosario speaks for the author seems justified by Cisneros's own statement: "the last speaker [Rosario], that's me!" (Dasenbrock and Jussawalla 292). Cisneros explains that, having been "raised with a Mexican culture that has two role models: La Malinche and La Virgen de Guadalupe," she recognizes that they are "part of her"; in her writing she isn't trying to "exorcise them," which would be impossible, but "to make [her] peace with those ghosts" (Aranda 65, 67). Rosario seems to operate on the same assumption—that the Virgen "lives inside her" (Aranda 67); therefore, disidentification with the Virgen won't work. Rather, reconstructing the Virgen to endorse a wide range of femininities enables Rosario to embrace the Virgen and, in the same movement, learn to "love [herself]." A perspective that takes in the Virgen's complexity enables her to revision her mother's and grandmother's character traits as complex and various, too. Rather than being caught in an oscillation between the poles of disidentification and a totalizing identification with her mother, as Clemencia is, Rosario's work on gender enables her to make a more nuanced identification with her maternal line, a more differentiated appraisal of traits they share, traits they don't: "I wasn't ashamed, then, to be my mother's daughter, my grandmother's granddaughter, my ancestors' child" (128).

Judith Butler's *Gender Trouble* does us a service by debunking the notion of gender as an internal essence that governs the subject's actions and by drawing attention to its constructed nature as a social fiction. But the fact that gender is socially constructed does not render its hold less tenacious. In addition to being a discursive position in the symbolic order, gender identity is a central element of one's sense of self, as Lynne Layton and Stephen Frosh point out (Layton 10, Frosh 1). A dialogue with the Virgen may be a culture–specific way of dealing with gender, but Rosario's process of negotiating with gender—over many years, from many different angles—remains a useful model, for anyone, of the cultural work necessary to modify a gender identification that is both restrictive and an integral part of oneself.

So Rosario models the work necessary to changing the gender identifications that inhabit us. But gender is a position in social discourse, too, as Butler emphasizes. Changing the social definition of gender requires a different kind of cultural work, in the public sphere. In revising the figure of la Virgen so that, in her biculturalism, she endorses many different ways of being a woman, Cisneros is expanding the social definition of gender for the Chicana community. (And her recent essay, "Guadalupe the Sex Goddess," shows that Cisneros's project of giving new dimensions to the Virgen is an ongoing one.) Cisneros sees the reconstruction of the icons and the gender identities tied to them as a communal project, shared with other Chicana feminists, for " 'reinventing ourselves,' revising ourselves. We accept our culture, but not without adapting [it to] ourselves as women" (Aranda 66).[10]

IDENTIFICATION WITH DIFFERENCE IN "WOMAN HOLLERING CREEK"

Cisneros's title story revises a third icon of Mexican femininity, La Llorona. In a way the story also revises the paradigm of identification: it suggests that, unlike the pathological identifications studied in previous chapters, cross-cultural identification can be salutary, a means to flexibility and change; and it can provide these benefits without erasing the specifics of the cultural other's subjectivity. At the end of "Woman Hollering Creek," the Mexican protagonist Cleófilas identifies with a Chicana. That identification releases her from a debilitating identification with La Llorona, a Mexican icon of eternal suffering. The Chicana, Felice, is a border subject whose gender identifications are mixed, playful, and empowering—as distant as can be imagined from Cleófilas's single-minded embrace of (what Cisneros presents as) the monocultural Mexican gender ideal of suffering womanhood. How is it possible for Cleófilas to make the leap into identification with a woman whose gender position defies everything Cleófilas has absorbed from a lifelong acculturation to the damaging gender identity of suffering woman?

Cleófilas has an aptitude for identification. In the opening sections set in her Mexican hometown, Cleófilas incorporates the images of the *telenovela* stars, mapping her clothes, makeup and haircuts on them and taking in, unawares, the gender doctrine that women must suffer for love: "Somehow one ought to live one's life like that" ... because "to suffer for love is good. The pain all sweet somehow" (45). After her marriage to Juan Pedro and her move across the border to a small Texan town, Cleófilas is isolated. Human models being scarce, Cleófilas identifies with the creek called La Gritona, or Woman Hollering Creek. The victim of her husband's physical abuse, she hears in the creek's rippling murmur the voice of La Llorona (the weeping/lamenting woman.)

While the oral tradition to which La Llorona belongs is lively, generating ever new versions of what she suffered (three of my Chicana students related three different versions of the legend, told them by their mothers), what remains consistent through all the different versions is the sound of La Llorona's eerie wail and the fact that she drowned her children. In one version, for instance, she kills her three children because they get in the way of her wild living; after her own death, God sends her back to seek them eternally. In another version, the figure is fused with La Malinche: when Cortez wanted to take their son back to Spain with him, Malinche killed the son, then herself, rather than be separated from her child; since then, her spirit roams, moaning "Aayy!" (Shular 105, 99–101). La Llorona usually appears by the shore of a river or lake (she drowned her children); and sometimes she acts as siren, enticing men into the water to die (Agogino 27).[11]

Although the circumstances of her story change, La Llorona's cry of sorrow remains. That wail of inarticulate pain, reflected in the river's indeterminate *grito*, or shout—which Cleófilas repeatedly reads as "pain or rage" (47, 56)—offers Cleófilas an analogue to her own inarticulate, baffled misery. And when the text juxtaposes Cleófilas's baby, playing on the creek bank, with Cleófilas's growing belief that "La Llorona [is] calling to her," driving her "to the darkness under the trees" (51), the reader begins to fear that the identification with La Llorona will become total—that Cleófilas will drown herself and her child and so enter into La Llorona's eternity of mourning.

"Pain is sweet," say the *telenovelas*; and the traditional figure of La Llorona is caught up in eternal sorrow. Thus Cisneros indicts Mexican culture for offering, through both folklore and contemporary popular culture, a single monolithic definition of femininity: Woman is she who loves and suffers for love. Identifying with La Llorona's frozen sorrow and with the *telenovela* heroines immobilizes Cleófilas in the posture of beaten wife, "suffering for love," unable to articulate her experience or to find release through action. Of course, Cleófilas is trapped in the abusive marriage by material circumstances as well: a lack of money and mobility, a dependent child, a new pregnancy, and isolation in a social climate that condones violence to women (the men who drink with her husband in the ice house joke about how one of them killed his wife). But identification with old and new Mexican icons of suffering womanhood immobilizes her, too.[12]

Identification can also enable escape from gender interpellation, as the story's abrupt turnaround illustrates. At a prenatal clinic where, for once, she escapes her husband's surveillance, Cleófilas joins forces with two Chicanas—the nurse-practitioner, Graciela, and her friend, Felice—to effect an escape from abuse. Felice agrees to drive her to the Greyhound bus terminal in San Antonio, where Cleófilas and her small son can get a bus back to her father's house in Mexico. As they drive across Woman Hollering Creek on their way to San Antonio, the distance between Chicana and Mexican culture becomes apparent:

> When they drove across the *arroyo*, [Felice] opened her mouth and let out a yell as loud as any *mariachi*. . . . Every time I cross that bridge I do that. Because of the name, you know. Woman Hollering. *Pues*, I holler. Did you ever notice, Felice continued, how nothing around here is named after a woman? Really. Unless she's the Virgin. I guess you're only famous if you're a virgin. She was laughing again. That's why I like the name of that *arroyo*. Makes you want to holler like Tarzan, right? (55)

Felice "said this in a Spanish pocked with English and laughed" (55). Felice, a *mestiza* accustomed to going back and forth between Anglo and Mexican signifying systems, has acquired a flexibility of mind which allows her to go back and forth across the gender border, too—from the Virgen to Tarzan—and then, laughing at both, move on. That movement is creative, as Anzaldúa says, because it "keeps breaking down the unitary aspect of each . . . paradigm" (80), enabling new combinations to emerge. The story sets up a contrast between the border subject and a woman like Cleófilas who, subjected to a single culture, is locked into that culture's "unitary paradigm" of femininity—locked into the frozen pose of weeping woman. The cultural screen curves around a woman encased in a single national culture, Cisneros seems to say, so there is no seeing any alternative model of womanhood beyond it. A border subject like Felice, on the other hand, can play with gender identities and recombine them in new ways.[13]

The story ends with Cleófilas identifying with Felice. At first, Cleófilas responds cognitively to Felice's triumphant shout:

> Can you imagine, when we crossed the *arroyo* she just started yelling like a crazy, she would say later to her father and brothers. Just like that. Who would've thought? Who would've? Pain or rage, perhaps, but not a hoot like the one Felice had just let go. Makes you want to holler like Tarzan, Felice had said. (56)

Already the example of Felice's loud self-assertion is liberating, as Cleófilas begins to shake off the mutism of the abused woman by shaping the narrative she will tell her family.

Beyond this cognitive appreciation of Felice as a new kind of woman comes a leap into identification. The story ends:

> Felice began laughing again, but it wasn't Felice laughing. It was gurgling out of [Cleófilas's] own throat, a long ribbon of laughter, like water. (56)

Cleófilas seems to laugh with Felice's laughter, confused at first about whose throat the laughter issues from. And the text privileges this conflation of self and other as a mode of change: in laughing with Felice, in laughing *as* Felice, Cleófilas slips out of her interpellation as the woman who weeps to become a woman who laughs. The further description of her laughter as a "gurgle," a "ribbon of ... water," suggests that this is a three-way merger. The promised identification with the creek has occurred—an identification no longer destructive now that the river's voice can be heard not as eternal lament, but as a celebration of female freedom and exuberance.

The text privileges border consciousness as a means to gender flexibility: the multiple identity positions available to a woman living between two cultures like Felice encourages her to move beyond the unitary definition of woman, to put together a composite of the gender positions that best express herself. Felice hollers like a man, Tarzan, but she does so *as* a woman, responding to the creek's invitation to imitate a "woman hollering." She thus appropriates for women the privileges of freedom and mobility usually associated with masculinity and comically exaggerated in Tarzan's hypermobility and freedom from all social constraint. I would argue that identification opens to Cleófilas a similar range of gender positions: through identification, she gains access to Felice's model of a hybrid gender identity and to a border culture's expanded range of possibilities for female self-definition. Cleófilas's laughter expresses a release from interpellation—or, more precisely, from the grip of a singular culture's directive to be one kind of woman only.

Cleófilas's ability to identify with Felice is surprising, given the univocity of the various cultural representations that have interpellated her into the gender position of the woman who (only) cries. How are we to explain this capacity to identify with difference? The model of melancholic identification that Freud offers in *The Ego and the Id* suggests that identification could lead not to the stasis ascribed to identification in previous chapters, but rather to a subjective flexibility and multiplicity. Identification is a way of mourning loss, Freud says in this text. "An object which was lost has been set up again inside the ego—that is, ... an object-cathexis, has been replaced by an identification" (*Ego* 23). Through this internalization, the subject can hang on to the lost one, now become part of the ego. (This model does not contradict the notion of identification as primary, for Freud usually specifies that melancholic identification is "regressive"—a reversion to an earlier mode of relating. Identification is available to the subject as a means to cope with loss precisely because he or she has already established the pattern of identification, as "the earliest and original form of emotional tie" [*Group* 107]).[14] Freud says he used to think that melancholy, or compensatory, identification was pathological, but now he thinks it is quite common. Indeed, "it may be that this identification is the sole condition under which the id can give up its objects" (*Ego* 24). The ego tries "to make good the id's loss by saying: 'Look, you can love me too—I am so like the object'" (*Ego* 24); in other words, the libidinal energy originally directed at the loved one is channeled in a new direction—toward the ego which now houses the lost object.

What makes this model of identification relevant to Cleófilas, who has not suffered the loss of a love object but rather gained an identificatory object, is the underlying presumption of a plurality of identifications. Freud says that the process of compensatory identification is "a very frequent one." Indeed, he pictures the ego as an amalgam of numerous identifications—"a precipitate of abandoned object-cathexes" (24). I would add that the objects chosen for identification are necessarily varied because the selection of identificatory models is not governed by a principle of compatibility; rather, the ego takes into itself any object that is loved and lost, and over the course of a lifetime one's love objects necessarily vary. Freud himself says that the identifications, becoming "numerous ... and incompatible with one another," may produce "conflicts between the various identifications" (*Ego* 25). Although Freud remarks only on the down side of this multiplicity—it can produce a "multiple personality" (*Ego* 25)—his vision of heterogeneity can also be viewed as positive. His description suggested that the ego becomes a field of diverse, contradictory, and competing identifications—a kind of psychological border zone where one moves between the various identity positions modeled on disparate love objects as different situations call for different perspectives.[15] There are the makings of a theory of multiple subjectivity in the Freudian text, then, although he did not develop them fully.

The melancholy model of identification also suggests a capacity for identification with difference: one identifies with any and all of those who are loved and lost, and one does not always love people who are similar to oneself. To think about difference only along the axis of gender, the axis most relevant to "Woman Hollering Creek": if the subject identifies with a love object always as a compensation for loss, she will be identifying sometimes with persons who occupy different gender positions from her own. To start with, the oedipal crisis entails the loss of the opposite-sex object and therewith, as Freud himself specifies, a cross-gender identification: "often . . . a little girl, after she has had to relinquish her father as a love-object, will bring her masculinity into prominence and identify herself with her father (that is, with the object which has been lost)" (28). In later life, too, the subject is likely to lose friends and lovers of both genders, so the clutter of identificatory objects that Freud describes as the ego is likely to include diverse gender identities. According to Freud's model of compensatory identification, then, one can identify with difference—and indeed *must* identify with difference, in order to cope with loss. Because the unconscious preserves from early times both the wish to identify with multiple gender positions and the capacity to do so, "the fluidity of gender through access to different types of identification becomes a possibility," as Jessica Benjamin has argued (Sweetnam 445).[16]

On this model, Cleófilas's aptitude for identification gives her a tool for attaining gender flexibility. Practiced in identifying with the most diverse objects (even a river), she is equipped to identify with Felice even though Felice's gender position is at odds with Cleófilas's whole discursive formation. The story presents identification as a saving grace, a means to change, growth, and liberation.

Can we call Cleófilas's identification with Felice a heteropathic identification? Max Scheler labels an identification "heteropathic" when "the subject identifies his own self with the other," as opposed to assimilating the other into him- or herself (Laplanche and Pontalis 206). I would add that to qualify as heteropathic, the identification must be based on a clear perception of the other's differences. Otherwise, as in the cross-race identifications analyzed in chapter 4, the subject may well idealize the other and so identify with her own ideal of self-sufficient wholeness, projected onto the cultural other. Does Cleófilas idealize Felice? Here is the paragraph that precedes the concluding identification:

> Everything about this woman, this Felice, amazed Cleófilas. The fact that she drove a pickup.... when Cleófilas asked if it was her husband's, she said she didn't have a husband. The pickup was hers. She herself had chosen it. She herself was paying for it.... Felice was like no woman she'd ever met. (56)

The word "amazed" suggests idealization. But I would argue that Cleófilas's perceptions do not add up to idealization as I have defined it in chapter 4. Cleófilas does not identify with a figure of wholeness and perfection, represented by the specular outline of the woman's body. Rather, Cleófilas lists Felice's specific differences—differences that do not necessarily add up to a noncontradictory whole. Amazement is not directed at what Felice *is*, globally, but at what she does. The short declarative sentences record specific actions, as in: "A woman can own a pickup. A woman can pay for it herself!" I would argue, then, that this is a heteropathic identification: Cleófilas perceives Felice's difference within the context of Felice's own life circumstances; and she perceives her difference not globally, not as a unified perfect whole, but as a host of particular characteristics and acts. It is precisely Cleófilas's clear perception of Felice's differences that enables her to change by identifying with her.

Cisneros's story thus suggests the transformative potential of using identification as a bridge to cultural difference. But "Woman Hollering Creek" ends on the celebratory note of liberating identification, so readers do not know whether Cleófilas perceives Felice as separate and distinct after the moment of fusion—as she certainly does before it. So the story avoids a central question of identification: Can one achieve identification with a person from a different culture without occluding that person's difference, without assimilating her into oneself and so losing sight of her as a separate subject? The next chapter considers the possibilities for heteropathic identification across cultural borders in a multiethnic feminist community, taking into consideration the risks that previous chapters have shown accompany identification and that Cisneros's optimistic ending dodges: tendencies to assimilate the other to the self or to idealize her difference.

Part III

Heteropathic Identifications

Part III moves away from the inescapably negative implications of both Freud's and Lacan's models to consider the potential benefits of identification. Even in its infantile beginnings identification is, after all, not only an incorporation of the other (Freud) or an appropriation of the other's bodily form (Lacan) but also, from the first, a means of overcoming the barrier between self and other, of participating imaginatively in an other's experience. Acknowledging identification's tendency to assimilate difference to the same need not preclude the recognition that identification also opens us up to difference. Max Scheler has defined an alternative to Freud's incorporative identification: in "heteropathic identification" the subject moves out to identify with the other, to stand in her shoes, rather than assimilating the other into the self (Laplanche and Pontalis 206). In my view an identification would qualify as heteropathic only if the subject managed, even in the act of identifying, to remain aware of the model's particularity as a different subject, within the context of her own life situation. Yet even an identification with difference like Cleófilas's in "Woman Hollering Creek," one that seems to be based on a clear perception of the other subject, risks falling into assimilation on the one side or idealization on the other—both functions of the tendency to confuse self and other. In analyzing how identification functions in the politics of multiracial community, the following chapter confronts some of the ethical as well as psychological issues implicit in the notion of heteropathic identification.

Chapter 7

Toward Cross-Race Dialogue
Cherríe Moraga, Gloria Anzaldúa, and the Psychoanalytic Politics of Community

In this final chapter I brave the conventional wisdom that psychoanalysis is antithetical to community by using Lacan's three registers—imaginary, symbolic, and real—to explore the problematics and possibilities of identification in a multicultural community. It would seem that in such a community being able to identify with someone from a different cultural or racial background would facilitate hearing what she has to say and seeing things from her point of view. Yet even the most partial or benign identification with the other risks occluding her specificity as a separate subject, since, as Roy Schafer says, "merging is involved in every identification, even in the higher-level identifications" (153): identificatory processes tend toward a unity of self and other that erases difference and threatens the perception of the other as other. Feminists have argued both sides of this issue. Crossing disciplinary boundaries, I invoke the theories of standpoint epistemologists Sandra Harding and Paula Moya and feminist political theorists Seyla Benhabib and Iris Marion Young to help me explore two competing needs of a pluralistic community: on the one hand, hearing what the other says in her own terms requires temporarily adopting her perspective; on the other hand, hearing what the other says in her own terms requires some corrective to the imaginary tendency to draw the other into identification and so confuse her perspective (and interests) with one's own.[1]

Aligning psychoanalytic ideas with principles of standpoint theory, discourse ethics and political analysis enables me to approach the following question from a richer and more complex theoretical base. If imaginary processes of identification were sufficiently tempered by symbolic functions and by an acknowledgment of the real as it operates in community, could identification be modulated so that one could identify with the other's perspective without usurping or distorting it?[2]

I begin with an assumption: that it is a good thing, even a responsibility, for a human being (who is inescapably social, who necessarily lives within a community) to understand persons from different cultural backgrounds. But the effort to understand immediately engages us in the traps of "knowing" and "identification." Cognitive processes work by fitting new information into established mental schemas, so there is a built-in tendency to assimilate the other to the same. I can understand you fully only by subsuming your experience into cognitive structures based on my experience, not on yours. And "knowing" another person may become bound up with identification. As both Freud and Lacan have asserted, identification is integral to the constitution of the ego; and as the present text has claimed throughout, that early tangle of self and other, that early desire to be the other, leaves as its legacy a strong desire to identify with the other. Striving for understanding triggers not just cognitive processes, but the unconscious desire to feel what the other feels, to experience what the other experiences, to be the other. If cognitive processes tend to reduce the new to the familiar, unconscious processes of identification tend to reduce the other to the self. Therefore, a respect for the other's otherness requires both a limit on our expectation of what we can know of another person and a conscious brake on identification. In this chapter I address the problematics of knowing through an evocation of the Lacanian real as it would operate in community; and I theorize various ways that an emphasis on the symbolic, if translated into social institutions and procedures, could counter imaginary desires for identification.

In what specific ways does the symbolic block the imaginary tendency to reduce the other's complexity to an illusory perfection and wholeness? What role does the real play in an encounter with someone from a different culture? I approach these questions through a simulated "dialogue" between an Anglo reader (myself) and two Chicana feminists' texts: Cherríe Moraga's "From a Long Line of *Vendidas*" and Gloria Anzaldúa's *Borderlands/La Frontera*. Although they are to be sure literary transactions, these readerly dialogues are meant to model ways that imaginary, symbolic, and real processes inflect identification in the embodied conversations that take place in feminist communities.[3]

"Like You/Not You": Cherríe Moraga's "From a Long Line of *Vendidas*" and Symbolic Identification[4]

In Lacanian theory symbolic processes function as a constraint on the idealizing, simplifying and assimilative tendencies of imaginary identification, as Lacan explains in Seminar I. "Each time the subject apprehends himself as form and as ego, . . . his desire is projected outside. . . . But, thank God, the subject inhabits the world of the symbol, that is to say a world of others who speak. . . . Each time that, in the phenomenon of the other, something appears which once again allows the subject to reproject, to recomplete, to *feed*, . . . the image of the *Idealich* [ideal ego], each time that the jubilant assumption of the mirror stage is retrieved along similar lines, each time that the subject is captivated by one of his fellow beings, well, then the desire revives in the subject. But it is revived verbally" (S I 171). Explicating the conceptual terms in this passage will enable me to review the process of imaginary idealization I describe at length in chapter 4, as well as to introduce a description of some ways that symbolic processes counteract the force of the imaginary in cross-race dialogue.

The *Idealich* (ideal ego) is the nucleus of the ego assimilated originally from the mirror image and become, in later life, the source of all identifications in the visual field (*Écrits* 2). Because the subject first glimpsed the possibility of a unified self in an image external to the self (in the mirror image or in the bodily outline of the fellow human being) she or he continues throughout life to seek in the outside world an image of perfect wholeness. Because of the discrepancy between the seeming unity and coherence of the ideal ego and the actual incoherence and fragmentation of subjectivity, the ego is always "hungry," always in need of supplements to "feed it," to "recomplete it," to shore up a self-image of wholeness and consistency. The subject is "captivated" by the bodily outline of the other because it appears to incarnate the fullness of being once detected in the mirror image; and so the "desire revives" to acquire that fullness of being in the primitive fashion of the mirror stage—through incorporating "the empty form of the other" (S I 170) into the ideal ego.

Racial difference plays into the process of imaginary identification because difference itself props up the faith in the other's wholeness and self-consistency: if the other were just like me, then she would be fragmentary and shifting and inconsistent just like me; to embody my ideal of self-completion she must be different. The comments of the white feminists quoted in chapter 4 betray a tendency to attribute a self-possessed authority and integrity to black feminists; and because the writers project these idealized qualities onto the body, onto the corporeal presence, of the other woman, their comments seem to me to indicate the presence of imaginary identification. As the responses of the black feminists to their white idealizers attest, being the object of someone's idealizing fantasy is not flattering, for one is not recognized as a subject. Nor does it lead to fruitful dialogue: the missed communications between white women and black women show the dangers to feminist community of the impulse to perceive the other in terms of one's own need for an ideal self-possession.

Such misrecognitions hamper effective political action as well. One of the differences eclipsed by a white woman's imaginary identification with a woman of color is of course the power differential between them. To project a wished-for power and authority onto a black woman, as the white feminists surveyed in chapter 4 do, is to obscure and distort the existing power relations between white and black and so to prevent the white idealizer from feeling any urgent need to change the racially skewed distribution of power and resources in the United States—or to give up the benefits that she derives from it.

How does the symbolic register ("the world of the symbol," "the world of others who speak") check the desire "to recomplete, to *feed* . . . the image of the *Idealich* [ideal ego]"? How exactly does the symbolic counter the imaginary appetite for identification with the bodily form of the other? In the following reading of Cherríe Moraga's "From a Long Line of *Vendidas,*" I explore various ways that the dominance of the symbolic in a conversation between persons on different sides of a race border can curb identification and yet, perhaps, provide a bridge to difference.[5]

I encounter Moraga entirely as words on a page, so the symbolic is by definition foregrounded. The symbolic, the register of language and verbal interaction, functions through difference. On the level of language, signifiers mean through their difference from each other, and that meaning is always in motion as signifiers shift in relation to other signifiers. On the level of dialogue, each speaker reveals different aspects of herself over time. Imaginary identification is grounded in a vision of the other as a perfectly integrated body: she seems complete, arrested in the moment of perception; there is no more to be said. In a conversation, "there is always something more to be said": "the identity of the subject becomes a term that is always to be determined, always yet to be defined in a further movement of the signifying chain." This presentation of self as "the unfolding of a history" challenges the desire to see the other as a static whole, checking the impulse toward imaginary identification (Boothby 354). In the cross-race dialogue I model through the following reading of Moraga's autobiographical essay, I perceive the speaker piecemeal, over time, each passage revealing a new and different aspect of her subjectivity. And Moraga's self-presentation as a multiple and heterogeneous subject—she is one of the women of color who originated the concept of multiple subjectivity—enhances the symbolic and invites a different kind of identification.[6]

Moraga's description of a telephone conversation with her mother gives me an opening for identification. After an alienating gap of separation, Moraga's mother calls her, and Moraga is about to accept her mother's return and declare her great love for her—"I am big as a mountain! I want to say, Watch out Mamá! I love you and I am as big as a mountain!"—when she hears the other phone in her mother's house ring. Her mother, returning, says it is Moraga's brother on the other line: "Okay *mi'jita*. I love you. I'll talk to you later,'" she says, and hangs up—"cutting off the line in the middle of the connection. My brother has always come first" (177). This scenario of rejection draws me into identification: my mother (I felt) loved me till my brother was born and then transferred all her love to him, forsaking me. But Moraga's next statement cuts me off from identification: "What I wanted from my mother was impossible. It would have meant her going against Mexican/Chicano tradition in a very fundamental way. You are a traitor to your race if you do not put the man first" (177). Moraga moves to a dimension foreign to me by placing her mother's betrayal in a cultural context that explains it: loyalty to the race is first and foremost loyalty to the Chicano male. My mother was a traitor to me, period. I am thrown out of identification, reminded of difference: I am Anglo, she is Chicana. Identification is not uniform and all-consuming, but shifting: I am like her, then not her, moving in and out, making a partial identification.[7]

The Lacanian symbolic order encompasses sociocultural structure as well as linguistic structure. Moraga likewise situates her own experience always within an overarching cultural order. She argues that gender and sexuality must be understood "within a context formed by race, class, geography, religion, ethnicity, and language" (187). And that idea does not remain at the level of abstract principle. Rather, Moraga thinks of herself in terms of "a complex web of personal and political identity and oppression," each node of the "web" consisting of a nexus of discourses (181). Even what seems most private, sexual desire, is not isolated as a property of her own corporeal experience but is conjoined with race, culture, and family. For example, Moraga's erotic preference for women constitutes a betrayal of Mexican culture, which always privileges the male: "The Chicana's sexual commitment to the Chicano male... is proof of her fidelity to her people"; "You are a traitor to your race if you do not put the man first"; "I... betray my race by choosing my sexuality which excludes all men, and therefore most dangerously, Chicano men" (178, 177, 184). Mexican historical myth also weighs heavily on her individual sexual choices: being lesbian puts her in the position of La Malinche, using sexuality to betray the race.[8] Thus sexuality, she says, can be understood only in a "culturally-specific context" (189). The way that Moraga names her own sexuality—"my/our racial/sexual identity" (175)—says it all. Even something so personal as sexual desire can be understood only as it is spliced with race. And "my" must be spliced with "our"; the "I" cannot be extracted from the cultural context in which it is embedded.

This is the Lacanian symbolic, although Lacan says it differently: the signifier "I" situates the subject within a structure of sociocultural signifiers that governs the subject's relation to others. Or, as Shoshana Felman puts it, "Language... articulates a pre-established sociocultural system governed by a Law that structures relationships and into which [the subject's] own relations must be inscribed" (124). Although Moraga describes her experience and her culture in a more intimate and familiar discourse, she subscribes to this view, referring elements of her personal affective life always to the symbolic laws that govern her culture—or, as she says, to "the specific cultural contexts that have shaped her" (188).

What is the effect on cross-cultural identification? How does an Anglo reader like me process Moraga's symbolic orientation? How does the overriding symbolic element shape reader identification?

Contemplating Moraga's cultural interpretation of her mother's behavior leads me to rethink my mother's betrayal. Although my first response protests absolute difference—"Well, my mother was a traitor to me, period"—Moraga's symbolic orientation begins to shift my attitude toward the memory of my own mother's failure of love. As Moraga locates family relations within the boxed structures of male dominance—a male-dominant family structure within the larger male-dominant

Mexican culture—I am led to think of my mother's rejection in similar structural terms. My mother, too, was putting my brother first within a larger cultural structure where the male is valued over the female. To put it in Lacanian terminology, Moraga influences me to think of personal relations as the relations of signifier to signifier (or subject to subject) within a signifying structure that governs them both. And that symbolic way of thinking tempers my rage against my mother, so that it begins to shift from a dual relation—I hate her, I love her—to a more mediated view of mother, son, and daughter as they figure within a larger relational structure.

The nature of my identification with Moraga changes, too: having located myself in a family structure similar to hers, I experience not so much the initial totalizing identification with her individual rage and resentment—"I feel exactly the same as you"—as an identification with her position: that of daughter in a male-dominant family structure. This is a symbolic identification—not between two individuals, but between two positions in a symbolic organization, "not accomplished by resemblance (projective identity) but by a parallel position in a structure" (Felman 116).[9] Yet the partial identification is useful to communication between women whose cultural backgrounds differ. Identifying with Moraga as underloved daughter, being "in" the text of her family experience—or at least in the entry hall—I am more apt to be engaged, more inclined to be open to what she says about her experience, than if her story seemed completely foreign to me. I am still alert to differences, though, in part because bumping up against the actuality of what it means to be a woman in Mexican/Chicano culture throws me out of the comfortable place of identification.

The Benefits of Pluralism: Standpoint Theory, Discourse Ethics, and Partial Identification

Epistemologists Sandra Harding and Paula Moya develop standpoint theory in a direction relevant to the dialogic shift in perspective I have just described. According to standpoint theory, social location determines what one knows: persons in different class, race, gender, sexuality, and nation positions have different understandings of reality. Further, standpoint theory holds that more reliable understandings of reality can be generated from the positions of oppressed people: they do not have the stake that dominant persons do in maintaining a status quo supported by the reigning ideology; and in order to survive they have to be able to understand the worldview of the dominants who control things as well as the knowledge generated by their own experience of the world; they therefore have access to a broader vision of social reality (Hartsock 232).

One might predict, starting from this premise, that feminist standpoint epistemologists would conclude that one is imprisoned in the understanding of the world determined by one's social position—and, as a corollary, that an unbridgeable gap exists between the knowledge of one in a dominant position and one in a marginalized position.[10] But Harding reasons, on the contrary, that someone in a dominant position can recognize that the knowledge generated by persons in oppressed positions comes closer to an accurate view of the way things work and therefore choose to base her own analysis on a theoretical framework produced from the other's marginalized standpoint (see Harding, 287). And one can use the insights gained from adopting the other's theoretical perspective to undermine the system that gives one privilege in the first place. For example, one can become an antiracist thinker even if one begins from a privileged white middle-class woman's position.

Paula Moya's recent development of standpoint epistemology toward what she calls "post-positivist realism" indirectly describes the way that such a close acquaintance with one another's standpoints can refine community members' grasp of political realities (Moya, "Chicana" 445). And because some standpoints work better as explanations of the world than others, exposure to the other's standpoint can "reveal the contradictions and mystifications with which members of those societies live" (Moya, "Chicana" 468).

Political philosopher Seyla Benhabib takes up this notion of the enrichment in collective knowledge that derives from a multiplicity of perspectives and applies it to community decision making. Benhabib maintains that members of a community need to "reverse perspectives" and "judge from the point of view of the other(s)" before reaching judgment on an issue (32). A community's first task is to establish a discursive space in which I listen to what you say, "I know how to understand your point of view, [and I] learn to represent to myself the world and the other as you see them" (52).

So far, my thinking about the benefits of cross-race dialogue resembles the concepts developed by Harding, Moya, and Benhabib. My partial identification with Moraga illustrates, as do their theories, the stimulus toward individual change and the enlargement of knowledge produced by the diversity of perspectives in a pluralist community. Occupying Moraga's standpoint as I interact with her narrative, I get a new, more inclusive view of my own standpoint. I begin to conceptualize my own subjectivity in the structural way that Moraga sees herself—as a node in a "web" constituted by the intersection of multiple discourses: not just "woman," but raced, classed, heterosexualized woman. It may well be painful to surrender the definition of myself as, simply, "woman"—one of the oppressed, one of the guiltless—in order to acknowledge my standpoint as raced: for in a racially stratified field of women I figure as a dominant, no longer innocent but occupying a position of privilege supported by the oppression of others. But viewing social realities from Moraga's standpoint during the course of my reading pressures me to do so. As Harding and Moya suggest, it is the opportunity to look at my own standpoint through the lens of the marginalized subject that enables me to see more clearly "the contradictions and mystifications" of my standpoint—among them a blindness to class and race that is a privilege of whiteness and that protects white women from an accurate knowledge of the power relations in which they participate.

What then would a psychoanalytic perspective add to feminist standpoint theory and discourse ethics? I would say, first, an increased insistence on the necessity for instituting formal discourse procedures and specific protocols to foreground symbolic processes at the expense of imaginary ones. Second, someone with a psychoanalytic background might also feel a higher degree of anxiety about the potential for appropriation in "thinking in the other's place" (Benhabib 168, 133).

Cultural Assimilation, Difference, and the Real

Both Benhabib and Harding conceptualize the act of thinking from the other's standpoint as a purely cognitive act and so discount its potential for identification and assimilation (Benhabib 168; Harding 294–95). But even at the level of the intellect, is there not a risk of assimilation? When I incorporate the other's theoretical standpoint is there not a danger of my co-opting it, subordinating it to the premises of my own conceptual schemas, even warping it into a support for my belief system—so that it is distorted beyond recognition? To acknowledge, respect, and protect difference, some reminder that "social differences by their nature are not entirely comprehensible" may be necessary (Sommer 27).[11] Under the rubric of the real, I will discuss one way that subjects of marginalized cultures have set limits on being known and have resisted appropriation.

The real is the most difficult of Lacan's registers to turn to political uses because it falls outside social discourse by definition. The Lacanian real is not the material world; what we perceive as "reality" is structured by the symbolic order. Rather, the Lacanian real encompasses that which is excluded from the symbolic order. It is there in the world. But it resists signification: it cannot be understood. The appearance of the real throws the subject's reality into confusion because the symbolic structures that the subject relies on to make sense of the world no longer work to generate meaning.

I want to argue that certain long passages in Spanish in Gloria Anzaldúa's autobiographical/cultural text, *Borderlands/La Frontera*, create the effect of the real on a non-Latina reader. As I, a monolingual English speaker, read Anzaldúa's text, I am usually able to process the interspersion of Spanish among the English words because the Spanish is sometimes translated and always minimal compared to the islands of English where I am at home. And my readerly pride is gratified by my seizing Anzaldúa's point that I am being asked to occupy the position of the border subject Anzaldúa's text describes—called on to code switch at a moment's notice, to move back and forth across a linguistic border. But certain passages entirely in Spanish resist me. These passages tend to be long and to employ complex Spanish syntax, so there is no island of English where the reader can find respite for a moment. I argue that to a non–Spanish speaker these passages function as the real: they are there on the page, but they remain opaque to meaning; they resist absolutely integration into a monolingual English speaker's symbolic system.

Strictly speaking, the Lacanian real is always outside the linguistic. Nonetheless, I would argue, these dense Spanish passages produce effects of the real on a monolingual English reader. To encounter a lengthy passage in untranslated Spanish is to encounter a sudden failure, a sudden break in the reader's symbolic system. Something is there, a concrete presence, but to an English-only speaker it is immutable into signifiers, outside the symbolic structures of cognition. There, inert, it blocks the reader's symbolic progress; it is, like the real, "the rock upon which every attempt at symbolization fails" (Žižek, *Sublime* 169). (Of course these passages constitute an impediment only for a monolingual

English speaker; for a Spanish reader, they participate in the smooth circulation of the symbolic.)[12]

What Anzaldúa describes in the longest of these passages (43–44, 72) is an experience that a Western frame of reference would classify as madness: for days she remained closed up in her room, scratching her face and tearing out her hair. But Anzaldúa wishes to understand her despair within a pre-Columbian cosmic scheme where madness is a sign of being in the grip of Coatlicue. In the second passage, it becomes clear that the state of being "consumed" by Coatlicue is not one of despairing madness only, but of creative ferment also. In previous passages in English, Anzaldúa has informed us that Coatlicue ("Serpent Skirt") is a pre-Aztec "goddess of birth and death . . . she gives and takes away life" (46); "before the change to male dominance, Coatlicue . . . contained and balanced the dualities of male and female, light and dark, life and death" (32). She is thus "a symbol of the fusion of opposites (47)." The form of Anzaldúa's address to the goddess—*musa bruha* (Muse/Witch)—indicates how inextricable are the malevolence and the beneficence of Coatlicue, how intertwined her destructive and creative aspects. It becomes clear that the way down is also the way up, that to be pulled down into the underworld where madness, chaos, and Coatlicue reign is to find inspirations to bring up into the light. A Western perspective would tend to sort into binaries the factors that are established in the Spanish as indivisible; the positive and the negative, dark and light, despairing madness and joyous creativity. Anzaldúa's use of Spanish can be read as a means of protecting her cultural standpoint, and with it her most intimate spiritual experiences, from assimilation to the binary logic of a Western reader's thought.[13]

One advantage of this interpretation is that it turns an awareness of the real into an ethical act: if a reader becomes sensitized through impenetrable passages such as these to what remains forever beyond her ken in the experience of a woman with a different cultural formation, she may learn to respect the limits of both knowledge and identification. The implicit message of the Spanish, "You cannot know this," has a double valence. It is an empirical statement: You *cannot* know this—for cultural barriers prevent complete understanding. And it constitutes an ethical directive: You may not (must not) know this, because to know would be to appropriate and deform my experience, to reduce it to Western categories of thinking. What I am calling "the real" in Anzaldúa's discourse teaches a humble admission of the limitations on knowing an other.

In multicultural community, I would say that distancing strategies similar to Anzaldúa's refusal to reveal all to curious Anglo eyes could baffle the drive toward the assimilation of difference. A woman who belongs to a marginalized culture might for example respond to a probing question with silence, or an oblique response, or an answer that does not answer, or even some explicit statement of withholding like Rigoberta Menchú's recurring refusal, both in her writing and in her personal appearances, to let herself be known: "I'm still keeping my Indian identity a secret. I'm still keeping secret what I think no-one should know" (247; see also Sommer 119–20). Or take Patricia Hill Collins's seeming rebuke to those who would borrow an African-American standpoint: "Living life as an African-American woman is a necessary prerequisite for producing black feminist thought because within black women's communities thought is validated and produced with reference to a particular set of historical, material, and epistemological conditions" ("The Social" 539). In the present context, the statement can be read as a check on white feminist enthusiasm for borrowing the marginalized other's framework—not so much a total shutout of white feminist standpoint critics as a defense against appropriation, a healthy reminder that occupying the other's theoretical standpoint has its own built-in limitations, that historical and material conditions create epistemological differences that have to be respected.

As Diana Fuss states a central dilemma of multicultural community: "How can the other be brought into the domain of the knowable without annihilating the other as other—as precisely that which cannot be known?" (4).[14] Acts of knowing have their own tendencies toward assimilation. Our best effort to "know" the other's experience or the other's point of view places us on the inescapable ground of all our knowing: integrating the new into cognitive structures established by our own prior experience. Some forcible reminder that cultural difference is ultimately unknowable can provide the necessary complement to Harding's and Benhabib's notion of adopting the other's perspective.

IDENTIFICATION AND DIFFERENCE IN COMMUNITY:
USES OF THE REAL AND THE SYMBOLIC

I do not intend to debunk the possibility of thinking through the other's perspective. The hope for multicultural feminist community implicit in Benhabib's, Harding's, and Moya's theories and in my parable of a partial identification with Moraga is that adopting the other's analytic perspective and way of knowing would not only increase one's knowledge of social realities but also establish enough mutual understanding so that the group could work together effectively toward a common end. It would surely be useful to forging a common purpose in a cross-race alliance if its members could understand each other to a degree—and identify with one another to the extent of being able to perceive things from the other's standpoint. The trick is to put into practice the idea of identifying and understanding "to a degree."

It is not only interpersonal identification that tends toward totalization: the desire for an imaginary unity characterizes communities as well as individuals, and with a similar result—the suppression of difference. In "The Ideal of Community and the Politics of Difference," Iris Marion Young uncovers the workings of a drive to identify at the level of the group. Young reviews the writings of communitarian theorists and reports her own observations of specific feminist groups; she finds that both theorists and practicians cherish an ideal of unity and mutuality. In Michael Sandel's model of community, for instance, the claim is that individual identities will be constituted by the social practices, understandings, and goals of the community; because they are produced by a shared social vision, community members will mutually understand and affirm one another (Sandel 62–63, 173; qtd. in Young 305). Carol Gould, building on Marx's vision of a future society, similarly describes a community of subjects who, because they realize they all belong equally to a common species being, internalize an ideal of intersubjectivity such that each individual forms part of a communal subject; the notion of the other as an opaque external being disappears. The desire for identification here takes the form of a conviction that it is possible to form a community of others who understand each other as they understand themselves. But persons can be transparent to each other only if they are exactly alike—so this insistence on complete reciprocal understanding erases difference.

Young finds the same erasure of difference in the feminist groups she observed. The insistence on solidarity—on mutual identification and affirmation—outlaws disagreement and difference, which are "interpreted as a breach of sisterhood, the destruction of community" ("The Ideal" 311). The result is that difference is excluded: first, members of the group suppress their differences in order to express solidarity; and second, those who cannot identify with the others feel excluded (and, presumably, become disaffected and go away).

The threat to pluralism is clear. Given an ethos of solidarity (a social version of identification) groups quickly become homogeneous. In my description of a "dialogue" with Moraga, I have been implicitly arguing for the benefits of pluralism—to the individual and to the group. Each member of a community has a partial perspective on the world, conditioned and limited by her particular social location. My view of reality is ideologically skewed, as is yours; but since the ideology differs according to our social positions, a dialectical exchange of views between us has the potential to illuminate blind spots in both visions of the world. As long as everyone's "truth claims are understood in a realist way as fallible and subject to . . . revision," they can all "contribute dialectically to the development of reliable knowledge about the world," as Moya says ("Chicana" 445).[15] We are not stuck: learning from each other, we can revise our standpoints and move through "successive approximations to truth" ("Chicana" 477). And the more perspectives brought to bear on a particular issue, the richer will be the community's practical wisdom (Benhabib 137; Young, "Polity" 414). But it is specifically the *expression* of diverse perspectives that enriches a community's collective understanding of social realities. Enabling all voices to be heard requires conscious efforts to correct for unconscious tendencies, in both the individual and the group, to reduce difference to the same.

Endorsing Lacan's claim that the symbolic supplies at least a partial corrective to the imaginary tendency to appropriate the other's image to one's own purposes as I do, I would support Benhabib's contention that the first imperative for a feminist community is to institute a discursive space that enables the "concrete other" to speak. For, as she says, "neither the concreteness nor the otherness of the 'concrete other' can be known in the absence of the voice of the other" (168). But, with Nancy Fraser and Iris Marion Young, I would add that it is not just the freedom to speak that requires a guarantee: to have an equal voice, one must also be able to get an equal hearing. There is no more ardent advocate of "coming to voice" than bell hooks, yet what she emphasizes is the difficulty of being heard: "Our speech was often the soliloquy, the talking into thin air, the talking to ears that do not hear you"; "for black women, our struggle has not been to emerge from silence into speech but to change the nature and direction of our speech, to make a speech that compels listeners, one that is heard" (*Talking Back* 6). Credibility is differentially distributed along the lines of power relations, resting on unexamined beliefs that certain kinds of people and certain styles of speaking have authority and command respect while others do not. So specific discursive protocols and structures are necessary to give weight to the speech of community members who do not belong to the dominant group. (See Jodi Dean; Fraser; Young, *Justice* and "Polity".)[16]

Yet although "principles, institutions, and procedures to enable the articulation of the voice of 'others'" are necessary (Benhabib 168), they may not always be sufficient to guarantee a fair hearing to all. Community discourses have a way of developing outside of institutional structures and exerting a powerful normalizing pressure on individuals' values and ways of thinking. Patricia Hill Collins describes a situation in which a shared discourse silences difference; her discussion prompts me to defend the value of disruptions—even rude breaks, or "fighting words"—in the accepted discourse of the community as a means to better communication. I will discuss two kinds of disruption that I claim carry the shock value of the real.

Collins points out that academic discourse often includes ideas that seem demeaning to people of color. These propositions have been taken for granted so long that they are more or less invisible to the academics using them. Although African-American women may experience subtle racialized assumptions as "fighting words," they often choose to remain silent rather than provoke a racist battle. "Rather than respond to each incident [of racist speech] the women chose to adapt to the acts of everyday racism and rarely talked back or complained" (*Fighting* 85–86). In Mari Matsuda's words, black women in this situation chose to "internalize the harm rather than escalating the conflict" (2355; qtd. in Collins, *Fighting* 85). Silent acquiescence does not always signal agreement, then—but it may seem to the dominant group that it does. Under these circumstances, where marginalized members swallow a discourse they find offensive and dominants assume from their silence that they are in agreement, genuine dialogue based on mutual trust is not a possibility. Nor is the articulation of difference.

If on the other hand a woman of color were to protest, even angrily, at some covert verbal violence that remains hidden to the speaker but is perfectly obvious to her, such an opening toward genuine dialogue would be healthy and should therefore be welcome to all. But the original speaker, intending no offense and blind to the offensive assumption underlying her discourse, might well experience such a protest as, precisely, "fighting words."

June Jordan articulates the grounds for such an outburst. Referring to her participation in cross-race alliances, Jordan says, "If you make my life horrible then, when I can tell the truth, it will be a horrible truth; it will not sound good or look good or (God willing) feel good to you, either" ("Civil Wars" 180). Politeness is meant to make everyone feel comfortable. As I understand her words, Jordan is implying that if she were to make the white members of the group feel good—about themselves and their relations with women of color—that would be counterproductive because they would feel less urgency about changing the racist structures from which they benefit and people of color suffer. Sometimes, Jordan suggests, politeness is inappropriate.

Explosions through the polite surface of community relations such as June Jordan describes clearly break up a discourse of solidarity by emphatically reminding people of their differences. That kind of reminder disrupts cross-race identification and assumptions of complete mutual understanding.

I want to argue that such a rupture of the "civility" defined as such by community practice can have a shock effect akin to that of the real. When the real emerges in our everyday world, Lacan says, it throws our sense of reality into confusion because we habitually perceive the world around us through the scrim of the symbolic categories that organize our thinking, and the real is by definition that which eludes the symbolic. The real disrupts the subject's symbolic universe. The community equivalent of the individual's symbolic universe is the group's prevailing discourse—including its modes of speaking and thinking, its shared assumptions, its practices. From the perspective of most community members, a startling breach of friendly politeness such as Jordan describes might well seem like the real: a break in the shared symbolic system of the group through which appears some radical outside—something unacceptable, unassimilable.

And "unassimilable" is just the point: some rupture of the shared assumptions—and the assumption of sharing—in a community may be necessary to break the communal drive toward the assimilation of difference detected by Young. And the real in the same political sense of a rift in the prevailing discourse could also take the form of *not* talking, as in the withholdings of information I have suggested by analogy with the impenetrable wall of Anzaldúa's solid Spanish passages. I have argued that in a multicultural community various similar strategies—a silence, an oblique response, an open rebuff to the interlocutor's curiosity—could block the drive to know on the part of dominants. In offering an effective resistance to cultural assimilation, these various strategies of bafflement function like the real: they inform the dominant subject of the incomplete nature of her symbolic world, of a reality outside her culture's meaning structure. I want to argue here that such resistances function as the real in disrupting the discourse of solidarity as well: they break with the faith in complete reciprocal understanding that Young describes as a buttress to solidarity.

It may seem counterintuitive to embrace the "cold shoulder"—either the turn away from mutual understanding or the rupture of decorum—as constitutive of community.[17] But such a forcible reminder of difference may be necessary to disrupt a community's movement toward unity at the expense of difference. That drive toward unity would erase the benefits of pluralism, including the dialectic between different cultural perspectives I have been describing. As Chantal Mouffe maintains, the acceptance of pluralism *is* the acceptance of conflict (Worsham and Olson 176).[18] And acceptance is the operative word here: in order to allow the conversation to continue—and that is surely the main thing—a community would need to accept the idea that such moments of breach and disruption are necessary in order to ensure better overall communication and to enable an authentic multivoiced community to emerge.

Politicizing Lack: Moving from Imaginary Identification to Political Action

Because the impulse to idealize and identify with the other (racialized) woman is largely unconscious and so largely uncontrollable, it would likely survive such fixes from the symbolic and the real. It seems likely that in a multiracial community the tendency to idealize difference will continue. Is there a way to utilize imaginary identification itself in the service of political action? I will discuss two strategies for doing so: the first centers on transforming the energy of imaginary identification directly into political energy; the second posits a move toward the symbolic initiated by a recognition of the other's lack. Both solutions turn on Lacan's concept of lack.

Bell hooks's essay, "Eating the Other," is primarily a critique of white appropriations of black culture which, as her title suggests, leave no trace of the original behind: they "decontextualize" black cultural forms and erase their history (31). But her perspective on race relations is large enough to encompass a hope for the potential politicization of white desires for participation in black "being": "we can begin to conceptualize and identify ways that desire informs our political choices and affiliations" ("Eating" 39). Hooks speaks with approval of Traci's identification with black culture in the movie, *Hairspray*. Traci says, "I wish I was dark-skinned" and her boyfriend, Link, replies, "Traci, our souls are black even though our skins are white" (qtd. in hooks, "Eating" 36–37). Traci and Link would seem, then, to be idealizing and identifying with the other as a monolithic racialized identity. But although hooks has throughout the essay been critical of white "primitivism"—of the identificatory use of the black body coded as wild, sensual, and erotic to recharge a vitiated white subjectivity—she makes an exception for Traci and Link. "Their recognition of the particular pleasures and sorrows black folks experience does not lead to cultural appropriation but to an appreciation that extends into the realm of the political—Traci dares to support racial integration" ("Eating" 37). Traci meets with hooks's approval because rather than consuming black culture as a kind of vitality additive leaving no trace, Traci's identification with black culture becomes politicized. She identifies with the issues of African Americans, in a kind of heteropathic identification with their position that yet does not leave the self behind—for she "is concerned about her freedom and sees her liberation linked to black liberation and an effort to end racist domination" ("Eating" 37). (Indeed, the film graphically links white women's freedom with black liberation when Traci's white friend Penny is imprisoned, literally, by white racism.) The key to hook's approbation is: Traci acts. Having connected with black issues, she joins the African Americans in social protest aimed at overturning segregation.

What Traci does is perceive what black people lack—equal access and equal opportunity—identify that lack with her own, and thus broaden the sphere of personal concern to embrace others' issues. In hooks's words, "Traci shifts her positionality to stand in solidarity with black people" ("Eating" 37). She makes a "heteropathic identification," in Scheler's sense. What transforms Traci's imaginary infatuation with black people into political energy is the full realization of what black people lack.

Lacan's work suggests a similar way out of imaginary identification and idealization. In Lacan's thought, the subject is constituted by lack. And lack, as I have said, is what propels imaginary identification and idealization: one attributes to the other the fullness of being that is absent in oneself and strives to acquire that fullness of being through identification. To arrest the process, one would have to recognize, accept, and own one's lack. And one comes to that recognition, Lacan says, by accepting the fact that the idealized other with whom one identifies is also lacking. For example, the structure of psychoanalysis produces the analysand's imaginary identification with the analyst, who is idealized as "the subject presumed to know." To "cross the plane of identification," to deidealize the analyst, the patient has to be brought to acknowledge the "desire of the analyst" (S XI 273, 274). That is tantamount to recognizing the lack in the other. For lack and desire are coterminous in Lacan: simply put, one is a subject of desire because one is lacking; desire forever seeks the elusive thing that will fill up the gap in being. To be confronted with the fact that the idealized other has desires and is therefore lacking is to realize that no one is whole and self-sufficient, so it is impossible to achieve even a temporary respite from one's lacks through identifying with the other's wholeness. One has to accept one's own lack as irremediable.

To anchor the Lacanian concept of lack in cross-race politics: as the black feminists I cite in chapter 4 suggest, white idealizing fantasies cover over the material lacks in the lives of people of color. For instance, Ann duCille criticizes white writers for "tak[ing] symbolic wealth from the . . . romanticized black body but retain[ing] the luxury of ignoring its material poverty" (110). But idealization represents only the extreme case of a problem that women of color find, and have always found, endemic to white mainstream feminism. Historian Benita Roth shows that in the liberation movements of the 1970s, "Black feminists argued that white women's liberation's neglect of economic survival issues were time and time again the main stumbling block to joint work with white women on feminist issues" (76). Aida Hurtado maintains that today it is in large part because "other women's lived experience has not been central to the development of [white] feminist theorizing" that young Chicana feminists, for example, turn away from U.S. mainstream feminism (268); they fail to see any connection to the concrete situations of their lives in a "feminist agenda that avoids class issues" (311). Judging from this critique, constructing an effective integrated feminism depends on white women grasping in some immediate way the urgency of issues—and particularly "economic survival issues"— important to women of color. These feminists of color seem to be pointing white feminists in a direction similar to Lacan's—toward asking, What do women of color lack? And what do they desire?

The impetus for Traci beginning to ask such questions comes from her participation in a community with African Americans based on a shared activity—dance. It is everyday proximity to African–American people that shifts Traci's attitude from a global idealization of black culture to an action-oriented concern for what black people themselves lack and desire. I want to argue that participation in an ongoing multicultural community can similarly supply correctives to white ignorance of other women's concrete material conditions and provide the ground for a new and different feminist solidarity based on issues meaningful to women of color.

I have been writing about multicultural community as if it were an unproblematic notion, but in fact the ideal of multicultural community is often dismissed in contemporary academic circles as naive, idealistic, and outdated. Cross-race alliances are envisioned for the most part as temporary coalitions organized around a single political issue and destined to dissolution; and a preferred strategy for effecting social change is a shifting politics of identity like Chela Sandoval's "differential consciousness," where participants maintain fluid allegiances and move frequently between different sites of resistance to oppression (15; 59).[19]

I want to argue here, with Cynthia Franklin, that a "transformative politics" can emerge from multicultural community as well as the other way around (5). I have offered my simulated dialogue with Moraga as an example of the kind of interracial exchange between community members that can change the perspective of a white feminist. Moraga's narrative is thus persuasive and transformative because her articulation of oppression is grounded always in her "lived experience"—of her relationship to a particular mother and brother, of her particular sexual choices and their collision with her culture's values.[20] Such an exchange of personal information can effectively fill in the gap that women of color find in white feminists' grasp of their material realities. And I would argue that women from different racial/cultural groups are more likely to invest energy and time in such cross-race conversations if they know they will be continuing to live and/or work together for an extended period of time. A self-revealing conversation like the "dialogue" with Moraga is unlikely to take place unless trust has been built up over time. To state the obvious, trust cannot be taken as a given between women of racial groupings formed by centuries of slavery, land theft, and racism. In my experience at a small college with a racially diverse faculty and student body, it is the continuity of relations over time that creates trust: the repetition of casual and serendipitous conversations between faculty members from different racial and cultural backgrounds—on stair landings, beside mailboxes, on the way to adjacent offices—builds trust gradually. Over time, conversations that go beyond work-related concerns to an exchange of personal experience become possible and can lead to a more immediate understanding of each other's "lived experience"—including the material conditions that attach to being a woman of color in the United States and the daily toll of affronts and injuries inflicted by racism.

In addition to effecting a Lacanian cure for white idealizations that erase the lacks in the lives of women of color, in addition to satisfying the critique that white feminists ignore the concrete realities of being a woman of color in the United States, such a shift in the social perspective of white feminists can lead to more effective political action. For example, my response to Moraga's analysis of her personal experience does not necessarily end with a shift of perspective, with a new understanding of my own standpoint. The pressure to notice that race and class are part of my gender position is simultaneously a pressure to take responsibility for both the privileged position itself and the racial oppression that supports it—and, ultimately, a pressure to *do* something: for example, to use my new insights to undermine the system that grants me privilege in the first place and to work toward a more equitable distribution of power and resources. I would suggest that cross-race dialogues in an ongoing community could likewise politicize its members.

A political alliance to combat racial injustice is more likely to hold and to be effective if the allies can trust in one another's grasp of the concrete realities of living in a racist society. And women have a better chance of learning about the specifics of each other's everyday experience when they participate in an ongoing community than they would if the alliance were known to be strictly strategic and temporary. As a group of Boston black and white feminists write, "We need both a political understanding of racism and a personal-political understanding of how it affects our daily lives.... You simply cannot do political action without personal interaction" (Cross et al. 11; qtd. in Breines 1122–23).[21] I would add that the continuity of affectional ties and emotional support afforded by community can sustain a prolonged political action in the face of prolonged discouragement.

To give politics a Lacanian turn: we can start by listening to what feminists of color say they lack and say they desire. It is not as if feminists of color have concealed this information. Audre Lorde, for example, speaks directly to white feminists when she says, "Some problems we share as women, some we do not. You fear your children will grow up to join the patriarchy and testify against you, we fear our children will be dragged from a car and shot down in the street, and you will turn your back upon the reasons they are dying" (Lorde 119). Lorde here clearly articulates the difference in power and position between white and black women and clearly states what people of color lack: social justice. And bell hooks voices what some black feminists desire: only when white feminists "actively struggle to resist racist oppression" will there be "a foundation for the experience of political solidarity between white women and women of color" (*Feminist Theory* 55).

The kind of solidarity that hooks is evoking—as in the essay on *Hairspray*—is quite different from the pressure toward collective merger that Young detects in communities, and especially in feminist communities. Here solidarity means, in Sonia Kruk's words, "support for other women where one's own immediate well-being is not at issue" (151). The shift in definition pivots on a shift from imaginary to symbolic, from a vision of the other as the desired mirror of the self made whole to a focus on what the other lacks, and *says* she lacks. Antiracism based on the all-too-real lack of social justice could provide a more solid grounding for cross-race feminist solidarity than the imaginary yearning for identification.

Appendix

The Challenges of Infant Research and Neurobiology to Traditional Models of Primary Identification

Freud described identification as primary in human life: that is, the baby's first tie to the other is one of identification, rather than love (*Group* 105–07). The findings of infant research, based on laboratory observations of mother-infant interactions, pose a formidable challenge to the theory of primary identification, citing empirical evidence to show that a baby has an emergent sense of self as distinct from the other almost from birth and disputing the notion of identification between parent and child. In this appendix I explore the question of whether primary identification—a fusion or confusion of self and other in infancy—might still be a valid concept if one accepted the paradigm of mother-infant relations that emerges from infant research.

The issue is of obvious importance to this book, as the foregoing chapters are based on the premise that the desire for identification founds many affective relational structures. Freud's idea that identification occurs early helps to explain the primitive intensity of the desire to be the other which, in moments of envy, idealization and primary identification, overrides the rational awareness that one cannot be the other. More broadly, theories of parent-infant relations are important because psychoanalytic models, filtering down through cultural representations into everyday consciousness, inform not only our notions of correct child-raising procedures, but also our models of subjectivity and of social relations. In the Freudian model, the infant wants to be the parent, and because it processes experience in an oral mode, it imagines becoming the parent through eating him or her. Relations of self and other begin, then, in ambivalence: I love you and so want to be you; I want to be you, so I destroy you in order to take your place. The prospects for peaceable human relations appear to be negligible, if one's primary impulse is to reduce the other to the same or to appropriate the other's difference to oneself. Given this foundation, the possibility of a relation to the other that recognizes the other's separate and complex subjectivity seems unlikely. Infant research's observations of mothers and infants suggest a more positive basis for social relations. According to Daniel Stern, the baby is born with a bias for discriminating between the actions that it authors and the actions that come from another— with a bias, then, for discriminating self from other. Beatrice Beebe and Frank Lachmann study facial and vocalizing games between mother and child which lay down internal patterns of "mutual interlocking responsivity" (Beebe, "Mother-Infant" 39, 43). The paradigm emerging from infant research would predict the possibility for adult relations between self and other based on mutual recognition. So the prognosis for social relations is radically different from the Freudian model. I argue, however, that infant research tends to overlook the role of fantasy in human life and so to ignore the basis for relational structures that are not so positive, such as envy and idealization.

What I propose to do here is not to refute the findings of infant research, but to consider how primary identification might figure in a baby's psychic processes if one adopted the infant research model of a development that proceeds not through internalization but through the infant's integration of repeated daily experiences of self and other.

THE HISTORICAL DEBATE ON INFANCY: DOES PRIMARY IDENTIFICATION EXIST?

The paradigm of primary identification described by Freud in *Group Psychology* was taken up by W. R. D. Fairbairn and Margaret Mahler in the 1940s and 1950s, and under the name of symbiosis became so embedded in psychoanalytic thinking that Nancy Chodorow, summing up object relations theory in 1978, could write with perfect assurance: "Analysts call this aspect of the earliest period of life primary identification, aptly emphasizing the infant's object cathexis of someone it does not yet differentiate from itself.... [the infant] experiences itself as within a common boundary and fused, physically and psychologically, with its mother" (61–62). Margaret Mahler is the principal authority for Chodorow's description of the infant's prolonged primary identification. And it is against Mahler's notion of symbiosis that Daniel Stern is writing in *The Interpersonal World of the Infant* (1985). Mahler claimed that the infant between two and seven months "behaves and functions as though he and his mother were an omnipotent system—a dual unity within one common boundary" (Mahler 78). Apparently targeting Mahler's thesis, Stern strongly states: "There is no symbiotic-like phase"; "There is no confusion between self and other in the beginning or at any point during infancy" (*Interpersonal* 10). Rather, children come into the world prewired to sort out self from other: "the infant's first order of business . . . is to form the sense of a core self and core others, . . . [a task] largely accomplished during the period between two and seven months" (*Interpersonal* 70).

What is "primary" in Stern's model is a capacity for self-organizing experiences. The baby locates a sense of self over time by perceiving the invariants in its experience that demonstrate the existence of a continuous active and feeling self. For example, the baby notices that when its eyes shut it gets dark; it learns to recognize the intention (shut your eyes), the physical sensation of shutting the eyes, and the effect (when you shut your eyes it gets dark). By recognizing itself as author of its acts, the baby quickly (at 2–4 months) arrives at a sense of agency, together with a sense of a self that "goes on being," that has continuity over time.

This emergent self is, however, always in relationship. "[The] infant's life is so thoroughly social that most of the things the infant does, feels, and perceives occur in different kinds of relationships" (*Interpersonal* 118). But these relationships are—emphatically—not identificatory: "These important social experiences are neither primary nor secondary mergers. They are simply the actual experience of being with someone (a self-regulatory other) such that self-feelings are importantly changed" (*Interpersonal* 105).

Stern's theory, and the infant research it is based on, stress the reciprocity of infant-mother relations and thus credit the infant with a measure of agency and control. Infant research focuses on the baby as well as the mother *doing* things—making faces at each other, or building up a structure of vocal echoing. "When watching the gazing patterns of mother and infant during this life period," Stern remarks, "one is watching two people with almost equal facility and control over the same social behavior" (*Interpersonal* 21).

What happens to the desire for identification in such a model of infancy? Psychoanalytic theorists have traditionally located the desire for primary identification in the discrepancy between a baby who is passive and powerless and a parent who is active and effective, able to regulate the baby's emotional and physical state. Freud emphasized the infant's primal helplessness by referring again and again to the immaturity of the newborn, coming into the world "prematurely," "unfinished" relative to the young of other mammals (*Inhibitions* 154–55). Otto Fenichel summarizes Freud's insights on infancy thus: "The human infant is born more helpless than other mammals. He cannot live if he is not cared for. Innumerable stimuli pour out upon him which he cannot master. He is not in a position to move voluntarily and is not able to differentiate the encroaching stimuli. He knows no object world and has no ability yet to 'bind' tension" (34). W. R. D. Fairbairn understood this helplessness as the motivation for primary identification: "The inclination to merge with the mother derives from the infant's total and unconditional helplessness and dependency. His survival is contingent upon the mother's presence and ministrations, and he experiences himself either at one with her, or striving to be at one with her" (Fairbairn, *Object-relations*, as paraphrased by Greenberg and Mitchell 160–61).[1]

What becomes of the motivation for primary identification if the baby has a measure of control over itself and its world? In Stern's model, the baby of two months already has at its disposal various forms of self-regulation. For example, through a battery of tactics infants can regulate the level of stimulation they are subject to in mutual gazing with the mother: "They can avert their gaze, shut their eyes, stare past, become glassy-eyed"—all behaviors evidently used "to reject, distance themselves from, or defend themselves against mother" (21). They can also initiate facial communication by "gazing, smiling, and vocalizing" (22). From this evidence, Stern says, "it is difficult not to conclude that they sense their capacity to alter the behavior of the other as well as their own experience" (75). On Stern's model, babies develop very early (at two months) a sense of agency. If the rationale for imputing a desire for identification to the baby rests on the disparity between the neediness of the infant self and the apparently unlimited resources of the parental figure—so that the Freud baby or the Fairbairn baby might well want to "be" the other whose ability to answer its need makes her or him seem omnipotent—the Stern baby's experiences of agency, mutuality, and a degree of control over self and other seem less likely to inspire the desire to incorporate a figure of omnipotence.

THE INFANT RESEARCH MODEL OF EARLY REPRESENTATIONS AND PRIMARY IDENTIFICATION

The infant research theory of psychic development is based on a neuronal model of memory borrowed from contemporary neurobiology, notably from the work of Gerald Edelman (whom Stern often cites.) In Edelman's model, the baby is born with certain basic survival "values," or biases (such as "eating is better than not eating" or "seeing is better than not seeing"), but there are no predesigned programs in the brain. Rather, experience and behavior cause neurons to form neuronal groups, and the repetition of particular activities strengthens the synapses within and between the neuronal groups that correspond to those activities. "Neurons that fire together wire together," to borrow the colloquial phrase; and repeated firings create increasingly strong synaptic connections within and between neuronal groups, making certain pathways stronger, more capable of conducting neural signals. If there are no prewired programs in the brain and no preset instructions for certain mental formations, if neuronal groups form only in response to environmental stimuli, then repeated experiences alone form internal structure. Likewise, in the infant research model of development the baby constructs mental schemas of interactive events that recur with regularity in daily life, such as feeding and play. Over time, the specific schemas of a repeated event are abstracted to a more generalized, prototypical schema of an interactive event. Stern calls these RIGs, "Representations of Interactions that have been Generalized" (*Interpersonal* 97). Infant research emphasizes that it is interpersonal activities, and more specifically the "moment-to-moment interplay [of mother and baby]," that form early mental representations (Beebe and Lachmann, "Representation" 131; see Stern, *Interpersonal* 118). Stern, Beebe, and Lachmann put the capacity for memory at a much earlier age than developmental psychologists—at two or three months rather than the traditional eight to twelve months (Beebe and Lachmann, "Mother-Infant" 139–40; Stern, *Interpersonal* 91–94).

The neuronal model of memory replaces the psychoanalytic notion of internalization as the engine of psychic development. Stern, Beebe, and Lachmann emphatically deny the validity of internalization.

Mental representations, Stern says, "are not formed from external events or persons that have been internalized. They are not put inside from the outside. They are constructed from the inside, from the self-experience of being with another" (*Motherhood* 81). Likewise, Beatrice Beebe and Frank Lachmann maintain that the linear sequence implied by the concept of internalization is no longer meaningful: rather than making what is first an external structure of love and discipline into an internal one, internal organization is built up all the time as an inseparable part of interaction, with the baby contributing its part to the regime of mutual regulation ("Representation" 156). There is no conceptual need, and no conceptual room, for the idea of internalization: "Nothing is taken in" (Stern, *Motherhood* 81).

In disputing the traditional notion of "'taking in the functions of the other'" (Beebe and Lachmann, "Representation" 156), Stern, Beebe, and Lachmann are challenging a conceptual pillar of psychoanalysis—identification. For psychoanalysis has traditionally considered identification as a form of internalization: the other (the object) exists in external reality, and the subject "carrie[s] the object into the inner world," altering "the self along the lines of the object" (Schafer 154). The representation of the self is transformed by internalizing and integrating traits of the other, or the representation of the other as a whole. The baby learns to soothe itself, for example, by means of internalizing the mother and her soothing functions. In the Stern model the maternal figure does not become part of the baby: "representations . . . are not about objects (human or other), nor about images"; rather, they are "constructed from interactive experience with someone" (*Motherhood* 81). There is no experience of the other as an internal object; the sense of a core self is never breached. Thus Stern's insistence on the baby's autonomous sense of self extends to the structure of its memory traces. Just as the baby experiences itself in daily life as separate, face to face with a separate other, so the baby's internal representations are always structured as "I-experience[s] *with* an other" (*Interpersonal* 115).

If I pick up the challenge of infant research by abandoning the idea of internalization and positing an internal world of representations built on repeated interactions with the parent, there may still be a place for primary identification. The two events that I will be tracking—play and hunger/feeding—are candidates for mnemonic representation on the infant research model of memory: each is a dynamic interpersonal event repeated thousands of times—in Stern's words, "a microplot which is characteristic and frequently repeated" (Stern, "Early" 71). So both the self-other pattern of play and the self-other pattern of hunger/feeding will, according to the infant research model, become foundational mental schemas. But these two repeated events will, I argue, represent quite different experiences of self and other.

To paraphrase Michael Eigen, "The Freudian baby and the [Stern] baby are not identical. This doubleness points to the fact that no human baby is one baby. We do not know what to do with this multiplicity, but we are not free to evade it" (Eigen xxiii). Infant researchers, on the one hand, and theorists of primary identification like Mahler, Chodorow, and Borch-Jacobsen, on the other, seem to be describing two different species of baby. But perhaps, as I will argue, the two schools are only addressing different facets of the baby's daily experience. Infant research videotapes the microprocesses of mother and baby at play. It is, rather, hunger followed by feeding, and other processes that lead to physiological state changes, that have served as the chief observational basis for psychoanalysts who follow Freud's lead in positing that an infant "experiences himself either at one with [the mother], or striving to be at one with her" (Greenberg and Mitchell 160–61). Both hunger and play recur in daily life, but each represents a different kind of interaction with the caretaker. In moments of exchanging smiles or cooings with their mothers, infants may indeed experience themselves as equal partners in a game to which both contribute, as Stern says; but in moments of frustrated need, as in hunger or physical discomfort, the cognitive and perceptive capacities that Stern tracks may be overridden by feelings of helplessness. In such states of (perceived) deprivation, infants might well wish to identify with a parental figure—with an other who appears to have the resources necessary to meet all needs and to erase all discomfort. Stern presents persuasive evidence that infants are in possession of cognitive equipment that enables them, early on, to distinguish between self and other, but that does not mean that they always *want* to make that distinction.

The mother-infant games that Stern, Beebe, and Lachmann videotape facilitate self-differentiation. Difference drives these games. In games of facial display, in which mothers and babies from two to six months make faces at each other, it is the difference in the mother's contribution as she elaborates on the baby's facial expression that catches and holds the baby's attention. (Experiments have shown that babies quickly tire of simple mirroring but maintain their attentiveness when divergence is introduced.)² It is the opposite of the desire for "oneness" that founds these games, then: the mother can create something new out of what the baby offers only if she is different. On the other hand, the mother's acknowledgment, through her imitation, of the baby's facial expression recognizes the baby's act, affirming what it has made. Facial and vocal play thus depend on a recognition of difference. According to Stern, it is only at nine months that the baby gives indications of grasping the idea that the other has an internal world and can participate in shared feelings (*Interpersonal* 9, 124–42). But it would seem that the interlocking patterns of response recorded by Stern, Beebe, and Lachmann establish the ground for later dialogues of creative reciprocity and mutual recognition between subjects.

Power and agency appear less symmetrically distributed in moments of hunger and feeding. The child's state is one of distress, and the mother has the power to transform it (or not); agency is on the side of the mother, with need the lot of the infant. Through feeding, the parent can transform hunger pangs into gratification. "A dramatic shift in neurophysiological state is involved" (Stern, *Interpersonal* 103), testifying repeatedly to the parent's power in the face of the baby's helplessness. It is easy to see how the experience of hunger and feeding might give rise to the figure of an omnipotent mother. So there is ample motivation for the baby, driven by feelings of helplessness and depletion, to identify with a mother who possesses (seemingly) illimitable resources. But identifying with the mother would require a leap of fantasy—so there is a prior question to explore. Do babies have fantasies?

Fantasy

Infant researchers tend to overlook the grounds for and effects of fantasy in psychic life. For example, Stern maintains that the baby is attuned to reality at all times and that its early representational structures are created simultaneously with, and as a faithful representation of, actual events—always, of course, interactive events. Take nursing, for instance. The baby will first record a specific episode, consisting of a series of related actions: "being hungry, being positioned at the breast (with accompanying tactile, olfactory, and visual sensations . . .), rooting, opening mouth, beginning to suck, getting milk" (*Interpersonal* 95). As the episodes of nursing repeat, the baby "forms a generalized 'breast-milk' episode"—"an abstraction of many specific memories."

The generalized "breast-milk" episode cannot be said to reflect with accuracy any single experience, since it is "an averaged experience made prototypic" (*Interpersonal* 95–96); but the generalized representation is nonetheless firmly grounded in actual experience. Stern says that schemas record the affects, sensations, and perceptions attached to particular actions, but what *he* records are actions only.

Compare the tone of Stern's description with neo-Freudian Fred Pine's description of nursing: "The post-nursing moments of falling asleep at the mother's breast or in her arms against her body... are likely to be psychological high points of the infant's day.... These moments... look from the outside as though they could be accompanied by merging, melting, boundaryless experiences in the infant" (Pine 18). What Pine includes in the infant's (posited) experience is fantasy, in particular the fantasy of identification: you and I merge into one. The contrast points up how firmly anchored to reality the baby is in Stern's picture, how resolutely fantasy is banned from his hypothesis of the baby's experience. "Infants are... concerned with events that actually happen," Stern insists. "There are no wish-fulfilling fantasies.... Reality at this stage is never distorted" (*Interpersonal* 11). There can be no schema of "I am you" because internal representations correspond to daily experience, and the experience of being the other never occurs in actuality.[3]

Ten years later, in *The Motherhood Constellation*, Stern does theorize fantasy. But, as might be expected from his descriptions of infancy, fantasy is established as functionally subordinate to reality. Stern explains fantasies as montages constructed of some combination of the mental schemas based on lived experience: "the network of schemas-of-being-with is, in fact, the only reference for elaborating fantasies." Fantasies arise by means of "refiguration," in which the attention "move[s] back and forth freely between the various schematic formats, [creating] virtual sequences, virtual overlaps" (*Motherhood* 94). And what motivates fantasy? "The exact form of the fantasy is mostly determined by the immediate present context," determined indeed by its "function" in the immediate context: "each [fantasy has] functional values for adaptation" (*Motherhood* 96). Stern thus moves fantasy into the realm of the rational, functional, and adaptive. Fantasies as well as memory structures are securely fastened to lived experience, to both the memory of actual experience and the contingencies of the present moment.

The fantasy, "I want to be you," could not exist in the internal world either of the infant or of the adult subject, according to Stern's model; for if both memory and fantasy are constructed from actual experience only, there is no basis for such a fantasy. No one lives out a literal merger of self and other.

To put Stern's reality-based infant in a comparative context, I cite Borch-Jacobsen's contemporaneous (1988) theory of infantile subjective life. Freud left the theory of primary identification behind when he went on to elaborate the model of identification as a melancholy compensation for lost love objects; Borch-Jacobsen takes up the the theory that Freud abandoned and develops the characteristics of primary identification described by Freud in *Group Psychology and the Analysis of the Ego*. He begins from Freud's assertion that "identification is . . . the earliest expression of an emotional tie with another person" (*Group* 105) and elaborates that premise to its logical extreme. Identification is "primary" in the sense that incorporation of the other is the founding act of the subject: "the ego forms itself or is born in this devouring identification with the other" (*Emotional Tie* 60). Before the act of primary identification there is no internal world. The organism is an empty shell, and what comes to fill it is the image of the other. The ego emerges from this state where one is the other.

For Borch-Jacobsen, the infant's first experience *is* a fantasy: "I am you." That founding fantasy constructs a subject governed by the desire to be the other. "Desire . . . does not aim essentially at acquiring, possessing, or enjoying an object; it aims . . . at a subjective identity. Its basic verb is 'to be,' not 'to have'" (*Freudian* 28). While Borch-Jacobsen's picture of human desire is perhaps incomplete, his adoption of primary identification as the founding moment of subjectivity does explain, better than Stern's description of a relentlessly reality-based infant, some aspects of human psychic life: for example, fantasies of envy and idealization that involve an underlying desire, conscious or unconscious, to be the other.

The question raised by the contradiction between Stern and Borch-Jacobsen is then, Can one have a fantasy about something one hasn't experienced (except in fantasy)? And is a baby capable of generating a fantasy of identification? My own hypothesis is that fantasy is often produced by what the subject lacks, rather than by what the subject experiences in actuality. Lacan is of course the major theorist of lack, but his work emphasizes the lack established at the point of entry into language rather than the lack that a preverbal baby might experience. It is Freud, rather, who locates the origin of fantasy in the nursling, specifically at the moment that it experiences lack and cannot get what it wants: the absence of the breast leads to the wish for the breast and to the evocation of its image as the shortest path to fulfillment ("Interpretation" 565–67; see also Laplanche and Pontalis 482–83). Absence, or lack, generates desire, and desire generates a fantasy of fulfillment. Here and there, throughout his essays, Freud assumes lack as the engine of identificatory fantasy. In "Creative Writers and Daydreaming" he writes: "A child's play is determined by... a single wish.... the wish to be big and grown up" (146); and in "Family Romance" he says, "The child's most intense and most momentous wish during these early years is to be like his parents (that is, the parent of his own sex)" (237). The child wants to be "big and grown up" because it is not big and grown up. The fantasy of being the parent originates in a desire driven by lack.

Likewise, I would argue, the baby could have a fantasy of being the powerful other because it lacks power—or, more specifically, the sense of emptiness associated with helpless hunger could generate a fantasy of being the all-providing mother and thus possessing her infinite resources. Such a logic of identification motivated by lack would be in line with what Freud says about babies. Freud followed a conceptual line from lack to fantasy to identification: when the baby is hungry and the breast is not there, the baby hallucinates the breast in an effort to find satisfaction. Then the baby goes one step further to fantasize "I am the breast," as Freud says in "Findings, Ideas, Problems," (299). It would be consistent with this line of reasoning to theorize (as post-Freudians Chasseguet-Smirgel and Fairbairn did) that the baby in a state of hunger, depletion, and lack perceives the other as all-powerful and so identifies with the other in order to make that omnipotence its own.

It could be argued that the Stern baby's sense of a bounded self equipped with agency is itself a fantasy. In some ways the fantasy of identification with a parent figure is closer to the "reality" that the baby is utterly dependent on the other for its very existence—attached, or, in Freud's term, anaclitic, "leaning on" the parent for survival. The parent has to act as an extension of the infant because, as Freud says, the baby is born "prematurely"—its bodily functions still incomplete relative to the young of other animals. So when Stern claims that at two to three months infants appear to have "an organizing perspective that makes it feel as if there is now an integrated sense of themselves as distinct and coherent bodies, with control over their own actions, ownership of their own affectivity, a sense of continuity, and a sense of other people as distinct and separate interactants" (*Interpersonal* 69), he is attributing to them a *fantasy* of agency and autonomy. But he does not acknowledge the component of fantasy in this picture, continuing throughout *The Interpersonal World of the Infant* to insist that the infant is infallibly "an excellent reality-tester; reality at this stage is never distorted" (*Interpersonal* 11).

Philip Cushman contends that Stern's "marvelous infant" is in fact a cultural fantasy, one that Stern's readers share. "Masterful, bounded, interior, full of feelings, eager to share its subjectivity—relentlessly relational," this infant "is extremely appealing to modern Western readers. Why? Because it *is* them" (208). Cushman points out that the characteristics of the "core self" that Stern claims the infant integrates in the period between two and seven months—agency, self-coherence, affectivity and self-history, or continuity (*Interpersonal* 71)—"sound suspiciously correspondent to the characteristics of the current configuration of self predominant in the United States today. What is agency if not mastery, coherence if not boundedness, affectivity if not emotions, and history if not continuity?" (Cushman 210). "The degree to which Stern's (1985) description appears accurate is the degree to which his interests, methods, and ideas fit with the dominant social construction of the time" (209). According to Cushman, then, Stern's own value system generates the fantasy of a bounded, agentic, self-possessed baby.[4]

Of course, infants are not talking. In the absence of firsthand reports on what is going on in a baby's subjective world, every conceptual schema of an infant's interior life is to some extent a fantasy. As Jane Flax says, interpretations of infants' inner worlds are likely to "tell us far more about contemporary, culturally specific adult fantasies than [about] innate universal qualities of infancy" (1042). Stern's denial of the major role of fantasy in psychic life seems all the more incongruous when it is clear that a theorist of infancy has to use his own imagination quite liberally to interpret data bearing on an infant's internal world.

I do not wish to disparage infant research: the large and compelling body of empirical evidence that infant researchers have assembled on the relations of mothers and children is convincing and widely accepted; and infant researchers' integration of relational theory into current scientific models of the brain and memory constitutes a major contribution to our knowledge of how psychic structures are formed in an interpersonal field.[5] But since a central axis of psychoanalytic theory has from the beginning been a recognition of the extent to which fantasies shape and order mental life, it would seem to impoverish our understanding of human dynamics to leave it out.

Empirical Evidence for the Capacity for Identification

If there is no way to produce conclusive evidence that babies have fantasies, there is room to explore whether babies have the capacity for fantasies of identification. Despite infant researchers' repudiation of primary identification, some infant research studies suggest both that babies have the ability to identify with the other and that they do so identify. In studies by Cohn and Tronick infants of three months mirrored the mother's positive expression—smile or bright face—with a like expression: "the change from a neutral expression to a positive expression follows the mother's becoming positive" (69; cited in Muller 22). In Haviland and Lelwica's study, at two and a half months infants responded to their mothers' presentations of joy and anger with matching facial expressions of joy and anger; in response to their mothers' sad expressions, they responded by looking downward and sucking their lips and tongue, which the authors interpreted as self-soothing behaviors (103; qtd. in Muller 23).

Since we have no access to the subjective world of infants, it is difficult to show evidence that their facial expressions correspond with internal emotional states—but these researchers assume that there is such a correlation. Haviland and Lelwica state that "the mothers' expressions seem to have caused an emotional experience in the infants corresponding to the expression presented" (103); and they hypothesize that "even an infant younger than three months might respond with an emotion that mirrored the emotion stimulus" (97). In a further attempt to ascertain what is going on inside, a study by Davidson and Fox correlated the facial expressions that were shown to babies with their brain activation patterns. As Beebe, Lachmann, and Jaffe describe the study, "First they demonstrated that certain portions of the left frontal lobe are specialized for positive affect, and of the right for negative affect.... A 10-month-old infant watches a videotape of an actress. When the actress smiles and laughs, the infant's EEG shows the pattern characteristic of positive affect... When she appears to be in distress, the infant's EEG shows the pattern of negative affect. Thus, ... the baby's brain reflects the emotion of the other" (Beebe, Lachmann, and Jaffe 161).

Infant researchers do not, of course, draw the conclusion from this data that primary identification exists. Instead, they refer somewhat disparagingly to the automatic quality of these "induced-affect" or "coerced" responses (Haviland and Lelwica 103). Wolff, for example, speaks of "the quasi-obligatory facial response of six-week-old infants to faces" and seems to prefer the baby's "choice" of affect after four months of age (239). John Muller, contemplating the results of some of these studies, concludes: "The earliest empathic responses ... are automatic, almost coerced in constraining one's subjective state and behavior to match that of a model. The affective presentation is contagious, captivating, and produces a replica in the other" (24). From my point of view, however, the immediate, unthinking, and global nature of the infant's sympathetic resonance with the emotional world of the other suggests a capacity for primary identification. For it seems a mistake to call the infant's responses "empathic," as Muller does: in empathy, as it is commonly defined, one retains a sense of separation between self and other; and, according to Stern, empathy requires "the mediation of cognitive processes," including "the abstraction of empathic knowledge from the experience of emotional resonance" (*Interpersonal* 145)—capacities that Stern says are beyond the infant's capabilities.[6] I would say, rather, that the immediacy of the infant's emotional resonance with the other's feeling states implies an erasure of the boundary between the other's affective world and its own—a confusion of self and other that Freud called primary identification.

Oddly enough, then, given most infant researchers' exclusion or denial of primary identification, these infant research findings on the automatic, seemingly unavoidable nature of the infant's mimesis of the other's feelings—"The baby cannot escape the mother's emotion as reflected on her face" (Beebe, Lachmann, and Jaffe 161)—seem to corroborate Freud's description of identification as a primary response to the other.

If the baby does make such an imaginative leap into the other's emotional world, how would that identification play out within the infant research model of early representations? The notion of primary identification has traditionally been coupled with the idea of internalization: the baby takes in the mother, making her *imago* part of its internal structure. To counter this traditional view Stern contends that it is not figures or images, but interactive events that are recorded in memory (*Motherhood* 81). I would argue that even within the infant research paradigm that posits an internal world of representations formed from repeated daily events, there is room to understand how a fantasy of primary identification might be processed. Stern, Beebe, and Lachmann agree that hunger followed by feeding is a routine event whose repetition qualifies it to become a mental schema, a neuronal structure corresponding to "a generalized or prototypic happening" (Stern, *Motherhood* 81); further, the state transformation involved in the satisfaction of hunger makes it more likely that the event will be selected for internal representation. (See Beebe and Lachmann, "Representation" 149–51). Stern says in *The Motherhood Constellation* that affect is also recorded as part of a "temporal feeling-shape": a feeling that is habitually attached to one of the unfolding moments of a recurrent, predictable temporal sequence becomes part of the mental schema.[7] If states of hungry depletion habitually gave rise to the wish to be the all-resourceful mother or to the fantasy that one was the all-resourceful mother, that wish-fulfilling fantasy would be mnemonically represented as a part of the temporal sequence of rising hunger. Rather than internalizing, or introjecting, a maternal figure that then becomes part of the internal world, a baby might well schematize the repeated experience of fantasizing "I am the mother," along with the sequence of actions to which it is attached. Even if one embraces infant research's substitution of a neuronal model of representations for internalization, primary identification can survive as a usable concept. (Indeed, when Stern refers to his own patients in *The Motherhood Constellation*, he seems to contradict his own theory by referring to primary identification as if it were a given: it is as if clinical work with actual patients required the concept.)[8]

The Prospects for Adult Relational Structures

What then would be the implications for adult affective life? Since recurrent interpersonal experiences activate and strengthen discrete networks of interconnected neuronal groups, it is more likely that the neurobiological model of memory would lead to the establishment of a subject composed of discrete self states, or subject positions, than that it would lead to the singular, unified self pictured by Stern.[9] The existence of discrete schemas based, as infant researchers say all early representations are, on "many specific ways of being with mother" (Stern, *Interpersonal* 118), would logically lead to quite disparate figurations of self and other. If we consider only the relational patterns I have been reviewing in this paper—and of course there are many other relational schemas—it is clear that the neuronal networks constructed by different interactions with the same person may be quite different. The distinction between self and other may be fairly sharp, and the sense of agency and control foregrounded, as Stern says, when the infant plays a vocalizing or face-making game with its mother. In situations of hunger and feeding, though, the power relation is likely to be perceived as quite different—a helpless self in relation to the figure of an omnipotent mother.

Freud says that identification is primary, "the earliest expression of an emotional tie with another person" (*Group* 105), and "Stern considers play to be the first object relation" (Beebe, "Mother-Infant" 29). In my view, these two premises do not cancel each other out, but describe two successive moments in the baby's day and, perhaps, two founding positions of the subject in his or her relation to the other. Accepting both Freud's and Stern's descriptions of infant experience as accurate—as sequential rather than antithetical—prepares the way for accepting adult subjectivity as a dialectic between different modes of being with the other. On this model, different situations will call up different self-other schemas. For example, when the present context is one of unequal power relations with an admired other, the schema first associated with hunger and feeding may come into play, activating a desire to be the seemingly all-powerful other. Indeed, the reductive, concrete thinking associated with envy and idealization—the conception of the other as altogether powerful, autonomous, and self-sufficient, and the wish to acquire his or her desired qualities directly, magically, through identification—would seem to betray an origin in primitive thought processes. When the situation is more comfortable and the relationship more egalitarian, one could expect the pattern absorbed from the reciprocity of play to emerge. According to Beebe, what the baby encodes from repeated incidents of face-to-face play is a "process of both partners fine-tuning to each other," so that "what will be internalized is the temporal pattern of connectedness or of mutual interlocking responsivity" ("Mother-Infant" 39, 43). Such a schema of mutual adjustment and responsiveness founds the possibility for interactions in later life in which each participant is attuned to the other as subject.

The model I have constructed would predict that just as moments of primary identification and play succeed each other in the baby's daily life, so in adult life moments of dealing with the other as a fantasy object, subject to one's own internal processes of identification and projection, alternate with perceiving the other as a separate subject within his or her own life context. Or, as Jessica Benjamin puts it, subjects move between intrapsychic and intersubjective modes of relating to people, now treating others as mental objects subject to internal processes of incorporation and expulsion, now seeing others as distinct but related beings (*Bonds* 20–21).[10]

Notes

INTRODUCTION

1. Studies of physiological changes in sports fans during games confirm this bodily identification with athletes. A *New York Times* article by James C. McKinley, Jr. (August 11, 2000) reports on studies of rises and falls in testosterone levels in sports fans during games. One researcher, James Dabbs, a psychologist at Georgia State University, tested the hormone levels in the saliva of basketball fans and concluded that "the results suggest fans empathize with the competitors to such a degree that they mentally project themselves into the game and experience the same hormonal surges athletes do" (C24). See also Lauren Wispé's review of experimental evidence suggesting that people respond to seeing others in pain with "muscle mimicry," as if in immediate holistic identification with the other's suffering (135–55).

2. Freud was of course not the first to consider the entanglement with the other at the origins of self-consciousness and the resulting confusion of self and other. In *The Phenomenology of the Spirit*, Hegel was already asking, as Diana Fuss frames the question: "How is it that only through the other I can be myself, only in the place of the other I can arrive at a sense of self?" (3). The thinking of Hegel and the nineteenth- and twentieth-century theorists influenced by him provide a larger philosophical framework for psychoanalysis's focus on identification and the problem of alterity. See Fuss (16, note 8), for a list of authors who consider the relation between self and other within the larger philosophical tradition influenced by Hegel.

Lacan's early work was influenced by Hegel's thinking, filtered through Kojève's *Introduction to the Reading of Hegel: Lectures on the Phenomenology of the Spirit*; the book is founded on a series of lectures given by Kojève that Lacan attended. But Lacan rethought Kojève's terms within a psychoanalytic framework, transforming Kojève's picture of the subject into a more complex and differentiated model. See Charles Shepherdson's careful distinctions between Kojève's and Lacan's thinking on need, demand, and desire (Shepherdson, "The Epoch"). Mikkel Borch-Jacobsen, on the other hand, argues that Lacan remains trapped within a Kojèvian model in *Lacan: The Absolute Master*.

3. I have chosen to theorize identification from a base in Lacan's published work rather than using the unpublished Seminar IX (1961–1962), entitled "Identification," because the published seminars and *Écrits* are accessible to all and form the basis of current Lacanian discourse.

4. Stavrakakis goes on to say, "Since the objects of identification in adult life include political ideologies and other socially constructed objects, the process of identification is revealed as constitutive of socio-political life" (30). His book constitutes an exciting and thought-provoking reinterpretation of the political through key Lacanian concepts.

5. See, for example, Mary Ann Doane ("Misrecognition") and Anne Friedberg.

6. In her seminal essay on the potential uses of psychoanalysis to analyze race and class, Elizabeth Abel "ask[s] how labile psychoanalysis is, how far its boundaries can expand to incorporate issues of social difference into a discourse useful, if not for changing the social order, at least for theorizing this order's intervention in the production of diversely gendered subjects." ("Race" 185). For accounts of psychoanalysis's troubled historical relationship to race, see also Spillers ("Mama's Baby"), Gilman, and Walton. For a Lacanian analysis of race, see Seshadri-Crooks. For a wide-ranging analysis of identification and race, see Cheng; for melancholic identification and race, see Eng and Han. For discussions that combine psychoanalysis and race, see Bhabha ("Other Question" and "Mimicry"), Tate, *Psychoanalysis*, Silverman, *Threshold*, and the essays in *Psychoanalysis and Race*, edited by Lane.

7. Robyn Wiegman describes the visual economy of race in the United States. See especially pages 1–42.

8. After a comprehensive review of white-to-black mimesis in the "films, poetry, fiction, painting, photography and journalism" of the twentieth-century United States, Susan Gubar's *Racechanges* concludes that despite the variety of fantasies that motivate them, white impersonations of black Americans "almost always seem historically to have resulted in the subordination, muting, or obliteration of the Other" (244). Her study thus sadly confirms, at the level of cultural appropriation, Freud's initial insight that identification results in the assimilation, and thus the effacement, of the other.

9. "Scripts of confession" and "scripts of accusation" are Susan Stanford Friedman's terms for the statements of white feminists and black feminists in the impasse of dialogue that characterized the feminist movement in the 1980s and 1990s ("Beyond" 8–16; *Mappings* 41–43).

10. For an excellent survey of the issues raised in current debates on identification see Diana Fuss's "Introduction: Figuring Identification" in *Identification Papers* (1–19).

11. Elin Diamond and Diana Fuss give comprehensive descriptions of all Freud's notations on identification (Diamond, *Unmaking Mimesis* 109–12; Fuss 21–51; see also Borch-Jacobsen, *Freudian* 27–52).

12. Esther Rashkin uses Abraham's concept of the phantom, a guilty and unverbalized secret transmitted from one generation to the next, to study the concealed presences in literary works that drive the words and acts of certain characters and generate narrative action.

13. Jessica Benjamin likewise states that Freud's rigid separation of identification and desire does not "adequately represent the unconscious relations of desire." She suggests that we recognize "that identificatory love and object love can and do exist simultaneously. Why not see the movements from identification to object love, from object love to identification, as ongoing alternations throughout life?" (*Like Subjects* 79). In "White Skin, Brown Masks" Kaja Silverman suggests that identification should be conceptualized "not so much as the 'resolution' of desire as its perpetuation within another regime" (24). In a chapter called "On Being and Having" Marcia Ian points out that Freud's separation of identification and desire "denies not only same-sex desires but also heterosexual identifications, as if a man and a woman must automatically desire each other as other, and never respond to each other as in some way the 'same.' But it now appears that this assumption was one of Freud's great mistakes" (4).

14. David Eng and Shinhee Han likewise ground racial melancholia in a "suspended assimilation." "Asian Americans are typically seen by the mainstream as perpetual foreigners based on skin color and facial features. Despite the fact that they may be United States–born . . . [they] are continually perceived as eccentric to the nation." So they are enjoined to assimilate, yet are perceived and treated "as perpetual foreigners" (236). "To the extent that ideals of whiteness for Asian Americans (and other groups of color) remain unattainable, processes of assimilation are suspended, conflicted, and unresolved. . . . For Asian Americans, ideals of whiteness are continually estranged. They remain at an unattainable distance, at once a compelling fantasy and a lost ideal" (236). The lost object that is preserved, then, through melancholic incorporation is the lost ideal of whiteness. Eng and Han also define a "national melancholia" based on the repression from history of a series of laws that barred Asians from immigration and citizenship from 1882 to 1943. The "model minority" stereotype covers over the history of these exclusions and "works as a melancholic mechanism facilitating the erasure of repressed Asian-American identities [which] return as a type of ghostly presence" (239).

See also Homi Bhabha's classic essay on the colonial structure of mimicry, which demands that "other" (colonized) subjects mime whiteness, but fail in the attempt: "Colonial mimicry is the desire for a reformed, recognizable Other, *as a subject of a difference that is almost the same, but not quite. . . . Almost the same but not white*" ("Of Mimicry" 86, 89, Bhabha's emphasis).

15. In one chapter, Fuss does use Freud's original model of primary identification. She focuses on the violent aspect of primary identification, taking to its concrete extreme what is in Freud's model a description of the orientation of an infant who is capable of imagining identification only as a process of oral incorporation. Her examples literalize that model: Jame Gumb and Hannibal Lecter in *Silence of the Lambs* and Jeffrey Dahmer eat the objects of their affection and identify with them by wearing their skin. Fuss's point in these

analyses is that the media's representation of gay male identity as "insatiable oral sadist" does the cultural work of propagating "the specter of a perverse and monstrous homosexuality" (96).

16. Anne Cheng turns Borch-Jacobsen's concept of mimesis toward an analysis of speech and hearing in order to argue that primary identification is already cultural identification—that is, interpellation; she thus "blur[s] the lines between ontic and social formation" (159). "The infant mimes the sound he/she hears and, in that act of mimicry, experiences him/herself as at once possible and other ... A linguistic invasion can occur at [an] ontological level" (162). There is no subject that "is not already an echo" (162). Using Cha's *Dictee* as her text, Cheng argues that the first sounds an infant makes are an echo of the other, that "there is no subject without the 'others in place of her' " (162). One is always already reciting a "dictation" from social authority when one becomes a speaking subject. "The point is to understand the constitution of the subject as always already political"; "the injunction without is always already an echo of something within" (162, 158). Resistance is possible, as Cha shows—but only from within this "cultural relay" (159).

17. Ruth Leys's genealogy of trauma charts the tension between mimetic (identificatory) and antimimetic theories of trauma throughout the history of psychoanalysis. Her own clear preference is for a mimetic interpretation of trauma, which rests on the Freudian notion of primary identification. According to Leys's interpretation, the subject is born in an identification with the other, in "an identification that can never be remembered by the subject precisely because it precedes the very distinction between self and other on which the possibility of self-representation and hence recollection depends" (32). If this merging with the other occurred at its origin, the subject is primed to fall back into that state again, to become subsumed in another's personality. Leys defines trauma as exactly this experience, as *"imitative or mimetic identification itself,"* a return to the effacement of the self in the other (32; italics in original). The impossibility of recovering traumatic memory would rest, then, not on a defensive repression (or foreclosure) of the violent event, but on the fact that there was no subject present at the event and hence no self-representation or representation of an other to record. Indeed, the trauma "strictly speaking cannot be described as an event since it does not occur on the basis of a subject-object distinction" (33); trauma is, rather, a state of being, "an abyssal openness to all identification," "the vacancy of the traumatized subject or ego in a hypnotic openness to ... identifications occurring prior to all self-representation and hence to all rememoration" (32). Leys deconstructs a founding text of multiple personality, Morton Prince's *The Dissociation of a Personality*, arguing that "Sally," one of the alternative personas of Prince's patient, Miss Beauchamp, may be an impersonation of the analyst himself, the result of Miss Beauchamp's totalizing identification, or mimesis, with him under hypnosis, rather than a proof of multiple personality.

18. Schafer contrasts the potential for growth and change through ongoing identificatory relations with others with melancholic identification, which he

reads as pathological. The effort to preserve a loved person who is lost through the (unconscious) stratagem of keeping his or her image alive as part of the ego is a strategy of desperation that keeps the subject's affective world static, delays renunciation and mourning, and evades reality in favor of fantasy (154–55). Schafer's *Aspects of Internalization* gives full and helpful descriptions of various kinds of identification, from primary identification to the most highly developed forms of empathy.

19. Benjamin argues that the daughter, like the son, wants to identify with the father and so become what he is (in contemporary Western family culture): a subject of agency and desire. But a father in a traditional patriarchal nuclear family usually refuses identification with the daughter; and it is only when, rejected, the daughter has to give up on paternal identification that she turns to ideal love, displacing the wish to be an autonomous subject of agency and desire onto an idealized male figure. Benjamin likewise refuses the normative psychoanalytic assumption that sons must disidentify with their mothers in order to achieve masculinity, arguing for a healthier oedipal process of masculine gender differentiation that would admit a degree of similarity—and identification—with the mother, that would allow a "playful, secondary identification with femininity" (*Bonds* 169; *Like Subjects* 65). In general, she sees the child's identification with the mother's position as a crucial step in enabling the subject to enter into a dimension of intersubjectivity where the other is no longer an object to be controlled, but "a center of subjective experience not unlike [one's own]" (*Like Subjects* 93; see also 42–43).

In *Like Subjects* Benjamin also argues that multiple gender identifications in childhood provide the potential for adult gender fluidity. Young children formulate their self-representations through identifications with both genders; the unconscious retains a multiplicity of gender identity positions which can subvert the subject's conscious conformity to an exclusive model of femininity or masculinity. See chapter 6, note 16, for an elaboration of Benjamin's model of flexibile gender identifications as well as citations to other feminist relational psychoanalysts' theories of gender fluidity.

Chapter 1

1. Jessica Benjamin, makes this point concisely: "Unlike jealousy, envy is about being, not having" ("A Desire" 89).

2. Jacques-Alain Miller and Slavoj Žižek postulate that the source of racism is just this suspicion that the racial other participates in jouissance, enjoys the forbidden object a, "has access to some specific enjoyment" from which the subject is forever barred [Žižek, *Sublime* 187]. "Racism calls into play a hatred that is directed toward what grounds the Other's alterity, in other words, its jouissance . . . true intolerance is intolerance of the Other's jouissance"

(Miller, "Extimité" 79–80). Marshall Alcorn expands on this insight to argue that the logic of racism "operates not according to the logic of the symbolic, ... but according to the real and the drives, in the jouissance of the body" (88). He argues that racist attitudes do not give way to new meanings, no matter how persuasively presented, because racism is attached to the drives, not to language and the symbolic. In Alcorn's book, *Changing the Subject in English Class*, he contends that effecting changes in such deeply invested libidinal positions requires not persuasive rhetoric, but a process of mourning.

3. Feminists of color have pointed out the inadequacy of the 1970s movement's exclusive focus on gender oppression. Their critique of white middle-class feminists' insensitivity to the material effects of class and race oppression on the lives of women of color has been so successful that, as Benita Roth says, "the phrase 'the intersection of race, class and gender' is axiomatic now for doing feminist work" (75). For an alternative historical narrative of the part race and class issues played in 1970s feminism, see Breines.

4. In her essay on Iago's envy of Othello, "Iago's Alter Ego," Janet Adelman says that what is distinctive about Klein's notion of envy is that it is the good breast that draws the infant's rage. "For most analysts of infantile destructiveness and rage, the source and target is the frustrating 'bad' object—a maternal object that doesn't provide enough; ... but in Klein's reading of envy, the source and target of rage is ... the good breast, and it is exactly its goodness that provokes the rage ... [and] the need not to possess but to destroy it." The fantasized destruction takes place "through the violent projection of bits of the self and its contaminated objects—often localized as contaminated bodily products—into the good object. By means of this projection, the self succeeds in replicating its own inner world 'out there' and thus in destroying the goodness it cannot tolerate; at the end of the process ... 'There is nothing left to envy.'" (136–37). Hence the particular bitterness of envy: all sources of good both internal and external having been destroyed, all that is left is despair (136). Adelman brilliantly adapts Klein's model to race, showing how Othello's race functions for Iago (and thus implying how racism functions generally through projective identification). Hating Othello's goodness, Iago seeks to spoil it by projecting his own inner "poisons" into Othello. And Othello enacts the Kleinian recipient: he "really does change, ... begin[ning] to experience himself as contaminated and hence to act out Iago's scenarios" (143).

For contemporary Kleinian theories of envy and gender, see Kavaler-Adler, Kittay, and Olivier. Nancy Burke's "The Debate Broadens" provides a useful survey of current theories of envy (Burke 153–58).

Teresa Brennan, in *History after Lacan* (excerpted in Burke 285–96), refers to Lacan's model of Augustine's small boy, but follows the reference in a different direction from mine. Building on Freud's, Klein's, and Lacan's notions of envy, she develops a definition of the foundational fantasy that underlies commodity capitalism: "I am positing the desire for instant gratification, the preference for visual and 'object'-oriented thinking this entails, ... the envious desire to imitate the original, [and] the desire to control the mother, ... constitute a foundational psychical fantasy" that "tallies with the desires encapsulated in commodities" (Burke 294). See also Etchegoyen, Lopez and Rabih; Schneider; and Berke.

5. *Schadenfreude*, the pleasure in someone else's misfortune, is obviously related to the spoiler side of envy: if the envied other falls from grace, the release from the compulsion to envy results in an emotional charge experienced as pleasure. For a book-length account of the motivations and history of *Schadenfreude*, see Portmann.

6. See Johnson. Byatt reviews the opinions on envy of classic authors from Ovid and Spenser to Dickens and Balzac. For a full description of the virulence and destructiveness of envy, see Harris 299, 312–315.

7. Adrienne Harris and Helena Michie both theorize envy and competitiveness between women. Harris notes in her patients the inability to admit competitiveness "except as shameful loss of goodness" (298); and she discusses the threat that envy poses to the "idealized affiliations" between women promoted by feminism (315). Michie points out that feminism's idealization of sisterhood ignores the prevalence of envy, competition, and resentment in the dynamics of biological sisterhood. She makes a plea similar to that of the present chapter, arguing that "contemporary feminists need . . . to provide rhetorical and political room for the expression of female difference, for anger and mistrust among women" (21).

8. Many established feminists, accustomed to powerless self-images, do not experience themselves as powerful and fail to incorporate a realistic sense of their actual authority and influence into their self-conceptions. As Diane Elam says, "Power is not something women are supposed to have. It is what they lack, and their lack drives the struggle of feminism" ("Sisters" 57). Gallop, Hirsch, and Miller, in the "conversation" from which I have been quoting, inadvertently point up this blind spot in feminism through their reluctance to own their own power. The three do discuss feminism's lack of an analysis of power, and more particularly feminists' "reticence to recognize the power of the mothers," meaning the generation of Chodorow, Gilbert and Gubar, Gilligan, and Showalter discussed earlier (Gallop 366). But while recognizing the need for such a recognition, they back away from any acknowledgment that they themselves might now occupy the position of "mothers": that is, the position—which all three do indeed occupy—of famous and influential feminist theorists. As Linda Zwinger comments on their conversation, "They are clearly more interested in displaying, discussing, and acknowledging their own and one another's vulnerability . . . than they are in their positions as representative and established feminists," as "famous-established-feminist[s]" (189, 188). While shrinking from the acknowledgment of power, however, Hirsch does articulate the inappropriateness of feeling powerless: "We never really feel in power. . . . I don't know what it would mean to feel in power. Women—and feminists in particular . . . find it extremely difficult actually to acknowledge that at times we are the powerful person, or in the powerful position" (355).

When women in positions of power deny that power, they arouse resentment in less established women who want their elders to use power competently, and on their behalf (see Keller and Moglen 28). Not knowing what to do with power is no longer a badge of innocence, but a liability and a source of disruption to feminist community. In a fascinating response to this dialogue and to Nancy Miller's *Getting Personal*, Zwinger reacts to Gallop's, Hirsch's and Miller's display of vulnerability as a bid for the identification of younger feminists like herself, and she expresses her resentment of their "insistently offering themselves as just like me . . . despite superficial differences (of mere fame and glory!)" (189). She points out the perils of trying to set up such a mirroring relation with the reader and then goes beyond reading to reflect on the ambivalence that accompanies identifications between established academic feminists and less well positioned junior faculty (190–91). Diane Elam asserts that such "generational conflict is a structural necessity," since the established generation cannot control what the next generation will do with the feminist tradition they are handing down, and the younger generation of feminists feels that a feminist tradition whose making they did not control is being imposed on them. She states the underlying problem. Feminism, which in its origins occupied the moral high ground of the oppressed, the marginalized, the disinherited, "has yet to come to terms with what it would mean for it to have power and to put that power to good use." She recommends approaching the complexities of feminist power through an understanding of "tradition," "the act of handing down" ("Sisters" 63–64).

In her assessment of feminism at the turn of the twenty-first century, *Critical Condition*, Susan Gubar describes the perplexing conflicted loyalties of an academic feminist who is in an established senior position. Listing the many fissures within an academic feminist community—"between women of different ranks; between older and younger women; between women within traditional departments and those in multidisciplinary programs"—she adds that the imperative of sisterhood merely exacerbates the confusion and anger over such conflicts (*Critical* 101). See also the essays describing generational conflict within feminism collected in Looser and Kaplan.

Naomi Wolf's *Fire with Fire* critiques women's power aversity and power illiteracy. Wolf astutely analyzes the gratification and safety of the "good girl" role, describes women's motivations for "clinging to the idea that women are innocent of the will to power" (265), and advocates that women overcome their power aversity, lay claim to the power they already have, and use it (237–51). She recommends that feminists retire the model of a group bound by extended ties of friendship and intimacy and replace it with the model of "power group" or "resource group."

9. Atwood invites the reader to explore the multiple meanings of words through the example of her character Tony, who constantly plays with words and even ponders the possible sources of Zenia's name. She comes up with nine different derivations, among them "*Xenia*, a Russian word for hospitable" and "*Xeno*, Greek, a stranger, as in *xenophobic*" (517).

10. It is no secret that Zenia functions as a double for each of the protagonists. In addition to hints scattered through the novel, Atwood says as

much in a *New York Times* interview: Zenia is a "shadow" like the shadows to be found in Hoffman's tales; she is "the Mr. Hyde to our Dr. Jekylls" (Graeber 22). I argue here that Zenia functions as a double not in the usual sense of the subject's mirror image, but in Lacan's more specific sense of the uncanny double as an incarnation of the subject completed by the object a. Atwood documents her fascination with doubles and her sense of her own doubleness as a writer in "Duplicity."

11. Kalpana Seshadri-Crooks clearly explains the subject's relation to the object a: "The speaking subject suffers from the unconscious thought that he has lost some primal object necessary to his being. While the pursuit of this object at a safe distance from satisfaction sustains the subject in desire, it is the unconscious strategies or symptoms evolved by the subject to obtain satisfaction that cause suffering" (64). See also Joan Copjec's lucid explanation of the object a (128–29).

12. Lacan designates Claudius "the phallus" or "the real phallus" interchangeably with the figure completed by the object a. As Tim Dean says, "at the level of the real the phallus stands for castration as loss of jouissance" (14)—so the term points in the same direction as the object a, to a loss that founds the subject. I prefer to use the term "object a" in my work because Lacan uses it to mean one thing only, whereas the phallus means something different in each of Lacan's structural dimensions—the imaginary, the symbolic, and the real. As Tim Dean says, other, more precise, Lacanian terms can substitute for the phallus at each of these levels, and "one eliminates confusion by eliminating the concept of the phallus" (13). For a discussion of the various meanings of the phallus, see Tim Dean (12–17).

13. For a lucid explanation of all the complex meanings of jouissance, see Evans, "Jouissance." The original *père jouissant* is the father of the primal horde in Freud's *Totem and Taboo*, who was not subject to symbolic castration, and, recognizing no social code, had all the women in the tribe and exercised violence at will. After his sons murder him, his figure is abstracted into the Name-of-the-Father, the master signifier of the symbolic order, and in his place the Law of the Father rules. Slavoj Žižek discusses the *père jouissant* and the symbolic father (the Law of the Father) in a commentary on *Totem and Taboo* in *The Ticklish Subject* (313–22). He ties the *père-jouissant* to the figure of the double in "Grimaces" (53–56). See also Tim Dean (16). Todd McGowan analyzes contemporary versions of these fathers: he contends that the prevailing father figure is no longer the symbolic father (the Name-of-the-Father), but the *père-jouissant* or "anal father," who commands jouissance instead of prohibiting it; he follows the manifestations of the anal father in contemporary U.S. cinema (*The End of Dissatisfaction* chapter 2.)

14. Žižek similarly defines the double as the one who "embodies the phantom-like Thing in me," the one whose figure exceeds the mirror-image by incorporating the object a ("Grimaces" 55). See also Mladen Dolar, "I Shall Be" 13–15: "The object a is precisely that part of the loss that one cannot see in the

mirror, ... the nonspecular. ... the double is that mirror image in which the object a is included" ("I Shall Be" 13). Joan Copjec clearly explains both the normal functioning of the object a and the uncanny dimension produced by the encounter with a double whose body contains the object a (128–9).

15. The Lacanian real does not refer to the material world; it encompasses all that is excluded by the symbolic. Indeed, through its exclusion, the real enables the symbolic; it gives the symbolic a limit, and a lack. From the standpoint of the symbolic order, the real is the impossible—that which cannot be put into words, that which escapes articulation within the sociosymbolic order, that which evades the Law of the Father. Tim Dean gives a clear explanation of the real. See also Žižek, *Sublime* for a comprehensive and useful definition of the real (161–73). More recently, Charles Shepherdson has distinguished between a presymbolic real in the earlier texts of Lacan and a later Lacanian version of the real as a product of the symbolic—a remainder that escapes representation ("Intimate Alterity").

16. I give a full account of the dysfunctional family relations in Charis's and Tony's childhoods that prepare them for identification with Zenia in "I Want to Be You."

17. Zenia—who denies no impulse, who puts the self first always, who takes what she wants without regard for others' feelings—constitutes Atwood's protest against the reduction of women to goody-goody wimps who are denied half their human capacities. In the "Address to the Booksellers" Atwood explains, "If all women are well behaved by nature—or if we aren't allowed to say otherwise for fear of being accused of antifemaleism—they are deprived of moral choice"; "Where have all the Lady Macbeths gone? Gone to Ophelias, every one, leaving the devilish tour-de-force parts to be played by bass-baritones" (11). Like Roz's twin daughters, who demand that all fairy tales be reconfigured so that women play all the parts, Atwood is presenting a reconfigured "Robber Bridegroom" fairytale that restores women's ability to play all the roles, including those of the powerful and the evil. In the Graeber interview she remarks, "Women are tired of being good all the time.... When you deprive women of any notion of threat, it pretty much puts them back in the Victorian age. All innocent, and without power, except the power of being good" (22). (A conversation with Pam Bromberg suggested this line of thought.)

Elaborating on the theme of power that Atwood articulates here, J. Brooks Bouson views Zenia as a vehicle for Atwood's exploration of "women's collective fantasies of female power" ("Slipping" 149). Lynn Bloom and Veronica Makowsky similarly understand that "Zenia is so important to Tony, Charis, and Roz because she represents power to them: the power within each woman.... They are, however, ambivalent toward her since they are confused about the power within themselves" (172). Bloom and Makowsky quote Atwood in interview to explain women's ambivalence about assuming power: "'People can be morally superior when they are in a position of relative powerlessness. For instance, if you're a woman being victimized then you can afford moral superiority. But once you have power, you have to take responsibility'" (Twigg 122). When Tony, Charis, and Roz begin to take responsibility for their own power, Bloom and Makowsky say, "Zenia dies because they no longer need her to embody that power so that they can demonize it" (176).

18. Atwood has said that "Zenia's engines run on envy" (Graeber 22).

19. Jane Brown writes that the difficulties of female friendship have figured centrally not only in *The Robber Bride*, but in *Cat's Eye* and *The Handmaid's Tale* as well.

Chapter 2

1. On the autobiographical level, all accounts suggest that it is Lawrence's relation to his mother, not his father, that the *Rainbow*'s extraordinarily detailed account of a child's relation to an overbearing parent reflects. Barbara Schapiro says that Lawrence's *Sons and Lovers* both reflects Lawrence's mother's need to live through her sons and is "a moving testament to Lawrence's... deeply empathic identification with his mother" ("Dread" 154, 152). Indeed, Paul's feelings for his mother in *Sons and Lovers* echo Ursula's feelings about her father in *The Rainbow*: "It was as if the pivot and pole of his life, from which he could not escape, was his mother" (*Sons* 261). See also John Worthen's biography of Lawrence's early years. Notwithstanding the probable maternal source of Lawrence's nuanced insights into how an overbearing parent affects a child, his extension of the dynamic of demand to include fathers and daughters does point to a psychological reality: where the father has a need for identification, he may well demand that his daughter mirror his desires and ambitions, that she function as an extension of himself. Lawrence's portrait opens up Lacan's model of demand to a wider range of gender.

2. Kalpana Seshadri-Crooks provides this lucid explanation of "Man's desire is the desire of the Other" when Other is read not as the original representative of the Other, the mother, but as the symbolic order itself. "Insofar as language pre-exists each of us, the subject in his or her specificity can come into existence only by borrowing the signifiers of its desire from the Other. It follows, then, that desire is always the desire of the Other" (24).

3. While this explanation of separation is mine, worked out in conversation with Frances Restuccia, it is consonant with Bruce Fink's description of what "man's desire is the desire of the Other" means when the Other is taken to be the parent (the first representative of the Other) (*Lacanian* 53–54) and with his description of separation (*Lacanian* 61).

4. In *A Clinical Introduction* Fink identifies the structure of demand with perversion: "The pervert... plays the role of object: the object that fills the void in the mOther" (175). His description of the effects of demand on the child is clear and helpful (175–78).

5. William Walsh has remarked that Will's need to possess Ursula stems from some "profound inadequacy in himself" that prevents his acknowledging her separate autonomy. As for the effect on the child, Walsh says that Will's demands for support and accord "put an intolerable strain on the child. The relaxed rhythm of childhood is shattered, and the child ... is jerked too early into a sharpened awareness" (164, 167). Linda Ruth Williams sees this passage as positive. Basing her interpretation on Lawrence's *Fantasia of the Unconscious*, she emphasizes "the importance of vision in the growth of the self" and understands the moment of seeing and recognizing the parent in the passage quoted above as the decisive moment of individuation: "At this moment she comes into her own as a visual and conscious little girl.... She takes her place in the Symbolic ('her consciousness woke up').... What she is learning is how to be a *woman* who sees" (29, 28).

6. Bruce Fink translates this passage perhaps more clearly: "the relationship through which he comes to be—on the basis of lack which makes him desire—is most perturbed when there is no possibility of lack, when his mother is constantly on his back" (*Lacanian* 53).

7. Marguerite Beede Howe points out that images of metal and stone characterize both lovers, emphasizing their lack of a "blood connection" (48, 49). I am violating Lawrence's practice of showing lovers always in a reciprocal relation by focusing exclusively on Ursula here. Skrebensky is meant to be a poor creature, devoted to social surfaces, hollow at the core ("there was no core to him" [360]), the last and most dependent of *The Rainbow*'s three generations of dependent men. Howe comments that "when he has Ursula destroy Skrebensky, Lawrence is exorcising both the deadened social self that is cut off from a living relationship, and the dependent self that seeks only to exist at the living center ... Skrebensky suffers the nightmare fate of the ontologically insecure: his being is sapped by the very person who sustains it" (48). See also Kinkead-Weekes 35–36.

8. See Elizabeth Abel's perceptive analysis of how Steedman explicitly makes class the determining factor in the structure of these two "primal scenes" ("Race" 192–93).

9. In "The Watercress Seller," an essay in *Past Tenses*, Steedman acknowledges that her search into the life of Mayhew's little watercress girl enabled her to write *Landscape for a Good Woman*: "I see [the watercress girl] now as the shade of *Landscape for a Good Woman*, the means by which I allowed myself to recall my own childhood, and write another account of working-class childhood.... The Little Watercress Girl is what I want: the past, which is lost and which I cannot have: my own childhood. She is my fantasy child" (*Past Tenses* 201). The desire to be the watercress girl is half-acknowledged here to be compensatory—for Steedman's childhood did not include the key ingredient of the little watercress girl's, a mother who extends recognition to her daughter for her competence. Victoria Rosner makes a similar point: "Through her identification with the girl, she can reproduce and

repair her own textual childhood—as recounted in *Landscape for a Good Woman*" (13). Steedman goes on to acknowledge, albeit indirectly, in a general comment on historiography, her identification with the little watercress girl— what she calls a "transferential relationship": "I would argue... that the historian has a massive transferential relationship to the past. I would say that this transference becomes particularly acute and particularly interesting when children are the subjects of historical research" (*Past Tenses* 200). Rosner has elaborated both of the themes Steedman broaches here: she describes Steedman's relation to the little watercress girl as a mothering of a fantasy daughter; (13–17); and she defends identification with one's subjects as a valid component of historical research: "both [Steedman and Bell Gale Chevigny] found their historical work enriched by the identification [with their subjects]" (28). Rosner describes in detail Steedman's obsessive historical researches into the life of the little watercress girl.

10. Christian Dior introduced the New Look in 1947. The expansive shape of the New Look contrasted with the frugal lines of the World War II suit for women, which emphasized broad shoulders with shoulder pads and featured short slim skirts to conserve material. (Fabric was rationed during the war so it could be used for soldiers' uniforms). The New Look featured a "feminine" look, accentuating a small waistline and rounded hips and bust. Skirts were full, with a midcalf hemline, so that a New Look coat or dress required an extravagant expanse of material.

11. For Laura Marcus, the absence of a follow-up to Steedman's statement that "that dream is... my interpretative device, the means by which I can tell a story" (28)—the absence, that is, of a full interpretation of the dream and its relation to Steedman's "story"—is symptomatic of a central problem in Steedman's attempt to tell a story "for which the central interpretative devices of the culture don't quite work" (*Landscape* 6). "If the 'interpretative devices' of a culture are constituted by the dominant class, there is no form of access to interpretations through which those on the outside can understand their conditions of existence in their own terms" (87). Thus for Marcus the dream remains "opaque" and so does Steedman's personal story: "The personal and familial story is not presented as a microcosm of the public: it is seen to be opaque and enigmatic and exists in disjuncture from its apparent background"; "Steedman's adoption and rejection of a plethora of different theoretical positions reflects this felt absence of an authentic perspective" (86, 87). The lacunae in Steedman's story thus represent for Marcus the failure of her attempt to invent a narrative form for working-class childhood. Stephen Yeo, on the contrary, sees the "bits of history" that make up Steedman's story as a positive form for the histories that have not yet been told—"bits of history of the post-war welfare state as experienced by its children; bits of history of the traffic in women, their experience as objects of exchange but now 'owning something, even if it is only their labour and the babies they produce'; bits of history of men as uneasy in or unequal to roles structured by them and for them; bits of history of envy" (43). Telling history like this, "more open than shut," invites

other stories from other people who have been marginalized, Yeo says. He is disappointed only in Steedman's "exclusivity"—in her rejection of the work of other working-class authors and thus of the beginnings of a communal project of recovering the history of the marginalized (45).

12. While a reader might be tempted to see the figure in the New Look coat as the mother—elusive, giving confusing and contradictory signals—it is not Kay's mother but the woman her mother envies. Years later, Steedman identifies the woman in her dream as the legitimate wife of her father— Steedman and her sister were illegitimate—whom the child made up from confusing whispered references to "she, she" in her parents' conversations (*Past Tenses* 40). Consonant with the definition of envy in chapter 1, the mother wants to be in the place of the woman who is whole—in this case, in the place of the wife who has everything: New Look clothes, husband, and legitimacy. Even with this additional information about the identity of the woman in the dream, the analysis remains the same: the child dreamer Kay stands in the place of the mother, and the dream expresses the envy of the mother, not an envy of her own.

13. Bina Freiwald is sympathetic to Steedman's claim that her exclusion from her mother's love is part of a wider social exclusion. "Material want, the loss of social standing, and, ultimately, the emotional deprivations that these produce" combine, in Freiwald's view, to deprive Steedman of the belief "in the worth of [her] self and its very right to exist" (28, 29). Freiwald calls *Landscape for a Good Woman* "a doubly resisting discourse: not only does it talk back to such representatives of the hegemonic order as the health inspector, but it also talks back to an internalized devalued self," yet not even "this personal-reflective narrative can fully rid her of the doubts that threaten her sense of self" (29).

14. Steedman refers to her sister's "preciser sense of what we lacked, ... [she] wanted what she did not have" (118). (See also 46.) And here the wanting and the deprivation are not material, but stem from a shortage of good mothering—although, again, Steedman avoids mentioning her mother directly even here, where the feelings of deprivation are safely displaced onto the sister.

15. Steedman mentions only in passing that she had written a letter to her mother saying that she would not be seeing her for a while "because she upset me so much" (60).

Chapter 3

1. Psychoanalysis is well suited to the study of disturbances at the crossroads of language and the body, which is where Morrison locates the psychic distortions imposed by slavery. The originating discoveries of psychoanalysis took place at this intersection of body and language, in Freud's work with hysterics. And psychoanalysis has gone on to elaborate a unique perspective on

the relation between the signifier and the flesh, described by Charles Shepherdson in "The Epoch" and *Vital Signs* (3–8).

Nicolas Abraham offers a non-Lacanian paradigm for the intergenerational transmission of family secrets, the theory of the "phantom": the child doesn't consciously know what the parent's secret is because it has never been put into words; the child nonetheless acts it out, driven by a thing lodged in its unconscious which fits in with neither its conscious wishes nor its unconscious fantasies. "What haunts are not the dead, but the gaps left within us by the secrets of others" (75). For a lucid explanation and application of Abraham and Torok's theories, see Esther Rashkin's *Family Secrets*. For an account of the intergenerational transmission of ethnic hatreds associated with collective trauma in contemporary international relations, see Vamik Volkan's *Bloodlines*. J. Brooks Bouson uses trauma theory and shame theory to show how *Beloved* "uses the device of the ghost to convey the power of trauma to possess and trap its victims" (134). Laurie Vickroy assesses the effects of collective trauma in *Beloved*. Morgenstern discusses the conflict in *Beloved* between the need to tell the traumas of slavery and their untranslatability into language.

2. The novel withholds judgment on Sethe's act and persuades the reader to do the same, presenting the infanticide as the ultimate contradiction of mothering under slavery: the only way for a slave mother to "protect" her children, to "put [her] babies where they'd be safe," is to kill them (164). "It was absolutely the right thing to do . . . but it's also the thing you have no right to do," as Morrison comments in interview (Rothstein). Readers learn about the infanticide a bit at a time from different perspectives, a technique that prevents them from making simple judgments. Maggie Sale shows that Morrison's narrative strategy forces readers to see the event from multiple perspectives and to recognize that each version depends as much on the needs of the speaker and listener as on the historical "facts." The lack of a single definitive account "challenges readers to examine their own responses" both to Sethe's act and to the circumstances that force her to it (44).

Darlene Hine discusses infanticide as one of the strategies with which slave women resisted their sexual oppression. "Far from viewing [infanticide] as murder, and therefore indicating [it] as lack of love, slave parents who took their children's lives may have done so out of a higher form of love and a clearer understanding of the living death that awaited their children under slavery" (Hine 125; qtd. in Bouson, *Quiet* 232). Sally Keenan claims, as I do, that the infanticide allows Morrison "to capture the horrific contradiction of the slave mother" (70).

Stephanie Demetrakopoulos, comparing Sethe and Beloved to mythic counterparts, remarks that "Sethe attempts to return the babies to perhaps a collective mother body, to devour them back into the security of womb/tomb death . . . as the ultimate act of protection" (52). Helene Moglen understands Morrison's project to be lifting "the primal mother" out of the ahistorical prehistory of the subject and placing her in social history: "Deprived of a social identity and placed outside the law, Sethe conceives of herself as the primal mother has been conceived: not in and for herself but in relation to her children.... For a moment, she claims the right to be the primal mother, giving and taking life without responsibility to another with a subjectivity not her own" (210). Barbara Hill Rigney aligns Sethe with the African Great Mother, "the giver of both life and wisdom, who is *nommo*, the creative potential and the sacred aspect of nature itself.... Also like nature, the African Great Mother can kill as well as create" (68–69). She also attributes to Sethe the power of Demeter to bring back the daughter from the dead (70).

3. See my account of the way that the language of *Beloved* reflects the mirrorings and mergings of Beloved with her mother (Wyatt, "Giving" 480–82). Rebecca Ferguson uses D. W. Winnicott's essay, "Mirror-role of Mother and Family in Child Development,' to explain Beloved's fixation on her mother's face (117–18). Barbara Mathieson also cites D. W. Winnicott as support for her claim that Beloved's monologue mirrors the conviction of a preoedipal child that her identity and her mother's "flow into one another as interchangeably as their faces" (2).

Barbara Schapiro discusses the novel's images of orality and the gaze in the context of slavery, pointing out that "the emotional hunger, the obsessive and terrifying narcissistic fantasies" are not Beloved's alone; they belong to all those denied both mothers and selves by a slave system that "either separates [a mother] from her child or so enervates and depletes her that she has no self with which to confer recognition" ("Bonds" 194). Thus when Sethe complains, "There was no nursing milk to call my own," she expresses her own emotional starvation in the absence of her mother, and that emptiness in turn prevents her from adequately reflecting her own daughter, Denver ("Bonds" 200, 198).

Jennifer FitzGerald criticizes the use of psychoanalytic theory to analyze *Beloved* because psychoanalysis "focuses intensively on the interaction of infant and mother as if this existed as a free-standing relation, independent of the economic, political, or social conditions which affect the circumstances of parenting" (669). Claiming that object relations theory lends itself to an analysis that includes these socioeconomic factors, she describes the relations between Sethe, Beloved, and Paul D according to a Kleinian model. See also Demetrakopoulos, Hirsch *(Mother-Daughter),* Horvitz, and Bouson *(Quiet).*

4. Claire Kahane points out that Freud added, as an afterthought, the mechanism for Dora's homoerotic desire: "a series of footnotes" reveals that "the secret of the hysteric was... an unacknowledged identification with [the father]" (Kahane 22.) Parveen Adams argues that in Dora's identifications "object choice is not primary"; what is primary for Dora is "the identification itself," together with the pleasure of imagining now "what is it like to be the man for the woman," now "what is it like to be... the woman for the man?" (22–23). In "Intervention in the Transference" Lacan goes on to say that Dora is fascinated by Frau K because she believes that she can discover in Frau K the mystery of femininity; and most interpreters of Lacan's version of hysteria have fastened on this line of thinking, defining the hysteric as she who is forever asking the question of sexual difference: Am I a woman? Am I a man? I prefer to foreground Lacan's first interpretation: the desire of the hysteric is an imita-

tion of the desire of the Other. For the hysteric's confusion about sexual difference, see: Adams 11–24; Lemoine-Luccioni; Shepherdson *Vital*, 17–27; Martha Evans 178–99.

5. Although she is not commenting on Lacan's treatment of Dora's homosexuality, Judith Butler points out that making female homosexual desire rest on identification with a man is a function of the heterosexual matrix that insists that all active desire and all desire for a woman are the properties of the man, so that a woman must usurp phantasmatically the heterosexual masculine position in order to desire a woman. That idea effectively denies the possibility that a woman could desire a woman *tout court*—denies the possibility of female homosexual desire. "This is the predicament produced by a matrix that accounts for all desire for women by subjects of whatever sex or gender as originating in a masculine, heterosexual position. The libido-as-masculine is the source from which all possible sexuality is presumed to come" (*Gender Trouble* 53).

Commenting on the case histories of Dora and "the homosexual woman" as exemplary of Freud's attitude toward female homosexuality, Fuss points out that Freud's metaphors of falling and regression consign homosexuality to identification and reserve the "healthy" space of desire for heterosexuality. "In Freud's reading of identification and desire, homosexual desire is not even, properly speaking, desire. Rather, homosexuality represents an instance of identification gone awry—identification in overdrive (or, one might say, oral drive)... While desire is the province and the privilege of heterosexuals, homosexuals are portrayed as hysterical identifiers and expert mimics." Because identification and desire finally cannot be kept separate but keep turning into one another, Fuss says, Freud's effort to pathologize homosexuality as identification and validate heterosexuality as desire ultimately fails (*Identification Papers* 77).

6. In "Direction of the Treatment and the Principles of its Power" Lacan confirms this interpretation, rereading Freud's account of the "Witty Butcher's Wife's Dream" to uncover "the key to the fields, the key to the field of the desires of all the witty hysterics"—namely, "hysterical identification" (261). Without recounting the convolutions of the witty butcher's wife's dream, which has been admirably interpreted by Fuss, Catherine Clément, and Cynthia Chase, I limit my discussion here to Lacan's conclusions. The wife's underlying question, Lacan says, is "How can another woman be loved?" and she tries to solve that enigma by identifying with the position of the male desirer (in this case, with the position of her husband the butcher, who desires her friend); more precisely, Lacan adds, the wife identifies with the position of the phallus, in its guise of (sexual) desire." "To be the phallus.... Was not that the ultimate identification with the signifier of desire?" (262). And he concludes with the reiteration of his formula for desire as such, so admirably concretized in the case of hysterics: "man's desire is the desire of the Other" (264). See Diana Fuss, chapter 2, "Identification Papers," for a clarifying account of hysterical identification and for a summary of Freud's, Lacan's, Clément's, Chase's, and her own interpretations of this dream (27–32). See also Adams (14–19).

7. Ruth Leys deconstructs Caruth's theory of trauma as a literalization resistant to representation, as well as the neurobiological model of traumatic memory on which it is based—primarily that of Bessel van der Kolk (229–307). She thus contests the prevailing paradigm of contemporary trauma theory.

8. For Rushdy, Denver is "the signifyin(g) daughter" (579)—the one whose mission is to learn how Sethe's act fits into "the larger communal history of slavery's suffering" and to give meaning to that act within the context of "her shared history—her family's, her community's, her culture's" (581, 585).

9. For a discussion of how Freud's psychoanalytic perspective on hysteria emerged from and interacted with contemporary psychiatric, physiological, and sexological discourses that also bridged psyche and body, see Dianne Sadoff's *Sciences of the Flesh*.

10. Hortense Spillers's "Mama's Baby, Papa's Maybe" describes slavery as a system of domination that mandated slaves' "absence from a subject position," while imprinting the terms of their subjugation on their bodies (67).

11. For the importance of language and literacy to slaves, see Henry Louis Gates, "Introduction" xxiii–xxxi and Houston Baker. Baker writes, "Only by grasping the word could [the slave] engage in speech acts that would ultimately define his selfhood" and release him from the slaveowners' definition of him as "silently laboring beast" (245, 247). Jennifer Fleischner points out how influential Gates has been in establishing an "interpretive tradition" of slave narratives that foregrounds the importance of literacy to slaves (15–17).

12. Contrary to most readings of *Beloved*, which celebrate the entry of the pain and suffering into language as a means of healing, Boudreau argues that "the novel refuses to celebrate the pain that has produced" the fragmentation of Sethe and Paul D by insisting on "the incapacitating effects of slavery." As a result of slavery's torture, she says, "the characters in Morrison's novel have no access to the methods of ordered narrative. Their language, their reasoning powers, even their sense of self have been dismantled by the process of torture" (453).

13. Saidiya Hartman writes that "pain is essential to the making of productive slave laborers"; "pain is a normative condition that encompasses the legal subjectivity of the enslaved that is constructed along the lines of injury and punishment" (51). Richard Brodhead similarly emphasizes the centrality of whipping to the slave system: "Whipping *means* slavery. It emblematizes both an actual practice and the whole structure of relations that identify Southern slavery as a system" (142).

14. Caroline Rody reads *Beloved* "as a historiographic intervention, a strategic recentering of American history in the lives of the historically dispossessed" and stresses the affective aspect of this historical reconstruction: it is a "structure of historiographic desire, attempt[ing] to span a vast gap of time, loss, and ignorance to achieve an intimate bond, a bridge of restitution or healing, between the authorial present and the ancestral past" (94, 97).

15. Robert Samuels likewise understands that Morrison wants "to locate slavery and racism as the repressed heart of American culture and history" and to persuade American readers to process them in a new way; yet *Beloved* also acknowledges that the real of slavery's trauma cannot be fully entered into the symbolic (*Writing* 121). Lisa Garbus also writes on "the impossibility of *Beloved*'s subject matter and its telling," invoking the Lacanian real to describe what eludes its symbolic structures (54–55).

16. Valerie Smith comments that the disconnected linguistic units of Beloved's monologue "place all the moments of Beloved's sensation and recollection in a continuous and eternal present"; "this section of the novel resists explication, [prompting], rather, the recognition that what is essentially and effectively unspoken can never be conveyed and comprehended linguistically" ("'Circling,'" 351, 352). Brenda Marshall comments on this passage, "Perhaps the most obvious critique here of traditional history in the form of countermemory is the blurring of pastpresentfuture. There is nothing in *Beloved* that denies the past" (183).

17. Morrison herself says that the ghost is both Sethe's daughter, "her child returned to her from the dead," and "a survivor from the true, factual slave ship" (Darling 5). Naomi Morgenstern maintains that if one could pinpoint an origin for this intergenerational tragedy, it would have to be "the trauma of the Middle Passage, which establishes a pattern of separation and desertion" that is then repeated through generations of slave mothers and daughters (113–15). Deborah Horvitz thinks that it is Sethe's mother who speaks in Beloved's monologue from the slave ships, wanting to reunite with her own mother (162–63). Horvitz sums up Beloved's collective meaning thus: "The powerful corporeal ghost who creates matrilineal connection between Africa and America, Beloved stands for every African woman whose story will never be told. She is the haunting symbol of the many Beloveds—generations of mothers and daughters—hunted down and stolen from Africa.... [She] weaves in and out of different generations within the matrilineal chain. Yet... she is rooted in a particular story and is the embodiment of specific members of Sethe's family" (157–58). Caroline Rody states that "part of Beloved's strangeness derives... from the emotional burden she carries as a symbolic compression of innumerable forgotten people into one miraculously resurrected personality, the remembering of the 'sixty million' in one youthful body" (104). Iyunolu Osagie also analyzes the narrative strategies that allow the reader to see and accept the contradictory identities of Beloved: according to Osagie, she is both Sethe's daughter and a sexually abused slave who came over on a slave ship.

The variety of identities that various critics have assigned to Beloved testifies to her multiplicity. Elizabeth House argues persuasively that Beloved was the daughter of a mother captured in Africa and separated from her on the slave ship; once on American soil, Beloved was locked up by a white man and used for sexual purposes. Beloved "mistakenly thinks that Sethe is her long lost mother" (121), as Sethe mistakenly takes Beloved for the infant she killed. Denise Heinze sees Beloved as Sethe's double, more psychological than supernatural, who embodies Sethe's "own unforgiving memory" and "grows obese with Sethe's guilt" (208). Trudier Harris interprets Beloved as a supernatural creature—a demon, a succubus, a vampire—who is driven by a "desire for vengeance" (for her murder) and who, as a "female body reduced to desire," has all the demonic characteristics ascribed to female desire by a patriarchal imaginary (157, 155). To Karen Fields Beloved embodies "need itself—need for human connection, for warmth, for identity, for stories and on ad infinitum through all the things one human can willingly give to another, and more than that" (160). J. Brooks Bouson helpfully summarizes several more interpretations: "Morrison's character has been variously interpreted as 'the incarnated memory of Sethe's guilt'; as 'the objectification of the angry and revengeful ancestral spirits'; as an embodiment of 'the ghost of slavery that must haunt both personal and historical memories'; and as 'a complex metaphor for black America's relationship with its enslaved past'" (Rushdy 578, Bowers 71, Carmean 88, Keenan 48; qtd. in Bouson 234.)

18. Sethe still leaves out of mind and out of language the crucial trauma of her own abandonment: her mother was probably hanged for running away, and in escaping she had left Sethe behind. Sethe thus joins the many daughters in *Beloved* torn away from their mothers by slavery's disruptions. (See Morgenstern).

19. Barbara Christian calls on West African cosmology to explain the significance, for their descendants, of those lost on the Middle Passage. Since in the West African belief system family continuity and individual identity depended on keeping the ancestors present through remembering and feeding them, the loss of the "ancestors" in the Middle Passage was a "monumental collective psychic rupture for the African American slaves and their descendants" ("Fixing" 364). She understands *Beloved* as a "fixing ceremony," a memorial "for those who did not survive the Middle Passage and whose names we did not know" ("Fixing" 367).

20. Sethe's inability to tell her story leaves the account of the infanticide in the rhetoric of the masters (*Beloved* 148–151). As Mae Henderson points out, "the first [and I would add, the only] full representation of the events surrounding the infanticide [is] figured from a collective white/male perspective, represented by schoolteacher and the sheriff" ("Toni Morrison's *Beloved*" 78). The killing of the baby remains caught up in "the dominant metaphors of the master('s) narrative—wildness, cannibalism, animality, destructiveness" ("Toni Morrison's *Beloved*" 79). My PMLA article, "Giving Body to the Word," traces in more detail Sethe's failure to enter into language (and tell the story of the baby's death) as a refusal of substitutions related both to her self-image as nursing mother and to her refusal to acknowledge the loss of the nursing baby.

Had she access to it, Sethe would find in the discourse of actual slave mothers a language better suited to a perverse system which dictates that putting her children "where they would be safe" (163) can only mean transporting them out of this world. Harriet Jacobs, writing from within the paradoxes of the "peculiar institution," indeed connects maternal love to infanticide: "I would rather see [my children] killed than have them given up to [the slaveholder's] power"; "death is better than slavery" (80, 62).

21. There are many problems in extrapolating from one collective historical catastrophe to another, as Stanley Elkins's *Slavery: A Problem in American Institutional and Intellectual Life* shows (See Fleischner 11–13). But elements of the environment in which the second-generation Holocaust children grew up were similar to the household in which Denver grew up. The present life of the family was overshadowed by a traumatic past that was not spoken about, was not transformed into narrative. Dedicated to the renewal of life, most of the parents—the Holocaust survivors—imposed "a pact of silence" about their horrific past on themselves and on their children. And the parallels with Denver's coping strategies are striking. When their children offered hypotheses of what had happened to their parents, the parents dismissed these as fantasies. The children, instead of dismissing or repressing the guessed-at trauma, tended to make a global identification with the parent at the level of the body and "act out the traumatic aspects of their parents' lives as if it were their own story." The children's identification with their parents is extreme and totalizing, "characterized both by the totality of the immersion in another reality and by the involvement of the body" (Grubrich-Simitis 310–11; 303).

22. Morrison's narrative structure also respects the incomprehensibility of trauma, its resistance to sequential logic, by revealing the past out of temporal sequence—a bit here, a bit there. That fragmentation mimes the disconnected, involuntary nature of flashbacks. Such stylistic devices enable Morrison to honor the "truth" of traumatic experience, which "may reside not only in its brutal facts, but also in the way their occurrence defies simple comprehension" (Caruth 153). Philip Page shows how the circularity and fragmentation of Morrison's narrative structure parallels the indirect, piecemeal remembering of the characters.

23. Margaret Homans's notion of literalization enabled me to see how Morrison's metaphors work. "Literalization . . . occurs when some piece of overtly figurative language, a simile or an extended or conspicuous metaphor, is translated into an actual event or circumstance" (*Bearing the Word* 30).

24. Samuels "read[s] the ending of the novel as an extended address that is made to all of America. *Beloved* can . . . be read as reminder of a part of American history that has never been fully dealt with and so it rests 'disremembered and unaccounted for.' . . . In order for the broken fragments of Beloved's history to be re-membered and reorganized, we as a nation need to face up to the facts and begin a form of communal healing" (*Writing* 132). Avery Gordon says that *Beloved* is "about the lingering inheritance of racial slavery. . . . Slavery has ended, but something of it continues to live on, . . . propelling, as it always has, a something to be done. Such endings that are not over is what haunting is about" (139). The ghost Beloved, like all

ghosts, "forces a reckoning," a revisioning of "the lost subjects of history" and their continuing effects in the present (139, 195).

25. James Phelan gives a perceptive and detailed reading of the coda to *Beloved*, interpreting all the variations of "This is not a story to pass on," as well as all the indications of Beloved's absent presence, all the "negatives [that] suggest her ineradicable presence beneath all the denials of her" (273). He characterizes both the character Beloved and the novel's ending as "stubborn," presenting the reader with a "recalcitrance that will not yield" (714)—a refusal of the reader's desire for mastery, a reminder of our inability to grasp the history of the millions lost to slavery.

26. The failure of narrative closure to contain Beloved leaves the reader haunted, too, as Linda Krumholz says: "Beloved ... defies narrative closure or categorization, foreclosing the possibility of a complete 'clearing' for the reader. As the reader leaves the book, we have taken on slavery's haunt as our own" (396). Linda Anderson describes Morrison's "exploration of history's absences, of how what is unwritten and unremembered can come back to haunt us" (137). James Berger says that the ending reminds us that in the logic of trauma and symptom that has informed the novel, "traumatic memories that are repressed or denied return." He quotes Theodor Adorno to make the point that "even if the story is not passed on, the ghosts will return to inhabit each succeeding present 'until the causes of what happened then are no longer active. Only because these causes live on does the spell of the past remain ... unbroken'" (Adorno 129; Berger 415). See also Teresa Heffernan, who argues that "Beloved's ghostly return testifies to the untranslatable ... and disrupts the order of the symbolic" (569). Heffernan argues that the novel foregrounds "counter-memory," which disputes the efficacy of the "accounting-memory," which "seeks redemption from and reconciliation with the past" (562). She maintains that *Beloved* disputes the possibility of translating loss into language.

Chapter 4

1. Wini Breines responds to the question of why no integrated women's movement emerged from the liberation movements of the 1960s and 1970s by "examining white and black feminists' political histories as a way to understand why we were unsuccessful in crossing the color line" (1099). According to the many documents from the time that Breines quotes, white women and black women in the civil rights movement and early second-wave feminist movement appear to have fought for widely divergent ideals and goals, to have understood events in very different ways, and consequently to cherish far different memories of the two movements. Perhaps most relevant to the present focus on multiracial community is Breines's finding that while white women in the civil rights and early feminist movements believed, then and now, that they were working toward an ideal of a "universal, racially integrated sisterhood and

brotherhood ... a truly interracial community," "such idealism, a romanticization of interracial harmony, ... is not common among African Americans. Most did not see it that way. They wanted to be free; they wanted equal opportunity, justice, and peace, to be able to live any life they chose. Integration was not necessarily the goal; neither was building community with whites. Equality was" (1096, 1097, 1099). The range of texts by black and white women that Breines consults, together with her "insider/outsider" mode of analysis, provide an important historical context for understanding the difficulties that beset efforts to establish cross-race feminist alliances today.

For Hazel Carby's historical analysis, see note 26, below.

2. Elin Diamond describes the obscuration of the other that takes place in this process somewhat differently than I do by focusing on the perception of the self in the other that the mirror stage process engenders: "Here is the thralldom of what Lacan calls the mirror stage: the investment in a superior version of the ego—the image—that becomes fixed in one's psychic repertoire as an ideal ego.... the notion of 'projecting before' suggests that one's relation to the other is always, to some extent, a relation to oneself" ("Rethinking" 88); having glimpsed the perfected image of the self in an external form, one continues to see in the other the perfected image of the self. Either way—through the idealization of the other's form or through the perception of the idealized self in the other—the other's own subjectivity is eclipsed. (See also Diamond, *Unmaking Mimesis* 113.)

In emphasizing the desire for identification, I downplay the aggressivity that, Lacan says in the "Aggressivity" essay, always accompanies identification with the mirroring other. Jane Gallop puts it this way: "For Lacan, aggression is produced in response to the mirror image. There is a rivalry over which is the self and which the other, which the ego and which the replica" (*Reading* 62). See footnote 4 to the Introduction.

3. According to Seshadri-Crooks's Lacanian analysis, race is a system of signifiers governed by the master signifier, Whiteness. The signifier of whiteness is embedded in the unconscious, where it becomes imbricated with the fundamental fantasy ($\mathcal{S} <> a$) and its promise of wholeness. The belief in the absolute mastery and wholeness of whiteness sustains the whole race system. Seshadri-Crooks courageously addresses the most intractable aspect of race, the seeming incontrovertibility of visual evidence of race in skin color, hair, texture, and facial features. She contends that these bodily marks arise from the viewing subject's racial anxiety: when one is confronted with the historicity of whiteness, with evidence of its purely social construction, one becomes anxious at the dissolution of one's racial belief system and projects the bodily mark of race onto the other.

4. My thinking on the conflict between the stasis of the ideal ego and the temporal flux of the body has been influenced by the essays (on, respectively, Lacan and Irigaray) of Richard Boothby and Ewa Ziarek ("Toward a Radical"). Elizabeth Grosz has also speculated that the "form of fixity ... is an attempt to arrest rigidly the tensions of the opposition between the fragmented perceived body and the unified specular body" (43).

5. Cheng's analysis of Linda's (Nancy Kwan's) infatuation with her mirror image in the movie version of *Flower-Drum Song* brings out the potential complexity of a woman of color's assimilation to an ideal of white beauty. In Linda's relishing of her figure in the mirror is more than self-alienation: "Yes, interpellated, subjected, mediated, but something in the subject produced here exceeds that subjection, and that excess is the pleasure and source of self-identification: *I enjoy being [a girl]*. The celebration may be ... about transforming the abject state of being a (racialized) girl into celebrated materiality" (57).

6. Here again Morrison seems to be stealing a page from Freud. Freud says that the only explanation for man's use of the word "dog"—"his most faithful friend in the animal world"—as the ultimate derogatory term of abuse is his contempt for an animal dominated by the sense of smell (*Civilization* 47, n. 1). Freud does not say, but we can extrapolate, that humans are projecting their own repressed and repudiated "animal" sense of smell onto the dog.

7. Wilfred Samuels and Clenora Hudson-Weems also read the night women as a positive force, "interested in healing Jadine of her inauthenticity, trying to restore the ancient properties she has lost as a result of losing touch with her culture.... The night women simply want to nurse Jadine into a healthy mental attitude toward her culture" (91). Likewise, Cynthia Edelberg says that the night women are "the keepers of 'sacred properties'" who want to restore Jadine's cultural loyalties and natural urges (232).

8. The spirits who dwell there (the *vieilles*) could well be the spirits of slave women, since it is reputed that they have sexual relations with the spirits of the blind slaves who ride horseback over the mountains of the island.

9. J. Brooks Bouson discusses all the meanings that "tar" has for Morrison—in the first instance, "the positive qualities [that Jadine lacks]: both the maternal, nurturing qualities that act as a social 'glue,' and also the 'tar' of blackness that comes from being in touch with one's African-American roots." Bouson also quotes Morrison, in the LeClair interview, saying that "At one time, a tar pit was a holy place ... because tar was used to build things.... For me, the tar baby came to mean the black woman who can hold things together" (LeClair 122; qtd. in Bouson, *Quiet* 104). See also Bouson, *Quiet* 104–05, 121–22, 124. Marilyn Mobley's article explores "the dilemma Morrison faced in trying to depict the potential consequences of success predicated upon disconnection from one's racial identity and cultural heritage" (285). Evelyn Hawthorne comments on Morrison's "deep concern" for the loss of traditional African and African American values represented by the "modern woman" Jadine's assimilation to white Western culture. She contrasts Jadine's artificial mannequin persona with the embodiment of authenticity and origin in the African woman in yellow (103–04). James Coleman characterizes Jadine as "a hard-driving, selfish, materialistic Black woman with no strong connections to ... the folk past" (68). Lucille P. Fultz describes Ondine's attempts to instill (belatedly) a "womanist" sensibility in Jadine, a sense of loyalty to traditional black communal and familial values (238–41).

10. The text's endorsement of maternity as a "natural" instinct that Jadine is repressing could well be troubling to feminists, who have fought hard to decouple women from biology and from the notion that a "real woman" is defined by motherhood. In interview, Morrison backs up the novel's insistence on a corporeal "fertility and nurturing" (269): "That quality of nurturing is essential... she cannot nurture and be a career woman... [that is] not at all what her body was for. She does not intend to have children" (Ruas 104–05). It is risky to represent maternity as a denied instinct of Jadine's body, since that idea returns women to the traditional definition of woman as mother and implies that she who is not a mother is not "a real woman." It should be said, however, that Morrison's fiction as a whole does not carry this prescription for motherhood, but offers a broad spectrum of maternal representations, from the antimaternal (in *Sula*) to the inadequate (in *The Bluest Eye*) to the overmaternal (in *Beloved*).

11. Trudier Harris likewise understands the three groups of mythic female figures—the swamp women, the night women, and the woman in yellow, as "suppressed parts of [Jadine's] basic nature," like the "'smells' that she will not admit into her consciousness" (144; see also 142–43).

12. Although most commentators on *Tar Baby* (including Morrison herself [Dowling 53, Ruas 102]) have identified Jadine as the tar baby, made by the white man (the farmer/Valerian) to ensnare the trickster figure (Br'er Rabbit/ Son), I prefer to interpret tar as a symbol of African American cultural traditions and argue that Jadine's struggles with tar express her ambivalent relation to that tradition. Despite her self-proclaimed liberation from the "backward" legacy of black history, Jadine is not free of her black cultural heritage: it clings to her by way of her attraction to it—as the tarpit imagery suggests. See note 9 above, for a survey of the meanings of tar.

13. Kalpana Seshadri-Crooks uses the language of the symbolic register to describe all aspects of the mirror stage and of (what I have been calling) imaginary identification. She asserts that the mirror-stage experience is entirely governed by the symbolic, that the visual form taken in at the mirror becomes the ego ideal (rather than the ideal ego), and that accordingly the ego ideal is the source of all secondary identifications. I think that in the passages I quote from Seminar I and the "Mirror Stage" essay in the introduction to this chapter, Lacan clearly labels "ideal ego" the self-image derived from the mirror, specifies this ideal ego as the source of all secondary identifications, and describes as "imaginary" the identifications based on mirror-stage processes (see pp. 88–89, above, *Écrits* 2, Dylan Evans, *Dictionary* 52). When in Seminar XI Lacan includes the symbolic in the mirror stage he is careful to keep imaginary and symbolic positions separate, so that the admiring mother's gaze comes from a symbolic position and the baby has to make a symbolic identification with her as the ego ideal before it can admire, and take in, its own image as ideal ego. I would argue that maintaining these distinctions between imaginary and symbolic positions enables Lacan to define psychic processes more precisely and to describe with more exactitude the complex interactions of imaginary and symbolic.

14. While I interpret Jadine's adoption of a lean male body-image as an embrace of white American individualism taken to the masculinist extreme of defensive autonomy, Sandra Paquet aligns Jadine with the figure of the black male who flees responsibility and connection for freedom and adventure: "Jadine takes flight, literal and metaphoric, in a spirit of repudiation, substituting personal freedom, self-reliance, and a 'black male' spirit of adventure for rootedness in the ancestral way of black women as nurturers and keepers of hearth and home. Her flight is another version of Milkman's self-centered, self-serving plane flight in *Song of Solomon*" (202).

15. The ending contains only one contradictory note of hope: Jadine resolves to "tangle with the woman in yellow—with her and with all the night women" (290); the verb "tangle" promises a struggle with the repudiated body and cultural heritage on a closer, more intimate level than the specular—for, as Br'er Rabbit discovered, to tangle with tar is to become ever more entangled in its embrace. Despite this one note of ambiguous promise, the ending of *Tar Baby* is surely among the most pessimistic of Morrison's conclusions. Ideally, the novel would end with a consolidation of the loving couple, Jadine and Son—the "new woman's" ambition and energy grounded in an attachment to the African-American cultural heritage represented by Son. Instead, the future (Jadine's ambition and determination to "make it" in the world as it is) is split off from the past (Son's cherished connection with black tradition and black history). The link to the past, Son, becomes immured in myth—for the ending suggests that Son joins the mythic slave horsemen of the island—so it cannot infuse the world of the present; and the future, the modern woman, ends literally "up in the air"—rootless, "cut off" from the ancestors and their "ancient properties" (305).

Denise Heinze perceptively interprets the pair, Jadine and Son, as the representation of "the schizophrenia—the double-vision—inherent in being black in a white America. She is the persona, the public mask struggling to gain acceptance. He is the soul, the anima keeping alive a culture threatened by extinction. That they cannot resolve their differences... is a manifestation of the psychic fragmentation of the culture as a whole" (36–37).

16. In *Fair Sex, Savage Dreams* Walton contributes to this project by uncovering the racial fantasies that construct whiteness in seminal essays on femininity and sexuality by 1930s feminist analysts like Marie Bonaparte, Melanie Klein and Joan Riviere. Although race infused the case histories of the patients on which they based their theories of femininity, race played no part in these analysts' interpretations. That exclusion is typical of psychoanalysis, Walton argues. Through analyses of texts by Margaret Mead and H.D., as well as the above theorists, she shows how processes of racialization are indissolubly linked to processes of sexuation in female subjects' development.

17. Lauren Berlant gives one explanation for this corporeal idealization: a white woman splits off her sexually marked corporeal identity as a strategy for living up to the demand, reified in the U.S. Constitution, that a citizen be

a disembodied abstract individual; thus bourgeois white femininity hides the body beneath sex-denying clothes in an effort to meet that definition of abstract "person." But then, since she is denied body, the white bourgeois woman looks with envy at the African-American woman—irrevocably embodied because of the skin color that, in our color-coded social hierarchy, precludes invisibility—and she longs for reembodiment through the fantasy of being a black woman.

Margaret Homans contrasts three postmodern white feminists' use of black women to represent embodiment with two African American women's "identification of the black woman with her body" ("Women of Color" 90). While Judith Butler, Diana Fuss, and Donna Haraway use the figures of African American women "to do the work of embodiment," but also, paradoxically, to make the case for a poststructuralist disembodied subject ("Women of Color" 86–87), Alice Walker and Patricia Williams celebrate the body playfully, as the site of a potential reconciliation for the disparate "selves" inevitably coexisting in a professional woman of color who must meet the demands of disparate race, gender, and professional discourses.

18. Jennifer Fleischner's analysis of nineteenth-century antislavery romance shows that white idealizations of black women have a long history, particularly as white reading and writing strategies. The romances' idealized portrait of the mistreated but virtuous slave woman "manage[d] the fear of difference" for the white female reader while an emphasis on the black woman's inferior station prevented a too complete identification and thus obviated "the threat to the integrity of white womanhood implied by total sameness. This could be done by idealizing difference and transforming it into a mode of identification" (39). That mode of identification tended toward pity rather than empathy, maintaining a measure of distance (40).

19. The intersection of class, gender, and culture makes for a continuum of "femininities," of course; middle-class Jewish and Italian American women could not be said to be indoctrinated with self-effacing gestures to the degree that WASP women are.

20. The projection of an ideal wholeness onto the other woman's body is particularly marked in the essay "The Love Letter" ("La lettre d'amour") by Annie Leclerc, which Jane Gallop has critiqued in "Annie Leclerc Writing a Letter with Vermeer." In "The Love Letter" the other woman is set apart from the writer by class rather than by race: Leclerc devotes much of the letter to the praises of the servant-woman in her favorite painting, Vermeer's "Lady Writing a Letter, with her Maid." Annie Leclerc perceives the servant-woman as "whole unto herself" (Gallop, "Annie" 151), and she locates that wholeness in the body. She wants nothing, for in "the well-being of her body" she has everything (Leclerc 128; my translation). Leclerc dwells on the body, on the way it curves in on itself in self-enclosure: "Here the curve of the round arms, the warm, secure closure of the forearms, the hands tenderly joined. . . . wedded" (Leclerc 136). As Gallop says, this closure figures the servant's "erotic self-sufficiency" (Gallop, "Annie" 150). Not just erotic, I would add: Leclerc repeats that "she

knows, she knows," and by not specifying the nature of that knowledge, she implies that the servant knows, in and through her body, everything worth knowing about being alive. Corporeal plenitude becomes "une plenitude toute-savant," an all-knowing plenitude: as in the excerpts from the white American feminists, above, a fullness of knowledge is lodged in the body. It would seem that in all these cases, the vehicle for idealization echoes the illusion of self-presence at the mirror—the outline of a body that is self-enclosed and apparently self-consistent.

21. Mary Ann Doane quotes this sentence from Fanon, commenting that the white gaze "fixes the black person, producing a subjectivity which is fully aligned with a process of reification" (*Femmes Fatales* 224). Indira Karamcheti similarly protests against the reduction of black professors on college campuses to a corporeal schema that denotes (only) otherness: "We are, in fact, encased in the personal and visible facts of our visible selves, walking exemplars of ethnicity and of race ... We are flesh and blood information retrieval systems, native informants who demonstrate and act out difference" (Karamcheti 13–17; qtd. in duCille 96).

22. DuCille comments sensibly on Gallop's conversation that if she really wanted McDowell's approval, she could include her and other black feminist scholars "in the category of feminist theorists"—in other words, respect their work, "treat black feminist critics as colleagues to be respected, not feared" (101).

23. On the social construction of black women, see also Elsa Barkley Brown, Hazel Carby, Patricia Hill Collins *(Black Feminist Thought)*, Angela Davis, Paula Giddings, Joyce Ladner, and Claudia Tate *(Domestic)*.

24. Radford-Hill enumerates the traits of this new maternal version of Strong Black Woman:

> Attitude—Don't take abuse. Call the question.
>
> Altitude—Don't settle. Have lofty aspirations.
>
> Image—Look good. The worse you feel, the better you need to look. Have style.
>
> Faith—Never give up. Love yourself, your people, and your community. (1086)

25. Morgan distinguishes carefully between the stereotypes of strong-blackwoman and the historical reality of black women's strength: "I draw strength daily from the history of struggle and survival that is a black woman's spiritual legacy" (87). And she agrees with Radford-Hill's assessment of the gender role's utility as "emotional inoculation" against the ravages of sexism and racism (104); but "this myth also tricks many of us into believing we can carry the weight of the world" (104).

26. Slave system ideology constructed black slave women as sexually insatiable bodies in order to impute to them the initiative for sexual relations

with the white slave-owners who raped them; racist ideology continued after slavery to justify the rape of African-American women by representing them "as sexually permissive, as available and eager for the sexual assaults of any man" (hooks, *Ain't* 52). Contemporary idealizations of black women's bodies from the site of white femininity also ignore the painful history of African American women's relation to the requirements of white femininity. As Hazel Carby has shown, the nineteenth-century hegemonic ideal of the spiritual, pure white lady rested on a contrast with the sexualized body of the African-American slave woman (23–34). See also Davis 5–12; Giddings 43.

Bell hooks claims that United States culture is marked by an unbroken historical continuum of white "primitivist" projections of "wildness" and natural spontaneity onto black bodies that extends into contemporary cultural productions ("Eating" 34). Hooks calls this white appropriation of black bodies "eating the Other" to emphasize its incorporative nature and points up its dehistoricizing effects: "consumer cannibalism... not only displaces the Other but denies the significance of that Other's history through a process of decontextualization" ("Eating" 31). The psychic mechanism operating here seems to be the whites' need to recharge a vitiated body by means of identification with an African-American body phantasmatically endowed with untamed vitality and sensual energy, with some "secret access to intense pleasure, particularly pleasures of the body" ("Eating" 26). Eric Lott's study analyzes the vulgar excesses of the "black" body portrayed in nineteenth-century black-face minstrelsy as the vehicle for white working-class spectators' vicarious enjoyment of the bodily transgressions denied them by the newly instituted ethic of industrial "morality" and "workday rationality" (148, 145). Lott gives a historical and psychological account of the dialectic of "racial insult and racial envy" in blackface minstrel shows (18), demonstrating how the projection of repellant but enjoyable bodily pleasures onto the other constituted and reinforced white subjectivity (See especially 148–50). Susan Gubar points out that minstrelsy's exclusive emphasis on "the black body... excludes African Americans from rationality, reducing them instead to physicality, desire, animality, entertainment" (*Racechanges* 96). The Harlem of the 1930s provides another historical example of white projections of the desire for a lost primitivism onto blacks: Harlem became a place where white Americans could rediscover their own primitive selves. Marianne Torgovnick describes the source of primitivism as a desire for "overcoming alienation from the body, restoring the body, and hence the self, to a relation of full and easy harmony with nature or the cosmos" (228).

27. Silverman buttresses her contention that one can "idealize and identify at a distance" in two ways: first, in addition to Lacan's mirror stage, she draws on Wallon's alternative model of the mirror stage as a moment when one both identifies with the mirror image and recognizes its distance from the observing self: "the visual imago remains stubbornly exterior" (*Threshold* 23). Secondly, she specifies that the cinema she envisions should play with idealization, showing that idealization is an aura bestowed by the spectator. The object of idealization should "seem not so much [to] incarnate ideality as [to] wear it, like a cloak" (*Threshold* 37). She requires that the new cinema perform the

difficult operation of idealizing a figure—so as to enchant the viewer and compel identification—while simultaneously drawing attention to the very process of idealization, so that the viewer becomes aware that idealization is a gift that the observer bestows on the object. The film that Silverman finds exemplary for her purposes is *Looking for Langston* (see especially 104–08).

28. Of course, the visual evidence that the other woman is black is itself culturally determined. While the certainty with which we identify the body as either black or white seems to rely on the simplicity and authority of the visible, that certainty itself rests on an Enlightenment convention that, as Foucault has explained, started with the seventeenth-century natural scientists' equation of seeing with knowing. The other's skin color seems to be a matter of immediate perception, "given as a function of the most visible organ—the skin" (Doane, *Femmes Fatales* 224), but the enormous range of skin colors that fall under either "black" or "white" belies the absoluteness of racial categories and so (had we but eyes to see) undermines the myth of absolute racial difference. See Robyn Wiegman for an account of the visual economies that underwrite the racial binary (especially 8–10; 21–42). See Brody for an account of the role of hybridity in the production of "pure" categories of racial difference in Victorian culture (11–13; 59–97).

29. Paul Gilroy argues that the visual regime of racial difference is becoming obsolete as a result of new technologies which redefine the body, such as medical imaging, which focuses on the interior of the body and genomic study, which refigures the body as code and information. "When the body becomes absolutely penetrable, and is refigured as the transient epiphenomenon of coded invisible information, . . . that aesthetic, that [racializing] gaze, and that regime of power are irrecoverably over" (47).

30. Hortense Spillers also protests white culture's appropriation of the African-American "body in its material and abstract phase [as] a resource for metaphor" ("Mama's Baby" 66). The account that Spillers offers of the black body is, on the contrary, concrete and material, grounded in the historical actuality of the markings, mutilations, and rapes that black Americans experienced at the hands of white slave-owning Americans ("Mama's Baby" 67–73).

31. As Gallop points out, Marjorie Pryse and Hortense Spillers, coeditors of *Conjuring*, write on African-American women writers from very different perspectives in, respectively, the introduction and the afterword to the anthology. From my perspective, the Pryse introduction, though it works on a body of literary works rather than on the body of a black woman, bears some marks of an idealizing process that align it with the idealizing comments of the white feminists in the present study (and Pryse is herself a white feminist academic). Pryse works hard to unify an African-American women writers' tradition, untiringly tracing the inspiration of individual authors to a single source, "the genuine power of the folk tradition" (17). "By their combined recognition and mutual naming, based on magic, oral inheritance, and the need to struggle against oppression, black women writers . . . affirm the wholeness and endur-

ance of a vision" (5). Pryse's reading of the entire sequence of African–American women writers as "affirm[ing] the wholeness ... of a vision" betrays the tendency of idealization to construct the other as whole and self-consistent. And as totally other: Gallop finds her desire for an "exoticised, idealized other" answered by Pryse's insistence that the tradition of African-American women writers, rather than betraying any influence by the European novel or by the white male American literary tradition, is based on something entirely different—on oral tradition, magic, and folk wisdom. Again, the vision of the other (here, a body of literature) as whole and self-completed comes linked to the vision of the other's racial purity.

In the epilogue, Hortense Spillers by contrast explains the collected writings of African American women in terms of discontinuities and the confluence of various traditions, including that of white male American writing: "What these breaks and interstices in the pattern of woman-making would argue is that these writers engage no allegiance to a hierarchy of dynastic meanings that unfold in linear succession and according to our customary sense of 'influence.'" It is, rather, "contradiction and rupture" that characterize the "serial array" of black writers ("Afterword" 258). See also DuCille 102–05.

Chapter 5

1. In *The Psychic Life of Power,* Judith Butler theorizes the following issues: "How are we to account for the desire for the norm and for subjection more generally in terms of a prior desire for social existence, a desire exploited by regulatory power? ... How is it, then, that the longing for subjection, based on a longing for social existence, recalling and exploiting primary dependencies, emerges as an instrument and effect of the power of subjection?" (*Psychic Life* 9–20). See also Mladen Dolar's analysis of the circularity in Althusser's argument: the acceptance of the hail assumes the existence of a consenting subject who accepts the call from the symbolic order that creates him as subject ("Beyond" 90).

2. See also Lisa Loew's revision of Althusser to make room for a multiply interpellated subject, "hailed by several ideologies whose conditions of production are heterogeneous and incommensurable" (146).

3. "Man's desire is the desire of the Other" opens up to many interpretations. Here, "the Other" is the symbolic order—the usual signification of the big (capitalized) Other. And the signification of the phrase, then, is that one desires to be the object of desire of the Other. Or, as I explain later in the chapter, the desire of the Other is also the lack in the Other, the gap in the symbolic order called the object a (the gaze), and the phrase indicates a desire to be the object of desire of the gaze. In chapters 2 and 3 above, I read the "desire of the Other" to be the desire of the first representative of the symbolic order (the Other) in the baby's life—the parent: in that case, "Man's desire is the desire of the Other" means, as in Bruce Fink's reading, "Man's desire is the

same as the Other's desire," or "[Man] desires what the Other desires in the same way [as the Other] . . . Man learns to desire as an other, as if he were some other person" (*Lacanian* 54).

4. Frances Restuccia similarly describes how "the women's narrative conveyed by the *telenovela* naturalizes the sweetness of pain" and leads to Cleófilas's acceptance of Juan Pedro's beatings: " 'Woman Hollering Creek' links Foucauldian disciplinary power operating through soap operas to the success of Foucauldian spectacular power, such as that wielded by Juan Pedro Martinez Sanchez over Cleófilas" (117, 116). Restuccia traces connections between pain, the loss of language and the final liberating holler and locates the abuse Cleófilas suffers in the social context of the acceptance of violence to women.

5. Bourdieu claims that "photographic practice only exists and subsists for most of the time by virtue of its family function or rather by the function conferred upon it by the family group, namely that of solemnizing and immortalizing the high points of family life, in short, of reinforcing the integration of the family group by reasserting the sense that it has both of itself and of its unity" (*Photography* 19). Laura Wexler characterizes nineteenth-century photography as a "mode of domestic self-representation. It worked by staging affect or imagining relation—*seeing sentiment* as a way of organizing family life" (166).

6. Schema of the optical field (Diagram 2, S XI 91).

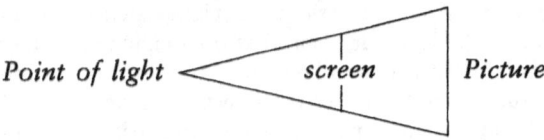

7. Schema of the optical field (Diagram 1, S XI 91).

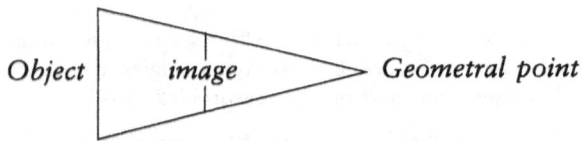

8. *The Magic Toyshop* goes on to dramatize a series of practices, discursive and familial, which transform a young girl into a feminine object—including a parodic version of the oedipal crisis and resolution. See my article, "The Violence of Gendering."

9. Robert Samuels also explains the gaze as object a, "the object that is eluded by all forms of representation and vision; it is the lack or the limit" of the visual field. "The gaze is precisely that part of the visual world that refuses to be controlled or mastered" because "the gaze as a form of the object (a) is

always without a specular image" (*Hitchcock's* 111, 112). Todd McGowan writes that traditional Lacanian film criticism ties the gaze to the imaginary: Lacanian film critics have treated "the process of spectator identification with the full presence of the cinematic image" as if it were a direct recapitulation of "the infant's relationship to the mirror in what Lacan calls the mirror stage." Traditional film criticism thus misses the function of the real, which manifests in the visual field as the gaze. McGowan argues that cinema has a potentially radical dimension: certain films lead the spectator to confront the gaze, which is the point of absence in the visual field, the point at which the symbolic structure giving meaning to the film fails: there is a hole, an absence in the seeming plenitude of the visual image (*Cinemas* 21–22). In the films "of desire" which enable such an encounter with the gaze, the recognition of the gaze "reveals... the inconsistent and incomplete nature of [the spectator's] symbolic world" (17) and thus provides a position from which the spectator can perceive the faultlines in the ideology that constructs his or her everyday reality. See also the discussion of the gaze and its radical potential in film spectators' experience in McGowan's article, "Looking for the Gaze."

10. See Joanne Creighton's discussion of Clara's relation to her mother and her mother's house (68–73). See also Ellen Lambert's location of the basis for Clara's "rapt and ferocious ambition" in the "stony ground" of north-of-England hopelessness; Lambert, however, defines Clara's ambition as above all a quest for love (40–43).

11. Linda Mizejewski describes the twentieth-century social construction of glamour, using the example of the Ziegfield Girls. "Concepts such as 'sexiness' and 'glamour' are constituted by... specific class and racial concerns." The Ziegfield Girls, for example, performed whiteness and a middle-class version of sexuality as glamour. A glamorous female icon is constructed by a combination of public visibility and inaccessibility, "producing the tension of desire" (11).

Chapter 6

1. The pressure to marry and have children is strong in Mexican and Mexican-American culture. Gloria Anzaldúa articulates the Mexican gender mandate: "Educated or not, the onus is still on a woman to be a wife/mother.... Women are made to feel total failures if they don't marry and have children" (*Borderlands* 17). Pilar Aranda agrees: "Even in the eighties, Mexican women feel there are all these expectations they must fulfill, like getting married, having children" (66).

2. Paula Moya supplies a historical context that explains the salience of La Malinche (as well as La Virgen and La Llorona) in the consciousness of contemporary Chicana feminists ("Chicana" 447–48). Moya vividly describes the conflicting ideologies that produce Chicana subjectivity as multiple.

3. Mexican and Chicana feminist writers have substantially revised the Malinche myth. Rosario Castellanos's "Malinche" (reproduced in Cypess, 139–40) focuses on Malinche's feelings of betrayal as her mother sells her into slavery rather than on Malinche's betrayal of her race. Adelaida Del Castillo's essay, "Malintzin Tenepal: A Preliminary Look into a New Perspective," treats her as a woman of strong religious commitment who believed the destruction of the Aztec empire was part of an inevitable cycle that would lead to a new spiritual age for Mexico (Moraga 175). Sandra Cypess has written an exhaustive account of the changes rung on the Malinche legend over the centuries.

4. Katheryn Rios's essay on "Never Marry a Mexican" points out that Clemencia's alignment with the characteristics of Paz's *chingón* is a revolt against the passive figure of La Malinche. Paz's *Labyrinth of Solitude* is indicted by other Chicana feminists for helping to promulgate the myth of La Malinche as sexual traitor (Alarcón, "Chicana" 190 n.1; Cypess 11). His description of the gender dynamics of *el chingón* and *la chingada* is nonetheless relevant to Clemencia's sexual rhetoric.

5. For a brilliant exposition of the inevitable entanglement of disidentification with identification, see Cheng's explication of Maxine Hong Kingston's *The Woman Warrior*, especially her analysis of the bathroom torture scene (65–102).

6. See Gloria Anzaldúa's *Borderlands* for a history of the gradual splitting off of La Virgen/Tonantsin's darker, fiercer, more sexual and more powerful aspects through the successive male-dominated governing orders of Mexico, pre-Columbian through post-Conquest (27–31). "They divided her who had been complete, who possessed both upper (light) and underworld (dark) aspects" (27). Today, Anzaldúa says, the Virgen de Guadalupe "is a synthesis of the old world and the new, of the religion and culture of the two races in our psyche.... She is the symbol of the *mestizo* true to his or her Indian values" (30). See also Soto 13–14, Campbell 12–13.

7. In *Gender Trouble*, Butler argues that gender is not a property of one's core identity that expresses itself in certain behaviors; rather, the repeated performance of gender convinces the performer that she is enacting an intrinsic part of her subjectivity. "Repeated performances of gender norms that include certain ways of behaving, dressing, gesturing, and speaking create an illusion of essence, an illusion that there is something inner called femininity or masculinity that we—females and males—express in such actions" (Layton 210). Refusing to cite the norm, enacting an exaggerated parody of gender, or acting out an alternative gender position through counterhegemonic behaviors, would contribute to change, Butler says, by showing up gender as "drag," an imitation of an imitation that one "puts on" deliberately. "The possibilities of gender transformation are to be found precisely in ... the possibility of a failure to repeat, a de-formity, or a parodic repetition that exposes the phantasmatic effect of abiding identity as a politically tenuous construction" (*Gender Trouble* 141).

8. Butler clarifies and corrects misreadings of performativity such as Clemencia's in the introduction to *Bodies That Matter*. Performativity is not simply voluntaristic performance or role-playing. Performativity must be understood "not as the act by which a subject brings into being what she/he names, but, rather, as that reiterative power of discourse to produce the phenomena that it regulates and constrains" (2). For a clear and comprehensive discussion of the evolution of Butler's concept of performativity in response to critical responses to *Gender Trouble*, see Layton 210–22.

9. In "Blessings in Disguise" Susan Gubar argues that it does not strengthen female identity to leave it behind in favor of masculinity: masculine impersonation just calls attention to the weakness of being a woman, and it leaves the underlying femininity unaltered.

10. For other revisionary essays on the Virgen de Guadalupe, see the collection *Goddess of the Americas/La Diosa de las Americas: Writings on the Virgin of Guadalupe*. For a list of Chicana works that seek to restore the historical Malinche, see footnote 3, above.

11. In other legends, La Llorona as the ghost of La Malinche mourns her lost children, the Indians whom she betrayed to Cortez. La Llorona's wail is also said to have preceded Cortez, to have been one of the eight omens in Tenochtitlan that foretold the Conquest: in that case the children La Llorona grieves for are the Indians about to be slaughtered, and her cry continues through the centuries to mourn the loss of the indigenous civilization (Garza 447–54). Anzaldúa identifies La Llorona with "*Cihuacoatl*, Serpent Woman, ancient Aztec goddess of the earth, of war and birth, patron of midwives, and antecedent of *La Llorona*.... Like *La Llorona*, *Cihaucoatl* howls and weeps in the night, screams as if demented" (*Borderlands* 35). Likewise, Paz claims that the figure of La Llorona derives from Cihaucoatl (75).

12. Mary Pat Brady analyzes the political implications of spatiality in "Woman Hollering Creek," as well as in other stories in the collection. "Cisneros's title story explores ... how private violence is tacitly sanctioned by the arrangement of public space, [showing how the city's] spatial structure reinforces the patriarchal system that leaves Cleófilas bleeding and bruised" (140–41). On La Llorona and on "Woman Hollering Creek" as a "feminist revision of a powerful misogynist folktale," see Sonia Saldívar-Hull (117–23).

13. Extending Gloria Anzaldúa's account of the ways that living on the border enables creativity, Renato Rosaldo labels "transculturation" what he calls the "Chicano gift for improvisation and recombination within an array of disparate cultural elements.... Creative processes of transculturation center themselves along literal and figurative borders where the 'person' is crisscrossed by multiple identities" (215–16).

14. "First, identification is the original form of emotional tie with an object; secondly, in a regressive way it becomes a substitute for a libidinal

object-tie, as it were by means of introjection of the object into the ego" (*Group* 107–08; see also *The Ego and the Id* 31, "Mourning" 249). Mikkel Borch-Jacobsen makes a similar argument in *The Freudian Subject* (182–85).

15. Diana Fuss articulates succinctly this aspect of Freudian thought: "What Freudian psychoanalysis understands by 'subjectivity' is precisely this struggle to negotiate a constantly changing field of ambivalent identifications; indeed, subjectivity can be most concisely understood as the history of one's identifications" (34). As Elin Diamond says, "In Freud's account, it would seem that subjects are constituted by the (psychical) history of the cathected (social) objects that have transformed them. The humanist notion of identity as a stable model that the self enacts over time, that is unique, unified, and consistent, is belied by the occluded (never remembered) historicity of identificatory relations" (*Unmaking Mimesis* 111). Teresa Brennan makes a similar point relative to the ego ideal: "multiple identifications" with various ego ideal figures could "drag the subject into diverse social currents," moving the subject out of fixated ideals and into new ways of thinking (13, 11).

16. Benjamin's theory of "overinclusivity" can give the general theory of identificatory multiplicity I have been extrapolating from Freud an empirical basis in the observations of young children's gender identifications. Starting from Irene Fast's study of young children rather than from Freud, Benjamin argues that children before the age of four routinely identify with both genders, "formulating important parts of their self representations" through "cross-gender as well as same-gender identifications" (*Like* 126). The ability to make cross-sex identifications continues as an unconscious capacity which opposes the subject's conscious conformity to the cultural rule that one is either exclusively masculine or exclusively feminine. See Annie Sweetnam's article for a lucid summary of Benjamin's argument and that of other feminist relational theorists Muriel Dimen, Virginia Goldner, and Adrienne Harris. Sweetnam herself theorizes gender as sometimes fixed, sometimes fluid, depending on the requirements of the situation. See also Layton for an excellent discussion of Benjamin's theories. Layton proposes a "negotiation model" of gender identity: "men and women maintain multiple gender identities, and each gender identity is associated with its own modes of agency and relationship" (53). Subjects then have a broad repertoire of internalized gender positions to choose from. Layton points out that identifying with a range of women who are "crucially different in capacities" can be a rich source of multiple gender identifications for women, helping them "out of the painful confines of the gender binary" (60). Jacqueline Rose argues that the internalization of gender norms is always problematic because the subject is divided, and unconscious forces are always at odds with the subject's conscious assumption of a stable identity position: "Because there is no continuity of psychic life, so there is no stability of sexual identity, no position for women (or for men) which is ever simply achieved... there is a resistance to identity at the very heart of psychic life" (Rose, *Sexuality* 90–91).

Chapter 7

1. Feminist psychoanalytic critics and feminist philosophers have theorized the possibilities and hazards of using some form of identification to bridge race and culture differences. Thus Kaja Silverman in *Threshold of the Visible World* constructs a model of "heteropathic identification," or "identification-at-a-distance," that would, even in the act of idealizing the other, preserve an awareness of the other's difference. In *Like Subjects* Jessica Benjamin explores some of the same questions of identification and differences that I do, but from an object relations perspective. Diana Fuss *(Identification Papers)* and Doris Sommer *(Proceed with Caution)* warn against any attempt to use identification as a political tool for bridging difference because of its seemingly inevitable assimilation of the other to the self. Similarly, Elizabeth Spelman points out that empathetic identification with the pain of the other can be objectifying, inegalitarian, and unwelcome ("Changing the Subject"). Theorizing from a phenomenological perspective, Sonia Kruks proposes an ethic that balances "feeling-with" others and "respectful recognition" of difference as the basis for interracial feminist alliances *(Retrieving* 154, 172–6). And she points out the dangers of white women's "excessive identification" with women of color, obscuring as it does differentials of power and privilege (158). On similar issues of cross-race identification and empathy, see feminist philosophers Sandra Bartky and Maria Lugones.

2. In *Racechanges*, Susan Gubar asks this crucial question: "How can white people understand or sympathize with African Americans without distorting or usurping their perspective?" (246). At the end of her exhaustive study of cultural forms that pivot on white identifications with blacks, Gubar concludes that despite the proliferation of cross-race impersonations, imitations, and metamorphoses that she has studied in twentieth-century cultural representations, and despite the various fantasies and motivations that propel them, they "almost always seem historically to have resulted in the subordination, muting, or obliteration of the Other" *(Racechanges* 244).

3. Gloria Anzaldúa and Cherríe Moraga, with whose texts I carry on these experiments in cross-cultural dialogue, have themselves been seminal thinkers in theorizing inter-race coalitional politics. See *This Bridge Called My Back*, edited by Anzaldúa and Moraga, and Anzaldúa's anthology, *Making Face, Making Soul/Hacienda Caras*. Cynthia Franklin points out that in addition to theorizing coalitional dynamics, *This Bridge Called My Back* (1981) and *Making Face, Making Soul* (1990) "constituted new communities of and for women" that cross many of the borders drawn by identity politics (9, 5). Feminists of color have generally been more successful than white feminists in forging alliances across race. Chicana feminists, in particular, have a long tradition of theorizing the politics of such coalitions. See Paula Moya's and Chela Sandoval's accounts of the origins and history of women-of-color coalitions and the writings on coalitional dynamics they produced (Sandoval 42.2–62.4; Moya, "Chicana"

448–49). Among these theoretical writings on women-of-color movements, see Moraga and Anzaldúa; Moraga, "Preface"; Alarcón; Anzaldúa, "*Hacienda caras: Una entrada*"; Lugones. More recent Chicana discussions of women-of-color feminisms include Saldívar-Hull 2000; Sandoval; Moya, "Chicana" and *Learning*. While *This Bridge Called My Back* (1981) staged a dialogue across culture/race differences, its successor, *This Bridge Called Home* (Anzaldúa and Keating, 2002) is even more inclusive, containing essays by whites and males. See especially essays in *Home* that address issues of multiracial community, by M. Jacqui Alexander, Gloria Anzaldúa, Hector Carbaja, Cynthia Franklin, AnaLouise Keating, Toni C. King et al., Kimberly Springer, and Indigo Violet. (For a commentary on Moya's "post-positivist realism" see my article in *Signs*, "Toward Cross-Race Dialogue.")

4. I am borrowing, and reversing, the title of Trinh Minh-ha's essay, "Not You/Like You: Post-Colonial Women and the Interlocking Questions of Identity and Difference."

5. A caveat is in order here: it could be said that the following analysis idealizes the symbolic because it leaves out the many ways that the resources of the symbolic have been used to incite violence and aggression. Nonetheless, for purposes of sorting out the complex intertwining of imaginary and symbolic processes in cross-race encounters, I will be focusing here on the Lacanian idea that symbolic processes function as a constraint on imaginary identification.

6. From their daily experience of crossing cultural borders and inhabiting the several competing discourses that demand their allegiance, feminists of color have fashioned a self-definition as multiple, heterogeneous, and self-contradictory. Chicana feminists, especially, have insisted on that self-definition "as speaking subjects of a new discursive formation" in their writings (Alarcón 356), beginning with the 1981 publication of *This Bridge Called My Back*, which Moraga coedited. Many African-American feminists also stress the multiplicity of identity, of course. Perhaps the preponderance of African-American targets of idealization in white feminist texts can be ascribed in part to a culture that has historically represented African-American women visually, as bodily presences.

7. I am encouraged to make this experiment in partial identification by Moraga's own example: in an essay called "La Güera" she makes just such a cross-race and partial identification with Ntosake Shange, an African-American writer with whom she shares a single identity position ("La Güera" 32–33).

8. See chapter 6, above, for a discussion of the cultural and historical significance of La Malinche.

9. Tamise Van Pelt makes a useful and comprehensive distinction between imaginary identification and symbolic identification in her book on Lacan's three registers (57–63).

10. Joey Sprague provides a helpful summary of standpoint theorists who suggest ways of bridging this gap (530–31).

11. Doris Sommer's model of reading "minority" texts in *Proceed with Caution* has been very helpful to my thinking through the necessity for blocks against the totalizing takeover that comes along with "knowing" texts and women from other cultures.

12. I have circumvented Anzaldúa's implied prohibition on knowing through the kind offices of my colleague Adelaida Lopez, professor of Spanish, Occidental College, who translated them for me.

13. Anzaldúa's work seeks to transcend dualities like English-Spanish (Keating 1996, 70–71); she writes from a multilingual and multicultural perspective—indigenous, English, Spanish. (See also Friedman's analysis of *Borderlands'* multiplicity in *Mappings* 93–101). Indeed, Anzaldúa identifies Spanish as the language of the conquistadors. And her intended audience is not necessarily Western readers like me. But from my position as a monolingual Anglo reader an encounter with untranslated Spanish functions as the real. Then, too, I am emboldened to offer this explanation of the Spanish as a defense against assimilation into a Western frame of reference by Anzaldúa's own statements elsewhere in *Borderlands*. "White rationality" and in particular its guiding principle, "the consciousness of duality," has always posed a threat to her Indian/Mexican vision, she says. And she voices her indignation at whites' practice of appropriating the cultural practices of subordinate groups and transporting them into dominant systems of representation, erasing all traces of their indigenous meaning (36, 37, 69). For Chicana feminist interpretations of *Anzaldúa's* "Coatlicue State," see Alarcón (*"Anzaldúa's Frontera"*) and Saldívar-Hull (65–67).

14. Naomi Schor's concise summary of common ways of "knowing" the other is useful: "If othering involves attributing to the objectified other a difference that serves to legitimate her oppression, saming denies the objectified other the right to her difference. . . . If othering assumes that the other is knowable, saming precludes any knowledge of the other in her otherness" (45; qtd. in Sommer 283, n. 93).

15. Donna Haraway likewise states, eloquently, that an interchange of "partial perspectives" can sustain "the possibility of webs of connections called solidarity in politics and shared conversations in epistemology" (191). She also disputes the claim of standpoint theorists like Harding and Hartsock that oppressed standpoints automatically give one more complete access to truth (191).

16. Feminist discourse ethicists often point out this problem and suggest discursive structures for equalizing the space and weight granted to the expression of oppressed groups' interests with the space and weight accorded dominant speakers. For example, Iris Marion Young writes: "Only if oppressed groups are able to express their interests and experience in the public on an equal basis with other groups can group domination through formally equal processes of participation be avoided" (*Justice* 34). See also Fraser 46–47; Kaplan 9–10; Young, "Polity" 410–16). These feminist political theorists, including Benhabib, are writing in the shadow of a historical precedent, the famous

failure of the 1970s women's movement to make racial pluralism work. The practice of 1970s feminism, consciousness-raising, provides a paradigmatic example of a communal ethic of identification and empathy ("sisterhood") forcing out difference. See Dubey 15–16; hooks, *Ain't I*; hooks *Feminist Theory*. For a history of the 1970s women's movement and consciousness-raising, see Breines; the essays in DuPlessis and Snitow; Messer-Davidow; Michie; Ryan; Shreve.

17. I am borrowing the phrase "cold shoulder" from Doris Sommer (4).

18. Mouffe theorizes a democratic order based on "agonistic pluralism," a discursive ethic that would attempt to institutionalize, or as she says, "domesticate," the outbreaks of dissension that I have been calling the real (Olson and Worsham 183). Mouffe envisions a social bond that is based on a shared reverence for basic values like liberty and equality, but makes room for the articulation of quite different understandings of those values. Citizens would be linked by a consensus that encourages dissensus. See Mouffe, and Worsham and Olson 181–83. Ewa Ziarek's *Ethics of Dissensus* also theorizes the inevitability of antagonisms and conflicts in democratic politics. This rich and complex text brings together ethical questions of freedom and obligation with the implications of racial and sexual difference. It challenges the disembodied, desexualized notions of citizenship, rights and democratic community in traditional political discourse by considering, among other things, the ethical significance of embodiment and the ethical responsibility for the other based on accountability for racist, sexist, and economic oppression. The book also contains an analysis and critique of Mouffe's theorization of radical democracy, as well as an extended discussion of bell hooks's theories of postmodernity, race and feminism. For a discussion of the discomforts involved in cross-race alliances, see Bernice Reagon, 356; Dale Bauer and Priscilla Wald, 1299–1303.

19. See Friedman for a useful survey of contemporary feminist discourses of multiplicity and fluidity (*Mappings* 19–25). Friedman's own contribution to theories of multiplicity is "the relational discourse of positionality" (*Mappings* 22–23; *Beyond* 16–21).

20. See Moya's analysis of the distinctive qualities of Moraga's "theories in the flesh" (*Learning* 48–57).

21. African-American and white feminists' analyses of interracial political alliances in the 1960s and 1970s help to make the case that more effective political alliances can emerge from everyday knowledge of one another's lives. Based on her study of many documents from the period, Wini Breines concludes that although 1960s feminist socialist groups like Bread and Roses were genuinely antiracist, their antiracism was based on an "abstract theorizing" that "did not speak to [black women]," who continued to feel "invisible to white women." "Abstractness impaired white women's understanding of the reality of the lives of women of color" (Breines 1122–23). The root problem, writes Breines, was that "black and white women did not know each other ... [they] had little connection with each other" (Breines 1122).

Appendix

1. Mark Bracher writes that primary identification "is the inevitable consequence of human prematuration, which necessitates a degree and duration of reliance on the other that is unequaled elsewhere in the animal kingdom.... And because of this reliance, the Other plays a formative, constitutive role in the production of the human subject. This constitutive effect takes place through identification, which is an attempt to make the part of the Other that is necessary for survival into part of oneself" (4).

2. In addition to the many infant studies that demonstrate babies' longer attention span for games that introduce novelty (Stern, *Interpersonal* 73–74), Bahrick and Watson established that babies responded with more interest to a video playback of their movements when it was delayed than when it was simultaneous: that is, they seemed to prefer the disjunctive, the different, to the sameness of mirroring (cited in Benjamin, *Bonds* 259–60, note 79).

3. Stern deals with fantasy in the life of the child only briefly, and at a later stage—when the child acquires language and symbolic thinking, "toward the middle of the second year" (*Interpersonal* 163). "With the advent of language... children now have the tools to distort and transcend reality. They can create expectations contrary to past experience. They can elaborate a wish contrary to present fact." Prior to the acquisition of language, then, babies cannot "elaborate a wish contrary to present fact." Rather, they "are confined to reflect the impress of reality" (*Interpersonal* 182).

4. Taking a stand against what he sees as Stern's positivist, universalizing method, Cushman contends that psychological theorists should recognize the extent to which their models of human behavior are products of their cultural and historical context. Cushman suggests that Stern's data on parent-infant interactions would be better read as "a look into the very process of social construction itself.... Stern described the enactments of millions of behavioral microprocesses that lead, teach, and demonstrate to infants that they are little bounded, masterful, feeling selves" (210).

5. Jane Flax's skepticism about the universality of the truth claims that emerge from studies of infancy extends to infant research. "Despite its increasing volume and technical sophistication, empirical research does not validate... broad claims about early human being, cognition, or process." There is a large gap between "the observed phenomena... and the breadth of the deduced conclusion.... In such studies, observations and conclusions hang together because their coherence stems from a background set of premises" (1043).

6. Judith K. Jordan likewise writes that "empathy is a complex process, relying on a high level of ego development and ego strength.... In order to empathize, one must have a well-differentiated sense of self in addition to an appreciation of and sensitivity to the differentness as well as sameness of the other" (69). Jodi Halpern makes a complex and useful distinction between various forms of identification and empathy. (See especially 81–86). Her book as a whole defines the nature and uses of "clinical empathy" in medical practice.

7. In *The Motherhood Constellation* Stern elaborates the initial conception of infantile memory in *The Interpersonal World* to integrate feeling, as well as other dimensions; he describes "five different basic formats for representing the infant's subjective interactive experience"; the fifth category is composed of "schemas ... of affects (temporal feeling shapes)" (*Motherhood* 88). The "temporal feeling shape can be viewed as a plausible representational format for schematizing affective experience" (*Motherhood* 84). Feelings are recorded, then, attached to a temporal sequence of events. And "particular experiences, such as being hungry or waiting for the bottle, have their own individual, characteristic feeling shapes" (*Motherhood* 87).

8. Throughout *The Motherhood Constellation* Stern continues to deny the internalization of a maternal figure: "Such terms as *internalization* and *introjection*" are not useful," he says (*Motherhood* 19), for "nothing is taken in from the outside" (*Motherhood* 81); he thus extends the argument of *The Interpersonal World* that the mother is experienced from the beginnings of life as a core other. Yet when it comes to describing his clinical experience with patients who are new mothers, he unexpectedly refers to primary identification as if it were a given. The "new mother's stored memories ... include both sides of her interaction or relationship with her own mother when she was young: the parts that she experienced directly as a baby, while interacting with her mother, and the parts of her mother's experience of interacting with her that she experienced empathically (via imitation and primary identification.)" (*Motherhood* 181). Since Stern does not offer an explanation of primary identification here but only refers to it in passing, the term retains its original meaning—an infantile confusion or fusion of self and other. It would seem that primary identification becomes a valid, in fact a necessary, category of analysis when Stern is treating actual patients. Indeed, he says as much: "Certain mental operations ... are clinically indispensable, such as identification" (53).

9. To be sure, these neuronal groups are not located in a single place; one cannot say they form clusters that correspond to distinct self-states; rather, the various aspects of an experience are recorded in different maps, or collections of neuronal groups, which are located in different parts of the brain. And these maps are not static; rather, "the maps interact with one another and constantly recategorize information" (Rosenfield 184). But a familiar event—like hunger or playing—will activate all the maps that correspond to the prototype of that event, reinforcing the connections between maps.

10. Stephen Mitchell's model of multiple subjectivity is similar to what I have outlined here. "The same person may ... integrate a relationship in very different ways with the same person in different contexts.... We are, in a fundamental sense, quite different persons at different times.... At any given time we operate out of a particular way of representing ourselves to ourselves, in relation to a portrayal of a distinct sort of other with whom we are engaged" (*Hope* 106). The notion of subjectivity as a dialectic between quite different relational positions also has affinities with Thomas Ogden's paradigm of human being as a dialectic between the depressive position and the paranoid-schizoid position.

Works Cited

Abel, Elizabeth. "Black Writing, White Reading: Race and the Politics of Feminist Interpretation." *Critical Inquiry* 19.3 (Spring 1993): 470–98. Reprinted in *Female Subjects in Black and White: Race, Psychoanalysis, Feminism.* Ed. Elizabeth Abel, Barbara Christian, Helene Moglen. Berkeley: University of California P, 1997. 102–31.

———. "Race, Class, and Psychoanalysis? Opening Questions." *Conflicts in Feminism.* Ed. Marianne Hirsch and Evelyn Fox Keller. New York: Routledge, 1990. 184–204.

Abraham, Nicolas. "Notes on the Phantom: A Complement to Freud's Metapsychology." *The Trial(s) of Psychoanalysis.* Ed. Françoise Meltzer. Chicago: U of Chicago P, 1987. 75–80.

——— and Maria Torok. "Introjection—Incorporation: Mourning or Melancholia." *Psychoanalysis in France.* Ed. Serge Lebovici and Daniel Widlocher. New York: International UP, 1980. 3–16.

Adams, Parveen. *The Emptiness of the Image: Psychoanalysis and Sexual Difference.* New York and London: Routledge, 1996.

Adorno, Theodor W. "What Does Coming to Terms with the Past Mean?" *Bitburg in Moral and Political Perspective.* Ed. Geoffrey Hartman. Bloomington: Indiana UP, 1986. 114–129.

Agogino, George, Dominique Stevens, and Lynda Carlotta. "Doña Marina and the Legend of La Llorona." *Anthropological Journal of Canada* 2.1 (1973): 25–38.

Ahmed, Sara. "Tanning the Body: Skin, Colour, and Gender." *New Formations: A Journal of Culture/Theory/Politics* 34 (Summer 1998): 27–42.

Alarcón, Norma. "Anzaldúa's *Frontera*: Inscribing Gynetics." *Displacement, Diaspora, and Geographies of Identity.* Ed. Smadar Lavie and Ted Swedenburg. Durham: Duke UP, 1996. 35–38.

———. "Chicana Feminist Literature: A Re-vision through Malintzín: Putting the Flesh Back on the Object." *This Bridge Called My Back: Writings by Radical Women of Color.* Ed. Cherríe Moraga and Gloria Anzaldúa. New York: Kitchen Table, Women of Color P, 1983. 182–90.

———. "The Theoretical Subject(s) of *This Bridge Called My Back* and Anglo-American Feminism." *Making Face, Making Soul: Hacienda Caras: Creative and Critical Perspectives by Women of Color*. Ed. Gloria Anzaldúa. San Francisco: Aunt Lute Press, 1990. 356–69.

Alcorn, Marshall. "Talking with Jesse Helms: The Relation of Drives to Discourse." *Journal for the Psychoanalysis of Culture and Society* 1.1 (Spring 1996): 81–89.

Althusser, Louis. "Ideology and Ideological State Apparatuses." *Lenin and Philosophy and Other Essays*. Trans. Ben Brewster. New York: Monthly Review Press, 1971. 127–88.

Anderson, Linda. "The Re-imagining of History in Contemporary Women's Fiction." *Plotting Change*. Ed. Linda Anderson. London: Arnold, 1990. 129–41.

Anzaldúa, Gloria. *Borderlands/La Frontera: The New Mestiza*. San Francisco: Aunt Lute Books, 1987.

———. "*Hacienda caras: Una entrada*." *Making Face, Making Soul/Hacienda caras*. Ed. Gloria Anzaldúa. San Francisco: Aunt Lute Books, 1990. xv–xxviii.

———. Ed. *Making Face, Making Soul/Hacienda caras: Creative and Critical Perspectives by Women of Color*. San Francisco: Aunt Lute Books, 1990.

——— and AnaLouise Keating, eds. *This Bridge We Call Home: Radical Visions for Transformation*. New York and London: Routledge, 2002.

Aranda, Pilar E. Rodriguez. "On the Solitary Fate of Being Mexican, Female, Wicked, and Thirty-Three: An Interview with Writer Sandra Cisneros." *The Americas Review* 18.1 (1990): 64–81.

Arendt, Hannah. "Crisis in Culture." *Between Past and Future: Six Exercises in Political Thought*. New York: Meridian, 1961. 221.

Atwood, Margaret. "Address to the American Booksellers Association Convention." (Miami, Florida, June 1, 1993.) *Book Group Companion to Margaret Atwood's The Robber Bride*. Ed. Nan A. Talese. New York: Doubleday, 1994. 7–13.

———. "Duplicity: The Jekyll Hand, the Hyde Hand, and the Slippery Double: Why There Are Always Two." Margaret Atwood, *Negotiating with the Dead: A Writer on Writing*. Cambridge: Cambridge UP, 2002. 29–58.

———. *The Robber Bride*. New York: Bantam, 1995.

Baker, Houston A., Jr. "Autobiographical Acts and the Voice of the Southern Slave." *The Slave's Narrative*. Ed. Charles T. Davis and Henry Louis Gates, Jr. Oxford: Oxford UP, 1990. 242–61.

Bartky, Sandra. "Sympathy and Solidarity: On a Tightrope with Scheler." *Feminists Rethink the Self*. Ed. Diana T. Meyers. Boulder: Westview Press, 1997. 177–96.

Barzilai, Shuli. *Lacan and the Matter of Origins*. Stanford: Stanford UP, 1999.

Bauer, Dale, and Priscilla Wald. "Complaining, Conversing, and Coalescing." *Signs* 25.4 (Summer 2000): 1299–1303.

Beauvoir, Simone de. *The Second Sex*. Trans. H. M. Parshley. New York: Vintage, [1949] 1989.

Beebe, Beatrice. "Mother-Infant Mutual Influence and Precursors of Self and Object Representations." *Empirical Studies of Psychoanalytic Theories*, v. 2. Ed. J. Masling. Hillsdale, NJ: The Analytic P, 1986. 27–48.

Beebe, Beatrice, and Frank Lachmann. "Representation and Internalization in Infancy: Three Principles of Salience." *Psychoanalytic Psychology* 11 (1994): 127–65.

Beebe, Beatrice, Frank Lachmann, and Joseph Jaffe. "Mother-Infant Interaction Structures and Presymbolic Self and Object Representations." *Psychoanalytic Dialogues* 7.2 (1997): 133–82.

———. "A Transformational Model of Presymbolic Representations: Reply to Commentaries." *Psychoanalytic Dialogues* 7.2 (1997): 215–24.

Ben-Ephraim, Gavriel. *The Moon's Dominion: Narrative Dichotomy and Female Dominance in Lawrence's Earlier Novels*. East Brunswick, NJ: Associated University Presses, 1981.

Benhabib, Seyla. *Situating the Self: Gender, Community, and Postmodernism in Contemporary Ethics*. New York: Routledge, 1992.

Benjamin, Jessica. *The Bonds of Love: Psychoanalysis, Feminism, and the Problem of Domination*. New York: Pantheon Books, 1988.

———. "A Desire of One's Own: Psychoanalytic Feminism and Intersubjective Space." *Feminist Studies/Critical Studies*. Ed. Teresa de Lauretis. Bloomington: Indiana UP, 1986. 78–101.

———. "Commentary on Irwin Z. Hoffman's Discussion: Toward a Social-Constructivist View of the Psychoanalytic Situation." *Psychoanalytic Dialogues* 1.4 (1991): 525–33.

———. *Like Subjects, Love Objects: Essays on Recognition and Sexual Difference*. New Haven: Yale UP, 1995.

———. "The Omnipotent Mother: A Psychoanalytic Study of Fantasy." *Representations of Motherhood*. Ed. Donna Bassin, Margaret Honey, and Meryle Kaplan. New Haven: Yale UP, 1994. 129–46.

———. "The Shadow of the Other (Subject): Intersubjectivity and Feminist Theory." *Constellation* 1.2 (1994): 231–54.

Berger, James. "Ghosts of Liberalism: Morrison's *Beloved* and the Moynihan Report." *PMLA* 111.3 (May 1996): 408–20.

Berke, J. H. "Shame and Envy." *The Many Faces of Shame*. Ed. D. L. Nathanson. New York: Guilford, 1987.

Berlant, Lauren. "National Brands/National Body: *Imitation of Life*." *Comparative American Identities: Race, Sex and Nationality in the Modern Text*. Ed. Hortense Spillers. London: Routledge, 1991. 110–40.

Bhabha, Homi. "Of Mimicry and Man." *The Location of Culture*. London: Routledge, 1994. 85–92.

———. "The Other Question: Stereotype, Discrimination and the Discourse of Colonialism." *The Location of Culture*. London: Routledge, 1994. 66–84.

Bloom, Lynn Z., and Veronica Makowsky. "Zenia's Paradoxes." *LIT* 6 (1995): 167–79.

Boothby, Richard. "The Psychic Meaning of Life and Death: Reflections on the Lacanian Imaginary, Symbolic, and Real." *Disseminating Lacan*. Ed. David Pettigrew and Francois Raffoul. New York: State U of New York P, 1996. 337–63.

Borch-Jacobsen, Mikkel. *The Emotional Tie: Psychoanalysis, Mimesis, and Affect*. Trans. Douglas Brick. Stanford: Stanford UP, 1992.

———. *The Freudian Subject*. Trans. Catherine Porter. Stanford: Stanford UP, 1988.

———. *Lacan: The Absolute Master*. Trans. Douglas Brick. Stanford: Stanford UP, 1991.

Bordo, Susan. "The Body and the Reproduction of Femininity: A Feminist Appropriation of Foucault." *Gender/Body/Knowledge: Feminist Reconstructions of Being and Knowing*. Ed. Alison Jaggar and Susan Bordo. New Brunswick: Rutgers UP, 1989. 13–33.

Boudreau, Kristin. "Pain and the Unmaking of Self in Toni Morrison's *Beloved*." *Contemporary Literature* 36.3: 447–65.

Bourdieu, Pierre. *Outline of a Theory of Practice*. Cambridge: Cambridge UP, 1977.

———. *Photography: A Middle-Brow Art*. Stanford: Stanford UP, 1990.

Bouson, J. Brooks. *Quiet as It's Kept: Shame, Trauma and Race in the Novels of Toni Morrison*. Albany: State U of New York P, 2000.

———. "Slipping Sideways into the Dreams of Women: The Female Dream Work of Power Feminism in Margaret Atwood's *The Robber Bride*." *LIT* 6 (1995): 149–66.

Bowers, Susan. "*Beloved* and the New Apocalypse." *The Journal of Ethnic Studies* 18.1 (Spring 1990): 59–77.

Brady, Mary Pat. "The Contrapuntal Geographies of *Woman Hollering Creek and Other Stories*." *American Literature* 71.1 (March 1999): 117–149.

Bracher, Mark. "Editor's Column: Lacan's "Civilization and Its Discontents." *Journal for the Psychoanalysis of Culture and Society* (Fall 1996): 1, 2: 1–12.

Breines, Wini. "What's Love Got to Do with It? White Women, Black Women, and Feminism in the Movement Years." *Signs: Journal of Women in Culture and Society* 27.4 (Summer 2002): 1095–1134.

Brennan, Teresa. *History after Lacan*. New York and London: Routledge, 1993.

———. "The Foundational Fantasy." In Burke, 285–98.

Brodhead, Richard. "Sparing the Rod: Discipline and Fiction in Antebellum America." *The New American Studies*. Ed. Philip Fisher. Berkeley: U of California P, 1991. 141–70.

Brody, Jennifer. *Impossible Purities. Blackness, Femininity, and Victorian Culture*. Durham, NC: Duke UP, 1998.

Brown, Elsa Barkley. " 'What Has Happened Here': The Politics of Difference in Women's History and Feminist Politics." *The Second Wave: A Reader in Feminist Theory*. Ed. Linda Nicholson. New York and London: Routledge, 1997. 272–87.

Brown, Jane W. "Constructing the Narrative of Women's Friendship: Margaret Atwood's Reflexive Fictions." *LIT* 6 (1995): 197–212.

Burke, Nancy. *Gender and Envy*. New York and London: Routledge, 1998.
Butler, Judith. *Bodies that Matter: On the Discursive Limits of "Sex."* New York and London: Routledge, 1993.
―――. *Gender Trouble: Feminism and the Subversion of Identity*. New York and London: Routledge, 1990.
―――. "Imitation and Gender Insubordination." *The Second Wave: A Reader in Feminist Theory*. Ed. Linda Nicholson. New York and London: Routledge, 1997. 300–315.
―――. *The Psychic Life of Power: Theories in Subjection*. Stanford: Stanford UP, 1997.
―――, Seyla Benhabib, Drucilla Cornell, and Nancy Fraser. *Feminist Contentions: A Philosophical Exchange*. New York and London: Routledge, 1995.
Byatt, A. S. "Envy: The Sin of Families and Nations." *New York Times Book Review*. July 18, 1993. 3.
Campbell, Ena. "The Virgin of Guadalupe and the Female Self-Image: A Mexican Case History." *Mother Worship: Theme and Variations*. Chapel Hill, N.C.: U of North Carolina P, 1982.
Carby, Hazel. *Reconstructing Womanhood: The Emergence of the Afro-American Woman Novelist*. New York: Oxford UP, 1987.
Carmean, Karen. *Toni Morrison's World of Fiction*. Troy, NY: Whitston, 1993.
Carter, Angela. *The Magic Toyshop*. London: Virago Press, 1987.
Caruth, Cathy. "Introduction." *Trauma: Explorations in Memory*. Ed. Cathy Caruth. Baltimore: Johns Hopkins UP, 1995. 151–57.
Castellanos, Rosario. "Malinche." *Poesías no eres tu: Obra Poética, 1948–1971*. Mexico City: Fondo de Cultura Economica, 1972.
Chambers, Veronica. *Mama's Girl*. New York: Riverhead, 1996.
Chasseguet-Smirgel, Janine. "Some Thoughts on the Ego Ideal: A Contribution to the Study of the 'Illness of Ideality.'" *Psychoanalytic Quarterly* 45 (1976): 345–73.
Chavez, Denise. "The McCoy Hotel." *Growing Up Chicana/o: An Anthology*. Ed. Tiffany Ana Lopez. New York: William Morrow, 1993. 251–69.
Cheng, Anne. *The Melancholy of Race: Psychoanalysis, Assimilation, and Hidden Grief*. New York: Oxford UP, 2001.
Chodorow, Nancy. *The Reproduction of Mothering*. Berkeley: U of California P, 1978.
Chopin, Kate. *The Awakening*. New York: Norton (A Norton Critical Edition), 1976.
Chow, Rey. *Writing Diaspora: Tactics of Intervention in Contemporary Cultural Studies*. Bloomington: Indiana UP, 1993.
Christian, Barbara. "Fixing Methodologies: *Beloved*." *Female Subjects in Black and White: Race, Psychoanalysis, Feminism*. Ed. Elizabeth Abel, Barbara Christian, Helene Moglen. Berkeley: U of California P, 1997. 363–70. (Reprinted from *Cultural Critique* 24 [1993]: 56–59.)
Cisneros, Sandra. "Guadalupe the Sex Goddess." *Goddess of the Americas/La Diosa de las Americas: Writings on the Virgin Mary*. Ed. Ana Castillo. New York: Riverhead Books, 1997. 46–51.

———. *The House on Mango Street*. Houston: Arte Publico Press, 1983.
———. "Little Miracles, Kept Promises." *Woman Hollering Creek and Other Stories*. New York: Random House, 1992. 116–29.
———. "Never Marry a Mexican." *Woman Hollering Creek and Other Stories*. New York: Random House, 1992. 68–83.
———. *Woman Hollering Creek and Other Stories*. New York: Random House, 1992.
———. "Woman Hollering Creek." *Woman Hollering Creek and Other Stories*. New York: Random House, 1992, 43–56.
Cohn, J. and E. Tronick. "Mother-Infant Face-to-Face Interaction: The Sequence of Dyadic States at 3, 6, and 9 Months." *Developmental Psychology* 23 (1987): 68–77.
Coleman, James. "The Quest for Wholeness in Toni Morrison's *Tar Baby*." *Black American Literature Forum* 22.1 (Spring–Summer 1986): 63–73.
Collins, Patricia Hill. *Black Feminist Thought: Knowledge, Consciousness, and the Politics of Empowerment*. Boston: Unwin Hyman, 1990.
———. *Fighting Words: Black Women and the Search for Justice*. U. of Minnesota P, 1998.
———. "The Social Construction of Black Feminist Thought." *Feminism and Philosophy: Essential Readings in Theory, Reinterpretation, and Application*. Ed. Nancy Tuana and Rosemarie Tong. Boulder, Colo.: Westview Press, 1995: 526–47. Reprinted from *Signs: Journal of Women in Culture and Society* 14.4 (Summer 1989): 297–325.
Copjec, Joan. *Read My Desire*. Cambridge, MA: MIT Press, 1995.
Creighton, Joanne. *Margaret Drabble*. London and New York: Methuen, 1985.
Cross, Tia, Freada Klein, Barbara Smith, and Beverly Smith. "Face–to–Face, Day–to–Day—Racism CR." *Sojourner* (May): 11.
Cushman, Philip. "Ideology Obscured: Political Uses of the Self in Daniel Stern's Infant." *American Psychologist* 46, 3 (March 1991): 206–19.
Cypess, Sandra. *La Malinche in Mexican Literature: From History to Myth*. Austin: U of Texas P, 1991.
Darling, Marsha. "In the Realm of Responsibility: A Conversation with Toni Morrison." *Women's Review of Books* (March 1988): 5–6.
Dasenbrock, Reed Way and Feroza Jussawalla. "Interview with Sandra Cisneros." *Interviews with Writers of the Post-Colonial World*. Ed. Feroza Jussawalla and Reed Way Dasenbrock. Jackson: UP of Mississippi, 1992.
David-Ménard, Monique. *Hysteria from Freud to Lacan: Body and Language in Psychoanalysis*. Trans. Catherine Porter. Ithaca: Cornell UP, 1989.
Davis, Angela. *Women, Race and Class*. New York: Random, 1983.
Dean, Jodi. *Solidarity of Strangers: Feminism after Identity Politics*. Berkeley: University of California Press, 1996.
Dean, Tim. "Transsexual Identification, Gender Performance Theory, and the Politics of the Real." *Literature and Psychology* 39. 4 (1993): 1–27.
Delaney, Lucy. *From the Darkness Cometh the Light; or Struggles for Freedom*, c. 1891. Reprinted in *Six Women's Slave Narratives*. Schomburg Li-

brary of Nineteenth-Century Black Women Writers. New York: Oxford UP, 1988.
de Lauretis, Teresa. *Technologies of Gender: Essays on Theory, Film, and Fiction*. Bloomington: Indiana UP, 1987.
Del Castillo, Adelaida. "Malintzin Tenepal: A Preliminary Look into a New Perspective." *Essays on La Mujer*. Ed. Rosaura Sanchez and Rosa Martinez Cruz. Los Angeles: Chicano Studies Center, 1977. 124–49.
Demetrakopoulos, Stephanie. "Maternal Bonds as Devourers of Women's Individuation in Toni Morrison's *Beloved*." *African American Review* 26, 1 (1992): 51–60.
Diamond, Elin. " Rethinking Identification: Kennedy, Freud, Brecht." *Kenyon Review*, 15.2 (Spring 1993): 86–99.
———. *Unmaking Mimesis*. New York: Routledge, 1997.
Dimen, Muriel. "The Body as Rorschach." *Studies in Gender and Sexuality* 1.1 (2000): 9–40.
Doane, Mary Ann. *Femmes Fatales*. New York and London, 1991.
———. "Misrecognition and Identity." *Explorations in Film Theory: Selected Essays from Cine-Tracts*. Ed. Ron Burnett. Bloomington: Indiana U P, 1991. 15–25.
Dolar, Mladen. "Beyond Interpellation." *Qui Parle* 6.2 (Spring/Summer 1993): 73–96.
———. "'I Shall Be with You on Your Wedding-Night: Lacan and the Uncanny." *October* 58 (Fall 1991): 5–24.
Dowling, Colette. "The Song of Toni Morrison." *Conversations with Toni Morrison*. Ed. Danille Taylor-Guthrie. Jackson, MS: U of Mississippi P, 1994.
Drabble, Margaret. *Jerusalem the Golden*. New York: Popular Library, 1967.
Dubey, Madhu. *Black Women Novelists and the Nationalist Aesthetic*. Bloomington: Indiana UP, 1994.
duCille, Ann. *Skin Trade*. Cambridge: Harvard UP, 1996.
DuPlessis, Rachel Blau and Ann Snitow, eds. *The Feminist Memoir Project: Voices from Women's Liberation*. New York: Three Rivers P, 1998.
Edelberg, Cynthia. "Morrison's Voice: Formal Education, the Work Ethic, and the Bible." *American Literature* 58 (1986): 217–37.
Edelman, Gerald. *Neural Darwinism: The Theory of Neuronal Group Selection*. New York: Basic Books, 1987.
Eigen, Michael. *The Electrified Tightrope*. Northvale, NJ: Aronson, 1993.
Elam, Diane. *Feminism and Deconstruction*. New York: Routledge, 1994.
———. "Sisters Are Doing It to Themselves." *Generations: Academic Feminists in Dialogue*. Ed. Devoney Looser and E. Ann Kaplan. Minneapolis: U of Minnesota P, 1997. 55–68.
Elkins, Stanley. *Slavery: A Problem in American Institutional and Intellectual Life*. 3rd ed. Chicago: Chicago UP. 1976.
Eng, David, and Shinhee Han. "A Dialogue on Racial Melancholia." *Bringing the Plague: Towards a Postmodern Psychoanalysis*. Ed. Lynne Layton,

Carolyn Stack, and Susan Fairfield. New York: Other P, 2002. 233–67. (Originally published in *Psychoanalytic Dialogues* 10.4 [2000]. 667–700.)

Etchegoyen, R. H., B. M. Lopez, and M. Rabih. "On Envy and How to Interpret It." *International Journal of Psychoanalysis* 68.1: 49–61.

Evans, Dylan. "From Kantian Ethics to Mystical Experience: An Exploration of Jouissance." *Key Concepts of Lacanian Psychoanalysis*. Ed. Danny Nobus. New York: Other P. 1998. 1–28.

———. *An Introductory Dictionary of Lacanian Psychoanalysis*. London and New York: Routledge, 1996.

Evans, Martha Noel. *Fits and Starts: A Genealogy of Hysteria in Modern France*. Ithaca: Cornell UP, 1991.

Fairbairn, W. R. D. *An Object-Relations Theory of the Personality*. New York: Basic Books, 1952.

Fanon, Frantz. *Black Skin, White Masks*. Trans. Charles Lam Markmann. New York: Grove, 1967.

Felman, Shoshana. *Jacques Lacan and the Adventure of Insight: Psychoanalysis in Contemporary Culture*. Cambridge: Harvard UP, 1987.

Fenichel, Otto. *The Psychoanalytic Theory of Neurosis*. New York: Norton, 1945.

Fields, Karen. "To Embrace Dead Strangers: Toni Morrison's *Beloved*." *Mother Puzzles: Daughters and Mothers in Contemporary American Literature*. Ed. Mickey Pearlman. Westport: Greenwood, 1989. 159–169.

Fink, Bruce. *A Clinical Introduction to Lacanian Psychoanalysis: Theory and Technique*. Cambridge: Harvard UP, 1997.

———. *The Lacanian Subject: Between Language and Jouissance*. Princeton: Princeton UP, 1995.

FitzGerald, Jennifer. "Selfhood and Community: Psychoanalysis and Discourse in *Beloved*." *Modern Fiction Studies* 39.3–4 (Fall/Winter 1993): 669–87.

Flax, Jane. "Reentering the Labyrinth: Revisiting Dorothy Dinnerstein's *The Mermaid and the Minotaur*." *Signs* 27.4 (Summer 2002): 1037–57.

Fleischner, Jennifer. *Mastering Slavery: Memory, Family, and Identity in Women's Slave Narratives*. New York: New York UP, 1996.

Forter, Greg. "Against Melancholia." *Differences* 14.2 (Summer 2003): 134–70.

Franklin, Cynthia. *Writing Women's Communities: The Politics and Poetics of Contemporary Multi-Genre Anthologies*. Madison: U of Wisconsin P, 1997.

Fraser, Nancy. *Unruly Practices: Power, Discourse and Gender in Contemporary Social Theory*. Minneapolis: U of Minnesota P, 1989.

Freiwald, Bina. "Class, Subjectivity, Desire: Two Autobiographies." *RFR/ DRF* 25. 3–4: 26–33.

Freud, Sigmund. *Beyond the Pleasure Principle* (1920). *The Standard Edition of the Complete Works of Sigmund Freud*. Trans. James Strachey. London: Hogarth Press, 1958. 18: 7–64.

———. *Civilization and Its Discontents* (1930). *SE* 21: 57–146.

———. "Creative Writers and Day-Dreaming" (1908). *SE* 9: 168–75.
———. *The Ego and the Id*. *SE* 19 (1923): 1–66.
———. "Family Romance." *SE* 9: 236–41.
———. "Findings, Ideas, Problems" (1938): *SE* 23: 299.
———. "Formulations on the Two Principles of Mental Functioning" (1911). *SE* 12: 218–26.
———. *Fragment of the Analysis of a Case of Hysteria [Dora]* (1905). *SE* 7: 125–243.
———. "From the History of an Infantile Neurosis" (1918). *SE* 17: 7–122.
———. *Group Psychology and the Analysis of the Ego* (1921). *SE* 18: 69–143.
———. *Inhibitions, Symptoms and Anxiety* (1926): *SE* 20: 87–172.
———. *The Interpretation of Dreams* (Second Part) (1900–1901): *SE* 5: 339–627.
———. "Mourning and Melancholia." *SE* 14 (1917): 243–58.
———. "Negation." *SE* 19 (1925): 233–39.
———. *New Introductory Lectures on Psycho-Analysis* (1933): *SE* 22: 5–182.
———. "On Narcissism: An Introduction" (1914): *SE* 14: 73–102.
———. "The Uncanny" (1919). *SE* 17: 217–56.
Friedberg, Anne. "A Denial of Difference: Theories of Cinematic Identification." *Psychoanalysis and Cinema*. Ed. E. Ann Kaplan. London and New York: Routledge, 1990. 36–45.
Friedman, Susan Stanford. "Beyond White and Other: Relationality and Narratives of Race in Feminist Discourse." *Signs: Journal of Women in Culture and Society* 21.1 (Autumn 1995): 1–49.
———. *Mappings: Feminism and the Cultural Geographies of Encounter*. Princeton: Princeton UP, 1998.
Frosh, Stephen. *Sexual Difference, Masculinity and Psychoanalysis*. New York and London: Routledge, 1994.
Fultz, Lucille. "To Make Herself: Mother-Daughter Conflicts in Toni Morrison's *Sula* and *Tar Baby*." *Women of Color: Mother-Daughter Relationships in 20th-Century Literature*. Ed. Elizabeth Brown-Guillory. Austin: U of Texas P, 1996. 228–43.
Fuss, Diana. *Identification Papers*. New York and London: Routledge, 1995.
Gallop, Jane. "Annie Leclerc Writing a Letter, with Vermeer." *The Poetics of Gender*. Ed. Nancy Miller. New York: Columbia UP, 1986. 137–56.
———. *Around 1981: Academic Feminist Literary Theory*. London: Routledge, 1992.
———. *Reading Lacan*. Ithaca, New York: Cornell UP, 1985.
———, Marianne Hirsch, and Nancy K. Miller. "Criticizing Feminist Criticism." *Conflicts in Feminism*. Ed. Marianne Hirsch and Evelyn Fox Keller. New York: Routledge, 1990. 349–69.
Garza, Sabino. "La Llorona: An Omen of Doom." *El Quetzal Emplumece*. Ed. Carmela Montalvo, Leonardo Anguiano, and Cecilio Camarillo. San Antonio: Mexican American Cultural Center, 1976. 447–54.
Gates, Henry Louis, Jr. "Introduction: The Language of Slavery." *The Slave's Narrative*. Ed. Charles Davis and Henry Louis Gates. New York: Oxford UP, 1985. xi–xxxiv.

Giddings, Paula. *When and Where I Enter: The Impact of Black Women on Race and Sex in America*. New York: Routledge, 1984.
Gilligan, Carol. *In a Different Voice: Psychological Theory and Women's Development*. Cambridge: Harvard UP, 1982.
Gilman, Sander. *Freud, Race and Gender*. Princeton: Princeton UP, 1993.
Gilroy, Paul. *Against Race: Imagining Political Culture Beyond the Color Line*. Cambridge: Belknap Press of Harvard UP, 2000.
Goldman, Anne. "'I Made the Ink': (Literary) Production and Reproduction in *Dessa Rose* and *Beloved*." *Feminist Studies* 16 (1990): 313–30.
Goldner, Virginia. "Towards a Critical Relational Theory of Gender." *Psychoanalytic Dialogues: A Journal of Relational Perspectives* 1 (1991): 249–72.
Gould, Carol. *Marx's Social Ontology*. Cambridge: MIT Press, 1978.
Graeber, Laurel. "Zenia Is Sort of Like Madonna." *New York Times Book Review*. October 31, 1993. 22.
Greenberg, Jay R., and Mitchell, Stephen A. *Object Relations in Psychoanalytic Theory*. Cambridge: Harvard UP, 1983.
Greenson, Ralph R. "The Struggle against Identification." *Pivotal Papers on Identification*. Ed. George H. Pollock. Madison, CT: International UP, 1993. 159–75.
Grosz, Elizabeth. *Jacques Lacan: A Feminist Introduction*. London: Routledge, 1990.
Grubrich-Simitis, Ilse. "From Concretism to Metaphor: Thoughts on Some Theoretical and Technical Aspects of the Psychoanalytic Work with Children of Holocaust Survivors." *The Psycho-analytic Study of the Child* 39 (1984): 301–19.
Gubar, Susan. "Blessings in Disguise: Cross-Dressing as Re-Dressing for Female Modernists." *Massachusetts Review* (Autumn, 1981): 477–508.
———. *Critical Conditions: Feminism at the Turn of the Century*. New York: Columbia UP, 2000.
———. *Racechanges: White Skin, Black Face in American Culture*. Oxford: Oxford UP, 1997.
Halpern, Jodi. *From Detached Concern to Empathy: Humanizing Medical Practice*. New York: Oxford UP, 2001.
Haraway, Donna. "Situated Knowledges: The Science Question in Feminism and the Privilege of Partial Perception." *Simians, Cyborgs and Women: The Reinvention of Nature*. New York and London: Routledge, 1991. 183–202.
Harding, Sandra. *Whose Science? Whose Knowledge? Thinking from Women's Lives*. Ithaca, N.Y.: Cornell UP, 1991.
Harris, Adrienne. "Aggression, Envy, and Ambition: Circulating Tensions in Women's Psychic Life." *Gender and Psychoanalysis* 2.3 (1997): 291–325.
Harris, Trudier. *Fiction and Folklore: The Novels of Toni Morrison*. Knoxville: U of Tennessee P, 1991.
Hartman, Saidiya V. *Scenes of Subjection*. Oxford: Oxford UP, 1997.
Hartsock, Nancy. *Money, Sex and Power: Toward a Feminist Historical Materialism*. New York and London: Longman, 1983.

Haviland, J., and M. Lelwica. "The Induced Affect Response: 10-Week-Old Infants' Responses to Three Emotional Expressions." *Developmental Psychology* 23 (1987): 97–104.

Hawthorne, Evelyn. "On Gaining the Double Vision: *Tar Baby* as Diasporean Novel." *Black American Literature Forum* 22.1 (Spring 1988): 97–107.

Heffernan, Teresa. "*Beloved* and the Problem of Mourning." *Studies in the Novel* 30.4 (Winter 1998): 558–73.

Heinze, Denise. *The Dilemma of "Double Consciousness": Toni Morrison's Novels*. U of Georgia P, 1993.

Henderson, Mae Gwendolyn. "Speaking in Tongues: Dialogics, Dialectics, and the Black Woman Writer's Literary Tradition." *Changing Our Own Words: Essays on Criticism, Theory, and Writing by Black Women*. Ed. Cheryl A. Wall. New Brunswick: Rutgers UP, 1989. 16–37.

——. "Toni Morrison's *Beloved*: Re-membering the Body as Historical Text." *Comparative American Identities: Race, Sex, and Nationality in the Modern Text*. Ed. Hortense Spillers. London: Routledge, 1991. 62–86.

Henley, Nancy. *Body Politics: Power, Sex, and Nonverbal Communication*. Englewood Cliffs: Prentice-Hall, 1977.

Hine, Darlene. "Female Slave Resistance: The Economics of Sex." *Western Journal of Black Studies* 3 (Summer 1979): 123–27.

Hirsch, Marianne. *The Mother-Daughter Plot: Narrative, Psychoanalysis, Feminism*. Bloomington: Indiana UP, 1989.

——. *Family Frames: Photography, Narrative, and Postmemory*. Cambridge: Harvard UP, 1997.

Holloway, Karla. "*Beloved*: A Spiritual." *Callaloo* 13 (1990): 516–25.

Holmes, Kristine. "This Is Flesh I'm Talking About Here": Embodiment in Toni Morrison's *Beloved* and Shirley Anne Williams' *Dessa Rose*." *LIT* 6 (1995): 133–48.

Homans, Margaret. *Bearing the Word: Language and Female Experience in Nineteenth-Century Women's Writing*. Chicago: U of Chicago P, 1986.

——. "'Women of Color' Writers and Feminist Theory." *New Literary History* 25.1 (1994): 73–94.

hooks, bell. *Ain't I a Woman: Black Women and Feminism*. Boston: South End P, 1981.

——. *Black Looks: Race and Representation*. Boston: South End P, 1992.

——. "Eating the Other." *Black Looks: Race and Representation*. Boston: South End P, 1992. 21–39.

——. *Feminist Theory: From Margin to Center*. Boston: South End P, 1984.

——. "Sisterhood: Political Solidarity between Women." *Feminist Theory: From Margin to Center*. Boston: South End Press, 1984. 43–65.

——. *Talking Back: Thinking Feminist, Thinking Black*. Boston: South End P, 1989.

Horvitz, Deborah. "Nameless Ghosts: Possession and Dispossession in *Beloved*." *Studies in American Fiction* 17 (1989): 157–67.

House, Elizabeth. "Toni Morrison's Ghost: The Beloved Who Is Not Beloved." *Critical Essays on Toni Morrison's Beloved*. Ed. James Nagel. Boston: G. K. Hall, 1998. 117–26.

Howe, Marguerite Beede. *The Art of the Self in D. H. Lawrence*. Athens: Ohio UP, 1977.

Hurtado, Aída. *Voicing Chicana Feminisms: Young Women Speak Out on Sexuality and Identity*. New York: New York UP.

Ian, Marcia. *Remembering the Phallic Mother: Psychoanalysis, Modernism, and the Fetish*. Ithaca: Cornell UP, 1993.

Jacobs, Harriet. *Incidents in the Life of a Slave Girl*. Cambridge: Harvard UP, 1987.

JanMohamed, Abdul R. "The Economy of Manichean Allegory: The Function of Racial Difference in Colonialist Literature." *"Race," Writing, and Difference*. Ed. Henry Louis Gates, Jr. Chicago: U of Chicago P, 1986. 78–106.

Johnson, Samuel. *The Rambler* No. 183: "The Influence of Envy and Interest Compared." *Yale Edition of the Works of Samuel Johnson*. New Haven: Yale UP, 1969. vol. 5, 196–99.

Jones, Lisa. *Bulletproof Diva: Tales of Race, Sex, and Hair*. New York: Doubleday, 1994.

Jordan, Judith V. "Empathy and Self Boundaries." *Women's Growth in Connection: Writings from the Stone Center*. Ed. Judith V. Jordan, Alexandra Kaplan, Jean Baker Miller, Irene Stiver, Janet Surrey. Guilford P., 1991. 67–80.

Jordan, June. "Civil Wars." *Civil Wars: Observations from the Front Lines of America*. New York: Simon and Schuster, 1995.

———. *On Call: Political Essays*. Boston: South End P, 1985.

Kahane, Claire. *Passions of the Voice: Hysteria, Narrative, and the Figure of the Speaking Woman, 1850–1915*. Baltimore: Johns Hopkins UP, 1995.

Kaplan, Carla. *The Erotics of Talk: Women's Writing and Feminist Paradigms*. Oxford: Oxford UP, 1994.

Karamcheti, Indira. "Caliban in the Classroom." *Radical Teacher* 44 (Winter 1993): 13–17.

Kavaler-Adler, Susan. "Vaginal Core or Vampire Mouth: The Visceral Level of Envy in Women: An Exploration of the Protosymbolic Politics of Object Relations." *Gender and Envy*. Ed. Nancy Burke. New York and London: Routledge, 1998. 221–38.

Keating, AnaLouise. *Women Reading Women Writing: Self-Invention in Paula Gunn Allen, Gloria Anzaldúa, and Audre Lorde*. Philadelphia: Temple UP, 1996.

Keenan, Sally. "'Four Hundred Years of Silence': Myth, History, and Motherhood in Toni Morrison's *Beloved*." *Recasting the World: Writing after Colonialism*. Ed. Jonathan White. Baltimore: Johns Hopkins UP, 1992. 45–81.

Keller, Evelyn Fox, and Helene Moglen. "Competition: A Problem for Academic Women." *Competition: A Feminist Taboo?* Ed. Helen E. Longino and Valerie Miner. New York: Feminist P, 1987.

Kinkead-Weekes, Mark. "The Marriage of Opposites in *The Rainbow*." *D. H. Lawrence: Centenary Essays*. Ed. Mara Kalnins. Bristol, England: Bristol Classical P, 1986. 21–40.

Kittay, Eva Feder. "Mastering Envy: From Freud's Narcissistic Wounds to Bettelheim's Symbolic Wounds to a Vision of Healing." *Gender and Envy*. Ed. Nancy Burke. New York and London: Routledge, 1998. 171–98.

Klein, Melanie. "A Study of Envy and Gratitude." *The Selected Melanie Klein*. New York: Macmillan, 1986. 211–29.

Kojève, Alexander. *Introduction to the Reading of Hegel*. Assembled by Raymond Queneau. Ed. Allan Bloom. Trans. James H. Nichols, Jr. Ithaca: Cornell UP, 1980.

Kristeva, Julia. *Black Sun: Depression and Melancholia*. Trans. Leon S. Roudiez. New York: Columbia UP, 1989.

Kruks, Sonia. *Retrieving Experience: Subjectivity and Recognition in Feminist Politics*. Ithaca: Cornell UP, 2001.

Krumholz, Linda. "The Ghosts of Slavery: Historical Recovery in Toni Morrison's *Beloved*." *African American Review* 26.3 (Fall 1992): 395–408.

Lacan, Jacques. "The Agency of the Letter in the Unconscious or Reason Since Freud." *Écrits: A Selection*. Trans. Alan Sheridan. New York: Norton, 1977. 146–78.

——. "Desire and the Interpretation of Desire in *Hamlet*." *Literature and Psychoanalysis: The Question of Reading: Otherwise*. Ed. Shoshana Felman. Baltimore: Johns Hopkins UP, 1982. 11–52.

——. "The Direction of the Treatment and the Principles of its Power." *Écrits: A Selection*. Trans. Alan Sheridan. New York: Norton, 1977. 226–80.

——. *Écrits. A Selection*. Trans. Alan Sheridan. New York: Norton, 1977.

——. "The Function and Field of Speech and Language in Psychoanalysis." 1953. *Écrits* 30–113.

——. "Intervention in the Transference." *Dora's Case: Freud–Hysteria–Feminism*. Ed. Charles Bernheimer and Claire Kahane. New York: Columbia UP, 1990. 92–104.

——. "The Meaning of the Phallus." *Feminine Sexuality: Jacques Lacan and the Ecole Freudienne*. Ed. Juliet Mitchell and Jacqueline Rose. Trans. Jacqueline Rose. New York: Pantheon Books, 1985.

——. "The Mirror Stage as Formative of the Function of the I." *Écrits: A Selection*. Trans. Alan Sheridan. New York: Norton, 1977. 1–7.

——. "The Phallic Phase and the Subjective Import of the Castration Complex." *Feminine Sexuality*. Ed. Juliet Mitchell and Jacqueline Rose. Trans. Jacqueline Rose. New York: Norton, 1985. 99–122.

——. *The Seminar of Jacques Lacan, Book I: Freud's Papers on Technique, 1953–1954*. Trans. John Forrester. New York: Norton, 1991. (S I)

——. *The Seminar of Jacques Lacan, Book II: The Ego in Freud's Theory and in the Technique of Psychoanalysis, 1954–1955*. Trans. Sylvana Tomaselli. New York: Norton, 1988. (S II)

——. *The Seminar of Jacques Lacan, Book III: The Psychoses, 1955–1956*. Trans. Russell Grigg. New York: Norton, 1993. (S III)

———. *The Seminar of Jacques Lacan, Book VII: The Ethics of Psychoanalysis, 1959–1960*. Trans. Dennis Porter. New York: Norton, 1992. (S VII)

———. *The Seminar of Jacques Lacan, Book X: Anxiety, 1962–1963*. Trans. Cormac Gallagher. (Unpublished.) (S X)

———. *The Seminar of Jacques Lacan, Book XI. The Four Fundamental Concepts of Psycho-Analysis, 1964*. Ed. Jacques-Alain Miller. Trans. Alan Sheridan. New York: Norton, 1978. (S XI)

———. *The Seminar of Jacques Lacan, Book XX: Encore on Feminine Sexuality: The Limits of Love and Knowledge, 1972–1973*. Trans. Bruce Fink. New York: Norton, 1998. (S XX)

———. "Some Reflections on the Ego." *International Journal of Psycho-analysis* 34 (1953): 11–17.

———. "The Subversion of the Subject and the Dialectic of Desire in the Freudian Unconscious." *Écrits: A Selection*. Trans. Alan Sheridan. New York: Norton, 1977. 292–325.

Ladner, Joyce. *Tomorrow's Tomorrow: The Black Woman*. Lincoln: U of Nebraska P, 1995.

Lambert, Ellen. "Margaret Drabble and the Sense of Possibility." *Critical Essays on Margaret Drabble*. Ed. Ellen Cronan Rose. Boston: G. K. Hall, 1985. 31–52.

Lane, Christopher. "The Psychoanalysis of Race: An Introduction." *The Psychoanalysis of Race*. Ed. Christopher Lane. New York: Columbia UP, 1998. 1–37.

Laplanche, Jean, and Jean-Bertrand Pontalis. *The Language of Psychoanalysis*. Trans. Donald Nicholson-Smith. New York: Norton, 1973.

Laurent, Eric. "Alienation and Separation (I)" and "Alienation and Separation (II). *Reading Seminar XI*. Ed. Richard Feldstein, Bruce Fink, and Maire Jaanus. Albany: State U of New York P, 1995. 19–38.

Lawrence, D. H. *The Rainbow*. London: Penguin, 1989.

———. *Sons and Lovers*. Cambridge: Cambridge UP, 1992.

Layton, Lynne. *"Who's That Girl? Who's That Boy?": Clinical Practice Meets Postmodern Gender Theory*. Northvale, NJ and London: Jason Aronson, 1998.

Leclair, Thomas. "The Language Must Not Sweat: A Conversation with Toni Morrison." In *Conversations with Toni Morrison*. Ed. Danille Taylor-Guthrie. Jackson: U of Mississippi P, 1994. 119–28.

Leclerc, Annie. "La lettre d'amour." *La venue à l'écriture*. Ed. Helene Cixous, Madeleine Gagnon, and Annie Leclerc. Paris: Union Générale d'Éditions, 1977.

Lemoine-Luccioni, Eugénie. "The Fable of the Blood." *Returning to Freud: Clinical Psychoanalysis in the School of Lacan*. Ed. and trans. Stuart Schneiderman. New Haven: Yale UP, 1980.

Leys, Ruth. *Trauma: A Genealogy*. U of Chicago P, 2000.

Liscio, Lorraine. "Beloved's Narrative: Writing Mother's Milk." *Tulsa Studies in Women's Literature* 1.1 (Spring 1992): 31–46.

Looser, Devoney, and E. Ann Kaplan. *Generations: Academic Feminists in Dialogue.* Minneapolis: U of Minnesota P, 1997.

Lorde, Audre. *Sister Outsider.* Freedom, CA: Crossing P, 1985.

Lott, Eric. *Love and Theft: Blackface Minstrelsy and the American Working Class.* New York and Oxford: Oxford UP, 1993.

Lowe, Lisa. *Immigrant Acts: On Asian American Cultural Politics.* Durham: Duke UP, 1999.

Lugones, Maria. "Playfulness, 'World–Traveling,' and Loving Perception." *Making Face, Making Soul: Hacienda Caras.* Ed. Gloria Anzaldúa. San Francisco: Aunt Lute Books, 1990. 390–402.

Mahler, Margaret. "Symbiosis and Individuation: The Psychological Birth of the Human Infant" (1974). *Selected Papers of Margaret S. Mahler.* vol. 2. Northvale, NJ: Jason Aronson, 1994. 149–65.

Manzano, Juan Francisco. *Autobiography of a Slave.* Trans. Evelyn Picon Garfield. Detroit: Wayne State UP, 1996.

Marcus, Laura. "'Enough About You, Let's Talk About Me': Recent Autobiographical Writing." *New Formations* 1 (1987): 77–94.

Marshall, Brenda. *Teaching the Postmodern: Fiction and Theory.* New York: Routledge, 1992.

Mathieson, Barbara O. "Memory and Mother Love in Morrison's *Beloved.*" *American Imago* 47.1 (1990): 1–21.

Matsuda, Mari. "Public Response to Racist Speech: Considering the Victim's Story." *Michigan Law Review* 87 (August 1989): 2320–81.

McDowell, Deborah E. *"The Changing Same": Black Women's Literature, Criticism, and Theory.* Bloomington: Indiana UP, 1995.

McGowan, Todd. *Cinemas of Desire and Fantasy.* Under review at State U of New York P.

———. *The End of Dissatisfaction: Jacques Lacan and the Emerging Society of Enjoyment.* Albany: State U of New York P, 2003.

———. "Looking for the Gaze: Lacanian Film Theory and Its Vicissitudes." *Cinema Journal* 42.3 (Spring 2003): 27–47.

McKay, Nellie. "An Interview with Toni Morrison." *Conversations with Toni Morrison.* Ed. Danille Taylor-Guthrie. Jackson: U of Mississippi P, 1994. 138–55.

McKinley, James C. "It Isn't Just a Game: Clues to Avid Rooting." *New York Times* 11 Aug. 2000, national ed.: A1+.

Menchú, Rigoberta. *I, Rigoberta Menchú: An Indian Woman in Guatemala.* Ed. Elisabeth Burgos-Debray. Trans. Ann Wright. London and New York: Verso, 1984.

Merleau-Ponty, Maurice. *The Visible and the Invisible.* Trans. Alphonso Lingis. Evanston: Northwestern UP, 1968.

Messer-Davidow, Ellen. *Disciplining Feminism: From Social Activism to Academic Discourse.* Durham and London: Duke UP, 2002.

Michie, Helena. *Sororophobia: Differences Among Women in Literature and Culture.* New York and Oxford: Oxford UP, 1992.

Miller, Alice. *Prisoners of Childhood: The Drama of the Gifted Child and the Search for the True Self.* Trans. Ruth Ward. New York: Basic Books, 1981.

Miller, Jacques-Alain. ALL Conference, UCLA, Los Angeles, CA. March 1999.

———. "Extimité." *Lacanian Theory of Discourse: Subject, Structure, and Society*. Ed. Mark Bracher, Marshall Alcorn, Ronald J. Corthell, and Françoise Massardier-Kenney. New York: New York UP, 1994. 74–87.

Mitchell, Stephen. *Hope and Dread in Psychoanalysis*. New York: Basic Books, 1993.

———. *Relational Concepts in Psychoanalysis*. Cambridge, MA: Harvard UP, 1988.

Mizejewski, Linda. *Ziegfield Girl: Image and Icon in Culture and Cinema*. Durham, North Carolina: Duke UP, 1999.

Mock, Michèle. "Spitting Out the Seed: Ownership of Mother, Child, Breasts, Milk, and Voice in Toni Morrison's *Beloved*." *College Literature* 23.3 (October 1996): 117–27.

Mobley, Marilyn Sanders. "Narrative Dilemma: Jadine as Cultural Orphan in *Tar Baby*." *Toni Morrison's Developing Class Consciousness*. Ed. Doreatha Drummond Mbalia. Selinsgrove: Susquehenna UP, 1991. 67–86.

Modleski, Tania. *Feminism Without Women: Culture and Criticism in a "Post-Feminist" Age*. New York: Routledge, 1991.

Moglen, Helene. "Redeeming History: Toni Morrison's *Beloved*." *Cultural Critique* 24 (1993): 17–40. (Rpt. in *Female Subjects in Black and White: Race, Psychoanalysis, Feminism*. Ed. Elizabeth Abel, Barbara Christian, and Helene Moglen. Berkeley: U of California P, 1997. 201–20.

Moon, Michael. "Memorial Rags." *Professions of Desire: Lesbian and Gay Studies in Literature*. Eds. George E. Haggerty and Bonnie Zimmerman. New York: Modern Language Association, 1995. 233–40.

Moraga, Cherríe. "From a Long Line of *Vendidas*: Chicanas and Feminism." *Feminist Studies/Critical Studies*. Ed. Teresa de Lauretis. Bloomington: U of Indiana P, 1986. 173–90.

———."La Güera." *This Bridge Called My Back: Writings by Radical Women of Color*. Ed. Cherríe Moraga and Gloria Anzaldúa. New York: Kitchen Table Press, 1981. 27–34.

———. "Preface." *This Bridge Called My Back: Writings by Radical Women of Color*. Ed. Cherríe Moraga and Gloria Anzaldúa. New York: Kitchen Table Press, 1981. xiii–xix.

——— and Gloria Anzaldúa. Eds. *This Bridge Called My Back: Writings by Radical Women of Color*. New York: Kitchen Table Press, 1981.

Morgan, Joan. *When Chickenheads Come Home to Roost: My Life as a Hip-Hop Feminist*. New York: Simon and Schuster, 1999.

Morgenstern, Naomi. "Mother's Milk and Sister's Blood: Trauma and the Neoslave Narrative." *Differences* 8 (Summer 1996): 101–26.

Morrison, Toni. *Beloved*. New York: Knopf, 1987.

———. *The Bluest Eye*. New York: Penguin (Plume), 1994.

———. "Memory, Creation, and Writing." *Thought: A Review of Culture and Ideas* 59 (December 1984): 385–90.

———. *Playing in the Dark: Whiteness and the Literary Imagination*. New York: Random House, 1993.

———. "Recitatif." *Confirmation: An Anthology of African American Women.* Ed. Amiri Baraka and Amina Baraka. New York: Random House, 1983. 243–61.

———. "Rootedness: The Ancestor as Foundation." In *Black Women Writers (1950–1980): A Critical Evaluation.* Ed. Mari Evans. New York: Doubleday, 1984. 339–45.

———. *Tar Baby.* New York: Penguin (Plume), 1982.

Mouffe, Chantal. *The Return of the Political.* London: Verso, 1993.

Moya, Paula M. L. "Chicana Feminism and Postmodernist Theory." *Signs: Journal of Women in Culture and Society* 26.2 (Winter 2001): 441–84.

———. 2002. *Learning from Experience: Minority Identities, Multicultural Struggles.* Berkeley: U of California P, 2002.

Muller, John. *Beyond the Psychoanalytic Dyad.* New York: Routledge, 1996.

——— and Richardson, William J. *Lacan and Language: A Reader's Guide to Écrits.* United States: International UP, 1982.

Muñoz, José E. "Photographies of Mourning: Melancholia and Ambivalence in Van Der Zee, Mapplethorpe, and *Looking for Langston.*" *Race and the Subject of Masculinities.* Eds. Harry Stecopoulos and Michael Uebel. Durham: Duke UP, 1997. 337–58.

Novak, Philip. " 'Circles and Circles of Sorrow': In the Wake of Morrison's *Sula.*" *PMLA* 114 (1999): 184–93.

Ogden, Thomas. *Subjects of Analysis.* Northvale, N.J.: Jason Aronson, 1994.

Olivier, Christiane. "In the Beginning was Freud." *Gender and Envy.* Ed. Nancy Burke. New York and London: Routledge, 1998. 199–212.

Osagie, Iyunolu. "Is Morrison also among the Prophets?: 'Psychoanalytic' Strategies in *Beloved.*" *African American Review* 28.3 (Fall 1994): 423–40.

Page, Philip. "Circularity in Toni Morrison's *Beloved.*" *African American Review* 26, 1 (1992): 31–40.

Paquet, Sandra. "The Ancestor as Foundation in *Their Eyes Were Watching God* and *Tar Baby.*" *Toni Morrison's Fiction: Contemporary Criticism.* Ed. David L. Middleton. 183–206.

Paz, Octavio. *The Labyrinth of Solitude: Life and Thought in Mexico.* New York: Grove P, 1961.

Phelan, Shane. "Towards a Rhetorical Reader-Response Criticism: The Difficult, The Stubborn, and the Ending of *Beloved.*" *Modern Fiction Studies* 39.3 (Winter 1993): 709–28.

Pine, Fred. "In the Beginning: Contributions to a Psychoanalytic Developmental Psychology." *International Review of Psycho-Analysis* 8: 15–33.

Portmann, John. *When Bad Things Happen to Other People.* New York and London: Routledge, 2000.

Pryse, Marjorie. "Introduction: Zora Neale Hurston, Alice Walker, and the 'Ancient Power' of Black Women." *Conjuring: Black Women, Fiction, and Literary Tradition.* Bloomington: Indiana UP, 1985. 1–24.

Radford-Hill, Sheila. "Keepin' It Real: A Generational Commentary on Kimberly Springer's 'Third Wave Black Feminism?'" *Signs: Journal of Women in Culture and Society* 27.4 (Summer 2002): 1083–89.

Rashkin, Esther. *Family Secrets and the Psychoanalysis of Narrative.* Princeton: Princeton UP, 1992.

Reagon, Bernice Johnson. "Coalition Politics: Turning the Century." *Home Girls: A Black Feminist Anthology.* Ed. Barbara Smith. New York: Kitchen Table P., 1983. 356–68.

Restuccia, Frances. *Melancholics in Love: Representing Women's Depression and Domestic Abuse.* Lanham, MD: Rowman and Littlefield, 2000.

Rigney, Barbara Hill. *The Voices of Toni Morrison.* Columbus: Ohio State UP, 1991.

Rios, Katheryn. " 'And I Know What I Have to Say Isn't Always Pleasant': Translating the Unspoken Word in Cisneros' *Woman Hollering Creek.*" In *Chicana (W)rites: On Word and Film.* Ed. Maria Herrera-Sobek and Helena Maria Viramontes. Berkeley, CA: Third Woman P, 1995. 201–23.

Rosaldo, Renato. *Culture and Truth: The Remaking of Social Analysis.* Boston: Beacon P, 1989.

Rose, Jacqueline. "Introduction—II." *Feminine Sexuality.* Ed. Juliet Mitchell and Jacqueline Rose. New York: Norton, 1985. 27–57.

———. *Sexuality in the Field of Vision.* London and New York: Verso, 1986.

Rosenfield, Israel. *The Invention of Memory: A New View of the Brain.* New York: Basic Books, 1988.

Rosner, Victoria. "Have You Seen This Child? Carolyn K. Steedman and the Writing of Fantasy Motherhood." *Feminist Studies* 26, 1 (Spring 2000): 7–32.

Roth, Benita. "The Making of the Vanguard Center: Black Feminist Emergence in the 1960s and 1970s." *Still Lifting, Still Climbing: African Amercian Women's Contemporary Activism.* Ed. Kimberly Springer. New York: New York UP, 1999. 70–90.

Rothstein, Mervyn. "Toni Morrison, in Her New Novel, Defends Women." *New York Times* Aug. 27, 1989.

Ruas, Charles. "Toni Morrison." *Conversations with Toni Morrison.* Ed. Danille Taylor-Guthrie. Jackson, MS: UP of Mississippi, 1994. 93–118.

Rushdy, Ashraf. "Daughters Signifyin(g) History: The Example of Toni Morrison's *Beloved.*" *American Literature* 64.3 (September 1992): 567–97.

Ryan, Barbara. *Feminism and the Women's Movement: Dynamics of Change in Social Movement Ideology and Activism.* New York: Routledge, 1992.

Sadoff, Dianne F. *Science of the Flesh: Representing Body and Subject in Psychoanalysis.* Stanford: Stanford UP, 1998.

Saldívar-Hull, Sonia. *Feminism on the Border: Chicana Gender Politics and Literature.* Berkeley: U of California P, 2000.

Sale, Maggie. "Call and Response as Critical Method: African-American Oral Traditions and *Beloved.*" *African American Review* 26, 1 (1992): 17–30.

Samuels, Robert. *Hitchcock's Bi-Textuality: Lacan, Feminisms, and Queer Theory.* Albany: State U of New York P, 1998.

———. *Writing Prejudices.* Albany: State U of New York P, 2001.

Samuels, Wilfred, and Clenora Hudson-Weems. *Toni Morrison.* Boston: Twayne, 1990.

Sandel, Michael. *Liberalism and the Limits of Justice*. Cambridge: Cambridge UP, 1982.
Sandler, Joseph. "The Concept of Projective Identification." *Projection, Identification, Projective Identification*. Ed. Joseph Sandler. London: Karnac Books, 1989. 13–26.
Sandoval, Chela. *Methodology of the Oppressed*. Minneapolis: U Minnesota P, 2000.
———. "U.S. Third World Feminism: The Theory and Method of Oppositional Consciousness in the Postmodern World." *Genders* 10 (Spring 1991): 1–24.
Sartre, Jean-Paul. *Black Orpheus*. Trans. S. W. Allen. Paris: Présence Africaine, 1963.
Scarry, Elaine. *The Body in Pain: The Making and Unmaking of the World*. New York: Oxford UP, 1985.
Schafer, Roy. *Aspects of Internalization*. Madison, CT: International UP, 1968.
Schapiro, Barbara. "The Bonds of Love and the Boundaries of Self in Toni Morrison's *Beloved*." *Contemporary Literature* 32 (1991): 194–210.
———. *D. H. Lawrence and the Paradoxes of Psychic Life*. Albany: State U of New York P, 1999.
———. " 'The Dread and Repulsiveness of the Wild': D. H. Lawrence and Shame." *Scenes of Shame: Psychoanalysis, Shame, and Writing*. Ed. Joseph Adamson and Hilary Clark. Albany: State U of New York P, 1999. 147–66.
Scheler, Max, *The Nature of Sympathy*. Trans. Peter Heath. Hamden, CN: Archon, 1970.
Schneider, M. "Primary Envy and the Creation of the Ego-Ideal." *International Review of Psychoanalysis* 15 (3): 319–29
Schor, Naomi. "This Essentialism Which Is Not One: Coming to Grips with Irigaray." *Differences* 1.3 (1989): 38–58.
Seshadri-Crooks, Kalpana. *Desiring Whiteness: A Lacanian Analysis of Race*. New York and London: Routledge, 2000.
Shepherdson, Charles. "The Epoch of the Body: Need and Demand in Kojève and Lacan." *Perspectives on Embodiment: The Intersection of Nature and Culture*. Ed. Gail Weiss and Honi Fern Haber. New York and London: Routledge, 1999. 183–212.
———. "The Intimate Alterity of the Real: A Response to Reader Commentary on *History and the Real*." *Postmodern Culture* 6.3 (May 1996).
———. "A Pound of Flesh: Lacan's Reading of *The Visible and the Invisible*." *Diacritics* (Winter 1997): 1–16.
———. *Vital Signs: Nature, Culture, Psychoanalyis*. London: Routledge, 2000.
Shreve, Anita. *Women Together, Women Alone: The Legacy of the Consciousness Raising Movement*. New York: Viking, 1989.
Shular, Antonia Castaneda, Tomas Ybarra-Frausto, and Joseph Sommers. *Literatura Chicana: texto y contexto*. Englewood Cliffs, NJ: Prentice Hall, 1972.
Silverman, Kaja. *Male Subjectivity at the Margins*. New York and London: Routledge, 1992.

———. *The Threshold of the Visible World*. New York and London: Routledge, 1996.

———. "White Skin, Brown Masks: The Double Mimesis, or with Lawrence in Arabia." *Differences: A Journal of Feminist Cultural Studies* 1.3 (Fall 1989).

Smith, Valerie. "Black Feminist Theory and the Representation of the 'Other.'" *Changing Our Own Words: Essays on Criticism, Theory, and Writing by Black Women*. Ed. Cheryl A. Wall. New Brunswick: Rutgers UP, 1989. 38–57.

———. *Not Just Race, Not Just Gender: Black Feminist Readings*. New York and London: Routledge, 1998.

Sommer, Doris. *Proceed with Caution, When Engaged by Minority Writing in the Americas*. Cambridge, MA: Harvard UP, 1999.

Soto, Shirlene. "Tres modelos Culturales: La Virgen de Guadalupe, la Malinche y la Llorana." *Fem* 10 (1986): 15.

Spelman, Elizabeth. "Changing the Subject: Studies in the Appropriation of Pain." *Overcoming Racism and Sexism*. Ed. Linda Bell and David Blumenfeld. Lanham, Md.: Rowman and Littlefield, 1995. 191–96.

Spillers, Hortense. "Afterword: Cross-Currents, Discontinuities: Black Women's Fiction." *Conjuring: Black Women, Fiction, and Literary Tradition*. Ed. Marjorie Pryse and Hortense Spillers. Bloomington: Indiana UP, 1985. 249–61.

———. "'All the Things You Could Be Now, If Sigmund Freud's Wife Was Your Mother': Psychoanalysis and Race." *Female Subjects in Black and White: Race, Psychoanalysis, Feminism*. Ed. Elizabeth Abel, Barbara Christian, Helene Moglen. Berkeley: U of California P, 1997. 135–58.

———. "Mama's Baby, Papa's Maybe: An American Grammar Book." *Diacritics* 17.2 (Summer 1987): 64–81.

Sprague, Joey. "Comment on Walaby's 'Against Epistemological Chasms: The Science Question Revisited': Structured Knowledge and Strategic Methodology." *Signs: Journal of Women in Culture and Society* 26.2 (Winter 2001): 527–36.

Springer, Kimberly. "Third Wave Black Feminism?" *Signs: Journal of Women in Culture and Society* 27.4 (Summer 2002): 1059–82.

Stallybrass, Peter, and Allon White. *The Politics and Poetics of Transgression*. Ithaca: Cornell UP, 1986.

Stavrakakis, Jannis. *Lacan and the Political*. London: Routledge, 1999.

Steedman, Carolyn Kay. *Landscape for a Good Woman: A Story of Two Lives*. New Brunswick, NJ: Rutgers UP, 1986.

———. *Past Tenses*. London: River Orams P, 1992.

Stern, Daniel. "The Early Development of Schemas of Self, of Other, and of 'Self with Other.'" *Reflections on Self Psychology*. Ed. J. Lichtenberg and S. Kaplan. Hillsdale, NJ: The Analytic Press, 1983. 49–84.

———. *The Interpersonal World of the Infant: A View from Psychoanalysis and Developmental Psychology*. New York: Basic Books, 1985.

———. *The Motherhood Constellation: A Unified View of Parent-Infant Psychotherapy*. New York: Basic Books, 1995.

Sweetnam, Annie. "The Changing Concepts of Gender Between Fixed and Fluid Experience." *Psychoanalytic Dialogues: A Journal of Relational Perspectives* 6.4 (1996): 437–59.

Tate, Claudia. *Domestic Allegories of Political Desire: The Black Heroine's Text at the Turn of the Century.* New York: Oxford UP, 1992.

———. *Psychoanalysis and Black Novels: Desire and the Protocols of Race.* New York: Oxford UP, 1998.

Taylor-Guthrie, Danille. *Conversations with Toni Morrison.* Jackson: UP of Mississippi, 1994.

Todorov, Tzvetan. *The Conquest of America.* Trans. Richard Howard. New York: Harper Collins, 1984.

Tolstoy, Leo. *Anna Karenina.* Trans. Louise and Aylmer Maude. Oxford and New York: Oxford UP, 1983.

Torgovnick, Marianna. *Gone Primitive: Savage Intellects, Modern Lives.* Chicago: U of Chicago P, 1990.

Trinh Minh-ha. "Not You/Like You: Post-Colonial Women and the Interlocking Questions of Identity and Difference." *Making Face, Making Soul: Hacienda Caras: Creative and Critical Perspectives by Women of Color.* Ed. Gloria Anzaldúa. San Francisco. Aunt Lute P, 1990. 371–75.

Twigg, Alan. "Just Looking at Things That Are There." *Margaret Atwood: Conversations.* Ed. Earl G. Ingersoll. Princeton: Ontario Review P, 1990. 121–30.

Tyler, Anne. *Saint Maybe.* New York: Alfred A. Knopf, 1991.

Van Pelt, Tamise. *The Other Side of Desire: Lacan's Theory of the Registers.* New York: State U of New York P, 2000.

Vickroy, Laurie. "The Force Outside/The Force Inside: Mother-Love and Regenerative Spaces in *Sula* and *Beloved.*" *Obsidian II* 8.2 (Fall–Winter 1993): 28–45.

Viramontes, Helena Maria. "The Moths." *Growing Up Chicana/o: An Anthology.* Ed. Tiffany Ana Lopez. New York: William Morrow, 1993. 117–26.

Volkan, Vamik D. *Bloodlines: From Ethnic Pride to Ethnic Terrorism.* New York: Farrar, Straus and Giroux, 1997.

Walker, Alice. "Beauty: When the Other Dancer Is the Self." *In Search of Our Mothers' Gardens.* New York: Harcourt Brace, 1983. 384–93.

Walker, Lenore. *The Battered Woman.* New York: Harper Collins, 1979.

Wallace, Michele. *Black Macho and the Myth of the Superwoman.* New York: Dial, 1978.

Wallon, Henri. *Les Origines du caractère chez l'enfant: les préludes du sentiment de personalité.* Paris: Boivin, 1934.

Walsh, William. *The Use of Imagination: Educational Thought and the Literary Mind.* New York: Barnes and Noble, 1960.

Walton, Jean. *Fair Sex, Savage Dreams: Race, Psychoanalysis, Sexual Difference.* Durham and London: Duke UP, 2001.

Wexler, Laura. "Seeing Sentiment: Photography, Race, and the Innocent Eye." *Female Subjectivity in Black and White: Race, Psychoanalysis, Feminism.* Ed. Elizabeth Abel, Barbara Christian, and Helen Moglen. Berkeley: U of California P, 1997. 159–86.

Wiegman, Robyn. *American Anatomies: Theorizing Race and Gender.* Durham, NC and London: Duke UP, 1995.

Williams, Linda Ruth. *Sex in the Head: Visions of Femininity and Film in D. H. Lawrence.* Detroit: Wayne State UP, 1993.

Willis, Susan. "Eruptions of Funk: Historicizing Toni Morrison." *Black Literature and Literary Theory.* Ed. Henry Louis Gates, Jr. New York and London: Methuen, 1984. 263–84.

Wispé, Lauren. *The Psychology of Sympathy.* New York: Plenum P, 1991.

Wolf, Naomi. *Fire with Fire: The New Female Power and How to Use It.* New York: Random House, 1993.

Wolff, Cynthia. "Margaret Garner: A Cinncinnati Story." *Discovering Difference: Contemporary Essays in American Culture.* Ed. Christopher Lohmann. Bloomington: Indiana UP, 1993. 105–22. (Rpt. *Massachusetts Review* 32 [1991]: 417–40.)

Wolff, P. *The Development of Behavioral States and the Expression of Emotions in Early Infancy: New Proposals for Investigation.* Chicago: U of Chicago P, 1987.

Worsham, Lynne, and Gary A. Olson. "Rethinking Political Community: Chantal Mouffe's Liberal Socialism." *Race, Rhetoric, and the Postcolonial.* Ed. Gary A. Olson and Lynn Worsham. Albany: State U of New York P, 1999: 165–201.

Worthen, John. *D. H. Lawrence and the Idea of the Novel.* London: Macmillan P, 1979.

Wyatt, Jean. "Giving Body to the Word: The Maternal Symbolic in Toni Morrison's *Beloved.*" *PMLA* 108.3 (May 1993): 474–88.

———. "I Want To Be You: Envy, the Lacanian Double, and Feminist Community in Margaret Atwood's *The Robber Bride.*" *Tulsa Studies in Women's Literature* 17.1 (Spring, 1998): 37–64.

———. "On Not Being La Malinche: Border Negotiations of Gender in Sandra Cisneros's "Never Marry a Mexican" and "Woman Hollering Creek." *Tulsa Studies in Women's Literature* 14.2 (Fall 1995): 243–72.

———. *Reconstructing Desire: The Role of the Unconscious in Women's Reading and Writing.* Chapel Hill, N.C.: U of North Carolina P, 1990.

———. "Toward Cross-Race Dialogue: A Lacanian Approach to Identification, Misrecognition and Difference in Feminist Multicultural Community." *Signs* 29.3 (Spring 2004).

———. "The Violence of Gendering: Castration Images in Angela Carter's *The Magic Toyshop, The Passion of New Eve,* and "Peter and the Wolf." *Women's Studies* 25.6 (1996): 549–70.

Yeo, Stephen. "Difference, Autobiography and History." *Literature and History* 14. 1 (Spring, 1988): 37–47.

Young, Iris Marion. "The Ideal of Community and the Politics of Difference." *Feminism/Postmodernism.* Ed. Linda J. Nicholson. New York and London: Routledge, 1990. 300–23.

———. *Justice and the Politics of Difference.* Princeton: Princeton UP, 1990.

———. "Polity and Group Difference: A Critique of the Ideal of Universal Citizenship." *Feminism and Politics.* Ed. Anne Phillips. Oxford and New York: Oxford UP, 1998. 401–29.

Ziarek, Ewa. *An Ethics of Dissensus: Postmodernity, Feminism, and the Politics of Radical Democracy.* Stanford: Stanford UP, 2001.

———. "Toward a Radical Female Imaginary: Temporality and Embodiment in Irigaray's Ethics." *Diacritics* 28. 1 (Spring 1998): 60–75.

Žižek, Slavoj. "Grimaces of the Real, or When the Phallus Appears." *October* 58 (Fall 1991): 45–68.

———. "How to Give Body to a Deadlock?" *Thinking Bodies.* Ed. Juliet Flower MacCannell and Laura Zakarin. Stanford: Stanford UP, 1994. 63–77.

———. *The Sublime Object of Ideology.* London and New York: Verso, 1989.

———. *The Ticklish Subject: The Absent Center of Political Ontology.* London and New York: Verso, 1999.

Zwinger, Linda. "Dancing through the Mother Field: On Aggression, Making Nice, and Reading Symptoms." *Generations: Academic Feminists in Dialogue.* Minneapolis and London: U of Minnesota P, 1997. 183–96.

Index

Abel, Elizabeth, 7, 8, 51, 63, 101, 102, 104, 105, 117; 210n6; 220n8; class, on, 59
Abraham, Nicolas, 223n1;
Adams, Parveen, 224–25n4, 225n6
Adelman, Janet, 214n4
Adorno, Theodor, 230n26
Agogino, George, 163
Ahmed, Sarah, 5, 100
Alain-Miller, Jacques, 2
Alarcón, Norma, 146–47, 242n4, 246n3, 246n6, 247n13
Alcorn, Marshall, 214n2
Alexander, M. Jacqui, 246n3
Althusser, Louis, 119; 239n1, 239n2
Anderson, Linda, 230n26
Anzaldúa, Gloria, *Borderlands/La Frontera*, 9, 17–18, 158–60, 164, 170, 171, 179–85; 241n1, 242n6, 243n13, 245n3, 246n3, 247n12, 247n13
Aranda, Pilar, 161, 241n1
Atwood, Margaret, *The Robber Bride*, 6, 15, 19–41, 216n9, 216n10, 218n16, 218n17, 219n18, 219n19; community in, 30–41; envy, and the feminist ethic of care in, 30–32, 37–41; identification and, 31–32; jouissance and, 31–32; object a, in, 32
autobiography, 15, 51, 53, 62; Moraga, 173–76; Steedman, 49–65

Baker, Houston, 226n11
Bartky, Sandra, 245n1
Bauer, Dale and Wald, Priscilla, 248n18
Beauvoir, Simone de, 5, 119
Beebe, Beatrice, 193, 196, 207
Beebe, Beatrice, and Lachmann, Frank, 193, 196, 197, 198, 199, 205, 206
Beebe, Beatrice, Lachmann and Jaffe, 204, 205
Benhabib, Seyla, 4, 170, 177, 178, 181, 183, 184, 247n16
Benjamin, Jessica, 13, 14, 23, 100, 110, 167, 208, 211n13, 213n19, 213n1, 244n15, 245n1, 249n2
Berger, James, 230n26
Berke, J. H., 215n4
Berlant, Lauren, 234n17
Bhabha, Homi, 211n14
Bloom, Lynn, and Makowsky, Veronica, 218n17; 219n17
body, 76, 85, 91–105, 111, 123, 148, 222n1, 226n10, 237n26; ideal ego, and, 89–105; in hysterical symptoms, 16, 66–67; in idealization, 85–91, 95–107, 237n26, 238n28, 238n29, 238n30, 238n31, 246n6; in slavery, 16, 75–84, 107, 108, 109; in torture, 74–77; maternal, 11, 20, 68–81, 93; mirror stage, and, 87; race, and 8, 95–108, 231n3,

275

body *(continued)*
  236n26; St. Augustine and, 20–23; trauma and, 74–84; visual form of, 87–93, 95–99, 111
Bonaparte, Marie, 234n16
Boothby, Richard, 95, 111, 174, 231n4
Borch-Jacobsen, Mikkel, 10, 13, 14, 89, 198, 199, 201, 209n2, 210n11, 212n16, 244n14
border subjectivity *(mestiza)*, 157–66; gender and, 157–66; definition of, 158–59; in Anzaldúa, 158–59, 243n13
Bordo, Susan, 103, 104
Boudreau, Kristin, 75, 226n12
Bourdieu, Pierre, 103, 104, 125, 240n5
Bouson, J. Brooks, 218n17, 223n1, 223n2, 224n3, 228n17, 232n9
Bowers, Susan, 228n17
Bracher, Mark, 249n1
Brady, Mary Pat, 243n12
Breines, Wini, 87, 190, 214n3, 230–31n1, 248n16, 248n19
Brennan, Teresa, 214n4, 244n15
Brodhead, Richard, 75, 226n13
Brody, Jennifer, 238n28
Bromberg, Pam, 218n17
Brown, Elsa Barkley, 236n23
Brown, Jane, 219n19
Burke, Nancy, 214n4
Butler, Judith, 11, 119, 131, 145, 151, 154–55, 157, 160–61; 225n5, 235n17, 239n1, 242n7, 243n8
Byatt, A. S., 215n6

Campbell, Ena, 242n6
Carbaja, Hector, 246n3
Carby, Hazel, 87, 231n26, 236n23, 237n26
Carmean, Karen, 228n17
Carter, Angela, 85; *The Magic Toyshop*, 6, 17, 119, 121, 126, 129–31, 240n8

Caruth, Cathy, 72, 78, 82
Castellanos, Rosario, 242n3
Chambers, Veronica, 108
Chase, Cynthia, 225n6
Chasseguet-Smirgel, Janine, 202
Chavez, Denise, 155
Cheng, Anne, 12, 119, 210n6, 212n16, 232n5, 242n5
Chevigny, Bell Gale, 221n9
Chicana feminist theory, 145–47, 155–56, 162, 163, 164, 174–76, 177, 179–80, 188, 241n2, 242n3, 242n4, 242n6, 243n10, 243n11, 243n12, 245n3, 246n6, 246n7, 247n13
Chodorow, Nancy, 29, 52, 193, 194, 198, 215n8; *Reproduction of Mothering*, 23, 40, 41; theory of mother-daughter primary identification, 52
Chow, Rey, 116
Christian, Barbara, 228n19
cinema, 6, 17, 85, 103, 120, 122–24, 217n13, 237n27
Cisneros, Sandra, "*Bien* Pretty," 152; "Eyes of Zapata", 152; "Guadalupe the Sex Goddess," 162; "Little Miracles, Kept Promises," 17, 145, 157; "Never Marry a Mexican," 7, 17, 146–58, 160–62; "Woman Hollering Creek," 7, 17, 119–20, 122–23, 126, 145–46, 162–69, 240n4, 243n11; *House on Mango Street*, 156; in interview, 146, 156, 161; *Woman Hollering Creek*, 145; class, 5, 15; assimilation and, 4; gender, and, 105; in *Landscape for a Good Woman*, 51–55, 58, 59, 61, 65; Steedman's insertion of, into developmental stories of psychoanalysis, 51, 52, 53, 54, 55; oppression, and, 214n3
Clément, Catherine, 225n6
Coatlicue, 160, 180, 243n11
Cohn, J., and E. Tronick, 204

Coleman, James, 232n9
Collins, Patricia Hill, 181, 184, 236n23
community, 7, 22–41, 113, 169–91; exclusion, and, 181–84; feminist academic, 3–4, 9, 15, 17, 22–41, 85, 86, 101, 102, 168–91, 215n8, 236n22; feminist ethic, and, 24, 30, 39, 41, 247n16; imaginary processes and, 9, 101–10, 171–73; multicultural feminist, 3, 9, 15, 17, 168–91; partial identification, and, 9, 14, 170–78, 181–83; pluralism in, 4, 176–86; real and, 9, 17, 18, 178–86; symbolic processes and, 9, 17, 170–91; theorists of, Benhabib, Seyla, 183, 184; Collins, Patricia Hill, 184; Fraser, Nancy, 184; Gould, Carol, 182; Sandel, Michael, 182; Young, Iris Marion, 182–84. *See also* multicultural community
Copjec, Joan, 25, 122, 133–34, 217n11; 218n14
Cortez, 146, 147, 156, 163, 243n11;
Creighton, Joanne, 241n10
Cross, Tia, 190
Cushman, Philip, 203, 249n4
Cypess, Sandra, 242n3, 242n4

Dabbs, James, 209n1
Dasenbrock, Reed Way, and Feroza, Jussawalla, 161
David-Ménard, Monique, 77
Davidson and Fox, 204
Davis, Angela, 236n23, 237n26
de Lauretis, Teresa, 6, 120
Dean, Jodi, 184
Dean, Tim, 217n12, 217n13, 218n15
Del Castillo, Adelaida, 242n3
Demetrakopoulos, Stephanie, 223n2, 224n3
desire, 33, 36, 119, 201, 226n14, 239n3, 241n9; fame, for, 25, 26; identification, for, 1–2, 4, 13–14, 19, 20, 31–32, 36–37; in *Hamlet*, 32–33; in *Landscape for a Good Woman*, 50, 53–56, 58, 59, 61, 62, 65; Lacan on, 16, 45, 49; 53, 55, 56, 57, 65, 67, 69, 70, 71, 131, 132, 133, 136, 137, 139, 140, 141, 142, 143, 144; maternal, 42–45, 49–50, 55–56, 149; *Beloved*, in, 68–84; of the Other, 3, 21, 41, 45, 53, 56, 57, 65, 67, 69, 71; subject of desire, development of, 45–49. *See also* identification and desire
Diamond, Elin, 67, 210n11, 231n2, 244n15
Diego, Juan, 159
Dimen, Muriel, 91, 244n16
discourse ethics, 176, 178, 180
disidentification, 145–57, 242n5; Butler, Judith on, 154; failure of, 149–57; gender identity, and, 145–62; Greenson, Ralph, on, 154, 155; in mother-daughter relations, 152–58
Doane, Mary Ann, 114, 123, 210n5, 236n21, 238n28
Dolar, Mladen, 34, 119, 217n14, 239n1
double, 34, 137; Lacanian double, 32–37; Hoffman's doubles, 34; Dolar, Mladen, on, 34, 217n14
Dowling, Colette, 233n12
Drabble, Margaret, 6, 17, 85; *Jerusalem the Golden*, 6, 119, 121, 131, 134–41,
Dubey, Madhu, 248n16
duCille, Ann, 8, 101, 105, 109, 115, 188, 236n21, 236n22, 239n31
DuPlessis, Rachel Blau, and Ann Snitow, 248n16

Edelberg, Cynthia, 232n7
Edelman, Gerald, 196
ego ideal, 88–89, 98–99, 126–27, 129
Eigen, Michael, 198
Elam, Diane, 215n8, 216n8

Elkins, Stanley, 229n21
Eng, David and Han, Shinhee, 210n6, 211n14
envy, 1, 6, 7, 8, 13, 14, 20–41, 50, 193, 201, 207, 213n1, 214n4, 215n5, 215n6, 215n7, 219n18, 222n12; class, 4, 5, 15, 51, 55, 105; in *Landscape for a Good Woman*, 51–55, 58, 59, 61, 65; definition of, 15, 20–22; ethic of care, and, 37–41; fame, and, 22–26, 29; feminist ethics, and, 20, 22–28, 30, 37–41; Freud, definition of, 28–30, 40–41; fundamental fantasy, and, 21–22; gaze, the, and, 25–26; intergenerational, 26–29; jouissance and, 21–22, 31; Keller, Evelyn Fox, and Helene Moglen on, 27, 30; Klein, Melanie on, 28; Lacan, on, 15, 20–22, 24; vs. jealousy, 20–21, 27–28, 149
Etchegoyen, R. H., 215n4
Evans, Dylan, 21, 88–89
Evans, Martha, 225n4

Fairbairn, W. R. D., 193, 195, 202
family, photographs and ideology, 123–26; identification in, *See* mother-daughter relations, parent-child relations
Fanon, Frantz, 105
fantasy, 33, 34, 36, 80, 213n18, 221n9, 224n3, 231n3, 249n3; fundamental, 13, 21, 32, 45, 46, 48;
—definition of, 21–22, 32–33;
—traversing the, 186–91; identification, and 199–208; infant research in, 199–205; nursing, 68–69, 73;
Fast, Irene, 244n16
Felman, Shoshana, 175, 176
feminist film theorists, 6; Doane, Mary Ann, 114, 123, 210n5, 236n21, 238n28
Fenichel, Otto, 195
Ferguson, Rebecca, 224n3

Fields, Karen, 228n17
Fink, Bruce, 43, 45, 48, 57, 61, 219n3; 219n4; 220n6, 239n3
FitzGerald, Jennifer, 224n3
Flax, Jane, 203, 249n5
Fleischner, Jennifer, 226n11, 229n21, 235n18
Forter, Greg, 12
Fragd, Lula, 103
Franklin, Cynthia, 189, 245n3, 246n3
Fraser, Nancy, 183, 184, 247n16
Freiwald, Bina, 222n13
Freud, 169, 171, 198, 201, 202, 205, 206, 207, 209n2; "Creative Writers and Daydreaming," 202; "Finding, Ideas, Problems," 202; "Mourning and Melancholia," 10; Dora, 70, 224n4, 225n5; *Group Psychology and the Analysis of the Ego*, 2, 10, 13, 28, 155, 166, 192, 193, 201, 207; hysterical identification, 66, 67, 71, 74–84, 222n1, 226n9;
—identification with a group, 67; *Interpretation of Dreams*, 67, 77; melancholic identification, model of, 9, 11, 165–67; multiple subjectivity, model of, 165–67; on dreams, 55; on envy, 28–30, 40–41; on smell, 91, 232n6; on the uncanny manifesting as "the double," 34; on trauma, 71, 74–75; primary identification, model of, 2–3, 9–10, 28–29, 41–42, 70, 136, 169, 192, 195, 211n15, 212n17, 214n4; talking cure, 74–77; *The Ego and the Id*, 10, 165, 166, 244n14
Friedberg, Anne, 123, 210n5, 247n13, 248n19
Friedman, Susan Stanford, 117–18, 210n9
Frosh, Stephen, 161
Fultz, Lucille, P., 232n9
fundamental fantasy. *See* fantasy, fundamental

INDEX

Fuss, Diana, 4, 11, 16, 181, 209n2, 210n10, 210n11, 211n15, 225n5, 225n6, 235n17, 244n15, 245n1; on race, 3

Gallop, Jane, 8, 26, 27, 28, 40, 101, 105, 106, 110, 115, 116, 117, 215n8, 216n8, 231n2, 235n20, 236n22, 238–39n31
Garbus, Lisa, 227n15
Gates, Henry Louis, Jr., 226n11
gaze, the, 6, 85, 98, 103, 104, 105, 119, 120, 121, 122, 130–34, 142, 236n21, 238n29, 239n3, 240n9, 241n9; definitions of,
—Lacan, 17, 25–26, 120–22, 130–34;
—Merleau-Ponty, 25, 121, 133–34;
—Silverman, 120–21; desire for, 25–26, 121–22, 131–44; double lure of, 131–42; envy and, 25–26; fame and, 25; in Drabble, *Jerusalem the Golden*, 131–42; interpellation, and, 143–44; universal, 25, 121, 133–34
gender identifications, 119–44, 145–68, 213n19; border negotiations of, 145–68; cultural representations of, 5–7, 119–44; flexible, 162–68, 213n19, 244n16;
—Benjamin, Jessica, on, 14, 213n19, 244n16; Butler, Judith, on, 11, 161, 242n7, 243n8; interpellation, 5–7, 85, 119–44, 162–65; melancholic, 11; liberation from, 157–68; performance of, 146–48, 161, 242n7
Giddings, Paula, 104, 105, 236n23, 237n26
Gilbert, Sandra, 29, 215n8
Gilligan, Carol, 29, 37, 215n8
Gilman, Sander, 210n6
Gilroy, Paul, 109, 238n29
glamour, 6, 85, 93, 144, 241n11
Goldberg, Whoopi, 103, 104
Goldner, Virginia, 148, 149, 244n16
Gordon, Avery, 229n24

Gould, Carol, 182
Graeber, Laurel, 217n10; 218n17; 219n17
Greenberg, Jay, R. and Stephen, A. Mitchell, 42, 69, 195, 198
Greenson, Ralph, "The Struggle against Identification," 154, 155,
Grosz, 231n4
Grubrich-Simitis, Ilse, 67, 80, 229n21
Gubar, Susan, 29, 210n8; 215n8; 216n8, 237n26, 243n9, 245n2

Hairspray, 187, 191
Halpern, Jodi, 249n6
Hamer, Fanny Lou, 104, 107
Haraway, Donna, 235n17, 247n15
Harding, Sandra, 4, 170, 176, 177, 178, 181, 247n15
Harlem Renaissance, 116, 237n26
Harris, Adrienne, 215n6; 215n7, 244n16
Harris, Trudier, 228n17, 233n11
Hartman, Saidiya, 226n13
Hartsock, Nancy, 177, 247n15
Haviland, J., and M. Lelwica, 204, 205
Hawthorne, Evelyn, 232n9
Heffernan, Teresa, 230n26
Hegel, *The Phenomenology of the Spirit*, 209n2
Heinze, Denise, 227n17, 234n15
Henderson, Mae, 228n20
Henley, Nancy, 104
Hine, Darlene, 223n2
Hirsch, Marianne, 26, 29, 105, 125, 215n8, 216n8, 224n3
Holloway, Karla, 77
Homans, Margaret, 229n23, 235n17
hooks, bell, 116, 183, 186, 187, 191, 237n26, 248n16
Horvitz, Deborah, 224n3, 227n17
House, Elizabeth, 227n17
Howe, Marguerite Beede, 220n7
Hudson-Weems, Clenora, 232n7
Hurtado, Aida, 188

INDEX

hysterical identification, 3, 11, 66–84, 224n4: *Beloved*, in, 66–84; group identification and, 66–67, 77

Ian, Marcia, 211n13
icon, 145, 158, 241n11
ideal ego, 16, 85–106, 114, 116, 127, 172–73, 231n4, 233n13; body and, 89–105, 111, 112, 172, 173; Lacan on, 89–90, 91, 95, 101, 111; secondary identifications, and, 87; *Tar Baby*, in, 87–101;
idealization, 1, 3, 13, 14, 86–89, 95, 97, 105–7, 110–12, 114–15, 117–18, 168, 186–87, 193, 207; African-American women, of, 8, 16, 104, 85, 86, 87, 89, 102–18, 235n18, 238n27; Black feminists on, 8, 86, 87, 105, 106, 107, 108, 109, 110; body, and, 87, 105–9, 234n17; ideal ego, and, 85–106; Lacan on, 16, 89, 90, 91, 95, 101, 111, 86–11; material conditions, and, 110–18, 188–91; mirror stage, and, 2, 16, 87, 88, 89; of sisterhood, 215n7; overcoming 186–91; race and, 16, 86–118; *See also* ideal ego.
identification, Abraham, Nicolas and Maria Torok on, 10, 11; assimilation, and 3, 4, 12, 178, 210n8; Borch-Jacobsen, Mikkel, on, 10, 13, 14, 89, 198, 199, 201, 209n2, 210n11, 212n16, 244n14; contemporary theorists on, 9–15; cross-race, 4, 8, 15, 17–18, 101–18, 170–91; culture and, 119–44; definition of, 1–3, 10, 14, 28, 87–88, 165–67, 172–76; desire, and, 1–2, 10–11, 15, 19, 32, 36, 42–65, 66–84, 211n13;
—Benjamin, Jessica on, 13–14;
—Fuss, Diana on, 11;
—Lacan on, 70; desire for, 1–2, 4, 13–14, 19, 20, 31–32, 36–37;

Diamond Elin, on, 67; empathy, and, 249n6; heteropathic, 14, 167, 168, 169–91, 245n1;
—definition of, 14, 169, 245n1;
—Silverman, Kaja on, 14, 245n1; interpellation and, 6, 119–44; maternal, 156, 160, 42–74; mirror stage and, 6, 14, 63, 87–88, 110, 122–23; neuronal networks, and, 18; parent-child, 3, 15, 42, 68, 74, 213n19; partial, 9, 14, 170–78, 181–83; race and, 5, 86–118, 170–91, 214n4, 244n16, 245n2; totalising, tendency of, 9; visual, 1, 3, 16–18, 85–144. *See also* gender identification; hysterical identification; ideal ego; imaginary identification; melancholic identification; partial identification; primary identification; race; symbolic identification
imaginary, definition of, 7–8
imaginary identification, 5, 9, 17, 18, 85–118, 120, 122, 129, 172, 173, 186, 233n13, 246n5; cross-race, 8, 101–10; definition of, 2, 8, 86–88; Lacan on, 2, 3, 85–87;
infant research, 192–208, 249n5; fantasy in, 199–205; neurobiological model of early representations, 196–97
interpellation, 2–3, 5, 13, 85, 119–44, 232n5; definitions of,
—Althusser, 16–17, 119–20;
—de Lauretis, 6, 119–20; desire for, 119–31; gaze, the, and, 6, 17, 131–44; ideal ego and, 127, 131; mirror stage and, 6, 16–17, 120–26; screen, the, and, 6, 17, 126–31; television and, 120, 122–26.
Irigaray, Luce, 231n4

Jacobs, Harriet, 228n20
Jan Mohamed, Abdul, 9
Johnson, Samuel, 29, 215n6
Jones, Lisa, 108

INDEX

Jordan, Judith K., 249n6
Jordan, June, 185
jouissance, 6, 21–22, 31–37, 132, 213n2, 217n12, 217n13; definition of, 21; racism and, 213n2

Kahane, Claire, 74, 75, 224n4
Kaplan, Carla, 247n16
Karamcheti, Indira, 236n21
Kavaler-Adler, Kittay, 214n4
Keating, AnaLouise, 246n3, 247n13
Keenan, Sally, 223n2, 228n17
Keller, Evelyn Fox, 26–27, 29–30, 216n8
King, Toni C., 246n3
Kingston, Maxine Hong, *The Woman Warrior*, 242n5
Kinkead-Weekes, Mark, 220n7
Klein, Melanie, on envy, 28, 214n4, 224n3, 234n16
Kohut, Hans, self psychology, 60
Kojève, Alexander, *Introduction to the Reading of Hegel: Lectures on the Phenomenology of the Spirit*, 209n2
Kristeva, Julia, 11, 74; melancholic identification, on, 10
Kruks, Sonia, 4, 191, 245n1
Krumholz, Linda, 230n26

Lacan, 21–22, 111, 133, 169, 171, 174, 175, 176, 185, 187, 188, 214n4, 217n10, 217n12, 219n1, 231n4, 224n4; definition of need, 56; desire, on, 16, 45, 49; 53, 55–57, 65, 67, 69–71, 131–33, 136–37, 139, 140–44; Dora, on 70, 225n5; double (Lacanian), on 32–37; *Écrits*, 3, 16, 44, 87–88, 172, 210n3; envy, on, 2, 20–21, 24, 29, 31; envy vs. jealousy, on, 20; demand, structure of, 15, 44; fort-da-parable, and symbolic, 43; gaze, on, 6, 17, 25–26, 127, 130–34; *Hamlet*, on, 32–36; hysteria, on, 70–71; ideal ego, on, 89–91;
95, 111; idealization, 7, 14, 16; identification and aggressivity, on, 28; imaginary identification, 2, 85, 87–88, 110, 117, 126; influence of Hegel, 209n2; lack, 186–91, 201; Law of the Father, 33; maternal desire, 42–43; Merleau-Ponty, and, 25, 121, 133–34; mirror-stage, 6, 8, 120, 122, 134, 231n2, 233n13, 237n27; parent-child relations, on, 3, 42–46, 48, 62; real, the, 8, 32–36, 82–84, 179, 218n15, 227n15; screen, on, 6, 17, 128–29; Seminar I, 3, 85, 88, 92, 111, 134, 172; Seminar II, 82; Seminar IX, 210n3; Seminar VII, 20, 21, 49; Seminar X, 15, 44, 45, 126; Seminar XI, 17, 25, 44–45, 82, 98–99, 119–21, 122–23, 126–38, 141, 188, 233n13; symbolic, on, 82, 83, 183; three registers, 7, 170, 246n9; uncanny, on, 34, 36; visual field, 2, 129, 130–34, 138;
—diagrams of, 240n6, 240n7. *See also* object a.
lack, 43–46, 186–91
Ladner, Joyce, 236n23
Lambert, Ellen, 241n10
Lane, Chris, 88, 210n6
Laplanche, Jean, and Jean-Bertrand Pontalis, 2, 167, 169, 202
Law of the Father, 33
Lawrence, D. H., *The Rainbow*, 15, 42–50, 59, 219n1; 220n7; desire in, 43, 48, 49, 50; Lacan's structure of demand in, 46; object a, in, 48, 49; parent-child identification in, 42–43, 46–50, 59, 68; primary identification in, 46; *Fantasia of the Unconscious*, 220n5; *Sons and Lovers*, 219n1
Layton, Lynne, 161, 242n7, 243n8, 244n16
Leclair, Thomas, 232n9
Leclerc, Annie, 106, 235n20

Lemoine-Luccioni, Eugéne, 225n4
Leys, Ruth, 212n17, 226n7
Llorona, La, 146, 162–63, 241n2, 243n.11, 243n12
Loew, Lisa, 239n2
Looser, Devoney, and E. Ann Kaplan, 216n8
Lopez, Adelaida, 247n12
Lorde, Audre, 191
Lott, Eric, 237n26
Lugones, Maria, 245n1, 246n3

Mahler, Margaret, 193, 194, 198
Malinche, La, 7, 17, 145–50, 152, 156, 161, 163, 241n2, 242n3, 242n4, 243n8, 243n11, 246n8
Malinche. *See* La Malinche
Malintzín. *See* La Malinche
Manzano, Juan Francisco, *Autobiography of a Slave*, 76
Marcus, Laura, 221n11
Marshall, Brenda, 227n16
Marx, 54, 55, 182;
maternal desire. *See* desire, maternal
Mathieson, Barbara, 224n3
Matsuda, Mari, 184
Mayhew, Henry, 52;
McDowell, Deborah, 8, 101, 105, 106, 236n22, "The Changing Same," 106
McGowan, Todd, 217n13, 241n9
McKay, Nellie, 112, 113
McKinley, James C. Jr., 209n1
Mead, Margaret, 234n16
melancholic identification, 9, 11, 165, 166, 211n14, 212n18; Butler, Judith on, 11; Cheng, Anne, on, 12; definition of, 10, 165–67; Fuss, Diana on, 11; queer theory and, 11–12; multiple gender identifications and, 165–67; race melancholia, 12, 211n14
memory, neurobiological model of, 196, 207
Menchú, Rigoberta, 181
Merleau-Ponty, Maurice, 25, 121, 133, 134, 139, 142

Messer-Davidow, Ellen, 23, 248n16
mestiza, 146, 158, 159, 164, 242n6. *See also* border subjectivity
Michie, Helena, 27, 116, 215n7, 248n16
Miller, Alice, 60, 61
Miller, Jacques-Alain, 213n2; 215n8
Miller, Nancy, 105, 216n8
mirror stage, 85, 87, 88, 89, 91, 112, 120, 172
Mitchell, Stephen, 10, 42, 69, 250n10
Mizejewski, Linda, 241n11
Mobley, Marilyn, 232n9
Modleski, Tania, 8, 101, 103, 104
Moglen, Helene, 26–27, 29–30, 216n8, 223n2
Moon, Michael, 12
Moraga, Cherríe, 146, 147, 245n3, 246n3, 246n6, 246n7, 248n19; "From a Long Line of *Vendidas*," 9, 17, 170–91; *Loving*, 155
Morgan, Joan, 107, 108, 236n25
Morgenstern, Naomi, 66, 67, 68, 72, 77–78, 80, 223n1, 227n17, 228n18
Morrison, Toni, *Beloved*, 5, 15, 19, 42, 43, 66–84; hysterical identification in, 44; imaginary identification in, 69; infanticide in, 66, 72, 74, 77, 84, 223n2, 228–29n20; jouissance, in, 71; Morrison on, 71, 80, 83; parent-child identification in, 42, 43, 68, 73; primary identification in, 44, 68, 69, 73; primary identification in, slavery, 15, 67; *Sula*, 12; *Tar Baby*, 5, 16, 85, 86–118, 127; body in, 91–105, 110, 112–14; ideal ego in, 87, 89–101; Morrison on, 90, 111, 112, 114; *The Bluest Eye*, 128, 233n10; "Recitatif," 102, 104
mother-daughter relations, African-American families, in, 107–8; Cisneros's fiction, in, 152–61; Lacan, on, 42–46; Moraga, on, 175–76; Morrison's *Beloved*, in,

66–74; Steedman's *Landscape for a Good Woman*, in, 49–65
Mouffe, Chantal, 186, 248n18
Moya, Paula, 4, 170, 176, 177, 178, 181, 183, 241n2, 245n3, 246n3, 248n19
Muller, John, 55, 204, 205
multicultural community, critique of, 189; defense of, 189–91; imaginary in, 101–18, 172–73, 182–83, 186; real in, 179–81, 184–86; symbolic in, 173–78, 182–84, 188–90; trust in, 189–91
multiple subjectivity, Anzaldúa, on, 158–59; border subjects (*mestizas*) and, 159–61, 164–65; Chicana feminist theory, on, 158–59, 174, 246n6; infant research model, potential for, 206–8; melancholic identification and, 165–67; relational psychoanalytic model of, 208, 244n16, 250n10
Muñoz, José, 12

Nahuatl, 145
Name-of-the-Father, 35, 83
neurobiology, 192
neuronal networks, 18
Novak, Philip, on *Sula*, 12
object a, 20–26, 32–34, 36, 42, 44, 45, 46, 49, 57, 70, 134, 144, 217n10, 217n11, 217n14, 218n14, 240n9; definition of, 21, 217n11; gaze, as the, 25, 121–22, 131–44

Ogden, Thomas, 250n10
Olivier, Christiane, 214n4
Osagie, Iyunolu, 227n17
Ovid, 215n6

Pacquet, Sandra, 234n14
Page, Philip, 229n22
parental-child relations, 42–65, 192
parent-child identification, *Beloved*, in, 42–44, 46; *The Rainbow*, in, 42–49; *Landscape for a Good Woman*, in, 42–65
partial identification, 9, 170–78, 181–82, 246n7
patriarchy, 6, 23, 27
Paz, Octavio, 147, 148, 242n4, 243n11
performativity, 146–48, 161, 242n7, 243n8
Phelan, James, 230n25
photographs, 85, 125, 240n5
Pine, Fred, 200
Pontalis, Jean-Bertrand, 2
Portmann, John, 215n5
posttraumatic stress disorder, 71
primary identification, 1, 2, 15, 19, 42–44, 46, 51, 57, 61, 65, 192–208, 249n1, 250n8; Borch-Jacobsen, Mikkel on, 10, 13, 14, 89, 198, 199, 201, 209n2, 210n11, 212n16, 244n14; class and, 15; desire, and, 13; Freud on, 2, 3, 9, 10, 19, 28; in *Beloved*, 15; infant research and, 18, 192–208; Lacan on, 2, 3, 19; mother and daughter, 23; oral fantasy and, 155; Stern, Daniel, on, 18, 192–204, 250n8; *The Robber Bride*, in, 40;
Prince, Morton, 212n17
Pryse, Marjorie, 115, 238–39n31

queer theory, 10

race, assimilation and, 3–4; authenticity, 112–14; cross-race feminist alliances, 18, 181–85, 186–91, 230n26, 245n3; cross-race idealization, 4, 86–88, 101–18, 172–73; cross-race identification, 3–5, 101–18, 169–91, 214n4, 244n16, 245n2; imaginary and, 86–88, 101–18; melancholia and, 12, 211n14; symbolic and, 8, 170–78, 181–84, 186–91; visual regimes and, 88, 114–15, 238n28, 238n29
Radford-Hill, Sheila, 107, 108, 236n24, 236n25

Rashkin, Esther, 211n12, 223n1
Reagon, Bernice, 248n18
real, the, definition of, 8, 218n15; gaze as, 25–26, 120–22, 131–44; Lacanian double and, 32–36; Morrison's *Beloved*, in, 82–84; multicultural community, in, 9, 17, 18, 178–86; and slavery, 82–84; 227n15
relational psychoanalysis, 18, 203
Restuccia, Frances, 219n3, 240n4, 243n12
Richardson, William J., 55, 204, 205
Rigney, Barbara Hill, 224n2
RIGs, 196
Rios, Katheryn, 242n4
Riviere, Joan, 234n16
Rody, Caroline, 226n14, 227n17
Rosaldo, Renato, 243n13
Rose, Jacqueline, 43, 56, 244n16
Rosenfield, Israel, 250n9
Rosner, Victoria, 51, 52, 220–221n9
Roth, Benita, 188, 214n3
Rothstein, Mervyn, 223n2
Rousseau, Jean-Jacques, 116
Ruas, Charles, 90, 95, 233n10, 233n12
Rushdy, Ashraf, on *Beloved*, 73, 226n8, 228n17
Ryan, Barbara, 248n16

Sadoff, Diane, 226n9
Saldívar-Hull, Chela, 243n12, 246n3, 247n13
Sale, Maggie, 223n2
Samuels, Robert, 142, 240n9
Samuels, Wilfred, 227n15, 229n24, 232n7
Sandel, Michael, 182
Sandoval, Chela, 189, 245n3, 246n3
Sartre, Jean-Paul, 25, 98, 122
Scarry, Elaine, 75
Schadenfreude, 215n5
Schafer, Roy, 12, 13, 14, 170, 198, 212–13n18

Schapiro, Barbara, 219n1; 224n3
Scheler, Max, 14, 167, 169, 187
Schneider, M., 215n4
Schor, Naomi, 247n14
screen, 17, 120, 121, 123, 127, 128, 130
secondary identification, 87; definition of, 3
Seshadri-Crooks, Kalpana, 8, 88, 217n11, 219n2, 231n3, 233n13; on race, definition of, 8
sexism, 12
sexual identity, 147
Shakespeare, William, *Hamlet*, 32–36
Shange, Ntosake, 246n7
Shepherdson, Charles, 42, 43, 62, 132, 134, 209n2, 218n15, 223n1, 225n4
Showalter, Elaine, 29, 215n8
Shreve, Anita, 248n16
Shular, Antonia Castaneda, 163
Silverman, Kaja, 14, 17, 121, 123, 127, 131, 138, 210n6, 211n13, 237n27, 245n1; *Male Subjectivity at the Margins*, 17, 120; *Threshold of the Visible World*, 14, 109, 110, 245n1
slavery, 5, 6, 222n1; 224n3, 226n8, 226n9, 226n11, 227n15, 228nn.17, 18, 19, 228–29n20, n21, n24, 230n25, 230n26, 236n26; in *Beloved*, 15; African-American, 15, 16, 66–84, 87, 94, 107, 108
Smith, Valerie, 8, 101, 108, 109, 112, 113, 114, 227n16
Sommer, Doris, 3, 5, 181, 245n1, 247n11, 247n14, 248n17
Soto, Shirlene, 146, 242n6
spectatorship, interpellation and, 6, 120, 122–24
Spelman, Elizabeth, 245n1
Spillers, Hortense, 7, 51, 76, 210n6, 226n10, 238n30, 238–39n31
Sprague, Joey, 246n10
Springer, Kimberly, 108, 246n3

St. Augustine, *Confessions*, 20
Stallybrass, Peter, 103
standpoint theory, 4, 170, 176, 177, 178, 181, 246n10, 247n15
Stavrakakis, Jannis, 4, 88, 210n4
Steedman, Carolyn Kay, *Landscape for a Good Woman*, 15, 19, 42–44, 46, 49–65; Chodorow, Nancy, in, 52; desire in, 49, 50, 53, 54, 55, 56, 57, 58, 59, 61, 62, 65; envy in, 50, 55; fairytales in, "The Little Mermaid," in, 63, 64; "The Snow Queen," in, 63, 64; fantasy in, 58; identification, desire for, 50; Marxist theory in, 54; mother-daughter relations in, 49–57; New Look, in, 50, 53–56, 58, 61, 62, 64, 221n10, 222n12; parent-child identification, 68; primary identification in, 49, 50, 51, 52, 54, 55, 56, 57, 61, 65; symbolic identification, in, 55, 61, 62; "The Watercress Seller," *Past Tenses*, *Landscape for a Good Woman*, 220–21n9
Stembridge, Jane, 8, 104, 105, 107
Stern, Daniel, 18, 193–207, 249n2, 249n3, 249n4, 250n7, 250n8
Stowe, Harriet Beecher, 106
Student Nonviolent Coordinating Committee, 104
Subjectivity, multiple. *See* multiple subjectivity
Sweetnam, Annie, 167, 244n16
symbolic identification, 9, 17, 88, 120, 172–91; definition of, 98–99, 172–76.
symbolic, the, 7, 8, 34, 35, 82, 117, 172–78, 181–84, 187–91

Tate, Claudia, 210n6, 236n23
telenovelas, 120, 162, 163, 240n4
television, 17, 120, 122–24
Todorov, Tzvetan, 146
Tolstoy, Leo, *Karenina, Anna*, 124

Tonantsin. *See Virgen de Guadalupe, La*
Torgovnick, Marianne, 237n26
Torok, Maria, 10, 223n1
trauma, 66–84, 212n17, 226n7, 228n18, 229nn.21, 22; body and, 5, 16, 69–71; theory, 68–75, 82, 226n7; hysterical symptoms and, 16, 66–74; intergenerational transmission of, 66–74, 223n1; representation and narrative gaps in *Beloved* and, 67, 80–82; theories of:
—Leys, Ruth, 212n17, 226n7
—Caruth, Cathy, 72, 78, 82; time, and, 71–74; talking cure, and, 74–82
Trinh, Minh-ha, 246n4
Truth, Sojourner, 106
Twigg, Alan, 219n17
Tyler, Anne, 17; *Saint Maybe*, 6, 119, 123–26, 129

van der Kolk, Bessel, 226n7
Van Pelt, Tamise, 246n9
Vickroy, Laurie, 223n1
Violet, Indigo, 246n3
Viramontes, Helena Maria, 155
Virgen de Guadalupe, La, 7, 17, 145, 146, 152, 157–62, 241n2, 242n6, 243n8, 243n10
—Tonantsin, 159, 242n6
visual regimes, 8, 85, 88, 92, 99, 105, 109, 114–15, 210n7, 236n21, 238n28, 240n9, 246n6
Volkan, Vamik, 223n1

Walker, Alice, 235n17
Wallace, Michele, 107
Wallon, Henri, 237n27
Walsh, William, 220n5
Walton, Jean, 102
Walton, Seshadri-Crooks, 210n6, 234n16
Wexler, Laura, 125, 240n5
White, Allon, 103

whiteness, 12, 16, 115, 178, 231n3, 241n11
Wiegman, Robyn, 210n7, 238n28
Williams, Linda Ruth, 220n5
Williams, Patricia, 235n17
Winnicott, D. W., 224n3
Wispé, Lauren, 209n1
Wolf, Naomi, 216n8
Wolff, Cynthia, 205
Worsham, Lynne, and Gary A. Olson, 186, 248n18
Worthen, John, 219n1
Wyatt, 224n3, 246n3, 240n8

Yeo, Stephen, 221n11
Young, Iris Marion, 4, 170, 185, 186, 191, 247n16; "The Ideal of Community and the Politics of Difference," 182; *Justice* and "Polity," 183, 184

Ziarek, Ewa, 89, 231n4, 248n18
Žižek, Slavoj, 35, 45, 56, 98, 126, 127, 129, 130, 132, 179, 213n2; 217n13; 217n14; 218n15
Zwinger, Linda, 29, 215n8, 216n8

www.ingramcontent.com/pod-product-compliance
Lightning Source LLC
Chambersburg PA
CBHW020639230426
43665CB00008B/244